Smoke on the Water

The Deep Purple Story

Published by ECW Press
2120 Queen Street East, Suite 200, Toronto, Ontario, Canada M4E 1E2

NATIONAL LIBRARY OF CANADA CATALOGUING IN PUBLICATION

David Thompson
Smoke on the water: the Deep Purple Story / David Thompson.

Includes index.
ISBN 1-55022-618-5

1. Deep Purple (Musical group) 2. Rock musicians — England — Biography.
I. Title.

ML421.D311T46 2004   782.42166′092′2   C2004-900615-0

Editing: Jennifer Hale
Cover and Text Design: Tania Craan
Production and Typesetting: Mary Bowness
Printing: Tri-Graphic

This book is set in Akzidenz Grotesk and Minion.

DISTRIBUTION
CANADA: Jaguar Book Group, 100 Armstrong Avenue, Georgetown, ON, L7G 5S4
UNITED STATES: Independent Publishers Group, 814 North Franklin Street, Chicago, Illinois 60610

PRINTED AND BOUND IN CANADA

ECW PRESS
ecwpress.com

Smoke on the Water

The Deep Purple Story

Dave Thompson

ECW Press

Acknowledgments

I'd like to thank everybody who threw something into the pot, but most especially Jim Worthley, for unstinting access to his own redoubtable Purple archive and knowledge, and Kevin Scott Collier, for shedding so much light on the 1980 Deep Purple "reunion." Neither could this book have been completed without the encouragement and enthusiasm of Amy Hanson, Jo-Ann Greene, Greg Loescher (*Goldmine* magazine), Brian Perera (Cleopatra Records), Peter Purnell (Angel Air Records), my agent Sherrill Chidiac, and everyone at ECW.

To the musicians who took the time to speak with me over the years, in and out of the interview room — special thanks to Roger Glover, Geoff Goddard, Dale Griffin, Ronnie James Dio, Bernie Tormé, Ray Fenwick, Mo Foster, Ian Gillan, Joe Satriani, Jon Lord, Cozy Powell, and Ian Paice.

Finally, thanks to everybody else who helped bring the beast to life — Anchorite Man; Bateerz and family; Biggie Squidge; Blind Pew; Mrs B. East; Ella and Sprocket; Gef the Talking Mongoose; the Gremlins who live in the furnace; K-Mart and Snarleyyowl; Geoff Monmouth; Nutkin; Sonny; a lot of Thompsons and Neville Viking.

CONTENTS

Introduction

It was back in 1970 that I first heard Deep Purple blasting out of British TV's pop flagship *Top of the Pops* with a purpose and power that few ten-year-olds had ever experienced; it was 1972 before I could afford to buy one of their LPs — *Made in Japan*, a double live package for the same price as a single disc (a crucial consideration in those pocket-monied days); and 1974 before I saw them live, in London, with David Coverdale and Glenn Hughes.

Since that time, following Deep Purple has veered between a lifelong vocation and a bitter cross to bear. But it has never failed in the one thing at which music always ought to succeed (but, sadly, frequently fails): it has always remained entertaining. Whether I was waiting for the band's next album, or digging through the leaves that litter the foot of the family tree, the music made by the fourteen musicians who have passed through the group's ranks over the last thirty-five years represents one of the most awe-inspiring catalogs in the history of rock'n'roll.

Deep Purple's own contributions to the catalog, of course, need no introduction. But step outside of the seventeen studio (and countless live) albums they have made, and you embark on a journey that leads from the scratchy beat that Ritchie

Blackmore played during his years with producer Joe Meek, to the lilting lutes and mandolins that fire his current band, Blackmore's Night; from the raw R&B of Jon Lord's first band, the Artwoods, to the grandiose classical edifices he concentrates on today; from the pure pop of Ian Gillan and Roger Glover's days with Episode Six, to the jazz rock of the Ian Gillan Band and the lyrical soundscapes of Glover's *Snapshot*. And those are only the extremes.

Babe Ruth and Black Sabbath, David Gilmour and the Dixie Dregs, Warhorse and Whitesnake — the story of Deep Purple intersects so many other careers that simply keeping up with it all is a full-time occupation. Telling the story takes even longer.

Nevertheless, that is what this book endeavors to do — and if Deep Purple's story might occasionally get lost within the manifold twists and turns that the narrative takes, all the better. It is a cliché to say that a great group is more than the sum of its parts, but Deep Purple are living proof of the truth of those words.

No band exists in a vacuum. No matter how hard the individual musicians might try to isolate themselves, the rest of the world still rotates around them, and it would be a sad sack of cynics who could carry on their own sweet path without ever noting anything that spun off in their direction. And though Deep Purple have been called a lot of things over the years, they have never been condemned as isolationist. Rather, it sometimes seems their eyes are open even wider than most bands', granting them an awareness that allows them to experiment with new ideas and principles the rest of the pack might not notice for months.

Not all of these discoveries come out in Deep Purple's own records. Every member of the band, past and present, has enjoyed a separate career and, with every change in the band's lineup, whether the introduction of brand-new blood or merely the return of a long-gone trouper, the sound, the sense, the very shape of the band has shifted, not only to accommodate the newcomer, but to absorb the newcomer's experiences.

That — all of that — is what this book is about. It is not an insider's tale of sex, drugs, and debauchery — that, if it needs to be told, is for the band members themselves to impart (and thank you, Ian Gillan, for an autobiography that makes a welcome start). Neither is it a fly-on-the-wall account of the ins and outs of the band's business practises, for that, again, is Deep Purple's own business.

Rather, this is the story of a band as it forms, develops, succeeds, and survives in a world filled with other bands; a document of the ideas, interactions, and inspirations that, for over forty years, have shaped and sharpened, shattered, and shadowed the musicians whose names will forever be associated with the one group that they all have in common.

Deep Purple's first LP was titled *Shades of Deep Purple*. This book could easily be subtitled *Shards Of*. But, like all shards, when they are reassembled with enough care and effort, they form a complete picture.

Chapter 1

Absolute Beginners

They were the war babies, a generation conceived while German bombs rained down on British cities and young marrieds snatched just a few days together before the men went back to the battle. None were old enough to retain any but the most fleeting memories of the war — a child born in 1941 was barely four when the fighting stopped. They were sufficiently aware to be conscious that something momentous had suddenly happened, but young enough to file it away among the favorite toys and elderly aunts that crowd every childhood mind.

It was only later, as relatives' talk and schoolteachers' lessons took their place alongside those filings, that anything more than experience became a part of the memory. And later still, as short trousers gave way to long ones, and the opposite sex started looking more cuddly than stuffed bears and zebras, before the sheer magnitude of all they had lived through struck home — the bluster and the blackouts, the fear and the fires, the restrictions and the rationing. And now the sense that England's pleasant green had turned to featureless gray, as though some higher power had mockingly decreed that winning the war was only the first step. Winning the peace was something else entirely.

That was the task the war babies faced — how to win the peace. Through the last years of the '40s, when the winters were colder and the meat rations shorter, they simply accepted life as it was laid out before them. Into the early '50s, too, adolescence stretched out like a looming no-man's-land, the final rite of passage before they stepped into their father's shoes and followed him to the office. But first, two years serving in the armed forces.

National Service, the compulsory induction of every able-bodied school-leaver into one of Her Majesty's Armed Forces, was introduced in 1948, in part to halt a massive upsurge in juvenile crime in the immediate postwar period; in part to ensure that Britain, so unprepared for Hitler in 1939, would never be caught napping again.

When the United Nations waded into Korea in 1951, National Servicemen supplied nearly 60 per cent of Britain's infantry force; when Britain marched into Egypt in 1956, the conscripts were in the frontline again. Everywhere that Britannia was perceived to be under threat, a fresh crop of eighteen-year-old boys was draped in green and dispatched to serve their nation — with their blood, if they had to. And there was very little they could do to prevent it, or even postpone it.

Maybe that's why rock'n'roll was so important to these youths, fourteen, fifteen years into a life that seemed to have been mapped out before it had even begun. The sounds that filtered out of the transistor radio, pressed tight to one ear beneath the bedclothes, had an unpredictability that wasn't simply exciting, it was liberating. No one had ever heard anything like it — no one had ever sung anything like it; and how satisfying it was, after a hard day's obeisance to a crinkled adult world, to simply let rip with the feelings you really felt meant something.

By the end of the decade, the vampiric shadow of two years of compulsory square-bashing was finally lifted, and National Service was consigned to the history books. In the meantime, rock'n'roll proved a potent antidote to the fears and uncertainty those words invoked. Rock'n'roll and, alongside it, the unexplored possibilities of being young.

But it wasn't only the energy and escapism of rock'n'roll that appealed. It was the sense of illegality as well, the knowledge that the older generation — anybody from an elder brother up to a grizzled great-grandmother — hated it with a passion they had hitherto reserved for the likes of Hitler and rickets. Rock'n'roll was unsafe, corrupting, evil, and American, and it was difficult to decide which offended them most.

For many kids, even hearing the new rebel yell was a battleground that only added to its outlaw allure. The BBC, the state-sponsored broadcaster that held a monopoly on British radio until as late as 1973, barely even registered the latest youth fad, and the family wireless was rarely tuned to anything but the Beeb's own brand of entertainment — light orchestral music, live dancing contests, prewar comedians, and mind-broadening lectures. Which is where the transistor under the bedclothes came in, furtively tuning in to the unregulated Radio Luxembourg that beamed in from the European coast, crackling with the atmosphere and fading with the wind.

That's where the new music held sway and that's how it traveled, on barely tolerated (but legally untouchable) waves of sound, from the heart of the Grand Duchy to the souls of English youth. It was years before the young minds that devoured the noise from Luxy came to realize they'd absorbed the sounds of the BBC, too, and years before they came to appreciate precisely how valuable that overspill was.

Fresh down to London from the Welsh town of Brecon, where he was born on November 30, 1945, Roger Glover was ten years old when rock'n'roll hit, and as smitten by the bug as any of his peers. Even at that age, he had no time for Sam Costa and Archie Andrews, Nat Gonella and His Georgians, Celia Lipton and Dorothy Carless, and all the rest of the BBC brew. But four decades later, he recalled, "Growing up in the '50s in England, we had the BBC, and they played every kind of music there was. And, though we complained about it, in retrospect that was a great education. Without the BBC, we'd not have heard gospel music and classical music, folk, blues, and jazz. They'd dip into everything and it wasn't done with any style or anything. But in retrospect it wasn't so bad, because you look at kids growing up now, they get force-fed a particular subgenre of music, and that's it. They don't have the wide overview. They're very channeled."

In 1955, Bill Haley rocked around the clock and Britain's teenagers — the word was not new, but its meaning certainly was — swarmed to the cinemas to see him. In 1956, Elvis Presley scored with "Heartbreak Hotel," and Lonely Street had never sounded so sexy before. By 1957, Britain's own first rockers and rollers were making their way up the charts, and the skiffle boom was underway — proto-folkies with a Woody Guthrie bent, predating the DIY ethics of punk by twenty years not simply by teaching themselves to play their instruments, but by teaching themselves to make them as well.

Stick a broomstick in a tea chest, arm it with a tight, strong string, and presto, you had a bass guitar. With thimbles on your fingertips and a washboard by your side, suddenly you were a percussionist. Not everybody did it; not everybody even liked it. But, again like punk two decades hence, skiffle wasn't simply the latest musical craze. It was symbolic of something else, a sense that, for the first time in a long time — certainly since before the war, and possibly since before time began — the present was no longer the blank state of stasis you ground through while waiting for the future. The present was suddenly a pleasure in itself.

Roger Glover was lucky. His parents moved to London to take over as landlords of a public house, the Richmond Arms on the Old Brompton Road, in Kensington, and live music was one of the venue's staples. "Skiffle bands used to come and play in the saloon bar," he remembered. "I'd get out of bed and creep downstairs to listen to them."

Other kids had to go further afield in search of such grand entertainment and, having got there, they made sure they found it. The cities erupted. Where once red brick and gray men held sway, and the sidewalks rolled up when dusk came to call, there now flashed a sea of color and kids. Pounding beats and exotic smoke, tailored suits and haute coiffure — the world that director Julien Temple conjured in *Absolute Beginners*, of garish neon and switchblade glint, may have been more *West Side Story* than West End London, but still the streets of Soho exuded everything a teenage heart could desire, from the jukebox pounding at the 2 I's Coffee Bar, to the promise-packed notice boards in the paper-shop window: "Established band seeks ambitious singer," "Guitar for sale: 10/- ono," "Pop group manager needs up-and-coming talent," "Discreet French-style massages."

The streets were paved with magnets. For the wilder kids, simply breathing the air and tasting the fruit was enough. For the ambitious ones, there were the crowds draped outside the gold-plated portals of the agents and talent spotters, busking whatever instrument they could play, or simply hanging around and looking cool, hoping the Great Man might spot them and whisk them to fame. For the serious ones, there were the late-night dives that stayed open all day, where earnest jazzmen and bohemian folkies gathered to plot the overthrow of rock. And for the practical ones, there were the music stores just a few short blocks away, crowding round the junction of Oxford Street and Tottenham Court Road, and straggling up Denmark Street — the home of the hits.

Twelve years old, Richard Harold Blackmore was one of the serious ones, journeying into the city every day he could to soak up the atmosphere and dream, his nose pressed against the glass of his favorite guitar emporiums. He came in from Heston, although his soft accent revealed more exotic, west-country origins. He was born in Weston-Super-Mare on April 14, 1945, but moved away when he was two, to a suburb of the West London suburbs, close enough to Heathrow Airport to hear the Comets streaking overhead, but still awaiting the umbilical line of the Underground railway to connect it to the world.

At that age, of course, all he could do was look, but even before he borrowed his first-ever guitar, the instrument captivated him. By the time he persuaded his parents to buy him one of his own, £5 for a black Framus acoustic, he'd already convinced himself that he was destined to play, and the year of classical lessons that were thrown in with the gift — the one condition laid down by his rock-loathing father — quickly convinced other people as well.

Blackmore accepted the lessons and did well at them. But he hankered for wilder sounds as well and, with the guileless optimism of ambitious childhood, he decided to chase his dream from the top, opening the phone book and looking up the address of his own favorite guitar player, Big Jim Sullivan. It turned out that the star of singer Marty Wilde's rocking band lived just a bus ride away in Hounslow, and so, while other would-be ax idols took their lead from the great American guitarists of the day and dreamed that one day they might actually see them playing in concert, Blackmore was knocking on his hero's front door, stars in his eyes and guitar in hand.

Sullivan wasn't immediately impressed by his young visitor, not on the first visit nor, apparently, on the multitude that followed. But he never did turn the boy away. "I think he used to get fed up with me hanging around, but he taught me a lot," Blackmore later reflected, with lesson one coming more or less the first time Sullivan heard the boy play. Any guitarist, Big Jim told his student, could parrot the solos others had recorded. But a great guitarist created his own.

Blackmore was still learning his instrument when he joined his first band, but, practical beyond his thirteen years, he had no intention of continuing his education in public. He turned instead to the ubiquitous tea-chest bass, the sonic foundation of the 2 I's Coffee Bar Junior Skiffle Group — named for, but never actually performing at, that most legendary of Soho learning centers. The group lasted six months, until skiffle itself had faded from view, and he returned to his first love.

Blackmore left school at fifteen in 1960 and found a job at the airport, learning to service radio transmitters, his eye for the task honed by the time he'd spent in the school science lab electrifying his guitar and building an amp from an old valve radio. It wasn't a job he was especially desperate to pursue, but the wage packet financed his love of music, and it paid for a new, "real" electric guitar, a Hofner Club 50.

Now he was ready to step out with his instrument. One of his old school friends, Mick Underwood, had recently taken possession of a drum kit and, together, they formed their first band. The Dominators took their place on a local youth club circuit that was already creaking beneath the weight of so many bands.

For reasons that have never been understood, the extremes of West London were a fertile breeding ground for so many of the musicians with whom Blackmore's path soon crossed: Ian Gillan lived in Hounslow, Nick Simper was born in Southall, Mick Waller was from Greenford. Without ever straying more than five miles from the Blackmore home, you could have formed the most spectacular band in the world, simply by following the sounds of the rehearsing hopefuls. And you'd have had your choice of guitarists as well — though they never knew one another at the time, Jimmy Page, too, hailed from Heston.

Bassist Nick Simper, on the other hand, was constantly bumping into Blackmore. He was seven months younger than the guitarist (he was born on November 3, 1945), and his first band, the Renegades, debuted on the circuit around the same time as the Dominators. Although the two bands never shared a bill, they often said hello.

Simper's own career moved slower than Blackmore's, edging from one short-lived group to another until finally he found one, he later laughed, that was proficient enough "not to have Coke bottles thrown at them." That was the Delta Five, a cover band that, according to legend, opened for Jerry Lee Lewis at the Hanwell Community Centre during the Killer's 1962 U.K. tour — his first visit since being drummed out of the country four years earlier, when details of his marriage to a thirteen-year-old cousin aroused one of those periodic witch hunts to which the British media is so prone.

Blackmore, by this time, had moved on through his own succession of local bands — the Satellites and Mike Dee & the Jaywalkers among them — before 1962 brought him his own taste of minor stardom as one of the Savages, the ultratheatrical backing band for arch-showman and rockabilly ghoul "Screaming Lord" David Sutch.

It was not the first time Blackmore had tried out for the band. The previous year, as rhythm guitarist with the Satellites, he found himself competing with his own lead guitarist, Roger Mingay, for the same vacancy. "Ritchie Blackmore, who could have only been fifteen at the time," Savages drummer Carlo Little recalled, "came along with his girl-friend and his dad. We heard about seven or eight blokes, but it was a toss-up between Ritchie and Roger Mingay. Roger just had the edge, because he was older and more experienced."

Mingay had long since moved on, and his replacement as well when, at long last, in May 1962, Blackmore got the call he'd been waiting for. He was a Savage and, nightly, was to have his normally reticent stage demeanor trashed and trampled as Sutch, having already dressed the musicians in whichever outlandish costume took his fancy, insisted they act the part as well.

Clad in nothing more than a loincloth, Blackmore quickly became accustomed to being dragged to stage center, often by his guitar neck. Quickly, too, he began developing moves and routines that were as flam-boyant as Sutch himself, a talent that the singer, speaking shortly before his death in June 1999, recalled with a delighted cackle: "When Ritchie first joined, all he wanted to do was play his guitar. [But] you could tell he was dying to join in with the madness and, by the time he left, he was an absolute wild man."

For many bands, the guitar-playing alone would have been enough — Blackmore's specialty, as Carlo Little put it, saw him executing "devastating runs up and down the guitar [that] left people gasping for breath." Soon, however, Blackmore was throwing himself across the stage as dramatically as Sutch.

Blackmore did not necessary relish his time with Sutch. Looking back, he told journalist Dave Ling, "The hungry days were mostly nice times, but I often played with musicians I hated, too. Some of them were real snobs who only wanted to see the negative sides of playing rock-'n'roll. This was really bad when I played with . . . Sutch. One half of the band consisted of rock'n'rollers, the other half were jazz soloists. They drove me nuts."

However, Blackmore later acknowledged, and Sutch readily confirmed, that much of his future stagecraft was learned at the Lord's knee. "The breaking guitars, the catching fire to amps, all that was just a part of the Savages show," said Sutch. "Years before anyone had heard of Pete Townshend and autodestruction, Ritchie would be out there smashing things."

Nick Simper, too, caught Sutch's eye. Though Simper never formally joined the Savages, there were several occasions when, having misplaced his regular bassist, Sutch asked him to stand in for a show. "That was a great lineup," Sutch reflected. "It was the start of Deep Purple. Ritchie and Nick, they didn't play together very often, but when they did, you could tell they had a spark going. I wasn't at all surprised when they formed a band together."

Blackmore remained with Sutch for six months, and when he departed, in October 1962, he didn't travel far. Across the string of now-classic singles, ignited in 1961 by the shock-horror rockabilly of "Til the Following Night," Sutch worked with maverick producer Joe Meek, the mastermind behind what emerged as among the most exciting slices of vinyl in British rock history. As of late 1962, however, Meek's schemes were on hold as he sought out a new drummer and guitarist for the Outlaws, the studio house band that, more than any other, brought a distinctive instrumental glow to the best of Meek's period recordings.

The musician grapevine put him in touch with the first half of the required combination, drummer Mick Underwood; he, in turn, naturally recommended his best friend, Ritchie Blackmore. By year's end, the pair had made their first appearance on record — and scored their first hit single, as Mike Berry's "Don't You Think It's Time" powered to No. 6 on the U.K. chart.

Had he lived, and had that life only conformed a little more to the music business norm, Joe Meek would today be ranked among the greatest producers of the rock'n'roll age. Instead, though a devoted cult following still bestows that lofty title upon him, his greater reputation is as a sad and lonely man whose creative genius, sparking across some still unmatchable music, was undermined at every step of the way by his unpredictability, his stubborn selfishness, and, ultimately, his self-destructiveness.

Even Meek's most indulgent biographers acknowledge that there are great swaths of Meek's catalog that they find utterly unlistenable; even his greatest fans will swear they could happily die tomorrow if it meant they would never hear some personal nightmare recording again.

What these otherwise reasonable viewpoints overlook, however, is the very thing that made Meek so important — the sheer unpredictability that was the nature of his game. For it was not the wavering of genius, nor the arrogance of ego, that prompted Meek to make some truly dreadful records. Rather, it was the same relentless drive and fervent imagination that also allowed him to make some great ones. It was just that sometimes the experiment failed.

And so, for every "Ain't Necessarily So," there is an "Early Bird"; for every "She's Fallen in Love with a Monster Man," there is an "I'm Not a Bad Guy"; and for every John Leyton, there was a Tony Dangerfield. But, in every instance, it was not the end result that mattered. It was the loving labor that went into the creation. Not for him the comfortable, well-equipped surroundings within which the other producers of the age did their jobs. Meek worked from home, from a sprawling warren of junk-piled cupboards that even he referred to as "the bathroom." Wires trailed wildly across every surface, and a visitor who managed to remain undetected while Meek worked his magic was as likely to see a musician striking an ashtray with a signet ring, as strumming a guitar or playing the drums. If he couldn't create the sound he wanted by conventional means, he looked for the unconventional.

The Outlaws were one of the few oases of normalcy within Meek's empire, a tight band that could play anything he threw at them, and play it well. Over the next two years or so, as the last gasps of the original rock'n'roll boom faded from memory in the face of a new onslaught launched by the Merseybeat of the Beatles, Blackmore played on more sessions for Meek than even he can remember. Meek himself disdained the new-fangled beat groups — was, in fact, one of the multitude of London-based producers and A&R men who turned away the then-unknown Fab Four when they first came knocking at his door.

He had long since forgiven himself that particular indulgence, but he certainly knew which way the musical breeze was blowing. The Outlaws, though they could (and did) turn their hand toward any style Meek asked of them, were responsible for the torrent of bouncing beat-styled singles that poured out of Meek's Holloway Road lair, a litany of crack-ling 45s by everyone from North London beat merchants the Honeycombs to a then-unknown and unsung Tom Jones, from John Leyton to Glenda Collins.

There were weeks when Blackmore and the band found themselves playing up to half a dozen sessions a day, simply waiting around the studio while Meek ushered in another young hopeful or old pro to record. And, when they weren't in the studio, the Outlaws were out on the road, backing one or another of Meek's protégés or, for a few weeks during 1964, accompanying the legendary Gene Vincent as he undertook another of his periodic comebacks.

The band recorded in their own right as well, making a glorious chain of singles under Meek's tutelage that included a positively violent rendi-tion of Jerry Lee Lewis' "Keep on Knocking" — subsequently termed, by British DJ John Peel, the first heavy metal record ever made. Maybe it was, maybe it wasn't — released all but simultaneously, the Kinks' "You Really Got Me" has been tarred with the same pioneering brush.

Not that such plaudits made much difference to the Outlaws. They broke up in spring 1964 and Blackmore moved on to the Wild Boys, the backing band assembled to accompany Meek's premier protégé, Teutonic bleached-bombshell heartthrob Heinz. There he continued playing on hit records, but suddenly Meek was no longer the only producer who sensed something special in Blackmore. Another freelance operative,

Derek Lawrence, was equally keen to work with the guitarist, hiring him first to play alongside a couple of ad hoc British Invasion–styled bands he was aiming at the lucrative U.S. market, then unleashing him across a de facto solo single, credited to the Ritchie Blackmore Orchestra and, today, rightly regarded as a Holy Grail among Deep Purple collectors. The distinctive fuzz tone that dominates "Little Brown Jug," incidentally, was attained via a six-inch speaker that Blackmore, deliberately or otherwise, had kicked and stamped into distortion overdrive.

The single did nothing, and neither did an attempt to get his own band going. Inspired by the madness of life with Sutch, Blackmore conceived a new act that would be just as colorful, adventurous, and explosive as any the Lord ever conjured. It was called the Three Musketeers, and the musicians were precisely that — swashbuckling swordsmen who just happened to be magnificent instrumentalists.

Jim Anderson and Avid Andersen joined him in this new escapade. He had worked with them in his latest gig, backing Jerry Lee Lewis on a short German stint. When Lewis returned to America, the Musketeers remained behind, booking a residency at the newly opened Star-Club in Bochum, to begin early in 1966.

It was a disaster. "We [came] onstage fencing," Blackmore recalled, "as the drummer played two bass drums, which was unheard of in those days, and [we were] a three-piece, which was also unusual. The band was excellent, but far too advanced for the German public, because we used to play very fast instrumentals." Too advanced? Maybe. But it's true that audiences never warmed to them and the band was no more than a week into its residency when the promoter called them aside and announced he was giving the remainder of their contract to another new band, High Society.

For the moment, that didn't seem to matter. Neil Christian, whose Crusaders were a permanent presence on the lower rungs of the British beat boom, was another fervent admirer of Blackmore's and, when his original guitarist, one Jimmy Page, moved on, Christian did not hesitate to invite Blackmore to fill his boots.

Blackmore agreed, but he was tiring of the endless grind of cold dressing rooms, drafty Transit vans, cabinless ferry crossings, and half-empty clubs in the back end of nowhere. Looking around him, he saw the music scene exploding with new sounds, new energies, new impetus

— and where was he? Still rattling around much the same circuit he'd been on since 1960, before half of the latest generation of red-hot musicians had even tuned their first guitars. He quit Christian's band and sat back to consider his options.

Blackmore was restless, bored. But, worse than that, he was stagnating, so accustomed to standing still while waiting for something to happen that he'd forgotten that sometimes you have to make it happen yourself. So, when someone asked him if he'd had a chance to catch this new black American guitarist who'd appeared in London, who could play the guitar with his teeth, Blackmore barely even shrugged his disdain. Another showman, another show-*off*: "How very musical."

But then someone else asked him the same question, and someone else after that. And the buzz never stopped. From the day in September 1966 when the newcomer first touched down, the name of Jimi Hendrix spread like a plague, not simply among the chattering classes who leap aboard any fashionable flurry, but among the very cream of the rock establishment — among Cream themselves, the self-reverently named virtuoso combo that already boasted the world's greatest guitarist, Eric Clapton, in its three-man ranks. Hendrix jammed with them within a week of his arrival in London, and Clapton confessed he was blown away by what he saw.

Jeff Beck, Pete Townshend, Paul McCartney, Brian Jones, Eric Burdon . . . There were so many luminaries already in attendance around Hendrix that Blackmore finally gave in and joined the queue. Days later, he was armed with his own Fender Stratocaster, a gift from Eric Clapton.

Later, Blackmore came to play down the effect that Hendrix had on him: "I was impressed . . . not so much by his playing, as his attitude — he wasn't a great player, but everything else about him was brilliant. Even the way he walked was amazing. His guitar-playing, though, was always a little bit weird. Hendrix inspired me, but I was still more into Wes Montgomery."

At the time, however, Blackmore was considerably less confrontational on the subject. Responding instinctively to the gauntlet that Hendrix's fiery showmanship and electrifying style threw down to every guitar picker of the age, Blackmore had learned another lesson. If you can't be the master, you can at least borrow his tools. And then you master them.

On October 7, 1966, midway through a tour of northern Britain, the car carrying Johnny Kidd and the latest incarnation of his Pirates backing band was involved in a horrific road accident. Kidd was killed, while his bassist, Nick Simper, broke an arm.

Since his days with the Delta Five and occasionally Sutch, Simper — like Blackmore — had bounced between bands. He was a member of the imaginatively named Some Other Guys for a time; he toured the Channel Islands with his first professional band, Buddy Britten and the Regents, and joined them on the mod bandwagon when they changed their name to the Simon Raven Cult; and he was a willing guinea pig when a local, Hanwell-based music store, Marshall's, marketed its first, giant, 4-by-12 speaker cabinets, then sought out local musicians to push them through their paces.

By early 1966, Simper was biding time in Cyrano and the Bergeracs, yet another lower-rung beat band scouring the West London circuit, but still keeping his eyes peeled for that increasingly elusive break. This time, it wasn't far away.

Pop memories were long in those days, and there was scarcely a soul on the British music scene who couldn't recall the fission of fear that spangled down their spine the first time they heard Johnny Kidd's "Shakin' All Over," the 1960 No. 1 that announced to the world that British rock had come of age.

There'd been homegrown rockers before, of course, from Tommy Steele to Marty Wilde, from Cliff Richard to Wee Willie Harris. Not one, however, had stayed the course, not one had realized there might be more to a life in music than a few quick rockers at the dawn of their careers before they marched on to embrace lighter, sweeter forms of entertainment. Steele had gone into musicals, Cliff was turning into slush, and most everyone else had faded away.

Kidd, however, never let up, not even when the hits dried up and his advisors insisted he take the showbiz route out. Nightly, he'd slide into his leather and eye patch, make sure the band was cranked up to kill, then put on the greatest rock'n'roll show in the world.

Nothing fazed him — not the lack of hits nor the lessening crowds, not even the diminishing financial returns. Even when his latest band walked out on him in a dispute over how much he paid them, he seemed completely unflustered. Something would turn up, he believed, and he was right. Days after Simper and Bergeracs drummer Roger Truth heard that the great Captain Kidd's crew had abandoned ship, the pair looked up his address and knocked on the door. And when Kidd himself answered, they told him why they were there: "We're the Pirates."

In fact, they became the New Pirates — the old ones, led by bassist Johnny Spence and drummer Frank Farley, still retained the original band name. But it didn't matter. Nightly on the road with Kidd, Simper recreated the thrill of the first . . . the fiftieth . . . the five-hundredth time you ever heard "Shakin' All Over," only for the accident to end it for all time.

The music industry flocked to Kidd's memory. In nightclubs and theaters around the U.K., bands paid and played their own tributes to an all-time inspiration; as far afield as Stockholm, Sweden, midway through a European tour, The Who performed the Pirates' "Please Don't Touch" in memory of the master. And Screaming Lord Sutch convened a whole new generation of Savages, converted them to Centurions, and announced the band would debut at a benefit for Kidd's widow.

Clad in a surprisingly lifelike approximation of ancient Roman armor, Ritchie Blackmore, Carlo Little, Matthew Fisher, Tony Dangerfield, and Joel James became Lord Caesar Sutch's Roman Empire, an extravaganza that spread to territories the original Romans never conquered, Sweden and Germany included, before petering out in the early spring.

Immediately, Neil Christian came knocking again. The singer had just scored a moderate hit, "That's Nice," and landed a short German tour that wound up in Hamburg in May 1967. The entire Roman Empire joined him on the journey, but it was there that Blackmore finally decided he had had enough. While the rest of the band returned home to England, Blackmore stayed behind in Hamburg, half-retired and half-planning a new band of his own, to be called Mandrake Root.

Since its heyday in the early 1960s, the seething years during which the Star-Club justly jousted with the U.K. for the title of "the cradle of British rock," Hamburg had slipped somewhat from the musical map. The Beatles, of course, cut their performance teeth there and, once they returned home and broke with such enormity, the Star-Club (or, for that matter, any venue in the vicinity of the Star-Club) became a compulsory rite of passage for every British hopeful of the age.

Bands were booked in for almost military, test-of-endurance–type campaigns; anyone bemoaning the repeal of National Service, and thinking kids were getting away with life far too easily, would have sneered on the other side of their faces had they only known the tours of duty that awaited these young musicians in Hamburg. Eight-, ten-, twelve-hour shifts were the norm, the bands playing for sixty minutes, resting for thirty, then back for another hour, all night long.

Some nights it was a bloodbath, physically, emotionally, musically, and chemically. For many bands, only the pills that circulated so freely kept them going until their shift was over — but then, when it was finally time to sleep, they'd be so wired they'd be up for half the next day, finally crashing just in time to start the circus over again.

Such horror stories did nothing to deter fresh meat. As the beat boom built, as new bands spilled out of every corner of the United Kingdom, and as Germany threw her own youthful talent into the same melting pot, every one of them set their sights on the Star-Club, convinced that the very floorboards exuded some kind of magical power. But lightning of that magnitude strikes only once and, its prestige long since tarnished by too many unprestigious acts, by 1967 the Star-Club lived on little more than its memories and flourished via its reputation, an attraction for every starstruck Beatles fan passing through Hamburg's St. Pauli district.

If you wanted to meet musicians, though, it was still the best gig in town, and though Mandrake Root never amounted to much more than a passing fancy, with its membership confined to whoever Blackmore was jamming, talking, or drinking with at any given moment, still the band's name is woven into the footnotes of the Star-Club's lingering legend. Indeed, a handful of musicians actually came close to joining, including drummer Carlo Little, back in town as part of Billie Davis' backing band, and his partner in this new group's rhythm section, Nick Simper.

One of the crop of girl singers who opened their accounts under Joe Meek's aegis, Davis was then recruited to Australian impresario Robert Stigwood's burgeoning stable of stars and, groomed to near-perfection, she was launched as the female antagonist on comedian Mike Sarne's

"Will I What?" — a cheerfully cheeky call-and-response song that went to No. 18 in Britain in 1962.

Months later, her cover of the Exciters' Stateside hit "Tell Him" brought her first solo success, but a broken jaw, sustained in a car accident while returning home from a concert in Worcester, effectively slammed her career to a halt. A follow-up single, "He's the One," foundered on Davis' inability to promote it and, by the time she was able to work again, her early momentum had long since dissipated.

She continued recording and touring, of course, and returned to the charts once more, in 1968. For now, however, she was playing where and when she could, with few illusions beyond putting on a great show — with a great band behind her. Guitarist Ged Stone and keyboard player Billy Davidson joined Simper and Little, and the group set off for Germany.

Of course, Simper and Little immediately reconnected with Ritchie Blackmore; and, of course, their conversation drifted from what they'd been doing to what they dreamed of doing. And that was the cue Blackmore was waiting for. It was the age of the powerhouse rock trio — Cream and the Jimi Hendrix Experience both made maximum noise with minimal instrumentation: guitar, drums, and bass, with one or the other to sing. Little, Simper, and Blackmore knew one another, could work well together. What if . . . ? What if. When the Billie Davis residency ended, so did Little and Simper's stay in Germany.

Another day in Hamburg, another band to check out. Back in January 1967, on the ferry across the North Sea, Blackmore got talking with another musician, the drummer with a band called the Maze. They were on their way to Italy for a three-month residency in Milan, but were planning to get up to Hamburg once the gigs were over. It appeared they had succeeded, scoring a three-week stay at the Star-Club, and Blackmore made a point of going to see them. Or, at least, going to see their drummer.

Ian Anderson Paice was born in Nottingham, England, on June 29, 1948. His father, Keith, was once pianist in a dance band, a road warrior of the prewar years, but gave it up when he started his family. Now Paice Senior was content simply to play around locally, and when he sensed his son was musical, too — an avid drummer even before he got his first kit — it was only natural to encourage him. By the time Ian reached his early teens, the two Paices were playing together at Saturday-night dances around the new family home in Bicester, near Oxford.

By 1964, Paice had joined his first beat group, Georgie and the Rave Ons; the following year, the same set of friends changed their name to the Shindigs and, though they remained steadfastly unknown beyond Bicester's borders, in town they were something else entirely. Particularly their drummer. So when another local group, the Horizons, found themselves in need of a new one in mid-1965, they had no hesitation in poaching Paice away with the promise that, though they were no bigger than the Shindigs at the time, they had one thing the other band seemed seriously to lack — ambition. They'd already decided to change their name, to the MI Five (after the British secret service). Their next step was to turn professional.

The Horizons were the first and only band vocalist Rod Evans ever played with. Born in Edinburgh, Scotland, on January 19, 1947, but raised in and around Slough, where the family moved while he was a toddler, Evans was still at school when the band formed around him — guitarist Roger Lewis, keyboard player Chris Banham, and bassist Lenny Hawkes. Since that time, Hawkes had moved on to chart success with the pop band the Tremoloes (he was replaced by Eric Keene); now, the MI Five looked destined to follow him up the ladder.

Things were certainly moving. By the summer of 1966, with Paice firmly installed in the engine room, the band had landed a recording contract with Parlophone, at that time universally renowned as the U.K. home of the Beatles. Their first single, "You'll Never Stop Loving Me," sold poorly, but the band quickly bounced back, abandoning the hidebound R&B sound that had been their forte, and delving into a psychedelic realm. And they changed their name once again. Now they were the Maze.

Again, the band seemed destined for success. "Discovered" by Stigwood again, the Maze were promptly signed to his Reaction label, label mates to The Who and Cream. Stigwood was a man accustomed to success, and he was adamant that the Maze would meet with the same thing, no matter how far they had to travel to find it. And so the Maze found themselves weaving, appropriately, a maze across Europe before washing up in Hamburg, where that three-week residency awaited them.

Cheerfully reunited early on in the band's stint, Blackmore and Paice met regularly to talk about music and discuss Mandrake Root with earnest enthusiasm. At least, Blackmore was earnest and enthusiastic. Paice's interest faltered when he learned that the band's membership at that time comprised just one player, Blackmore himself. He declined the offer of a place in the band and, when he returned to the U.K. with the Maze, Blackmore remained in Hamburg, still nursing his dreams.

Chapter 2

On a Carousel

A lot of crazy ideas floated to the surface of the psychedelic rock'n'roll psyche from 1967–68. The Beatles talked of opening a boutique, and handing out money to the musically needy. The Rolling Stones decided a circus big top was a suitable venue for amplified heat. The Who dreamed of writing a rock opera that would make a superstar of a deaf, dumb, and blind boy. And British pop veteran Chris Curtis wanted to launch a rock'n'roll carousel called, of course, the Roundabout.

Aesthetically, the daydream dovetailed perfectly with the predilections of the age. Nostalgia was "in," and what was more nostalgic than a good old-fashioned fun fair, with its echoes of youth and blissful hot summers? The Beatles had already tested the waters with the Victorian carnival of Mr. Kite; the Idle Race had fleshed out the spirit with the captivating "Skeleton and the Roundabout," and the first psychedelic happening of the 1967 season, the 24 Hour Technicolour Dream concert, had put the dream into practical use, by installing a giant helter-skelter in the center of the dance floor. Plus, anything was worth a shot if it freed the senses from another bunch of musicians standing around the stage while bubble lights bubbled and a stroboscope flashed.

The Roundabout was, all practical considerations notwithstanding, a brilliant concept, an audacious collision of the old-time touring routines that still plowed around the theater circuit, where a single band backed a host of solo singing sensations, and the new wave of superstar supergroups that was soon sweeping all before it. A fixed nucleus of musicians — a guitarist, drummer, keyboard player, and a bassist — would be located at the center of the roundabout. Other musicians would then leap aboard to join them, to play whatever they saw fit, then depart when their turn was over.

Curtis himself was almost as fascinating as the idea — his career had touched both the highest and the deepest extremes of musical fame and fortune: swings and, indeed, roundabouts.

It was back in 1960 that Curtis was first recruited to country pop singer Johnny Sandon's backing band, to plow the infant circuit of a local Liverpool pop scene that boasted any number of aspiring young beat combos — Kingsize Taylor & the Dominoes, Rory Storm & the Hurricanes, and, though they barely registered in the most generous local pecking order, the sometimes Silver Beatles. Sandon's own quintet slipped effortlessly into this community and, when Sandon departed to tour Germany with the Remo Four, his bandmates opted to remain together as the Searchers and make their own way across the North Sea.

Their destination was the Star-Club, at that time at the peak of both its powers and its demands on its entertainers. Most bands simply couldn't last the pace, and fled back to sanity the first moment they could. Those that did survive, though, quickly reaped the rewards — again, physically, emotionally, musically, chemically.

For the Beatles, Hamburg taught them the brutal work ethic that sustained them through the years of madness awaiting on the far side of fame. For the Searchers, though they never quite touched the same peaks of perfection as John, Paul, George, and Ringo, the experience made them mightier than they'd ever have been if they'd stayed at home. And when John Lennon described them as his favorite band in 1963, he was recalling all those steaming nights in the dockside sweatbox, watching the Searchers slam through a set that was as much inspiration as perspiration.

Buoyed by Lennon's words of love, the next couple of years saw the Searchers ride His Master's Vote to glory, igniting a sequence of fourteen hit singles that kept the group on the U.K. chart long after the beat boom had banged its final drum. Three of their first four singles went to No. 1 and the best of their output — "Needles and Pins," "Sweets for My Sweet," "When You Walk in the Room," "Don't Throw Your Love Away" — remains a staple of countless period memories and nostalgic compilations.

Slowly, however, the Searchers' star began to dip. The once sold-out theater tours gave way to underattended nightclubs and workingmen's clubs, the singles began struggling even to scratch the British Top 50. By late 1966, the Searchers were no more, and Curtis was looking to start afresh — a new band, a new vision, and a brand-new concept. The Roundabout.

It was Vicki Wickham, assistant producer of television's *Ready Steady Go!*, who introduced Curtis to the businessman who came to share his enthusiasm for the venture. She'd received an invitation to a dinner party being thrown by Tony Edwards, owner of the Alice Edwards fashion house and manager of model-turned-fledgling-singer Ayshea, and brought Curtis along with her. In the course of conversation, Curtis mentioned the Roundabout, and Edwards seemed interested — an impression Curtis carried around for much of the next year.

When Curtis first conceived the Roundabout, its greatest drawback had been its ambition. Now, however, it seemed — in the vernacular of the time — considerably less "far out." Sometime during the late summer of 1967, Curtis decided the time was ripe for the Roundabout and got back in touch with Edwards. Edwards agreed, and remarked that he might also be interested in financing the venture, should anything come of Curtis' plans. His attempts to launch Ayshea had come to naught, even though Island Records entrepreneur Chris Blackwell helped set up a new label, BRP, for her alone. Edwards was still fascinated with the music industry, though, and if the pop side of the business was proving unreceptive, maybe he'd have more luck at the heavier rock end of things.

While Edwards made the calls to marketing consultant John Coletta and Ronald Hire that brought him the partners he felt he needed for the new venture, Curtis was busy recruiting musicians to the Roundabout. The first band he approached was a Herefordshire outfit called the Shakedown Sound. Drummer Dale Griffin remembers, "We were hanging around the West End of London, wandering around and in and out of the many music shops there, salivating over the arrays of amazing amplifiers, PA systems, guitars, keyboards, and drums. You know . . . wishing and hoping.

"We noticed that a tall, skinny guy with a rather old-fashioned haircut and suit seemed to be everywhere that we went. Finally, we recognized him as Chris. Eventually he walked up to us and asked if we were a group. Immediately we were suspicious. We'd heard all about blokes like that! But he invited us to the Giaconda Café in Denmark Street, which was a real muso's hangout.

"He was amiable and good-humored and wanted us to form his new group, Roundabout. We walked to the offices of Polydor Records, where Chris walked up and down the corridors, knocking on doors, but not getting any joy, so he spoke with us a little more and said he'd meet us the next day, but he didn't show, and we were rather relieved, truth to tell." (Three years later, the group reemerged as early-'70s superstars Mott the Hoople.)

Other ears, however, were more receptive. Curtis had recently taken up residence in a flat on the same Chelsea street, Gunter Grove, that had spawned the infant Rolling Stones five years before, sharing the premises with three other musicians, the Moody Blues' Denny Laine, Procol Harum's David Knights, and the Artwoods' Jon Lord. Between the four of them, there was never any shortage of ideas and suggestions but, of them all, it was Lord toward whom Curtis was most drawn.

Musically, the two seemed ideally in tune; conceptually, Lord never tired of throwing new notions into the Roundabout's revolving evolution. He had ideas that rose far beyond the daily drudge of rock'n'roll, notions that flourished further every time he spoke.

Lord's background, like his imagination, was far from the late-'60s rock'n'roll norm. He was born in the midlands city of Leicester on June 9, 1941, the son of dance-band saxophonist Reg Lord, and was still a child when it became apparent that he'd inherited his father's love of music, graduating to the family's old upright piano and quickly picking up the rudiments. By the age of seven, he was taking formal piano lessons. Among his tutors was Frederick All, a local celebrity who frequently performed organ recitals for the BBC's Light Service (now Radio 2). A decade later, still devoutly taking his lessons, Lord passed the stringent exams set by the Royal College of Music and left school with an A-level.

His first job was as a clerk in a local solicitor's office, where he worked simply to make the money that would allow him to build his record collection. At first, his interests lay in the classics, with rock'n'roll little more than a distant annoyance to be decried with a smile. It was only when he set himself to tackle a rock song, Jerry Lee Lewis' "Whole Lotta Shakin'," that he realized that, maybe, there was more to the noise than he'd originally thought.

No matter how hard he tried to coax them out of the old upright piano, he simply could not master the first four bars of the song. He knew the chords, he knew the notes. But the feel — the clanging, clattering, visceral thrill of a piano screaming defiance — that was what he could not comprehend.

After two years with the solicitors, Lord left to study at the Central School of Speech and Drama in North London's Swiss Cottage neighborhood — music aside, his other great passion was acting and, aware that neither was exactly a steady profession, he opted for the one with the greatest chance of some success. He never abandoned the piano, though, and when he lost his college grant after quitting the Central for a new school being established by some of his favorite tutors, the London Drama Centre, he fell back on his first love to help pay the bills.

His first band was the Bill Ashton Combo, a jazz band that plied the North London pub circuit. From there he graduated to the Don Wilson Quartet, specialists in weddings and sports club receptions by day, denizens of the West End jazz clubs at night. As Red Bludd's Bluesicians, they were regulars at the famed Flamingo, playing short sets of their own and sitting in behind any visiting American jazz and bluesmen who needed them, a grueling apprenticeship, but one that would get the musicians noticed.

Art Wood, one of that coterie of half-forgotten faces who single-handedly brought British R&B kicking and screeching into the world, was one of the Bluesicians' closest admirers, and when his own Art Wood Combo broke up in 1963, it was suggested that they join forces — as the New Art Wood Combo. Over the next few months, the band weathered a couple of lineup changes, and a couple of name changes too — when Lord switched from piano to an electric Lowry organ, his bandmates celebrated by renaming themselves the Great Organ-ised and, over the next six months, they developed a fearsome reputation as one of the most intensive blues experiences the capital had to offer.

Certainly Mike Vernon, a house producer at Decca Records, thought so. A fount of blues knowledge and respectability, Vernon went on to discover Fleetwood Mac, Chicken Shack, and Duster Bennett, the very pillars upon which the late-'60s British blues boom was built. But even now, his understanding of the music was without peer, together with his understanding of the record-buying public. It was Vernon who suggested the band change its name once again, to the readily identifiable Artwoods, and in the summer of 1964, he signed the group to Decca.

The Artwoods' first single, a Terry Kennedy–produced cover of Leadbelly's "Sweet Mary," followed in October, but Lord had something else to celebrate that fall — a recording he had assumed was simply a one-off session for another all-but-unknown band, "You Really Got Me" by the Kinks, stormed to the top of the U.K. charts. Recorded in the studio basement beneath the Artwoods' publishers' Denmark Street offices, with Lord joined on the session by the young Jimmy Page, "You Really Got Me" ignited a twenty-year streak of hits for the Kinks, and ignited, too, that oft-debated argument over what was the first heavy record ever made.

Its magic, however, would not rub off on the Artwoods. Regular single releases over the next two years brought down a hail of great reviews (veteran rocker Billy Fury elected "Goodbye Sisters" his Pick of the Week in *Melody Maker*), but only once did they even nibble chart glory, when their fourth 45, "I Take What I Want," inched to No. 35 on the *Melody Maker* chart.

With Mike Vernon producing, the band cut their debut album in early 1966. It promised, according to the band's own plans, to be an ambitious affair. Lord had recently taken delivery of a Hammond organ (which he promptly cut in half, to make it easier to transport!), and talked enthusiastically about incorporating both established and newly composed classical themes into the music — live, he had been hurling snippets of popular classics into the mix for years. But that was only a part of it.

Sometime previous, Lord encountered *Dialogues for Jazz Combo and Orchestra*, the Dave Brubeck Quartet's 1959 collaboration with the New

York Philharmonic, conducted by Leonard Bernstein. A powerful classical/jazz hybrid composed by Brubeck's brother Howard, the album left Lord convinced that R&B and the classics could be similarly married. Immediately he began discussions with the New Jazz Orchestra, and period interviews frequently found him musing on the material he'd already penned for the collaboration.

Decca Records, however, saw little future in such collusion and forbade the band from sailing into such preposterous waters. The Artwoods album, when it was finally released, reflected the band's disappointment. *Art Gallery* comprised nothing but rootsy covers, and it was clear that the Artwoods' day was coming to an end. Dropped by Decca at the end of 1966, the group shifted over to Parlophone for one last 45, then commenced their final spiral — ironically, just as their own abandoned dreams finally began coming to fruition elsewhere.

First, Decca had second thoughts about the classical/rock combination and commissioned the Moody Blues to produce one — the Birmingham band's *Days of Future Passed* went on to become one of the best-loved and biggest-selling records of the age. Then, Keith Emerson, the mercurial and, like Lord, classically influenced keyboard player with Gary Farr's T-Bones, announced he was quitting to form a new group, the Nice, to explore even deeper the possibilities of a rock-and-classics fusion.

The Nice's greatest triumph was to rearrange existing classics to their own ends — a habit Keith Emerson subsequently translated into a way of life. Jon Lord, however, continued to scheme a partnership in which group and orchestra would be as one, and found a willing ear when he encountered German composer Hans Bregel. He, too, was thinking along these lines; indeed, not only did he suggest they write a piece together, he also spoke of linking the Artwoods with the German Symphony Orchestra to perform the piece that December.

But it never happened. Neither did a proposed link with Art Wood's brother Ron's band, the Birds, and the Artwoods' final act was to cash in on the American gangster craze swept up by the hit movie *Bonnie and Clyde,* change their name to the St. Valentine's Day Massacre, and record a suitably atmospheric version of the 1932 Rudy Vallee chestnut "Brother Can You Spare a Dime?."

It was, Art Wood later admitted, "a bloody stupid idea," and the single bombed in the U.K. Denmark, however, loved it, sending the St. Valentine's Day Massacre to No. 1, and that summer the Artwoods played their last shows, touring Denmark for a month from the lofty peak of a chart-topping novelty act. They then did what all chart-topping novelty acts should do — they broke up. Jon Lord was still pondering his next move when Chris Curtis swung into his life and, with the rudiments of the Roundabout fixed in their minds, the next step was to find the musicians who could set it in motion.

That summer of 1967 saw the entire Western world, it seemed, besotted with the concept of going to San Francisco, preferably with flowers in the hair. The seedy junction of Haight and Asbury had become a mecca for the hippie generation, a cop-free zone where acid grew on trees, grass was as common as . . . well, grass, and life was just one long party of uninhibited music, unrestrained laughter, and undulating bodies. Or so it seemed from a few thousand miles away, where the underlying social currents of the West Coast counterculture were little more than a subtext to the pictures of hippies in British newspapers.

So, when radio began playing "Let's Go to San Francisco," an innocuously lovely piece of pop fluff by the Flowerpot Men, British record buyers didn't hesitate to scoop it up by the bucketload. Within weeks, the song was at No. 4 on the charts and demand for the Flowerpot Men to hit the road was unquenchable. Unfortunately, as with so many hit groups of the 1960s, the Flowerpot Men existed only on paper — the record was recorded by session men. Undaunted, the song's masterminds, former Southernaires/Ivy League frontmen John Carter and Ken Lewis, began piecing together a "band" — the already-proven combination of Ged Stone, Billy Davidson, Carlo Little, and Nick Simper, from Billie Davis' backing group. Only when Davidson fell ill on the eve of the tour did they need to look any further. They called Jon Lord.

The Garden, as this combo was to be dubbed, was little more than a cabaret act, backing a troupe of four singers — led by session superstar Tony Burrows — through a repertoire that comprised little more than a battery of breezy covers and Carter-Lewis compositions. It was, by and large, an uneventful outing — except for Carlo Little, who met his future wife Iris at a Flowerpot Men gig at a South Shields casino. When they wed six months later, Lord played organ and Burrows gave the bride away.

On the road, meanwhile, Lord was enthusiastically discussing the Roundabout with anyone who'd listen and, by the time the touring was over, in January 1968, Nick Simper had thrown in his lot with the concept. And when Chris Curtis suggested they try to track down a guitarist he remembered from a few years back, one Ritchie Blackmore, Simper knew exactly how to contact him.

Blackmore arrived in London in the middle of a snowstorm, appearing at Lord's door with an acoustic guitar in hand and nowhere else to stay. The organist told *Mojo* magazine, "That night we came up with two . . . songs . . . 'And the Address' and 'Mandrake Root.'" Blackmore impressed Lord from the outset: "Right away I felt that he wouldn't suffer fools gladly, but it felt right. Ritchie seemed dark . . . he always seemed dark." It was that darkness, balanced by Lord's natural musical flamboyance, that came to flavor all that the pair went on to accomplish together. First, however, they had to locate the fellow players who would further color their own chemistry, at the same time as they wrestled with Chris Curtis' ever-expanding ideas for the Roundabout. Because it was all beginning to get a little silly.

Adamant that he was presenting a musical experience that no one could say was not "original," Curtis was apparently throwing all conventional wisdom out of the window. For example, upon discovering that, before he turned to bass playing, Simper was a mean guitarist, Curtis decided that the Roundabout would dispense with the bass altogether.

There was also a suspicion that, while Curtis' vision of a parade of guest musicians leaping on and off the Roundabout to take a song was certainly viable, he had yet to determine who any of them might be, a failing that made actual rehearsals a dodgy proposition. How, after all, can you make allowances for another musician's contributions if you don't know who that other musician might be — or even what instrument he might be playing? The only songs the Roundabout came even close to working out during November 1967 were that pair of Blackmore/Lord compositions, and a frankly bizarre rearrangement of the Beatles' "Help."

The group's newly formed management of HEC, as Hire, Edwards, and Coletta called themselves, were also wondering precisely how (or even if) their latest investment was going to pan out. Slowly, their interest in the Roundabout began to falter — at least in its current configuration. The mercurial Curtis seemed to be losing interest, too, and when the Flowerpot Men called Lord and Simper away to Germany, Blackmore alone remained in London to watch the dream finally fall to pieces.

Curtis took himself out of the picture. He would, in time, return to the Searchers as they prepared to launch a new career on the rock circuit of the early 1970s. Blackmore, in the meantime, decided simply to wait for Lord and Simper to return, resolute that something good would come out of the Roundabout experience.

HEC, too, were keen to continue working with the pair, although when they contacted Lord to discuss the future, he was just leaving for the first Flowerpot Men gig in Munich, Germany. Later, Lord described their call as "a key moment in my life." But it was another couple of weeks before he was finally able to show up, not only to affirm that he was interested in putting together a new band, but agreeing that both Simper and Blackmore should remain a part of the picture.

Blackmore introduced a drummer to the setup. He first met Bobby Clarke during his days with Screaming Lord Sutch and the Savages, when the shock rockers found themselves sharing a Paris bill with legendary rocker Vince Taylor, whose drummer Clarke was. The pair had fallen out of touch since then, but when they met again at London's Speakeasy, on Margaret Street, Blackmore was quick to invite Clarke into the new band.

With the musicians still toying with the name (if not the concept) of Roundabout, Tony Edwards offered to find them a secluded country retreat where they could rehearse and get to know one another. He settled on the picturesque Deeves Hall, an old farmhouse outside South Mimms in Hertfordshire, owned by one of his business associates, John Chalk. HEC stumped up, too, for instruments and amps, close to £10,000 worth of gear that included what was to become one of the key sounds in the entire band's arsenal, a Hammond C3 organ. Amazingly, it was the first keyboard Lord had ever owned — all the others he had played were either rentals or else owned by his past bands.

It was Bobby Clarke who recommended the band's first vocalist — Dave Curtiss, once the guiding light of beat boomers Dave Curtiss & the

Tremors but, more recently, a member of French rocker Michel Polnareff's band. As far as the rest of the group was concerned, Curtiss was an utterly unknown quantity, and would remain so as various holdups saw the delivery of the band's equipment delayed long past Curtiss' own window of availability.

For a week, the musicians sat in Deeves Hall waiting for their gear to arrive — and a week was all Curtiss could spare. He had another string of shows lined up back in France with Polnareff and no intention of giving up a good gig on the off-chance that this new band might work out. He departed without singing a single note, and Roundabout were back where they started, with Lord, Clarke, and Blackmore killing time they should have spent with their own group by returning to the world of sessions and guesting on a new single by Boz Burrell, covers of Bob Dylan's *Basement Tapes* outtakes "I Shall Be Released" and "Down in the Flood."

In March 1968, an advertisement appeared in the weekly music paper *Melody Maker*, offering "two months well-paid work" and a guarantee of success to aspiring vocalists willing to make their way out to Deeves Hall to meet with Roundabout. A series of intensive auditions were set up, with the band's newly appointed roadie, Ian Hansford, ferrying some sixty would-be singers back and forth from nearby Borehamwood railroad station.

Few of them were worth a second glance, and the band members' scouting missions around the pubs and clubs of London also turned up few possibilities. Even Rod Stewart, then a virtual superstar within former Yardbirds guitarist Jeff Beck's eponymous band, failed to meet Roundabout's exacting standards, while overtures toward Terry Reid simply brought back a stern "not interested" from his management. Newly recruited to producer Mickie Most's management and production company, Reid was being widely championed as the next great British vocalist. He was not about to sacrifice that to throw in his lot with an untried new group.

Unknown Ashley Holt was a possibility for a time — and so impressed Nick Simper that, three years later, they would indeed team up. In the end, however, it was the one vocalist who seemed at all close to Roundabout's ideal, Mick Angus, who provided the final piece to the jigsaw, although he himself was not to be included among them. Rather, Angus recommended the band consider replacing drummer Bobby Clarke with a player he knew — Maze percussionist Ian Paice.

Recognizing his old Hamburg drinking buddy's name, Blackmore was instantly enthused, so much so that, when Angus next ran into Paice and the rest of the Maze, he was convinced that he himself had got the vocalist job, and that Paice might well be joining him there. What the aspiring vocalist didn't know was that Rod Evans, too, had answered the *Melody Maker* ad — and had also recommended Paice as a replacement for Clarke. The band suggested Evans come back later in the week and bring this seemingly miraculous drummer with him. They, too, had determined that Clarke perhaps wasn't exactly the kind of drummer they were searching for.

The divisions between Clarke and the remainder of Roundabout were musical. As his past activities made perfectly clear, his grounding was in rock'n'roll, and a very long way from the ambitious blending of psyche-delic guitars and, at Lord's convincing behest, classical leanings that his bandmates were conspiring to fuse. He hankered for music that he could sink his teeth into — to his ears, the other three seemed more intent on creating cotton candy.

Clarke was in London the night Paice arrived at Deeves Hall for his audition. According to band legend, he was out buying cigarettes from the Speakeasy, the only place in town that carried his brand, French tabs Gitanes. He arrived back at the farmhouse, however, to discover the audition still underway — only now it had turned into a full-fledged jam session. And, if he didn't realize then and there that his days aboard Roundabout were over, he found out soon afterward, when Tony Edwards paid him off with £40 in expenses. (Edwards also made a pledge to keep in touch, enacted just months later when Clarke and the recently returned Dave Curtiss announced their own new band, formed with ex-Tomorrow guitarist Steve Howe. Canto — or Bodast, as they soon became — joined Roundabout on the HEC management roster before Howe, whose own underground renown was at least equal to any applause that Blackmore aspired toward, quit to join Yes.)

Evans, Simper, Blackmore, Lord, and Paice commenced rehearsals immediately, working up the songs that Blackmore and Lord had already jammed together, plus a lengthening repertoire of stylized covers. The Chris Curtis–era rearrangement of "Help" was dusted off, together with an assault on "Hey Joe," modeled after Jimi Hendrix's own revision, but distinguished by Lord's delightfully near-flamenco embellishments and a snatch of Manuel de Falla's "The Miller's Dance" ballet, and peaking with some decidedly non-Hendrix-styled guitar soloing.

From the Maze's back catalog, Skip James' "I'm So Glad" was unearthed, to be drawn even further away from the already-iconographic treatment meted out by the power trio Cream. The group also started playing around with "Hush," a song Blackmore first encountered in Hamburg via Dutch vocalist Kris Ife's recent monster European hit. As he recalled, "It was my idea to do 'Hush' . . . I mentioned it to the band, and we did it."

Witnessing many of the band's early rehearsals was Derek Lawrence, the producer who, three years earlier, had attempted cracking the lucrative American market with such Blackmore-led beat bands as the Lancasters, the Sessions, and the Murmaids. Now a staff producer at EMI's Abbey Road studios, Lawrence also had a clutch of connections that might pay off for the new band, beginning with Ben Nisbet, head of the music publishers Feldman's. Although Roundabout had still to graft together more than a handful of original compositions, HEC lost little time in aligning their future with the company, before following Nisbet's introductions to one Artie Mogull, head of the record division at the American Tetragrammaton label.

Never destined to become a major player on the American music scene, Tetragrammaton was nevertheless one of the more intriguing labels of the late 1960s. It was launched as an offshoot of a multimedia organization headed up by comedian Bill Cosby, film producer Bruce Campbell, and artist manager Roy Silver. Best known at the time for handling Tiny Tim, Silver's roster eventually swelled to include the nascent Sparks and the all-girl rock group Fanny — curios whose cultish staying power came to sum up the label's product. But Tetragrammaton was also the only American label courageous enough to release John Lennon and Yoko Ono's *Two Virgins* album, famed for the full-frontal nude portraits that draped its front and back covers, and the company's underground kudos were confirmed.

Right now, the label was looking to unearth some new talent in Britain, and Artie Mogull, briefed to find the next Jimi Hendrix or Cream, had already earmarked Derek Lawrence as a man he'd like to work with. Lawrence, in turn, recommended Roundabout as a band that might fulfil such lofty requirements. In March 1968, he took the quintet into the studio for the first time, to cut four demos that acted as the group's shop window — band originals "Shadows" and "Love Help Me," and a pair of covers, "Help" and "Hush."

It was not an altogether successful session. Having completed the recording to everyone's satisfaction, all concerned were mortified to receive the finished acetate back from the studio, there to discover that the painstakingly created "Love Help Me" had magically morphed from a dramatic vocal showcase into a tight instrumental. At some point in the cutting stage, an engineer had accidentally dropped Evans' contribution out of the mix.

No matter. The overall performance was powerful enough to persuade Tetragrammaton that the band was worth pursuing, while the demo was also attracting attention around London. Drawing on his own network of industry contacts, Jon Lord invited the Artwoods' old ally, Mike Vernon, to Deeves Hall to cast his own ear over the band.

Vernon was impressed and intended bringing the band up with his superiors at Decca. In the meantime, however, Derek Lawrence had played an acetate of Roundabout's "Help" to his associates at EMI and, before Vernon even had the opportunity to convene the promised meeting, EMI's Roy Featherstone was meeting with Coletta and Edwards, preparing to offer them a deal with the label's Parlophone subsidiary.

With so much action swirling around the group, Roundabout themselves were also busy. Again acting on one of Lord's initiatives, the band embarked upon its first ever live shows — an eleven-date tour of Denmark and Sweden in late April, set up by the same local promoter, Walther Klebel, who handled the St. Valentine's Day Massacre outing.

Roundabout's first show, at the tiny Vestpoppen Parkskolen club in Taastrup, Denmark, was scheduled for April 20, 1968, although it was touch-and-go whether the band would actually make it to the venue. Disembarking the ferry at Esbjerg, weighted down with a stageful of newly obtained equipment, the band and the two roadies employed to accompany them on this maiden voyage were aghast to discover that their work permits were not in order. Although the group was ultimately detained for no more than a couple of hours before the situation was sorted out, that was still plenty of time for the individual musicians to fill with visions of peremptory deportation — or worse.

Most of the shows took place in and around Copenhagen, before Roundabout moved on to Gothenburg, Sweden. All went down as well as could be expected, although the most lingering memory of this outing is the volume at which the band played. Back at Deeves Hall, rehearsals had grown louder as the songs grew more complicated — even this early on, the band members' future trademark of florid improvisation matched with primal volume was coming into focus, with Simper and Blackmore, in particular, working out the visual routines they enacted around Evans' already distinctive frontmanship.

The group's influences were wildly diverse. Blackmore's playing unquestionably still lay in the thrall of Jimi Hendrix, who continued opening sonic doors that mere guitarists had never ventured through before his advent. Just as predominant, however, was Jon Lord's newly consummated love for the American band Vanilla Fudge, maverick neoclassicists whose attempt to wed the weighty disciplines of "serious" music to the supposedly lightweight pretensions of pop ultimately washed up among the forefathers of a new school of rock, the progressive movement of the early 1970s.

With the Fudge's spectacularly baroque rendition of the old Supremes number "You Keep Me Hanging On" climbing up the U.K. charts, Lord had caught their first British gig, at the Finsbury Park Astoria on October 4, 1967. "They knocked me out," he admitted. As Roundabout took shape, and with his own musical ideas patently traveling in a similar direction to Fudge organist Mark Stein's, Lord was convinced, "We were going to be an English Vanilla Fudge."

Blackmore agreed: "We loved Vanilla Fudge — they were our heroes. They used to play London's Speakeasy and all the hippies used to go there to hang out — Clapton, the Beatles — everybody went there to pose. According to legend, the talk of the town during that period was Jimi Hendrix, but that's not true. It was Vanilla Fudge. They played eight-minute songs, with dynamics. People said, 'What the hell's going on here?

How come it's not three minutes?' Timmy Bogert, their bassist, was amazing. The whole group was ahead of its time. So, initially we wanted to be a Vanilla Fudge clone."

But not, the pair stressed, in terms of material and delivery. They intended to go even further, to tap the same rich vein of unfettered imagination that made the Fudge what they were. Neither were their bandmates averse to allowing them to spread their wings so far, so fast. They strove to invent something — a musical style that was uniquely their own. Jon Lord later recalled, "We took from jazz, we took from old-fashioned rock'n'roll, we took from the classics. We were musical magpies in a way, and I found that delightful. Ritchie and myself used to do things . . . that were taken purely from the style of modern jazz. We used to swap musical jokes and attacks. . . . He would play something and I'd have to see if I could match it. That provided a sense of humor, a sense of tension to the band, a sense of . . . what the hell's going to happen next? The audience didn't know, and nine times out of ten, neither did we!"

Blackmore had tired of the formulaic approach so many bands, even in the so-called liberated age of psychedelic rock, seemed content to take toward their music. In another world, after all, his own musical leanings might have cut him out for an esoteric folk band, reinterpreting the ballads and minstrelsy of three hundred years before. Aged nine or ten, he once recalled, he heard a choir boy singing "Greensleeves," a performance "that sort of touched a nerve with me. That meant a lot more to me than I could understand. That tune stayed with me and, as I got older, I got into David Munrow and the Music Consort of London, which played Renaissance music of the 1500s."

That was an interest he was not able to wholeheartedly pursue for another three decades. But the yearning was there, the influence was alive, and therein was spawned the restless curiosity that intuitively agreed with Hendrix's insistence that there was much more to electric-guitar-playing than six strings and an amp. As Lord reached out for ever more grandiose textures and treatments, Blackmore pursued him every step of the way. Soon, even the slightest song (and "Help," "Hush," and "Hey Joe" could all be so described) was rendered unrecognizably ornate, improbably vast.

"Hush," in fact, remained one of Blackmore's favorites. "The whole thing was done in two takes." He told journalist Mordechai Kleidermacher, "I liked the guitar solo — especially the feedback."

Alongside the reworking of "I'm So Glad" that was now regularly equaling Cream's improvisations in drama and impact, those three songs were the keystones of Roundabout's live set as they plowed on through their Scandinavian dawn — but they were by no means the sole highlights. Songwriting, once the quintet set to work, came easily to them, whether they pursued impromptu jams toward such peaks as the portentous "Mandrake Root" or meandered around the tightly buckled, neatly belted arty embellishments of "And the Address," and the period-twee psychedelic pop of "Love Help Me" and "One More Rainy Day."

Audiences who arrived at the venues out of curiosity, or even less than that, filed out again exhausted, overwhelmed by the sheer complexity the group was unleashing, but utterly invigorated, too, by the sheer power of their playing. At a time when so many British exports seemed intent on pursuing their homeland's natural inclinations toward morbid whimsicality and self-flagellating introspection to their darkest conclusions, here was a band that threw all of that aside, going for both the artistic and the physical jugular.

The band was still in Denmark when they finally made the decision to ditch the name Roundabout. None of the musicians were especially enthused by it, but their inability to agree on anything else had left them little choice. However, the walls of Deeves Hall had long since been redecorated with scrawled suggestions, most of which had enjoyed a brief moment in the sun — Concrete God and Fire were both in with a shot, as Jon Lord remembered. "'Orpheus' was [another] one," he said. "Bands used to name themselves what they were, like Fred Smith and the So and So's, but we were formed after that had gone out. But realize that once the band's accepted, you can use any name." Constantly, though, the group's attention kept returning to one of Blackmore's suggestions — Deep Purple.

It was his grandmother's favorite song, he explained — a mid-1930s piano solo that had developed into one of the postwar period's most cherished musical blossoms. The name was also common Stateside parlance for a popular strain of acid, thus squeezing a tiny in-joke past any authoritarian figures who might utter it. From the Small Faces celebrating "Here

Comes the Nice" to the Beatles advising "I'd love to turn you on," slipping cute drug references past society's moral censors was a popular pastime in the late 1960s.

But the name also put Blackmore in mind of one of the better bands to have emerged out of the United States in recent months. Blue Cheer's heavy blues reassemblage of Eddie Cochran's "Summertime Blues" was currently riding the American Top 20, and how shocked must they have been, as an entire generation of new bands began plundering the spectrum in search of names, to realize they had started the fashion. From Black Sabbath to Frijid Pink, Redbone to Greenslade, the entire rainbow was suddenly rocking. But from the moment Jon Lord announced his band's decision on a Danish TV show that saw them pre-Beatlesing the Beatles by performing "Hush" on the roof of the television studios, it was clear that Deep Purple intended coloring themselves brighter than anyone.

Chapter 3

Hush, We're Recording

Riffing on the name of one of Britain's best-loved candies, Ozzy Osbourne shrugged disdainfully in the early 1980s: "The nearest Sabbath ever came to Black Magic was a box of chocolates."

At the end of 1968, however, it was difficult for anybody, confirmed chocoholic or otherwise, to avoid some reflection on the dark arts. Scything out of the psychedelic underground as it searched desperately for fresh alternatives to the rules of the establishment, the successor to the Beatles' drive into transcendental meditation, Satanism was the counterculture's next big thrill and, from the Sunday tabloids to the Rolling Stones — opposite poles that had rarely agreed on anything — it lay upon everybody's lips.

"We have become very interested in magic," Stone Keith Richards warned the *Sunday Express.* "We are very serious about this." And, for anybody requiring further evidence of these intentions, one look at the two latest adherents to the Stones' entourage would serve well enough — occult filmmaker Kenneth Anger, who pronounced the group a conduit to powers that he had hitherto attributed only to the Great Beast, Aleister Crowley; and actress Anita Pallenberg, who rumor insisted was a practicing witch.

Richards' chauffeur, "Spanish" Tony Sanchez was only one of the band's longer-standing associates who claimed to have seen the heap of human relics with which the German beauty worked her malignant magic, and the visible disintegration of her earlier beau, Brian Jones, only added further fuel to the fire of speculation.

So did the group's latest music — the raging hustle of "Jumpin' Jack Flash," the seemingly unequivocal diabolism of "Sympathy for the Devil." Years later, Jagger would reveal the song's true inspiration, a reading of Soviet author Mikhail Bulgakov's *The Master and Margarita*. For now, he was content to allow the mystery and innuendo to swirl around him.

But the Stones were not the only exponents of this new musical consciousness. Even before Jack Flash began jumping, 1968 had already seen the Crazy World of Arthur Brown soar to the top of the charts with an invocation of the unholy God of Hellfire, while the murder/suicide that ended the life of producer Joe Meek in 1967 was inextricably bound up with rumors of midnight revels in a local churchyard, spectral voices and figures in his apartment, and a devilish bargain that had finally, violently, been called in.

And there was more still. Study the faces arrayed on the Beatles' *Sgt. Pepper's Lonely Hearts Club Band* sleeve, and Aleister Crowley peers out from there as well. British blues legend Graham Bond, whose Organization band proved the seminal training ground for some of the later 1960s' greatest instrumentalists (Cream's Jack Bruce among them) was a loudly practicing occultist; and Jimmy Page, at that time guitarist with the Yardbirds (but later to fly Led Zeppelin to glory), had friends all over the world seeking out diabolic literature for his personal library. It was already common knowledge that the devil had all the best music. Now it seemed as though he had the best of everything.

It was the age of the Hammer Studios' greatest epics, the seemingly endless litany of variations on Bram Stoker's *Dracula*; but, equally, it was an age that had been irrevocably flavored by the success of Roman Polanski's *Rosemary's Baby*, a genuinely frightening film that didn't simply tap into the prevalent counterculture zeitgeist, but stormed it in a manner that the Rolling Stones and Arthur Brown could only dream of.

The savage, tragic denouement of that achievement was still to come — in March 1969, Sharon Tate, Polanski's actress wife, had still a few more months left to live before followers of Charles Manson, a self-styled Satan of a far more earthbound kind, slaughtered her in her own home; months, too, were to pass before the Rolling Stones' flirtation with the darkest arts culminated in a ritual of blood at the Altamont Speedway.

Neither was it the cinema alone that was making money hand-over-cloven-hoof, nor merely the music industry that was so delightedly dancing with the devil. For every unreformed hippie kid who still sat in a park, his nose buried in *The Hobbit* or the *I-Ching*, there were now three times as many fearlessly devouring the works of Dennis Wheatley, the greatest of all Britain's pulp occult authors, or following Mick Jagger's example and marveling to *The Master and Margarita*, a satirical study of the day the Devil paid a visit to Communist Moscow.

Maybe it was simply the increased media surveillance; maybe there really was an explosion of occult activity across the Western world. But the Age of Aquarius, which had been so warmly welcomed in song, dance, and counterculture cliché, also seemed to be reawakening sensibilities that society had kept buried for over two hundred years.

The Manson murders were simply the most high-profile; the Zodiac killings in San Francisco that same season merely the most perplexing — across America, Britain, and Western Europe, witchcraft apparently lay at the root of everything, from horrific murders to brutal church and cemetery desecrations, from missing children to messy divorces. All of which, apparently, were on the increase.

In the face of such sensationalism, driven by speculative assumption or opportunistic criminality, the true nature of what is so readily tagged "witchcraft" wasn't simply overlooked, it was lost altogether. Even when no actual wrongdoing was involved, the press reveled in the so-called "confessions" of both white and black magicians. Maxine, one of several self-styled queens of England's witches, posed nearly naked for one of the Sunday tabloids, and gleefully spilled out her accounts of wild orgies and secret ceremonies, the involvement of well-known celebrities and highly placed politicians. *The Satanic Rites of Dracula*, a 1972 Hammer horror potboiler, in which vampire hunter Van Helsing stumbles upon an evil plot whose sponsors are in the uppermost echelons of government, could have been drawn wholly from the headlines of the previous three years.

From the war pigs snuffling in the trough of Vietnam to the hollow hell of famine in Biafra, civilization was bracing for an encounter with the Dark Lord, and more than one young, aspiring musician couldn't help but wonder — if people were willing to pay good money to be scared by a movie, how much would they pay to be scared by a rock band?

Ritchie Blackmore was no stranger to such thoughts. He already cultivated the look and leanings that would have the world referring to him as the Man in Black. The guitarist's interest in the occult has seen rumors (and, probably, lies) swirling around him throughout his career — culminating in 1984, when the British tabloid *The Sun* ran a two-page spread in which every aspect of Blackmore's professed fascination was outlined beneath the headline "He looks evil, even Satanic."

Fascinating, too, was his relationship with Joe Meek; Blackmore and his German-born wife, Margaret, rented an apartment from the producer, and Geoff Goddard, one of Meek's long-time friends and associates, remembered both attending seances with Meek and holding long, mystical conversations deep into the night.

"The three of them were fascinated by the occult," Goddard recalled. "Ritchie and Margaret's interest was more healthy . . . or, at least, it wasn't as destructive as Joe's. But they used to sit up all night talking, and they would scare the life out of one another." Margaret later spoke candidly of Meek's fears that he was being stalked by the spirit of Aleister Crowley, and admitted she was unable to alleviate those fears.

With an eye toward the prevalent mood that was now sweeping out of his personal iconography and onto the wider stage, Blackmore toyed with the idea of aligning Deep Purple with something as saleable as Satanism. He held back, however. Some things were just too precious, too private. Besides, the band was making ample headway under its musical colors alone.

Returning to the U.K. in April 1968, Deep Purple were welcomed with the news that Tetragrammaton had offered them a recording contract to go with the Parlophone deal — together with a $2,000 advance that went a long way toward recouping the money HEC had spent on equipment. Keeping the relationship within the family, as it were, Tetragrammaton also recommended that Derek Lawrence produce the group's first record, a suggestion Deep Purple were happy to go along with.

On May 11, Deep Purple moved into the Pye Studios in London's Marble Arch to record their debut album. The days when new bands debuted with a string of singles were receding into the distant past, but while Parlophone was accustomed to allowing bands to take their time with their records — a pervasive legacy, of course, of the Beatles' insistence that they work at their own pace — Tetragrammaton was less prone to relaxation.

The American label had issued just one LP so far, Murray Roman's *You Can't Beat People Up and Have Them Say I Love You*. *Shades of Deep Purple*, as the band's debut was to be titled, became the second, and was already on the July new-release schedules. No more than a weekend was mapped out for the band to record in, and though that is a mere pittance by modern standards (enough time to plug in the computers, perhaps, or sort out the sound on a hi-hat), it was ample time for a hot and hungry new band to run through its well-rehearsed and now stage-broken paces.

All of the songs performed on the Scandinavian tour were to be featured on the record, with Lawrence finding himself all but relegated to the sidelines as the group ran through its set, already confident with both their performance and their arrangements. Four songs were completed on the Saturday, three on the Sunday, the final one on the Monday, and Lawrence later admitted that his only real function in the studio was to keep an eye on the clock, making sure that neither Blackmore's nor Lord's solos overran.

Piecing the album together, too, fell naturally into place. The band had already decided on the running order before they even entered the studio, while their insistence that the eight tracks be linked by sound effects was addressed, quite simply, by taking a commercially available BBC sound-effects album and dropping the appropriate noises into the gaps between songs. Neither was it as crass a notion as it might sound today. The following year, Black Sabbath's "Black Sabbath" — an undisguised statement of intent from the band who did take that first step into rock'n'roll Satanism that Blackmore had disdained to take — opened with much the same storm effects as *Deep Purple*'s "One More Rainy Day," and a more effective intro to such a performance has yet to be devised.

Cruelly, however, it is easy to accuse the remainder of *Deep Purple* of having been likewise compiled from mere bits and pieces. Although the album as a whole does hang together, individual elements can be extracted from virtually every song and lined up against something someone had done before — the recurring hint of the *Thunderbirds* TV theme that interrupts the ever-so-Hendrixy "And the Address," the nicely Nice-ish "Prelude," the shades of "Foxy Lady" that pump through "Mandrake Root," and so on.

Nevertheless, Tetragrammaton was delighted with the album, and set up an appropriate photo shoot, posing the band in suitably moody lighting, tastefully togged out in the finest of designer Mr. Fish's mock-Edwardian threads. The clothes, Lord later laughed, "looked great for a good forty minutes. But then they fell off you."

No matter. Bang on schedule in July, *Shades of Deep Purple* was in the stores Stateside, to join the band's newly released first single. The group had pushed hard for Tetragrammaton to debut them with the baroque reassemblage of "Help"; label-heads prevailed, however, and plumped for the far more commercial-sounding "Hush." It was a wise decision, too. Though just fourteen months had elapsed since Billy Joe Royal's version, American FM radio promptly took the song to its heart, and with good reason. The difference between the two recordings, after all, was vast. While Royal's record twittered, Deep Purple emoted; while Royal whispered, Deep Purple roared.

Shades of Deep Purple would not register on the national charts until September, when it came to rest at No. 24. But "Hush" swept almost all competition aside as it marched to a resolute No. 4, entering a Top 10 dominated by the Beatles' "Hey Jude" and hanging around the chart for the next two months. It would also, however, have strange consequences for Deep Purple as they prepared for their British launch.

"Hush," released in Britain in late July, did nothing (a fate that also consumed every other version of the song — it would be twenty years before Deep Purple's own twentieth-anniversary rerecording finally shattered the country's antipathy), but perhaps it should never have been expected to. Grandiose it might have been, but it was grandiose in a manner wholly alien to British record-buyers, who thrilled at the time to the more visceral energies (and certainly rougher-shod charms) of Arthur Brown's "Fire" and Julie Driscoll/Brian Auger's "This Wheel's on

Fire" — records that matched "Hush" note-for-note in terms of musical versatility, but didn't try so hard to make sure people noticed. Of all the complaints leveled at the early Deep Purple by their homeland media, the whisper that, in the common vernacular, they fancied themselves just a little too much was paramount. It was a whisper that reached deafening volume before the summer was over.

On June 18, 1968, Deep Purple were invited to record a session for BBC DJ John Peel's *Top Gear* program, then regarded (as its modern equivalent is today) as the leading showcase for underground music in the country. The BBC had only launched a dedicated pop/rock radio station, Radio One, the previous August, and many of its scheduled programs were still struggling to find their musical feet.

Peel, however, simply took what he'd been doing for pirate Radio London and amped it up for national consumption, making his several-times-weekly session spots among the most avidly awaited segments on the network. Lined up alongside Deep Purple on the show's itinerary that month were additional sessions by Joe Cocker, Fairport Convention, Jethro Tull, Donovan, and Pink Floyd.

As was standard for any artist awaiting their first ever BBC broadcast, Deep Purple's first session also served as their audition tape. With just forty-five minutes at their disposal, a band was expected to set up their equipment, do a sound check, and then record up to three songs, for delivery (in an unlabeled box) to the Talent Selection Group, an eight-strong gathering of BBC staffers and producers who then weighed in with their opinions. A pass would free the session for broadcast; a fail would see it consigned to the dumper. Deep Purple passed. Their three songs — "Hush," "Help," and "One More Rainy Day" — were awarded an "enthusiastic, unanimous pass" for this "polished, commercial group."

Even before the *Top Gear* session was broadcast, on June 30, the group was invited back to Broadcasting House to record a second session on June 25, this time for DJ David Symonds' show. Four songs were on the agenda this time: reprises of "Hush" and "One More Rainy Day," plus a couple that had recently leaked into their live repertoire — a lively rendition of Neil Diamond's "Kentucky Woman" and a turbulent version of Ben E. King's "It's All Over." They would be aired one a day through the first week of July.

Deep Purple had not played any live concerts since the Scandinavian tour. Although the band readily agreed to undertake an American tour in September, they were reluctant to venture out onto British stages until they knew how their homeland would react to the album. Nevertheless, they were open to offers, and on July 6, two days after the last of the Symonds' sessions was broadcast, Deep Purple played their first U.K. concert, as a last-minute addition to what promised to be one of the summer's most eagerly awaited concerts, as West Coast country-folkers' the Byrds headlined London's Roundhouse Theatre.

Located in the slightly less than salubrious Chalk Farm neighborhood, just around the corner from Jon Lord's London Drama Centre stomping grounds, the loosely refurbished Victorian railway shed (and, for much of its lifespan, a Gilbey's Gin warehouse) had only recently been opened for live entertainment. Over the next fifteen years, however, from the tail end of the 1960s through the golden age of punk, it stood as perhaps *the* most important venue in London.

It wasn't the biggest, it wasn't the oldest, it wasn't the most prestigious. But it had an atmosphere like no other. When you breathed in, you tasted the same soot and oil that Patti Smith, Robert Calvert, Jimi Hendrix, and Jim Morrison once tasted. And when you looked into the darkest corners, the ghosts of old train drivers winked back at you, lined up alongside the hippies, greasers, and punks who, in turn, had called the Roundhouse home for so long. When the Roundhouse finally closed its doors in 1983 (it has since reopened), a lot of the magic went out of gig-going.

That warm July night in 1968, Deep Purple were the first act scheduled to appear, opening a bill that also included "Race With the Devil" hitmakers Gun, and the Deviants, the brutal mélange of post-Zappa experimentation and pre-punk agitation that charred a path through all the peace and love of the so-called hippie era.

It promised to be a great night of music, but it was a fractious occasion as well. Deviants frontman Mick Farren, now established among Britain's best-loved rock journalists and the author of a clutch of spellbinding science-fiction novels, recalls, "We turned up at the Roundhouse and discovered that Deep Purple had heavy management, brand-new custom Marshall stacks in purple vinyl, and an army of roadies who had set their gear up the same morning and didn't want anyone else's gear on the stage. I recall there had to be an intervention to prevent fistfights breaking out between our boys, led by Boss the Roadie, and their crew. What I don't remember is the music . . . my best recollection was of a slow and pompous din, somewhere between bad Tchaikovsky and a B-52 taking off on a bombing run."

Farren wasn't alone in his dismissal of Deep Purple's performance. Other ears, too, recoiled at what they saw as a calculatedly formulaic recounting of the worst excesses of Vanilla Fudge, a band that had never followed up their first British success with anything worth writing home about. Nor did it matter that the same excesses were eminently acceptable in the United States; in truth, that might only have made things worse. The baroque'n'roll interplay between Blackmore and Lord, soon to become so vital a component of the Deep Purple sound, appeared forced and rigid. It was a distant cry from the almost anarchic free-form improvisations that the likes of the Nice, in the able paws of Keith Emerson, were wringing from a similar diet of classically influenced rock, or the Plastic Penny, the latest additions to producer Larry Page's stable of supermen, whose raison d'être included indelibly heavyweight renditions of "Mac Arthur's Park" and "Hound Dog."

Undeterred by such a hostile reception, concerned only with warming up for their all-important American debut, Deep Purple agreed to a handful more shows, lower-key outings including a public house in the seaside town of Ramsgate, and the Red Lion, in Warrington, Yorkshire, a date organized by roadie Ian Hansford, himself a Warrington native.

There they opened the show for Fontana recording artists the Sweet Shop — soon to be the Sweet and destined, though one would never have guessed it in 1968, to become one of the kings of Britain's glam-rock scene. In that guise, too, they pursued a musical direction that often allied them with Deep Purple's own future peregrinations, a relationship that culminated when Blackmore jammed with them onstage in Santa Monica in 1974. There was another connection between the two bands that, again, nobody could have imagined in 1968 — the Sweet Shop formed from the wreckage of another band, the soul revue Wainwright's Gentlemen, after their vocalist quit to join Episode Six. That vocalist was Ian Gillan.

"I remember that show," the Sweet's Brian Connolly laughed years later. "It wasn't a big pub, more like a cozy local with a little stage at one end. And Purple came sauntering on with their American hit single, their purple amps, their flashy clothes. . . . They were a great band, lovely people, but they were *so* out of place that you really felt sorry for them."

Filing another disappointment away for future recrimination, Deep Purple switched their attentions to Europe, where they were to appear at a festival in Berne, opening for Dave Dee, Dozy, Beaky, Mick, and Tich. The event remains enshrined in local infamy after Swiss riot police stormed the stadium to quell a riot during the headliners' set. Deep Purple, meanwhile, moved on to the putative highlight of the band's summer, an opening slot at the Eighth National Jazz, Pop, Ballads and Blues Festival at the Kempton Park racecourse in Sunbury.

Soon to transplant to nearby Reading, where it became eponymous with its host, the festival was widely regarded as the crowning glory of the British rock year, a chance for established bands to confirm their success, and for new bands to tilt at their thrones — the previous year, both Fleetwood Mac and the Nice had emerged from the festival as superstars-in-waiting, with the latter confirming their ascendancy the next year, by coheadlining the second evening of the three-day festival, alongside the chart-topping Crazy World of Arthur Brown.

Joe Cocker, Ten Years After, Jeff Beck, and Tyrannosaurus Rex were also scheduled to play that evening, with Deep Purple buried deep in the running order, coming onto the main stage just a little after 7 PM. And, if the Roundhouse audience was hostile, the Kempton Park crowd was positively ruthless.

Deep Purple were playing solely on the recommendation of another of their well-connected friends, Jack Barrie, owner of the La Chasse after-hours club in London's Wardour Street, and the festival's catering manager. But Barrie's enthusiasm took a harsh knock that evening as, in his own words, "they died the proverbial death." Reviews of the festival in the following week's music press failed to even acknowledge the group's existence.

The band's problem, registered at the Roundhouse but amplified manifold by the wide-open spaces of the racecourse, was the volume at which they played, and the apparent arrogance with which they played it.

Word of the American breakthrough of "Hush" had, of course, filtered into English knowledge, if only via the handful of DJs who played the song on the BBC. With that word, however, traveled an unspoken assumption that the group was American — outside of the world of session musicians and keen-eyed club-goers, after all, not one member of the band could be termed a known quantity. Their music's strict adherence to Stateside archetypes did the rest. The "poor man's Vanilla Fudge" was the least of the harangues that flew that afternoon.

Once again, Deep Purple had failed in front of a homeland audience. More alarmingly, they had failed before their peers as well, as the Nice's Lee Jackson and Brian Davison were both in attendance, alongside *Melody Maker* journalist Chris Welch, as they ran through their set. Neither was impressed.

That said, Deep Purple were scarcely going out of their way to wow their homeland critics. Decked in their best color-coded clobber, the band's appearance on black-and-white television's *David Frost Show* in August was less memorable for a perfunctory lip-sync through "Hush" than for the nonappearance of Ritchie Blackmore, for whom his group's British television debut apparently took second preference to whatever else he had planned for that day. His place was taken by Mick Angus, passed over as the band's vocalist but retained on the road crew. He wasn't a guitarist, but he mimed with abandon and, truly, there could scarcely have been a viewer who noticed anything amiss.

The David Frost Show was Deep Purple's final British appearance of the season. Abandoning all hope that the U.K. edition of *Shades of Deep Purple*, set for release in September, might buck the odds and take off, but still with a few weeks to kill before their American tour, the group turned its attention — incredibly, by modern industry standards — to recording their second album.

It was Tetragrammaton's idea. Even though Deep Purple had yet to play a single American concert, press and radio interest in the group was high — so high that the label insisted on having a new album ready for release the moment the group set foot on American soil.

Back at De Lane Lea studios with Derek Lawrence, Deep Purple were faced with a considerable dilemma. So intent had they been on promoting their first album and rehearsing their show for the American tour, that writing new material was the last thing on their mind. Having to come up with another full album's worth of new material was daunting, to say the least.

Years later, the demands still struck Simper as incredible. "My main complaint about Deep Purple," he said, "is that when we did get some success, we were just worked to death by the management and the record company. We were just the products, and they were going to milk us as much as they could until we died. There was a hell of a lot of pressure on all the time. [Today,] people say, 'Well, you recorded other people's songs and you didn't write much of your own stuff.' We never had time! If we weren't on the road, we were in the studio. We never had time to do anything."

They returned, then, to the library of cover versions they most enjoyed playing. "Kentucky Woman" was revived from their last BBC session, while an extraordinarily portentous assault on "River Deep, Mountain High" bled straight out of a vivid rearrangement of the theme to the recently released movie *2001: A Space Odyssey*, "Also Sprach Zarathustra." Buoyed by rumors that the Beatles had loved their version of "Help," the group also worked up another Lennon-McCartney cover, "We Can Work It Out." The grumbling among British critics that such grandiose appropriations simply reeked of calculated gimmickry were never given a second glance.

Besides, against the band's repertoire of covers could be balanced the originals — "Listen, Learn, Read On," "Shield," the mellotron showpiece "Anthem," and the instrumental "Wring That Neck," four of the finest songs the early group ever accomplished. The musicianship, too, was exemplary, all the more so since Blackmore and Lord agreed to abandon their once deathless struggle to establish who was the greater virtuoso. For the first time, Deep Purple sounded like a real group.

There were still problems, of course. Seldom did the band simply lie back and relax into their music — there was always one more thing to prove, one more peak to scale, and, ultimately, one more nuance to sacrifice on the altar of musical perfection. Yet, what became *The Book of Taliesyn* emerged a far more distinctive album than its predecessor, dark in all the right places, conscious of the increasingly doomy mood of the times. The glittering optimism of the Summer of Love — so long ago, though just a year had passed — had withered and died; in its stead, the looming Age of Aquarius seemed peppered with portent and omen, violence and death.

Vietnam, Czechoslovakia, Paris, Detroit — flashpoints were igniting everywhere. And, as politics pushed into popular culture, pop pushed back just as hard. No longer the happy-go-lucky moptops of yore, the Beatles had just turned in their sprawling *White Album*, a set pregnant with promises one would rather they didn't keep: the still unrevealed holocaust of "Helter Skelter," the glowering foreboding of "Cry Baby Cry," the apocalyptic chaos of "Revolution 9." The Doors were mourning "The Unknown Soldier," and the Rolling Stones had delivered "Sympathy for the Devil." And when one of the best-selling singles of the year is by the God of Hellfire, the Crazy World of Arthur Brown's "Fire," you know society's in trouble.

Deep Purple followed the shift. Where once Vanilla Fudge had hung heavy over the proceedings, now the Doors were a pronounced influence, and the band's lyricism had slipped far from the winsome themes of *Shades of Deep Purple* to absorb the more mystic flavors prevailing elsewhere on the post-psychedelic scene. Taliesyn, of the album's title, was the bard at the Camelot court of King Arthur, and this "book," the sleeve notes explained, was "a modern representation of seven different feelings, with [the] musicians . . . establishing the musical moods under [Taliesyn's] spiritual direction."

The magical mood was confirmed by the album's cover art, a deliciously mystifying line-drawing commissioned from the coincidentally named English artist John Vernon Lord, a future professor of illustration at the University of Brighton whose work in the years since *Taliesyn* has included acclaimed editions of *Wuthering Heights* and *Aesop's Fables*, but who was best known at the time for his highly stylized work for magazines ranging from *House Beautiful* to *Holly Leaves*.

Tetragrammaton, for whom *Taliesyn*'s inherent mumbo jumbo surely spelled a second payday from the altar of hippie gullibility, was delighted with all that the band had wrought during just a few short days in the studio. The album was lined up for an October 1968 American release; EMI, for whom the group's American career was moving way too swiftly, opted to hold back the U.K. release until the following summer. Nobody, after all, could ever have predicted the seismic changes that would shake Deep Purple in the months before that.

Chapter 4

The Band Has Flown

With America drawing ever closer, Deep Purple undertook a handful more shows around the U.K. — their last dates were at Birmingham's Mothers on September 27, and Plymouth's Van Dyke Club the following evening. However, they certainly left the U.K. with something to think about. Asked by *Melody Maker* why Deep Purple's sudden American success showed no sign of being emulated in Britain, Ian Paice simply shrugged, "We've been given proper exposure over there. The Americans really know how to push records." Meaning, of course, that their British counterparts didn't.

He also made no bones about Deep Purple's opinion of their own worth. In an age when success was genuinely something to be worked for, usually via years of trudging up and down the country's antiquated highway system in the back of a dilapidated Transit van, Paice made it clear that his band had no time for such struggles. The five members had long since "paid their dues" in other groups. Now they demanded the rewards they were worth, and British venues, the drummer complained, "haven't . . . offered [us] the money we want. [So], unless there is some sort of prestige attached, there is no point in doing the general run of gigs. And, as far as we are concerned, dancing audiences" — the bread and butter of the ballroom scene that still dominated the live circuit — "are out. There are only about three numbers in our act that they can dance to. We make a point of warning promoters that we are not a dancing group."

Lord, too, seemed unwilling to endear himself to British ears. At a time when EMI was unleashing such masterpieces of creative freedom as the Pretty Things' SF *Sorrow*, Pink Floyd's *Piper at the Gates of Dawn* and *A Saucerful of Secrets*, and anything by the Beatles, Lord was claiming that American labels offered "far greater freedom, both financially and artistically, than we could ever have got from a British company . . . [who] won't spend any time or effort with you until you're an established name." And, of course, the only way to become an established name was to climb into the back of that van and establish it yourselves.

America, on the other hand, cared nothing for such niceties. There, where radio was all-powerful and hyperbole — a dirty, filthy word but still a power in the land — had no patience with such burdens as talent and worth, a band could readily burst through, fully formed and already massive. Tell enough people you were already huge and, sure enough, you could be. Tetragrammaton may not have had money to burn, but they certainly had a lot of hot air, and with just a handful of receptive DJs spinning Deep Purple in the markets that mattered, they already had most people believing the group was the Second Coming.

Further weight was added to the label's argument as the band's tour itinerary was unveiled. Tirelessly promoted by the label's in-house booking agent, Jeff Wald (the future Mr. Helen Reddy), Deep Purple were to make their American concert debut at the Inglewood Forum, California, on October 15, 1968, by slipping into the opening slot of Cream's already ten-day-old American farewell tour. That outing under their belts, Deep Purple then embarked upon their own headline adventure. But all eyes were on the first shows. It was, after all, a pairing to dream of. In the two years since they first emerged on the U.S. scene, Cream had relentlessly thrust themselves into a stratosphere that few bands, not even the Beatles, had entered in the past. As musicians, the trio had no peers — in the eyes of a slavering rock world, there was no better guitarist than Clapton, bassist than Bruce, or drummer than Baker. Nightly, Cream revealed their dexterity via solos and improvisations so lofty that time itself stood still to applaud. Now, however, they were going their separate ways and, ever since that announcement, the world's press had held its breath, trying to predict who would take their place. Deep Purple, though few outside the band's immediate circle believed it possible, were one of the handful poised to leap into the void. Inevitably, Vanilla Fudge were another.

America impressed the band from the outset — and so did Tetragrammaton. Until Deep Purple reached Los Angeles, the label's offices on Rodeo Drive were little more than an address on letterhead. Now the band saw Tetragrammaton's headquarters in all its splendor, set amid the palm trees that sprout like parking meters all across the city, and oozing the same opulence that would be lavished upon the band members themselves.

An on-site chef waited only for the latest visitor to demand a snack before rustling up dreamlike repasts. Twice a day, a nearby florist changed the flower displays around the building. Every night, the band was taken out on the town, to the Playboy Club one night, to a plush restaurant on another, and then whisked back to their hotel — the Sunset Marquee on Sunset Boulevard — aboard the fleet of black Cadillac limousines that were forever at their service and which they'd only ever seen in the movies.

Amid such luxury, the actual business of music seemed as far away as gray old London. Everything revolved around being seen, being talked about. Before they even made their concert debut, Deep Purple had the distinction of becoming the first rock band ever to appear on the *Dating Game* television network show, performing "Hush" — while Lord became the first musician to actually compete in the show. "One of us had to play the game, and I didn't step back quickly enough," he recalled.

Offstage, somebody mentioned that their performance had just been witnessed by more people than would ever see them in concert, even if they toured for the rest of the decade. But, looking back on their earliest television appearances, it seems hard to believe the band ever survived, let alone thrived. Of course, psychedelia was still the rage of the day, but the smartly laundered kaleidoscope that Deep Purple paraded before the cameras paid but begrudging lip service to the cosmic entities that controlled it.

With Evans in bright orange and Paice in neat purple, and Simper's hair so tightly teased you could have bred badgers within, the band looked like they'd stepped straight out of a fashion mag — and as uncomfortable as though they'd stepped in something even worse. Only Blackmore mustered anything more than a beguilingly grinning effervescence, his head perched upon vile emerald shoulders, his face locked into an eternal grimace. After he rebuffed a few early close-ups with a glance of total distaste, the cameras kept their distance for the rest of the performance.

"The idea was that we would look good," Lord told *Mojo* thirty years later. "We weren't going to be like a California hippie band. We were going to play loud and hard, and dress cool. [And] for a while, we looked incredibly cool — we thought. A lot of [other] people thought we looked like prats."

Even so, the sheer magnitude of the group's first U.S. shows could not help but take him aback. The National Blues & Jazz Festival was huge by British standards; it was an outdoor, once-a-year, three-day happening feted as a truly national event. Two nights at the Inglewood Forum were simply one stop in one town, but still there were 16,000 kids out there, paying between $3.50 and $6.50 a ticket, and all determined to have the time of their lives.

Back home, Deep Purple had worked up a live set that could stretch to ninety minutes without repeating itself. They would have no opportunity to display that prowess on the Cream dates. Rather, no more than half an hour lay at their disposal, during which they were expected both to promote their latest records — "Kentucky Woman" had just been unveiled as the follow-up to "Hush" — and maintain the air of musicianly cool that was expected from every major-league rock band. They succeeded with room to spare.

Cream were recording the concert for possible inclusion on their farewell live album; Tetragrammaton arranged to set the tapes rolling a little earlier, to capture Deep Purple's show as well. Released some three decades later as *Live at the Forum*, the tape finds the band opening with the two singles, giving the audience something recognizable to hold on to, and appearing a little rebellious as well, having some fun after they get the hits out of the way.

"River Deep, Mountain High" and "Help" both allowed the band to stretch out while maintaining that all-important sense of familiarity, and

"Hey Joe," the set-closer, served notice that Cream's throne was not the only part of the palace that Deep Purple intended storming. Jimi Hendrix, his future already cloaked in doubt as his Experience crumbled around him, was also firmly within Purple's sights.

Around such peaks, there was room for just two band originals — usually selected from among the virtuoso highlights "Mandrake Root" and "Wring That Neck" ("And the Address" was performed later in the tour), a twin tour de force during which Blackmore showed off precisely how much he had learned during five years as one of Britain's top session men, while Lord and Paice fired back with all the weight in their own personal arsenals.

It was a remarkable show, as loud as it was dynamic, as solid as it was skilful. And maybe that, voices in the Deep Purple camp mused afterward, was why the group's tenure on the tour was cut so brutally short — not because Deep Purple were actually upstaging the headliners, but because they could have been seen to be trying to. Either way, the band's third night on the Cream tour, in San Diego on October 20, was also their last. They had been kicked off.

It was not Cream's decision; according to Jon Lord, recalling the event for the *Leicester Mercury* newspaper in 2000, "We got on well with them. They had no idea we were to be taken off the tour — they were too stoned!" But neither could the headliners reverse the decision.

Stunned by such an unexpected development, Tetragrammaton pulled out all the stops to maintain Deep Purple's momentum. Reviews of their three shows so far were enthusiastic, and audience responses had certainly been powerful. Leaving the band to cool (or otherwise) their heels amid the multitudinous distractions of L.A. for a week, Jerry Wald worked flat out to schedule a new tour, booking them into venues up and down the West Coast, and finding them a berth, too, at the upcoming San Francisco International Pop Festival at the Alameda County Fairgrounds in Pleasanton, alongside the glittering likes of Creedence Clearwater Revival, Eric Burdon and the Animals, Iron Butterfly, and Canned Heat.

The majority of the shows on the band's itinerary were little better than any they could have mustered in Britain — if it's prestige and money you're after, there really isn't much difference between Seattle and

Southampton. But the value of these hastily arranged shows was incalculable. For the first time, the musicians were able to work in concert with an audience over a period of days, refining their performances beyond the boundaries imposed by the mirrors around their rehearsal rooms, and learning the little licks and tricks that separate a good band from a good show.

Blackmore, of course, had already sorted that out for himself, through his months alongside Screaming Lord Sutch. But now he was his own master and could decide for himself when it was time to let rip, luxuriating within the vast passages and avenues of his own imagination, translating his natural prowess to a flash and flair that truly allowed him to take his place among the guitar heroes of the age. By the time Deep Purple resumed their scheduled itinerary in November 1968, their performance had advanced light years from that which stepped out at the Inglewood Forum — now, had the occasion demanded, they really could give Cream a run for their money.

The original tour schedule planned for the band to return home in early December. Instead, Wald found himself adding so many fresh dates to the outing that it was early 1969, a full four weeks later, before Deep Purple saw England again, having spent Christmas and New Year's in New York. There, two nights sandwiched between — again — Credence Clearwater Revival and the James Cotton Blues Band, over December 20–21, gave way to a solid week's residency at the Electric Circus, a Polish social hall that had been magically transformed into the city's wildest psychedelic nitery. With the audience drawn largely and loyally from the crowd that had responded so enthusiastically to the Fillmore shows, Deep Purple completed their first year in absolute triumph.

December also saw the band in the recording studio, looking to cut a viable follow-up to "Kentucky Woman." Despite the success of the tour, neither single nor *The Book of Taliesyn* had come even close to outperforming the band's breakthrough releases, and, while Deep Purple's overall American sales were nudging a cool four million, they could still not overlook the need for another major hit single, something to establish the band permanently in the minds of the record-buying public.

Dutifully, the band set to work on three covers, each given what the press was already calling "the Deep Purple treatment." Less dutifully, however, they regarded the label's commands with somewhat less magnanimity than they had just a few months earlier. Ben E. King's "Oh No No," Neil Diamond's "Glory Road," and Bob Dylan's "Lay Lady Lay" were all laid out for inspection, but two months of solid live work had altered the band's own perception of what their music represented and the directions in which their ambitions lay.

All three recordings were regarded as unreleasable, if not unfinished. Even the cooperation of Diamond himself could not get the band through the hump; still best-known as the author of the Monkees' "I'm a Believer," and several years, therefore, from his transformation into the doyen of soul-sucking easy listening music, Diamond personally telephoned Lord to try and help him through a new arrangement of "Glory Road," but to no avail.

Back in London on January 3, the band returned to the studio, away from the helpful suggestions and prods of their L.A. paymasters, and this time they met with somewhat more success. "Emmaretta," an Evans song dedicated to an actress in the Broadway cast of the stage show *Hair*, and "The Bird Has Flown" (*not* a Beatles cover, despite lifting its title from their "Norwegian Wood") were both cut early on in sessions for what would become the group's third album, original compositions designed to haul Deep Purple out of the novelty-covers niche they still occupied in many British listeners' estimations.

Reflecting such intentions, they attempted only one cover on an altogether less overbearing album, a slight, if evocative, version of Donovan's "Lalena." Otherwise, material earmarked for the set was intended — whether by accident or, already, forward-thinking design — to reflect the talents not only of the band's musical engine room, Lord and Blackmore, but of Paice, whose drumming powered the near-tribal "Chasing Shadows." "The Bird Has Flown" was a grinding showcase for guitar and organ, while the percussion for "Blind" had a spectral menace that Evans' mannered vocal could not dispel.

Other ambitions, too, were highlighted, as Lord grafted a full orchestral passage onto "April," while Blackmore gave notice of his immediate intentions across the procontraceptive "Why Didn't Rosemary," a heavy R&B-beat–flavored stomper whose timeless riffing conjured up memories of every band that ever worked the London club circuit during the mid-1960s.

With these achievements still fresh on tape, Lord spoke of the group's frustration in an interview with *Disc*, one of the leading pop papers of the time. "We can be classed as an underground group," he reasoned. "But because we've had hits, I think the British underground devotees tend to look down on us." The band's major intention now, he said, was to put that reputation behind them and begin treating the U.K. to the kind of performances they'd granted the U.S..

They set the wheels in motion with a fiery BBC session, recorded on January 14, 1969, for broadcast by *Top Gear* on February 9. "Emmaretta," "Wring That Neck," and fresh reworkings of "Hey Joe" and "It's All Over" led the set, together with one brand-new song, "Hey Bob-a-Roo-Bob," which disguised behind its nonsensical title the rudiments of what would become "The Painter," one of the finest moments on the still-gestating third album. Two days after that set was broadcast, the band was back, this time at the behest of DJ Pete Brandon. "Emmaretta" and "Hey Bob-a-Roo-Bob" were reprised, "Hush" was reborn, and "The Bird Has Flown" was simply remarkable.

In the meantime, the group's first U.K. tour had got underway, with a Birmingham show that the BBC would also broadcast on *Radio One Club*, before the group marched out into the unknown. They were no longer concerned with prestige — nor, with payments rarely topping £150 a night, money; one interview even saw the group claim, with only a hint of pained martyrdom, that, compared to what they could earn in America, they were actually losing a couple of thousand pounds every night they played in Britain. But it mattered not. Tirelessly, Deep Purple ranged around the British midlands and the north, an arduous itinerary relieved only by occasional returns to London: University College, Goldsmith's College, and, as the outing drew to a close, the London music industry watering hole, the Speakeasy, on March 20.

There, in front of what might be termed an audience of their peers, Deep Purple turned in a performance that one onlooker, looking back from a couple of decades hence, described as proof that there *might* be more to Deep Purple than the ability "to bang a bit of Beethoven into a Beatles song and call it a new arrangement."

In fact, the rosy picture painted of the group's American pulling power was, to say the least, misleading. Close to a year had elapsed since

"Hush," during which time no subsequent single had so much as bothered the all-important Top 40. Instead, the band was indeed crossing into the underground, a favorable feat so long as one acknowledged that there was less money to be made in such hallowed circles — but not an accomplishment Tetragrammaton was exactly celebrating.

Having launched amid flamboyant hopes, the label had instead run into a series of increasingly dire financial holes. Though they received underground plaudits by the bucketload for releasing John and Yoko's *Two Virgins*, for example, and striking a major blow for the First Amendment and all that, it was later reported that Tetragrammaton spent more money placing every copy of the album into the brown paper bag that American morality demanded than they made from actually selling it. In other words, a lot of people supported free speech — just so long as they didn't have to pay for it.

Other label schemes, such as launching singer Elyse Weinberg with the release of five different singles on the same day, were similarly doomed to failure. It was difficult enough persuading radio jocks to play one record by a new artist, let alone five. Suddenly, the half-million dollars that the label allegedly spent on Deep Purple's first album cover seemed an extravagance that could easily have been dispensed with — especially after the company was forced to admit that, despite having the new Deep Purple album ready to go, they couldn't find the money to manufacture it.

Neither were plans for the U.S. tour going off as intended. Early hopes that the group might be booked onto the Rolling Stones' latest jaunt, their first American gigs in three years, were dashed when the Stones opted to spend their time in the recording studio and save the tour until November. Two months that could have been spent on top of the world now yawned ahead with all the allure of a money pit.

They opened in the Pacific Northwest, where shows at such prestigious piles as the Seattle Arena and Vancouver Agrodome were balanced against two weeks spent hauling around the universities and nightclubs of Seattle, Portland, and barely beyond. From there, the entourage shifted down to a similarly grueling micro-inspection of California's seats of learning. Considering the heights the band had hit on their first American tour, and the miles they were devouring as they traveled from one low-key show to the next, it was very much a low-budget outing. It was so low-budget that, at one point, Deep Purple seriously weighed sending manager John Coletta back to the U.K., simply to save on the nightly hotel bill.

The hubris that had once seen Deep Purple disavow any but the most important concerts was long behind them now, as the tour flipped to the East Coast and continued on as before. But audiences were receptive, material from the still-unreleased new album was going down well, and the forced activity of near-nightly shows saw the band's stagecraft shift up another few notches.

Recalling the band's Providence Warehouse show on May 4, journalist Mac Pingyouin marveled, "The difference between this show and their last local performance was staggering, and you can only imagine how great this band would be if they actually got more than a month or so of solid gigging under their belt at a time." In fact, the American tour alone would consume close to two months, but the individual musicians knew precisely what Pingyouin meant. However, they were also aware that for that trans-formation to take place, the band needed to undergo major surgery.

In the studio, Deep Purple had more or less clung in agreement with one another regarding the moods and textures they wanted to uphold. In concert, however, and with the experience of actually gigging on a regular basis, Lord and Blackmore sensed a growing gulf between what Deep Purple was capable of and what it was actually delivering.

No single incident can be isolated as the one that threw Deep Purple into finally exploring the energies and disciplines that haunted their ambitions. But there was one moment in which their course was irrevo-cably set — the day Jon Lord, toying with his Hammond organ, began wondering what might happen if he short-circuited the instrument's traditional means of amplification, through an internal Lesley speaker, and ran it instead directly into the same Marshall amps that Blackmore (and so many other guitarists of the day) employed.

What happened was a sound of such earthy, snarling, rambunctious aggression that even he was taken aback. "The beast," he later marveled, "was born." A beast that was so exhilarating, so powerful, and, most of all, so uncontainable that it was another two years before even he acknowledged that he had truly tamed it.

There were other considerations, too. February 1969 saw the release of the first album by Led Zeppelin, a band whose own constitution was not far removed from Deep Purple's. Like Blackmore and, to a lesser extent, Lord, guitarist Jimmy Page and bassist John Paul Jones had risen through the ranks of British session men — of course, Lord played alongside Page at the recording of the Kinks' "You Really Got Me" in 1964. And, like Blackmore and Lord, they were the only even partially known names in the band — vocalist Robert Plant and drummer John Bonham were lifted bodily from an underachieving beat group, Birmingham locals the Band of Joy.

What they created together, however, was infinitely more powerful than any examination of the component parts could ever have predicted: a blues-heavy, riff-roaring thunder that, as much as *Sgt. Pepper* a mere two years earlier, was destined to rewrite great swaths of the rock'n'roll rule book.

Blackmore later admitted, "It wasn't until Led Zeppelin came along that we had a direction." *Led Zeppelin I* — whose American success was so immediate that it was already playing every time you switched on the radio — certainly realigned Blackmore and Lord's perceptions of what could be done within the confines of a band. But it also alerted them to the possibilities of actually overstepping Zeppelin's boundaries. Zeppelin had keyboards, but they were little more than an occasional diversion for bassist Jones, never an integral part of the band's sound. But imagine what could be wrought if they were. And imagine what would happen if they sounded like the beast.

Deep Purple were still in America when, having isolated their own musical dreams, Blackmore and Lord turned their attention to the biggest problem of all — how to align Deep Purple to match them.

It was a problem that began, they were convinced, with vocalist Evans. A great singer, he was not necessarily a great rocker — and there was a difference. Bassist Simper, too, seemed increasingly out of step with the duo's dreams; again, he was great at what he did, but he seemed constantly to stumble when pushed to drive a little further. Taking Ian Paice to one side, Blackmore and Lord outlined their thoughts and, more importantly, the solution they had arrived at. Paice was in complete agreement.

Deep within the American midwest, the trio summoned manager John Coletta to an emergency band meeting — with two-fifths of the band necessarily absent. Coletta saw the point behind their planning, but cautioned the conspirators not to make any move until they had returned to the U.K.. Financing was already touch-and-go as the tour dragged on; a mid-schedule split, or even the suggestion of such change, might bring the entire edifice crashing down around them.

Although nothing was said, Simper and Evans knew something was in the wind. The last three weeks of the tour were torturous for everyone, with communication — even bare conversation — at a premium. By the time the tour ended on May 29, in Buffalo, N.Y., both camps — Simper and Evans in one, Blackmore, Lord, and Paice in the other — knew, without the words having ever been uttered, that the next time they visited the United States, it would be in very different company. And, most likely, for a different record company.

Blissfully unaware of the chaos tearing their biggest earners asunder, Tetragrammaton finally squeaked the band's third album, the simplistically titled *Deep Purple*, into the stores in June — days after the band left the country. Despite the friendships that the band had patently cultivated as they traveled the country, the album foundered badly, in and out of the charts in just six weeks and scraping to a derisory No. 162. Commercially as well as personally, Deep Purple had reached the end of the road. All they had to do now was stop moving.

With the proposed coup still under wraps, the group arrived home at the end of May to find *The Book of Taliesyn* finally approaching the eve of release. They were not necessarily thrilled by the news. Nine months old in America, the album was already stale in the band's estimation, and would be even staler by July, when it finally reached the stores.

They were beholden, nevertheless, to give it their best shot, and the next five weeks — time that could have been projecting the future that Blackmore, Lord, and Paice were now working toward — was instead spent flogging the dead horse that was the current lineup of the group through one last bout of touring.

It was not, after all, only the group's reputation that was at stake. *The Book of Taliesyn* also represented the birth of what EMI intended as a brand-new player in the world of underground rock, the Harvest label.

Parlophone had been good to Deep Purple, but that was all. There, the band had rattled around with too many others, as the label's pre-Beatles penchant for dabbling in every musical current that passed by left the company with a hopelessly unwieldy roster of acts, far too many and varied for even the best-intentioned PR department to handle. Parlophone's parent company, EMI, understood that dilemma as well as anyone — better, in fact, and in late 1968, producer Malcolm Jones had been given the go-ahead to launch a new label that would eschew such diversification once and for all.

Harvest Records was to be dedicated solely to the underground music then sweeping the U.K. — the unknown and unsigned groups that dominated the festival and university concert circuit and provoked high-and-mighty discussion in student common rooms the nation over. The creation of the label was, in many observers' eyes, a controversial move — as Jones himself remarked the following year, "Early critics . . . had always previously regarded [the underground] as a hallowed sphere of the music industry that was not to be entered by the commercial public companies."

Nevertheless, Harvest swiftly proved that its roster was to be dictated by what Jones, and fellow Harvest heads Peter Jenner and Andrew King, considered worthwhile, as opposed to any corporate notions of commerciality. The freak-form Edgar Broughton Band, singer-songwriter Michael Chapman, folkies Shirley and Dolly Collins, and former Cream songwriter Pete Brown were among the label's own initial signings, to be joined by the handful of renegade spirits that had hitherto toiled on EMI's more established labels — Pink Floyd, the Pretty Things, and Deep Purple.

Jones was reportedly less than enthusiastic about the recruitment of Deep Purple — like so many others at the time, he regarded them as little more than a gimmick-laden novelty, designed solely for the American market and many leagues removed from the relaxed neo-psychedelia of the acts he especially wanted Harvest to champion. EMI's insistence on transferring the band to his domain, then, was simply the price he had to pay for being given the label in the first place.

Behind the scenes, however, Blackmore, Lord, and Paice were working diligently to reshape the group closer to Jones' ideal.

Chapter 5

A New Episode in Rock

For any band, being remembered merely as an offshoot or precursor of some more successful outfit is a mixed blessing. On the one hand, an entire new audience will be drawn into orbit, in search of fresh thrills and secrets; on the other, an entire career's worth of endeavor is forever doomed to subservience, as though all those gigs, all those records, all those yesterdays were targeted toward just one objective: getting the hell out of Dodge and finding fame under another name.

Anybody looking back on the career of Episode Six could certainly be excused for feeling that way. In bassist Roger Glover and vocalist Ian Gillan, Episode Six boasted two men who would do much to shape the rock scene of the 1970s and beyond, just as the Maze, the Artwoods, the MI Five, and the Outlaws boasted their own future legends. But while those other bands had basked in little more than a brief flurry of underachieving excitement, and were scarcely mourned when they finally splintered, Episode Six were more accomplished.

Regulars on BBC's *Radio One Club*, where their rambunctious revue-like live show effortlessly shot a fresh jolt of excitement into the average listeners' living room, the band also enjoyed a three-year recording career that saw them at least flirt with the possibilities of mainstream success. That they never actually attained it would, of course, play a major part in the band's eventual demise. But, across a succession of singles released between 1966 and 1969, Episode Six did more than enough to assure their own immortality — regardless of where the band's members went next.

The roots of Episode Six lay in the July 1964 union of two West London bands, the Lightnings and the Madisons. From the first came vocalist Andy Ross, and the sibling team of Sheila and Graham Carter-Dimmock, playing organ and keyboards respectively; from the latter, drummer Harvey Shields, guitarist Tony Lander, and bassist Roger Glover.

Both bands were formed — and thrived — while the members attended Harrow County Grammar School. But now school was over, and the two groups might have splintered forever, as the members left to get on with the rest of their lives. Instead, they pooled their resources and, while the new band's first few months together saw activities confined to weekend gigs, by September, Glover was the only member who remained otherwise occupied, attending Hornsey College of Art.

Episode Six gigged constantly, their repertoire a fast-evolving mix of pop, R&B, and bluesy covers that brought them a firm reputation, both at home and abroad, as an exciting club act. Nobody doubted that they were going places — the band had its own office in London's Pimlico district, a full-time secretary, a thriving fan club, and the support of a string of pirate radio DJs. They even had a famous manager. Helmut Gordon was renowned for discovering the Detours, shortly before they became The Who.

Glover's academic ambitions finally came to a halt in April 1965, when Episode Six were offered a monthlong residency at the Arcadia Club in Frankfurt, Germany. It was a stamina-draining exercise — nightly, the band would play for forty-five out of every sixty minutes, from 7 at night until 3 in the morning. Furthermore, the club's promoter was so demanding that, when Glover's appendix inconsiderately burst three weeks into the residency, Episode Six had one-sixth of their earnings deducted for every night they performed without him.

Andy Ross quit the band the moment they returned to the U.K., but Episode Six already knew who they wanted to replace him. A few weeks before, they'd caught sight of Wainwright's Gentlemen, a six-to-eight-man soul-revue type band that was tracking around much the same pub and club circuit as they were. The group itself was very slick, very well-managed, very well-financed. But it was their singer that instructed Episode Six, a semi-cherub with a voice, oxymoronic though it seems, that was positively wasted on "Land of a Thousand Dances" *et al.*

Ian Gillan, for it was he, apparently agreed with that prognosis. Born in Hounslow on August 19, 1945, he arrived in Wainwright's Gentlemen in December 1964, from the string of youth-club-style bands he'd been performing with since he was sixteen — the Moonshiners, the Hi-Tones, the Javelins — and almost every one of them saw him adopt a new stage name: Garth Rockett, Jess Gillan, Jess Thunder. But, though Wainwright's Gentlemen were far better organized than any of them, Gillan later recalled, "they weren't as good. We'd play five nights a week . . . but I didn't enjoy it very much."

Gillan joined Episode Six in May 1965, just as Helmut Gordon handed the day-to-day running of the combo over to his assistant, Gloria Bristow. The band signed its first record deal with Pye soon after and got ready to record its first single, a cover of the Hollies' "Put Yourself in My Place," backed by Glover's "That's All I Want." It wasn't an altogether happy experience — the band arrived at the studio to discover a group of well-meaning session men waiting to record the music; all the band needed do was supply the vocal lines. Nevertheless, Gillan recalled, "despite all that . . . we were still glad to get our hands on our first piece of vinyl."

In fact, Episode Six would not play on either of their next two singles: a fine cover of the Tokens' "I Hear Trumpets Blow" in April 1966 and a lovely rendition of the Beatles' "Here There and Everywhere" in August. Neither would they make the charts and, that fall, it was decided they take a new course of action. With Gillan and both of the Carter-Dimmocks handling the band's lead vocals — a battery that contributed much to the sheer exhilaration of the Episode Six sound — the powers that be announced that subsequent singles would each highlight, by name, a different member of the band, beginning with "I Will Warm Your Heart," credited to Sheila Carter and Episode Six.

A considerably lighter-weight performance than any of the band's previous releases, this venture, too, went nowhere and the new scheme was quietly dropped. Gillan reflected, "Part of the problem was that we were still struggling to find an identity. We were neither the Hollies nor the Rebel Rousers nor, for that matter, the theatrical Barron Knights. We were Episode Six, a band of mainly copy musicians working with harmonies and showmanship." There was simply nothing there for record-buying audiences to get their teeth into and, in fairness, little about the band's records so far encouraged them to try.

Live, it was another matter entirely, as Bristow kept the band on the road almost perpetually, crisscrossing the U.K. both on their own and supporting other bands. One memorable outing saw Episode Six booked as the show-openers on a package tour headlined by Dusty Springfield; in the spirit of the times, the band was allocated four minutes at the start of the first half of the show and seven minutes at the start of the second. A visit to the Star-Club in Hamburg saw the band booked to play up to seven shows a night (with matinees on weekends), taking the stage for half an hour in between the other scheduled acts. Another memorable trip, over Christmas 1966, found Episode Six playing in Beirut. By the time they returned home, they had three singles in the Lebanese Top 10. "They didn't sell that many," Gillan later mused. "But it was our first taste of stardom."

So much work allowed the band to hone an act of incredible tightness and variety. They also began introducing comedy routines into their set — Gillan remembers donning outrageous false teeth for a Bee Gees pastiche, while Glover penned one of the all-time great Beach Boys parodies, in the form of "Mighty Morris Ten." Elsewhere, the growing influence of classical music on the rockers of the day prompted the band to unleash the ambitiously absurd "Mozart Versus the Rest."

Episode Six were capable of serious turns as well, though. Their live repertoire now included songs by the Doors, Bob Dylan, Jimmy Cliff, and Paul Simon, while their first single of 1967 was the distinctly raga-era Yardbirdsesque "Love Hate Revenge," followed in June by a powerful version of Tim Rose's "Morning Dew," a duet between Gillan and Sheila Carter that ranks alongside any of the song's better-feted covers. They also recorded a terrific assault on Love's "My Little Red Book" — absurdly left in the vault until 1991 brought the Sequel label's *Complete Episode Six* compilation.

Band originals, too, began to tighten (if not necessarily toughen) up. Glover's "Sunshine Girl," the B-side of "Morning Dew," is period pop-psych at its finest, a harmony-packed cross between the Hollies and the

Turtles that deserved far more than the absolute obscurity that awaited it. Other gems included "UFO," a distinctly bizarre number documenting a close encounter of some kind or another, that was placed on the B-side of the September 1967 single "I Won't Hurt You" — released as a Graham Carter solo effort, under the odd pseudonym Neo Mayo; "Gentlemen of the Park," a cracking little number featured on the movie soundtrack *Les Bicyclettes de Belsize*; and Glover's "I Can See Through You," a hyperambitious piece that conjured comparisons with the Pretty Things' recent (SF *Sorrow*-shaped) activities and has been described among Episode Six's finest accomplishments.

The arrival of BBC's dedicated pop channel Radio One in summer 1967 gave Episode Six a new outlet for their talents, as the group's support among the DJ community translated into a regular berth on *Radio One Club*, a live-in-the-studio pop jamboree show, and session appearances on other programs.

When a CD compiling many of the band's record-breaking eight appearances on *Radio One Club* was released in the U.K. in the mid-1990s, Roger Glover enthused, "I love it. I unashamedly love it. I cringed a few times, but it brought back so many memories. Episode Six has more or else disappeared for me — yes, I remember the singles, and yes, I remember that we spent twenty years on the road over the period of a few months, but it brought a lot of lovely memories back."

A mixture of covers and band originals, interspersed with interviews and other spoken-word material, the collection also resurrected performances that the band members had completely forgotten. "There's one song in particular, 'In the Morning,' continued Glover. "I remembered dimly that I used to love this Dusty Springfield song that we did, but I didn't know where it came from, I'd never heard it since that time. To hear it again, it's absolutely wonderful. I played it over and over again, and I think it could be a smash today. I loved it!"

Even this new dimension of exposure could not draw Episode Six to the next level, however, and with two years of overworked underachievement behind him, drummer Shields departed in fall 1967, to be replaced by John Kerrison. Pye Records was the next to bail, dropping the band following the failure of "I Can See Through You," while a new deal with MGM fell away after just one release, "Little One" — oddly credited simply to "Episode."

"The end was approaching," Gillan reflected from another far-flung one-night stand in the back end of nowhere. "After all our labors, why were we stuck out here, while the Moody Blues, The Who, and all the rest were riding the waves of success?" Any other band, all concerned knew, would have folded long before. Episode Six just kept plugging away, though, and when Kerrison quit in mid-1968, they simply shrugged, recruited former Outlaws drummer Mick Underwood in his stead, and moved on to a new label, producer Les Reed's Chapter One.

Their luck did not change. Two further singles, "Lucky Sunday" and the so-versatile "Mozart Versus the Rest," bombed as ignominiously as their predecessors. But for Gillan, at least, Underwood's arrival brought a world of fresh possibilities. Quietly, in the downtime between shows, the pair began scheming a complete overhaul of Episode Six, abandoning the old pop imagery (and, perhaps, even the name) in favor of a new, harder-hitting rock sound.

Before they could place their notions into practice, however, Underwood mentioned that his old Outlaws bandmate Ritchie Blackmore was looking for a new singer — and that he, Underwood, had recommended Gillan. A few nights later, on June 4, 1969, Lord and Blackmore dropped by the Ivy Lodge Club in Woodford, East London, to watch Episode Six perform. As the set neared its climax, Blackmore joined the band onstage for a jam and, immediately after the show, Lord asked Gillan if he'd be interested in joining Deep Purple. He was. Then they asked if he knew any decent bass players. He did.

Pledging to remain with Episode Six until they completed their scheduled shows, Gillan nevertheless started work convincing Roger Glover that he, too, should throw in his lot with Deep Purple. Episode Six, after all, were going nowhere, with little more to look forward to than however-many-more years trekking up and down the motorway en route to one more low-paying gig. Deep Purple, on the other hand, had a name, a reputation, a track record — and a record contract, something Episode Six might never sniff again. Of course, they also had vast bouffant hairdos, a feature of the group that Glover sometimes thought he'd never stop laughing at, but time can be a great healer. They were sure to grow out at some point.

Glover, however, was not easily swayed. Having played with the members of Episode Six in one form or another since his teens, he felt a loyalty to the group that Gillan never could. But he was well aware of the truth behind Gillan's predictions. The music scene was changing, the age of the play-anything-anywhere-anytime show bands was fast coming to an end, upended by the hard-rock specialists on the one hand and the out-and-out pop confections on the other. Plus, Gillan and Glover had recently begun writing together and both were well aware that their material deserved far more of an airing than Episode Six could ever grant it.

"Jon, Ritchie, and Ian . . . wanted to be writing their own stuff," Gillan explained, "so that's why they [wanted to bring] Roger and me in, because we were already a kind of songwriting team." And that became the carrot he used to draw Glover toward Deep Purple.

Still, it was not an easy sell. Beyond any sentimental attachment to his Episode Six bandmates, the bass player had not immediately taken to either Lord or Blackmore when they turned up at the Episode Six show, and he was utterly unimpressed when Blackmore joined the band onstage — in light of what the guitarist was planning, in fact, he considered it quite audacious.

Aware, however, just how much the decision meant to Gillan, he at least agreed to meet with Jon Lord, to show him some of their songs. Glover laughed, "We nervously played our songs . . . they were all about monkeys and lions. Monkeys always appeared in our lyrics in those days. But there was nothing that interested him. And then he pulled out a demo of [a song called] 'Hallelujah,' and said, 'What do you think of that?'"

The pair were too polite to tell him at the time, but later, they had no hesitation in confessing themselves absolutely appalled. Indeed, given all of Lord and Blackmore's grandiose schemes for the band, their dream of rewriting the rock landscape for the forthcoming decade, the song they were now listening to was little more than a limp joke. The idea that Deep Purple were even considering recording it was the most absurd thing they'd heard. Either that or the most challenging. Nobody mentioned the possibility of Glover actually joining Deep Purple at that point, and he would have refused if they had. But when Lord asked if he'd mind dropping by the studio later that same day, to play bass on a purely session basis, Glover readily agreed.

"Hallelujah" was the work of songwriters Roger Greenaway and

Roger Cook, once hit-makers in their own right as the David and Jonathan duo, and now the guiding force behind Blue Mink, a gaggle of Trident Studios session musicians set to become one of the biggest pop groups of early-'70s Britain. And, by those standards, it wasn't half-bad, a breezy little number with a tight chorus, a sing-along melody, and just enough semireligious intrigue in the lyrics to slide in alongside a few of the age's (and the band's) still-lingering mystic preoccupations.

Besides, "Hallelujah" was pop only on paper, which was why Derek Lawrence had handed the song over to the band after he received the songwriters' acetate demo. Turned over by Lord and Blackmore, it took on far greater depth and substance, and Deep Purple, with Evans and Simper still officially on board, had already booked a session at De Lane Lea Studios, to begin work on it. Any recording that they did that afternoon, however, was nothing more than a subterfuge. The band left the studio after just two hours — then Paice, Blackmore, and Lord doubled back, to start again with Gillan and Glover. And even before the session was complete, the trio knew their search for new musicians was over. Glover was invited to join the band that same evening: "I told them I'd think about it."

He took the question home with him that night, slept (or not) on it, then rang Lord the following day to accept the offer — only to be knocked down somewhat when, having impressed upon Deep Purple that he wasn't originally sure about joining, Jon Lord admitted that Deep Purple weren't certain about his recruitment either. Glover would be taken on three months' probation.

Neither was he to be allowed to settle once that initial period was over. A full year later, Glover recalled, "we were on a train going up to Scotland for a gig. We'd just come out of the studio the previous night, and I said, 'Ah, it's not as good as it could have been, if we'd been more together.' And Jon Lord turned round, gave me a sharp look . . . he was much more of a senior member in those days . . . and he says, 'Roger, you're wrong.' And that stopped me in my tracks. Then he said, 'If it could have been better, it would have been better. It is what it is and that's it. So shut the fuck up.'"

Gillan's position, too, was not secure. As late as November 1969, following a show at Bradford University, Lord was congratulating the support band's vocalist, one David Coverdale, on his performance and asking for his phone number — "Just in case things didn't work out with Gillan." He never made that call, but Coverdale would remember his words for the next four years.

Such uncertainties were only natural — very few bands are convinced that they have stumbled upon the ultimate chemistry after just a couple of meetings and a recording session. But still, there was a magic to the "Hallelujah" session that impressed upon everybody that they would need to travel far and wide to unearth another combination that felt so instantly alchemical.

"The amazing thing about it is that, in the beginning, Ian seemed like a stranger in the band," Jon Lord reflected twenty-five years later. "He didn't know what to do with his wonderful voice. Roger is somewhat like Ian's interpreter. I mean, Ian comes up with really weird ideas in his singing, just to see if they can fly. But then they crash and burn, and Roger's task is to extinguish the fires and pick up the pieces. Nobody in the band knows in which direction Ian wants to go with a song — except for Roger! Ian needs Roger to explain it to the rest of the band. They are really the perfect team."

What the team brought to the band was a sense of driving dynamism, something solid, unflustered, and, most of all, unfussed, topped by a Gillan vocal that was utterly without mannerism or idiosyncrasy, that was neither forced nor frenzied, but was capable of a dizzying array of emotions and moods regardless, and topped by an intensity that began in the bowels of the earth and then shrieked, literally, its way to the surface. In the studio that evening, the moment when he unleashed the first of what would become one of Deep Purple's greatest trademarks, a gravity-defying scream a minute and a half in, would later be ranked among the most crucial events in Deep Purple's musical history. In that split second, his stunned bandmates truly grasped everything the group was capable of — and the directions in which they were set to go.

Later, even Gillan would acknowledge that comparisons with Led Zeppelin, whose own vocal attack was led by Robert Plant's range, were valid. But, like Plant's, Gillan's personal style far outweighed his debt to anybody else. After two years and three albums, Deep Purple had finally found their voice.

The recording was completed over the course of a second clandestine session on June 12, 1969. Away from all such subterfuge, however, the official Deep Purple's zombie half-life continued with another U.K. tour, interspersed with a handful of European dates and, perhaps inevitably, a brace of fresh BBC sessions.

On June 24, Deep Purple recorded three songs for Pete Brandon's show, "Lalena," "The Painter," and "I'm So Glad"; the following week, they reprised "The Painter," "I'm So Glad," and, surprisingly, "Hush," for Chris Grant's immortally named *Tasty Pop Sundae* show. Four days later, on July 4, the original Deep Purple lineup played its final show, at the Top Rank in Cardiff. By the time *Tasty Pop Sundae* aired, on July 6, Ian Gillan and Roger Glover had been officially unveiled as the latest members of Deep Purple — with Simper learning of his dismissal from a news story in the *International Times*.

Both departing musicians were granted three months' wages, a share of the band's equipment, and the choice between a continued cut of the royalties on the three albums they'd recorded or a lump-sum buyout. Evans, who was already planning to move to America with his new wife, opted for the first course; Simper, however, took a third route and pursued Deep Purple into the courts, before finally accepting a £10,000 payoff in lieu of any future monies. That was not, it would swiftly transpire, the wisest decision.

Gillan and Glover made their live debuts with Deep Purple at the Speakeasy on July 10, and the difference between this showing and the band's last appearance there was phenomenal. Back then, they'd simply gone down well. This time, Gillan marveled, "as soon as we started, the place went wild. It was awesome, and I just coasted through, the feeling of power indescribable. *This was it!*"

Over at Harvest Records, while the changes wrought by the band's lineup caused only minimal concern, they did present the label with an administrative headache. *The Book of Taliesyn* was still scheduled as the label's first release, but it did beg the question of how a record company could claim to be on the cutting edge of the modern rock scene when its fanfare release was by a band that no longer even existed in the same form.

In a confusing maneuver, "Hallelujah" was hastily jammed into the release schedule, to appear in the stores on the same day as the album, with "April," a song from the still-unreleased and not yet even scheduled *third* Deep Purple album, on the B-side. Simultaneously, the band was booked into whichever TV and radio slots were available — a berth on the German television rock show *Beat Club* in early August, and another BBC session, for *The Stuart Henry Show*, in September.

And, while further gigs lay few and far between, time was not wasted, as the musicians focused on rehearsing and writing at their newly acquired home base at the Hanwell Community Centre, and getting to know one another, renting a couple of boats for a few days' cruising up the Thames. If all went according to plan, they'd be spending a lot of time together in similarly cramped conditions, charging from gig to gig. It didn't hurt to get an early heads-up on one another's notions of personal hygiene and the like.

The first new song the band came up with was "Kneel and Pray," a Mach 2 celebration of oral sex that would ultimately, and appropriately, develop into "Speed King." Half inspired by Blackmore's love of Jimi Hendrix's "Fire," and half drawing from Gillan's long-cherished hoard of old rock'n'roll records (he claimed his entire collection consisted of '50s-era classics), the song was earmarked for an immediate debut on the BBC session, where it was promptly retitled "Ricochet."

As July bled into August, the band seldom left the Community Centre, a venue that had long ago become a magnet for local bands in search of an isolated rehearsal space. Neither was it unusual, as the group's rehearsals progressed, for other bands to halt what they were doing and hearken instead to the amazing sounds emanating from Deep Purple's corner of the building.

David Byron, vocalist with another fast-evolving band, Spice, regularly listened in to Deep Purple's early rehearsals. He reflected, "It was interesting because, up to that point, we thought we were completely out on a limb." Having cut a less-than-sparkling single the previous year, "What About the Music," Spice had recently recruited a keyboard player, Ken Hensley, whose musical ambitions drifted in a distinctly classically tinged direction, at the same time as his bandmates pulsed a hard-rock vein. Byron admitted, "I know we listened to what Deep Purple were doing, and I'm sure they listened to us."

In later years, as Deep Purple's star soared into the very stratosphere while that of Spice — or Uriah Heep, as they were quickly renamed — remained at a more middling level, it became fashionable for rock critics to lambaste Byron and Co. for merely following Deep Purple's lead — even their decision to release a double live album in 1973, *Uriah Heep Live*, was written off as simply a desperate attempt to echo the success of Deep Purple's own *Made in Japan*.

Roger Glover does not dismiss such accusations: "I know Uriah Heep did get a lot from us. I remember coming back from a gig one time with Jon Lord; we got into the flat, turned on the TV, and there was a band on and we were watching it, and suddenly . . . our jaws just dropped, because they were doing everything we were doing! Long guitar solos, silly tunes, same sort of sound, the same organ and guitar mix. . . . 'What the fuck is this?'" It was Uriah Heep.

In fact, the two groups were to maintain the give-and-take — conscious or otherwise — that characterized their early days at the Community Centre; indeed, for close to four years, 1970–1973, Uriah Heep were to rank among the most reliable, and reliably consistent, bands on the circuit, responsible for a solid string of five albums that — aside from the occasional period nuance — stand as proudly effervescent today as they did in their prime.

One gigantic, grandiose step at a time, successive albums *Very 'Eavy . . . Very 'Umble, Salisbury, Look at Yourself, Demons and Wizards,* and *Magician's Birthday* pursued the band's development from their hard blues-inflected genesis to their destiny as what modern ears would describe as the extreme answer to Yes' contemporary peregrinations, with each release littering the landscape with a succession of still-classic performances.

By the time Heep paused for the May 1973 release of the in-concert double, they were averaging a new album every six to eight months, a breathtaking work rate that, sadly, sapped their creative spirit just as those years of hard work finally looked about to pay off. Even in their U.K. homeland, Uriah Heep were three albums old before they finally tasted chart success. But growing concert renown in America and a regular berth in the Top 40 saw them hovering on the very brink of superstardom — a brink upon which they would remain for the next three years and four LPs. Then the whole thing fell apart and, though various permutations of Heepers continue to play to this day, the most important part of the story was over.

Back in 1969, however, both bands — Uriah Heep and Deep Purple — were running neck-and-neck, spearheading precisely the new, and newly serious, school of heavy rock endeavor that Lord and Blackmore had foreseen six months earlier.

Musicianship remained paramount in this new arena. It was an age when great guitarists became gods, keyboard players became classical maestros, and the humblest band was expected to bisect its live show with breathtakingly complicated solos. But, in refusing to take their lead wholly from a variation of the heavy-metal blues espoused by Led Zeppelin and the Jeff Beck Group, which would develop into the solid, riff-based churning of Black Sabbath and Budgie, the likes of Deep Purple and Uriah Heep — as well as the rising stars of Atomic Rooster, Yes, Barclay James Harvest, Still Life, and the unequivocally named Greatest Show On Earth — carved a niche that shone, as the mood dictated, formidably distinctive, forebodingly primal, forlornly beautiful . . . and sometimes all three at once.

"It was a marvelous time, and it really was incredibly exciting," Jon Lord reflected. "It was a wonderful time to be a musician, because there were no rules and there were a whole number of different bands making new kinds of music. That post-Beatles period was a very special time for musical creativity."

It was, as it transpired, important that Deep Purple distanced themselves from the growing storms of the nascent heavy-metal movement. No matter that they would, in the end, be drawn into them anyway, as "Smoke on the Water" rose to become one of *the* all-time metal anthems. But the group's most formative years — 1969–71 — were spent keeping the skull-crushing battery of true metal firmly at arm's length, as they concentrated instead on creating textures and sustaining a musical momentum that was far from the power-chord palladium of the movement's true giants. Indeed, in later years Lord would insist that he never even heard the term "heavy metal" until the early 1980s, preferring instead to describe Purple's personalized variation on the prog ethic by the less accusatory (and certainly more appropriate) term "hard rock."

He might even be correct, though a bookshelf of metal encyclopedias and histories will doubtless creak in protest. Even within the progressive field of the day, Deep Purple's musical influences flew at sharp odds with those being espoused elsewhere on the scene, as the musicians proved when they discussed the genesis of "Child in Time," another of the songs that Deep Purple sketched out during those first days in Hanwell. It was rooted in "Bombay Calling," a cut from the recently released debut album by American West Coast band It's a Beautiful Day — although the percussive wash of Deep Purple's own "Lalena" was certainly caught up in its web as well. Lord was bowled over by the Dan Hicks song and frequently played around with it, until the day Gillan picked up on the melody and improvised his own lyrics: "Sweet child in time . . ."

As Gillan reflected in his autobiography, "Rock history was made! It was totally spontaneous and conceived without a storyline." Yet "Child in Time" would go on to become one of the most potent and poignant of all British rock commentaries on the then ongoing Vietnam War — and survive, too, to become a private anthem for many of the underground opposition groups forged within the political turmoil of 1980s–90s Eastern Europe.

Journalists, lost without a convenient peg to hang the new sound upon, raced to term this sound "progressive rock," then rushed faster to seek out the antecedents that would both validate the music's existence and vindicate their failure to predict its emergence in the first place. Elements of the early Pink Floyd and Moody Blues, hints of previous attempts to fuse rock with jazz (the Soft Machine) and the classics (the Nice), and the shadows of hot-wired world music (the Incredible String Band) and reheated psychedelia (too many to name) all dangled over this new sound. If, in later years, Deep Purple became more synonymous with heavy metal than anything so complex as prog, that proves only how all-encompassing this new genre originally was — and how one-dimensionally blinkered rock criticism so swiftly became.

The key to the absolute transformation that had engulfed Deep Purple wasn't solely the lineup changes, although they did make a difference. In the past, to awaken that grisly old specter once again, Deep Purple had simply sounded too American — selfish devotees of that school of musical thought that placed prowess and perfection ahead of every other consideration. Which, in layperson's terms, is probably a reasonable enough summation of prog rock in any form. What, after all, are such monstrosities as Yes' *Tales from Topographic Oceans* and ELP's *Works*, if not the gory crowning glory of an art form that has squeezed every last ounce of humanity out of itself?

There was, however, a difference. Prog is not about perfection. It is about the ability to transport the listener to plateaus that other forms of rock are incapable of reaching, because they lay beyond boundaries that rock is seldom willing to approach. And if, occasionally, that journey does lead to pomposity, peregrination, or worse, then at least others know not to take the same route.

Deep Purple's absorption into these necessarily convoluted waters was forever to be offset by other factors, not least of all their willingness to eschew many of the more obvious portents of prog. Gone, for instance, were the classical themes and chord structures that had once been the linchpin of the band's early grandiosity explorations — they had become "soul-less," Jon Lord complained, "too planned."

Now the group wanted to break into the opposite direction entirely, into the areas of spontaneity, experimentation, and orgasmic explosion. "We believe in experiment and excitement," Lord told *Beat Instrumental*. "We were trying to develop unnaturally before. We would grasp all sorts of different ideas at once, like a child in a garden full of flowers — he wants them all at once. When Ian and Roger joined, something very nice happened within the group." Joined by two musicians who'd spent their entire careers at the bottom of the rock'n'roll food chain, who'd eaten off some of the greasiest spoons that British motorway catering can offer, Deep Purple had finally learned to replace finesse with feeling, science with sensuality. And that translated to energies that kicked the group's earlier notions resoundingly out the window.

For Malcolm Jones at Harvest, his first inkling that he had misjudged Deep Purple arrived with "Hallelujah." Though the record itself did nothing, it at least racked up some encouraging reviews ("laden with mystique and compulsion," said *NME*), and from thereon, Deep Purple could do little wrong in his eyes — so little that, when he caught wind of the band's next project, Lord's so-called *Concerto for Group and*

Orchestra, he promptly gave it his blessing.

Of course, the notion that rock could — or even should — be successfully fused with the classics was one for which Jones could claim midwifery rights: the previous year, he had scored a major U.K. hit as producer of Love Sculpture's sonic, guitar-led demolition of Russian composer Khatchaturian's "Sabre Dance." In the months since then, the beckoning wraith of Nice organist Keith Emerson's next project, the Emerson Lake & Palmer supergroup, and Harvest's recruitment of the seriously classicist Barclay James Harvest had proven that, whatever doubts cynics might have entertained about colliding the two musical disciplines, it was a collision destined to happen.

For Jon Lord, the proposed *Concerto* was the fruition of close to four years of scheming, since the Artwoods' collaboration with the New Jazz Orchestra was struck down by the bean counters at Decca.

He never lost either the enthusiasm or the drive such a project would require, while rumors that labelmates Barclay James Harvest were themselves planning a major venture of a similar ilk, allying with classical pianist Robert John Godfrey and sundry Royal College of Music alumni to form the Barclay James Harvest Orchestra, could only have hardened his determination to see it through.

At the same time, however, Lord was well aware of the snake pit into which he was stepping, and thoughtfully conscious of the contradictions enshrined in the very concept of classical/rock couplings. He neither demanded his audience treat his work with the awestricken respect others might have claimed it deserved, nor once attempted to place it on a par with the masters. It was, simply, an idea "I had . . . about five years ago, but I've never been with a group I thought could do it until now."

Lord was also adamant that the concerto was not merely "a case of doing a pop version of suitable classical themes." He told *Melody Maker* in August 1969, "I am writing the whole lot from scratch," at the same time as acknowledging that he wasn't even certain whether he was capable of doing so. He had written for strings and woodwind in the past, but a full orchestra was a new experience — and adding a rock band to the brew only increased the project's edginess. As he later remarked, "One guitar chord can destroy a full orchestra very, very easily."

Any misgivings he may have felt, however, were swiftly put to rest not only by Malcolm Jones' encouragement, but also by managers Tony Edwards and John Coletta's unreserved enthusiasm, an excitement that had remained tangible since Lord first mentioned it to them, back before the band's last American tour. In fact, the pair booked the Royal Albert Hall and engaged the Royal Philharmonic Orchestra before Lord had even started writing. He told them he expected it would take him nine months to produce the work, and that is exactly how long they gave him. Lord laughed, "I mooted the idea and our manager . . . came to me a few months later and said, 'Are you serious about that *Concerto for Group and Orchestra*?' I said, 'Yeah, I'm working on it,' [and he replied,] 'Well, you'd better work harder because I've booked the Royal Albert Hall.'"

Conductor Malcolm Arnold, one of the U.K.'s foremost modern classical composers (his Oscar-winning soundtrack to the movie *Bridge over the River Kwai* is a masterpiece), was engaged and proved invaluable as the work progressed, assisting Lord with the mechanics of completing the score. A grateful Lord later described Arnold as "the cornerstone" of the entire project, "the man who'd stand between us and the fiercesome beast that was the Royal Philharmonic Orchestra."

Arnold, for his part, agreed to take on that task after reading just five pages of Lord's original score. "I have never heard before of a pop musician who could compose — and score — a work like this," he told the *Daily Express* newspaper in September 1969. "Even George Gershwin had to find someone [else] to score his 'Rhapsody in Blue.'" He continued, "Often when pop musicians compose more serious works, they become pretentious. But Mr. Lord's concerto is witty and lively." Lord originally intended writing just one movement; it was Arnold's unbridled encouragement that convinced him to expand to the traditional concerto format of three.

Lord's *Concerto for Group and Orchestra* was one of two new works premiered at the Royal Albert Hall on September 24, 1969 — Arnold's own long-awaited Symphony No. 6, performed by the orchestra alone, opened the bill. But it was the concerto that drew the most attention from both the pop press and the mainstream media — which, as Coletta later acknowledged, had been his intention all along.

As aware as anybody that Deep Purple needed to take a resolute stand against their own past, Coletta was also out to one-up the rest of the music scene, all the hundreds of other bands whose press-hungry publicists were chasing every available newspaper column inch by revealing ever more grandiose, absurd, or scandalous "truths" about their clients. Jon Lord saw the concerto in musical terms alone. Coletta and his partners regarded it as a publicity tool as well. And they were right to do so. Deep Purple received more British newspaper coverage in the month or so that lay on either side of the Albert Hall concert than they had in the previous two years combined.

Back at Hanwell, as summer 1969 wore on, Deep Purple were feeling pressures of a different kind, as Lord missed rehearsal after rehearsal in his rush to complete the concerto. Visitors to his ground-floor flat in Harbledown Road, Parsons Green, remember its very walls being coated in Lord's notes and thoughts, an elaborate filing system the composer himself could decode. Neither was he able to completely distance himself from the task when he did unite with his bandmates, for the clutch of live shows that had, thoughtlessly, been lined up for the band during the month or so prior to the Albert Hall show.

Lord recalled, "It was a difficult time orchestrating and writing the concerto. . . . I was getting back at 2 in the morning, putting on a pot of coffee, and working through till first light to get it finished, because parts of our management said we're booked and [we're gonna be in] trouble, aaaaargh!"

His actual playing did not suffer. But witnesses to the band's shows during those last few hectic weeks unanimously recall his look of absolute distraction, while the sheer fertility that exploded from the band's increasingly irregular rehearsals and jams seemed in constant danger of being undermined by the demands of the concerto.

It was a delicate period, after all. Songs being written now would prove the foundation for the band's next scheduled studio LP, and Gillan recalled, "I must admit that my attitude was all wrong. Roger and I had only just joined the band and we didn't really appreciate what working with the Royal Philharmonic Orchestra at the time could do for us. We were already writing for the [new] album, and this seemed like an unwanted interruption. Deep Purple have always tried to be challenging, yet here we were with something truly challenging and different, and we couldn't appreciate what we had."

Instead, the concerto hung over them like a trip to the dentist. "It was something we all found very difficult to cope with," Gillan continued. "Ritchie, in particular. . . . Words were spoken to the effect that we were a rock band making a major album" — not a plaything for Lord's more airy aspirations. They knew, after all, that it was the gestating album that would determine the group's future; that, for all its potential and portentousness, the concerto was little more than a one-off event into which the remainder of the band were co-opted by circumstance.

They gave it their all, nevertheless. Although Lord alone composed the music, Gillan supplied lyrics for the second movement — writing them on the day of the show, over lunch at an Italian restaurant, while Blackmore, Glover, and Paice would all find space in which to shine during the performance itself.

Lord recalled, "I would ask him, 'Ian, are you writing the lyrics?' 'Yes, Jon, I'm writing them.' Ian would say that day after day. And then we got to first rehearsal with the orchestra. 'Uh, I've got them somewhere, I've got them somewhere.' He wrote them just before the dress rehearsal. And he wrote them in an Italian restaurant over a large flagon of Chianti with Malcolm Arnold. Malcolm was a famous toter, he loved to drink. He doesn't drink anymore. But at the time he was famous for [that]. In fact, Gillan and he became soul buddies in that department. They turned [the lyrics] in about lunchtime.

"And what's lovely about the lyrics is that there is a genuine heartfelt thing on Ian Gillan's part in saying, 'What shall I do when they stand smiling at me? Look at the floor and be cool? What shall I do when it all goes wrong? How will I know and start singing my song?'"

In fact, if there were any problems with the proposed marriage of rock band and classical orchestra, the vast majority came from the orchestra, voiced vociferously during the week of rehearsals they managed to squeeze into the schedule. "The first session with orchestra and band," Gillan recalled, "ended with different emotions running high. . . ." Although none would come close to attaining the heights attained by the cellist who rose to her feet to denounce performing with "a second-rate Beatles."

Lord later admitted that the rehearsals were so appalling that he was reduced to the edge of tears, convinced the entire affair would turn into a bottomless debacle. It was Arnold alone, he said, who turned things around, when he rose to address his reluctant charges and informed them, "You're supposed to be the finest orchestra in Britain, and you're playing like a bunch of cunts."

The evening itself broke into three separate performances. First came Arnold's own symphony, after which Deep Purple arrived onstage to perform three numbers — "Hush," "Wring That Neck," and a darkly atmospheric "Child in Time." An interval followed before band and orchestra appeared together for the evening's main attraction.

After the disasters of the rehearsals, the performance itself was all but flawless. Looking back, Lord isolated certain passages as being executed with less style and panache than he might have hoped, but there was only one moment when the performance went seriously awry: when Ritchie Blackmore rose during the first movement to take what was intended as a ninety-second solo — and never stopped playing.

From the podium, Arnold stood in almost comical exasperation, attempting to catch the guitarist's eye and stare him into submission. Blackmore, however, was oblivious. "Ritchie had a statement to make," Lord laughingly reflected, "which was, 'This is just as much about rock-'n'roll as it is orchestral.' And he proceeded to play and play and play."

Finally, Blackmore came out of his reverie and hit the cue that Arnold and the orchestra had been waiting so long to hear, and the performance not only continued as scheduled, but required an encore that nobody had prepared for. Rather than disappoint the audience, then, Arnold waved the orchestra into a repeat airing of the tumultuous third movement, while Lord gazed in triumph as, with the hardest part of the evening behind them, all one-hundred-plus players on the stage performed with an abandon that pinpointed the most positive aspects of the event.

Drawing a line between the public and critical responses to the evening is difficult. Arnold himself told the orchestra during the final rehearsal, "We're going to make history tonight," and much of the audience — for whom attending a classical concert was a new experience — certainly attended the event with that sentiment in mind. The pop press, too, was impressed by the sheer magnitude of the event, acknowledging that, while further experiments in a similar vein needed to tread carefully around the multitudinous pitfalls that the concerto laid bare (volume paramount among them), the experiment was generally enjoyable. "A bold and inventive piece," as *Melody Maker*'s Chris Welch put it, was "probably the most advanced piece of writing produced by a pop musician."

It also ignited a fire beneath a host of similarly adventurous spirits. Within a year, the long-promised Barclay James Harvest Orchestra had come into brilliant, if short-lived being; both Pink Floyd and Caravan were being courted for ballet scores; and Soft Machine journeyed where even Deep Purple had not trod, when electronic musician Tim Souster secured them a berth at the Proms, the annual season of virtuoso orchestral performances that are to classical music what Woodstock is to rock. The world of stuffy classics, as *Musical Quarterly* didn't *quite* put it, had at long last returned one of the calendar's most cherished events to its original brief of "something for everyone, and . . . admitted that pop music is worthy of recognition."

Other mainstream voices, however, drifted between caution and downright dismissal. "The alliance of pop and symphony leaves me with one recommendation," advised Noel Goodwin, one of Britain's foremost classical reviewers. "Divorce by consent." The Deep Purple event had laid bare the compromise necessary for the two musical units to coexist, and it was one that denied the two ensembles the opportunity to function at anything approaching their peak. "As the orchestra yielded more and more of its capacity for sustained development of ideas, so the pop group had its fire steadily dampened."

BBC disc jockey John Peel was even more damning, professing himself so horrified by the very concept of the concerto that he refused ever again to play Deep Purple on his nightly show. "*Concerto* was, quite simply, spectacularly awful," Peel told author Paul Stump. "And the worst thing is, I thought it was crap then, too. People say, 'Oh, you used to play a lot of Purple on *Top Gear*,' which I did. But when they brought in an orchestra, I bailed out."

He later modified the reasons for his embargo, telling readers of his weekly column in *Disc*, "If . . . we stuck to records by Ten Years After, ELP and Deep Purple . . . we'd be guaranteed a huge audience. However, that's not what it's all about. Regardless of your own opinion on these . . . groups, you must admit they hardly need the limited exposure that *Top Gear* could afford them." But the end result was the same. Just once more would Deep

Purple's path cross with Peel's, when he helmed their appearance on the BBC's weekly *Sunday Concert* broadcast the following February.

All these, and sundry similar, opinions were given greater gravity following the release of a live recording of the event, the baldly titled *Concerto for Group and Orchestra*, in January 1970. Produced by engineer Martin Birch, it was a magnificent-sounding record, and the fact that its release date fell just weeks after the U.K. arrival of Deep Purple's long-delayed third album was no accident. The group had already made it clear that they were just as happy to see *Deep Purple* shelved altogether. The near-simultaneous appearance of what was already the most talked about new album of the season ensured that it might as well have been.

From the USA, Tetragrammaton announced that they, too, were eagerly looking forward to releasing the album, although the feeling around the HEC management offices was that they'd believe it when they saw it — and they hoped they never did. The continuing saga of the American label's financial difficulties was common knowledge now; royalty payments were already deeply in arrears. It was difficult to foresee a happy resolution to the entire mess — the only consoling thought was that Tetragrammaton would collapse sooner rather than later, and that Deep Purple might be freed to take their music elsewhere. Until then, they just had to grin and bear it.

Deep Purple would go on to perform the concerto on just three further occasions, in Vienna and Zurich in early 1970, during their next European tour, and at the Hollywood Bowl (with conductor Lawrence Foster) in August. It receded, then, into the realm of ancient history until its revival in 1999. In the meantime, the work of establishing Deep Purple as a rock band continued.

It was not going to be easy. In America, where Tetragrammaton's ongoing freefall into extinction rendered the existence of Deep Purple's back catalog all but immaterial, *Concerto for Group and Orchestra* served only to baffle any passersby who might have picked up a copy out of vague affection for "Hush." And at home, its appearance simply muddied waters that were already swirling toward a major identity crisis, from a fan's point of view, if not the band's.

In just six months, between August 1969 and January 1970, Deep Purple had released three albums — *Book of Taliesyn*, *Deep Purple*, and

Concerto — and one single, "Hallelujah." Each offered up a very different face, and each reveled in a very different sound. Then, in concert, as they continued gigging almost constantly in the run-up to the new year, there was a different group again, a steaming, screeching, pounding monstrosity that arose from a riff-addled stew of blues-blistered pomp, Wagnerian circumstance, and near-operatic screams, to pound the most hard-bitten onlooker into submission.

Few casual onlookers knew what to make of it all; many promoters were uncertain precisely what sort of group they were booking. As Deep Purple worked their way around the theaters and colleges that fall, several venues asked whether the band were supplying their own orchestra — and at least one, in Ipswich, went to the trouble of recruiting a local brass band to accompany the group, just in case.

Deep Purple themselves were similarly uncertain as to what was happening, fearing that whatever success the concerto had accrued might easily backfire upon the band and render it nothing more than a vehicle for further Jon Lord–led extravaganzas.

Lord himself was adamant that nothing could be further from his mind. "[The concerto] was never intended to be part of the direction of the group," he assured visiting journalists. "It was merely an experiment." The new sessions documented the true nature of the group: as Jon Lord was at pains to remind people, "We were actually already moving in [the hard rock] direction. We had already, back in April of that year, signed up Ian [Gillan] and Roger Glover and we were writing stuff that became *In Rock*."

But the uncertainty and disquiet of his bandmates remained a vivid reminder of the cost of that experiment, one that almost forced Lord out of the group — *not* because he intended pursuing his dream any further, but because he seemed unable to convince his bandmates of that fact. He later acknowledged that his determination to quit was so strong that, of all the crises the band's management had dealt with so far, this latest was far and away the most serious.

But somehow they smoothed the waters. Lord did not want to depart; he just felt like he ought to. The others didn't want him to leave; they were simply afraid that he would. But with Lord adamant that while he had one further, similar commission (from the BBC) to complete, he had no more need to write another concerto than his bandmates had to play one, the matter was dropped.

In fact, the concerto benefited the band far more than it did damage — at least in Britain. Hitherto, after all, the name Deep Purple had been synonymous with the overwrought, pseudoclassical covers that were still their best-known numbers. Though *Concerto for Group and Orchestra* did little to exorcise those earlier criticisms, it at least proved there was considerably more substance to Deep Purple than might otherwise have been assumed. Listeners who had written them off were piqued to give them a second chance — and, over the next six months, Deep Purple made every effort to afford them that opportunity, launching into a solid block of gigging that often saw them playing live five, even six, nights out of seven.

It was a punishing routine, but the band wouldn't have it any other way. Creatively — as writers, as players, as performers — the quintet was sparking. Songs like "Mandrake Root" and "Wring That Neck," long-established vehicles for onstage improvisation, now began stretching out even further, some nights moving toward the thirty-minute mark if the band felt the occasion deserved it. Elsewhere, although Deep Purple continued airing material from the early albums, new songs were slamming into the live set as soon as they were written, to be worked on in front of live audiences, until they could be considered complete.

Nightly, new components slipped into place — a solo here, a lyric change there, a drum fill somewhere else. And nightly, songs that just months earlier had been plucked out of the ether as mere jams or even jokes took on lives of their own. "Flight of the Rat" once existed merely as a jokey rearrangement of "Flight of the Bumble-Bee," while "Hard Lovin' Man" started life as a riff that Glover messed around with in rehearsal.

Necessity, as well as invention, contributed to the group's on-the-road workload. Staging the concerto had proven extravagantly expensive, all the more so given the continued absence of American royalties. Studio time was a luxury now, as the band toured simply to keep bread on the table and, while work on what would become the lineup's first album began at the IBC Studios in central London's Portland Place in October 1969, it would perforcedly stretch into the following May.

Gradually, however, the "new look" Deep Purple, Mark II, as the group's followers term it, took shape, with the band giving audiences further opportunity to trace their progress via regular returns to the BBC. Halloween 1969 saw them record near-perfect versions of "Living Wreck" and the now-retitled "Speed King" for broadcast on *The Stuart Henry Show*, alongside a work in progress that, although swiftly discarded by the band, has since seen release as "Jam Stew." At the time, it simply fell short of the maxim that Blackmore, early into the new album's gestation, insisted should be the group's one concern: "If it's not dramatic or exciting, it has no place on this album." Ironically, in light of the song's eventual prominence on the completed album, "Living Wreck" was also destined, at one time, to be left on the shelf.

Again, Martin Birch was working alongside the band in the studio. For the first time, however, Deep Purple were producing themselves, confident that they alone understood precisely what they were trying to accomplish on the record. Glover later insisted his most pervasive memory of the sessions was watching the VU meters march into the red, an overload that few producers — even those who prided themselves on their unconventionality — would have happily permitted. According to Blackmore, the overriding instruction to Birch was, "Make everything louder than everything else." The guitarist knew it was the journey into the unknown — or, at least, the unacceptable — that often drew the dividing line between magic and mundanity. His time spent alongside the great Joe Meek had not been wasted.

Birch's role would not go unnoticed, however. On the album's credits, he is described not only as an engineer, but also as a catalyst. What the band said they wanted, he ensured they got, and from the sessions there emerged, as Ian Gillan reflected with supreme understatement, "a pretty significant record" — one that completely redesigned the boundaries of progressive rock.

Birch's contributions to the show can best be comprehended by a quick listen to another project he worked on that momentous year, the self-titled debut album by Swiss blues rockers Toad. Recorded in December 1970 at De Lane Lea, with guitarist Vic Vergeat heavily to the fore, it echoes Deep Purple not only in execution, but also in intent, a witches' brew of influences and impacts that steadfastly refuses to be categorized — just, as Gillan felt, Deep Purple refused to be.

"If you listen to Jethro Tull," Gillan said, "[you] see that they're very obviously based in folk music. If you listen to Free, you see they're very obviously based in soul . . . and, if you listen to Zeppelin, it's blues. With Purple, it's kind of weird, because Jon grew up in the Royal College of Music, so his background's in orchestral music and jazz. Ian Paice grew up in the Buddy Rich school of music, so big band, swing — stuff like that — was the major influence in his life. Roger Glover was into Lonnie Donegan and every form of ethnic music you could imagine — folk music, basically. And Ritchie and I were pretty much pop, rock, sort-of-country, and then delving into blues and jazz. So we had a fairly diverse set of influences [and] when the band came together, it was enthusiastic and loud. . . . We just wanted to play music."

Which is exactly what they did.

Chapter 6

Black Nights
in White Satin

Nineteen-seventy was just weeks old when Tetragrammaton finally gave up the ghost, folding with Deep Purple still owed thousands of dollars. Worse yet, the band was still bound to their contract with the label, rendering them nothing more in the financiers' eyes than an asset of the shattered company.

It was a situation that has, on so many occasions, derailed — even destroyed — an artist's career. The accountants and bean counters who dispose of the wreckage of any failed business think only of making sure the creditors — anybody from the store that supplies the paper clips through to the taxman and beyond — see at least something of their money. Under those conditions, an artist is no more or less important than the coffee machine, and can be bartered with equal alacrity.

Deep Purple, like the remainder of the Tetragrammaton catalog, were fortunate in that the only people interested then in purchasing a record company were other record companies, with Warner Brothers swiftly moving to the head of the queue. HEC immediately got to work, negotiating with Warners an arrangement that would resolve their positions both as an asset and a creditor.

It took almost six months for the deal to fall into place, a hiatus that not only necessitated delaying the European release of the now-complete new album, but also forced the cancellation of the band's American tour in March. They had, after all, toured without the benefit of fresh product once before. Instead, Deep Purple carried on gigging, at home and across Western Europe, while Blackmore and Paice took a break of their own when they reunited with producer Derek Lawrence to partake in a project he called the Green Bullfrog.

Commissioned by the Decca label, who would release an album of the sessions the following year, the Green Bullfrog was carved firmly in the mold of the superstar jam sessions that so fascinated the rock cognoscenti of the late 1960s and early 1970s. With the entire crew adopting pseudonyms, both to avoid complications with their regular record contracts and to heighten the mystery that traditionally surrounded such aggregations, Blackmore ("Boots") and Paice ("Speedy") were joined by Blackmore's old guitar tutor Big Jim Sullivan (appropriately disguised as "The Boss"), the hard-drinking Tony Ashton (equally appropriately renamed "Bevy"), Blackmore's fellow former-Outlaw Chas Hodges ("Sleepy"), his Heads Hands & Feet colleague Albert Lee ("Pinta"), Procol Harum's Matthew Fisher ("Sorry"), Earl Jordan ("Jordan"), and Rod Alexander ("Vicar"). (Contrary to rumor and the inferences of sundry repackagings of the ensuing album, neither Roger Glover nor Jon Lord were involved.)

With such a stellar lineup, the musicianship was impeccable — at least, as impeccable as one would expect from a two-day studio party. A couple of Lawrence-penned numbers alone could be considered "originals"; the remainder of the album comprised blues-rock-inflected covers of such rock'n'roll staples as "Lawdy Miss Clawdy" and "My Baby Left Me," "Walk in My Shoes" by "Hush" songsmith Joe South, and a deliciously rough'n'ready version of '60s freakbeat mavericks the Creation's "Making Time" — a song for which Blackmore and Lawrence had been carrying a torch since the *Shades of Deep Purple* sessions.

With Blackmore, Sullivan, and Lee involved, it was naturally a guitar-heavy event, and there was certainly some searing playing amid the good-time grooves and loose-limbed energies. Based around the "Jam Stew" riff that Deep Purple had so recently discarded, the seven-minute title track was a particular tour de force. One had to admit, however, that unless ragtag armies of boogying buddies really were your cup of tea, there was little about *Green Bullfrog* to truly engage the attention. Just like every other superstar jam session, then.

Gillan, too, found himself in demand, when Tony Edwards sent playwrights Tim Rice and Andrew Lloyd Webber an acetate of "Child in Time" after hearing that they were seeking a rock singer to perform in their forthcoming musical, *Jesus Christ Superstar*. Meeting the pair, Gillan was less than enthused by Lloyd Webber, but hit it off so well with Rice that, despite reservations about the quality of the material, he immediately agreed to voice Jesus Christ on the production's accompanying soundtrack album.

With his commitment to Deep Purple forcing him to turn down the proffered role in the accompanying stage show (and, later, the movie), Gillan recorded his entire soundtrack contribution in a matter of hours. "It's not a project I got close to at all, although . . . there were two high points," he reflected. The first highlight was his performance of the song "In the Garden of Gethsemane," a moving piece set at the base of the cross; the second, Edwards' negotiation of royalty payments for the session, as opposed to the flat fee originally on offer. A Top 10 hit in Britain and an American chart-topper, *Jesus Christ Superstar* would go on to sell some eight million copies worldwide.

Of course, such diversions were little more than ways of filling (or killing) time around the activities of Deep Purple. Finally, the wait came to an end in May, as Warners and HEC agreed on a non-recoupable payment of $40,000, in lieu of the unpaid Tetragrammaton royalties. Warners celebrated with a rerelease of *Concerto for Group and Orchestra*, unavailable in America since a fleeting appearance in the new year, and were rewarded when it promptly climbed to No. 149 on the American charts, a fair improvement on the progress of its predecessor and a warm invitation to the band's forthcoming LP — the first in Deep Purple's history, the band felt, to truly represent what they were about. They intended calling it *Deep Purple in Rock*, and, if one bypasses the Rushmore-sized pun that serves as the album's jacket, there have been few more unequivocally titled LPs.

Deep Purple in Rock opens with a discordant overture of such cacophony that, when the album finally made it out in the United States, the record company sliced away the first ninety seconds, to protect local ears. "Speed King" thunders on regardless, a raucous celebration of every rock'n'roll keynote ever consigned to vinyl, from "Good golly, Miss Molly" to "Saturday night and I just got paid," a celebration that might, at one point, resolve itself into a gently twittering conversation between guitar and organ, but quickly picks up its basic thrust again, to conclude one of the most dramatic introductions to any album . . . *ever*.

What was remarkable, however — what divided *In Rock* from so many other albums that kick off with so dramatic a flourish — is that it never let up thereafter.

In Rock, for all its fame, is not perfect. While Blackmore's "If it isn't exciting" injunction was certainly adhered to throughout, there is a one-dimensionality to much of the album that, divorced from the time and place in which the record was conceived, renders it occasionally disappointing. The periodically plodding "Bloodsucker," "Living Wreck," and "Hard Lovin' Man" (Glover's favorite track!), after all, are little more than hard-rock showcases to which rudimentary lyrics have been grafted, while the anti-drug "Flight of the Rat" is more riff than roughage.

But no album that opens with "Speed King," wraps up its first side with "Child in Time," and then drops the grinding, slovenly funk of "Into the Fire" into the second-side mix can be readily discarded, any more than one would write off a mountain range because the peaks aren't all the same size. Put bluntly, those three songs set the bar so high that no band of the era (or any other) could have consistently matched them across the course of one album, and an alternate universe in which *In Rock* comprised only the "lesser" numbers would still have stepped back in admiration. *In Rock* might not have been the heaviest, loudest LP ever made. But, in that spring of 1970, it was difficult to think of many that could compete with it.

The secret of its success did not, however, reside merely in its woofer-warping volume. At a time when both Led Zeppelin and Free had punched hard-hitting blues rock into an entirely new realm of eviscerating drama, Deep Purple all but eschewed the bluesy half of the equation and concentrated on the rock, creating a sound that did not conform to any single genre, music that could not be comfortably filed alongside anything else on the market at that time.

Arthur Brown, whose "Fire"-breathing Crazy World were top of the bill at Deep Purple's now-far-away flop at the 1968 National Jazz & Blues Festival, later paid Deep Purple in general, and Ian Gillan in particular, an enormous compliment when he decreed, "Deep Purple . . . became the extension of the Crazy World sound." An *extension*, not a continuation, not a reinterpretation, and certainly not a mere photocopy.

Across the course of one mighty album, back in 1968, the Crazy World of Arthur Brown blueprinted a Hammond-heavy, percussion-powered, turbulent rock that was the absolute corollary of anything else that leeched from the psychedelic underground of the day — claustrophobic where elsewhere was expansion, stygian where others were breezy, taut where others were loose, and terrifying where others were simply a little edgy.

Deep Purple espoused similar principles: the same reliance on clashing dynamics and Herculean arrangements, the same tightrope interplay between voice and instrumentation, and, most of all, a similar approach to vocal technique — "the singing star with the high notes," as Brown put it. And he hit the nail right on the head. Though there were countless other acts whose debts to Brown were far more obvious (and far more frequently cited), from Alice Cooper to Kiss, and on to his own Crazy World bandmates' subsequent success as Atomic Rooster, Deep Purple alone truly comprehended the Crazy World's pioneering meld of hard blues, harder psychedelia, and absolutely impermeable rock'n'roll.

However, while Gillan's contributions were frequently isolated as Deep Purple's most recognizable element, Jon Lord, whose Hammond played such a pivotal role in the overall sound of the album, was swift to insist that *In Rock* was simply a summation of the direction in which Deep Purple had been moving all along. "We'd been working toward [it] for two years, even before [they] joined, and it turned out exactly as we wanted it," he told *Music Scene*, asserting that no single member of the group was more important than any other. At the same time, he confirmed the sense of competition that was so critical to the group's internal chemistry: *Make everything louder than everything else.*

In the face of making music of such intensity, relations in the studio frayed with timepiece regularity, as each musician battled to ensure that he shone at his personal best throughout the album. Playbacks were especially chaotic, as each listened hard for his own contributions, making it plain when he thought someone else was overwhelming him.

Occasionally, too, tempers frayed, as when Gillan pointed out that he could not hear his vocals on one track. According to Blackmore, that wasn't important: "Who the fuck do you think you are? Tom Jones?"

This was no place for grandstanding, no place for ego. Jon Lord later insisted that the band coined the title "in rock" to differentiate it from the previous "in concert." But, of course, the title meant so much more than that. *Deep Purple in Rock* was the sound of a band working its way, as one, up from the ground floor, discarding the baggage of both its distant and — remembering the concerto — recent past. It was the sound of a van haring up the M1 motorway en route to another college gymnasium; the smell of another tiny dressing room in another out-of-the-way backwater; the embodiment of everything that rock — in all its pigeonholed guises — was supposed to represent.

In a musical climate whose progenitors prided themselves not simply for being antistyle and antifashion, but also for their maverick disavowal of the glitter and glitz that attended pop stardom, Deep Purple had hiked themselves out of oblivion and into the hearts of what the industry regarded as the most hard-to-please audience, one whose very existence proved just how far the musical power base had shifted — not overnight, but certainly quickly enough to render obsolete the business practices that had reigned supreme just two or three years before.

No longer was the live circuit in the thrall of decrepit theatrical and ballroom agents who just wanted to put on "a good show for the people." Now it was students' union secretaries who booked the most meaningful shows, reacting to the demands of their constituency by attracting the weirdest, the wildest, the most way-out bands they could find.

Record labels, too, had changed. After a birth attended only by suspicion and cynicism, Harvest was now merely one of a battery of major-label subsidiaries dedicated to the progressive rock that might never set the world on fire, but was certainly too popular to be ignored. Decca established the Nova label, bringing the likes of Steve Hillage's Egg to the cognoscenti's attention; Pye launched Dawn, with such off-kilter delights as Demon Fuzz and Comus; Fontana ignited Vertigo, home to Dr Z, Caterpillar, Affinity, and Ben. But whereas once, even the hippest label would have been staffed by nothing more than company timeservers, now the department heads really were "heads" — characters who might happily drift round the office in jeans, who had long ago traded Cuban cigars for Lebanese hash, and who daily celebrated rock's absolute liberation from the constraints of a pop world that had lain unchanged since time began.

As the goalposts shifted, so did the goals. Once, a hit single was a band's shortcut to stardom — even if they never followed it up, they were guaranteed work in the ballrooms for at least a few more years, and from there, the workingman's clubs and cabaret circuit yawned lucratively before them. Now, however, "hit single" was a dirty two words — fine if the ballrooms were all you aspired for, but anathema to an artist who believed his art was worth more than that. Kids bought singles like they bought candy, toys, and dolls. Serious music fans, however, bought full-length LPS — and serious music fans were the lifeblood of the underground.

Such disdain was a fashion birthed, like so many other of the early 1970s' most sacred cows, by Led Zeppelin. Their own first album scheduled for release in 1969, both the band and their record label, Atlantic, were happily awaiting the release of their first single, "Communication Breakdown," when manager Peter Grant announced that, at least in Britain, it wasn't going to happen. His charges, he insisted, were too important to be bothered with the promotional rigmarole that would attend such a release, too musical to be cheapened by the roll call of embarrassing television guest slots that a "hit" would demand: kids' shows, variety slots, the special guests of ghastly MOR entertainers, a musical turn in a half-hour helmed by puppets. Even after the BBC launched *The Old Grey Whistle Test*, a weekly late-night digest of the best in album-oriented rock, music television remained one area that hadn't changed, no matter how much the rest of the industry had shifted. Led Zeppelin were not a singles band.

Where Zeppelin led, others hastened to follow. Emerson, Lake & Palmer would not release a British single until 1973, the time of their fifth album. Having had a handful of hits and misses during their earliest years together, Pink Floyd would not issue another U.K. 45 until 1979. In the words of the *New Musical Express*' Julie Webb, "It wasn't done to release singles because no one would take you seriously, man. 'And we're not into singles, anyway,' artists would say in all sincerity."

Floyd — then as now, a law unto themselves — aside, Malcolm Jones and Harvest never paid much attention to the prevalent mood, although that is not to say the label roster in any way benefited from their 45 releases. From Kevin Ayers' "Singing a Song in the Morning" to Syd Barrett's "Octopus," from Battered Ornaments' "Goodbye We Love You" to Forest's "Searching for Shadows," some magnificent music made it out on Harvest's distinctively green-labeled 45, but scarcely anyone even noticed. By summer 1970, the label's first anniversary, Harvest had racked up precisely one hit single, as the Edgar Broughton Band's compulsive freak chant "Out Demons Out" squeaked into the British Top 40.

Deep Purple were no more interested in singles than any of their peers. On both radio and TV, they moved the other way entirely, purposefully pulling the most challenging numbers from their repertoire for broadcast. A session for BBC radio's *Sound of the Seventies* in April 1970 brought "Hard Lovin' Man," "Bloodsucker," and "Living Wreck" out to play, while July's appearance on the TV show *Doing Their Thing* was dominated by Blackmore's improvisational histrionics, with even "Child in Time" sounding all but conventional when sandwiched between the wild jams that comprised the remainder of the band's half-hour performance.

No surprise, then, that throughout the sessions for *Deep Purple in Rock*, the band didn't give a second thought to any one song being pulled from the album to maybe give radio something to think about. But Harvest, with HEC in full agreement, had other ideas. No sooner had the proffered master tapes been given a listen than the band found themselves having to answer the question "Where's the single?" And when they admitted there wasn't one, they were promptly returned to the studio to come up with one.

The session, in the familiar surroundings of De Lane Lea, was a washout. All day long, the band played around with riffs and ideas, in search of that elusive commercial sound their advisors were so determined they discover. But evening came and they had accomplished nothing. Finally, around 8, the band gave up and went to the nearby Newton Arms pub, in the vague hope that liquid refreshment might deliver the inspiration that mere hard graft had so patently failed to provide. And, for Glover and Blackmore, it did. They returned to the studio after just a couple of hours and, when the others joined them later in the evening, the pair had conjured a riff that, if it didn't have "hit single" written all over it, at least had an indefinable something that made it stand out. Glover called it "Black Night."

The basic riff revolved around an old Ricky Nelson song, "Summertime," that Blackmore had dragged from his memory banks — and echoed, too, the Blues Magoos' "We Ain't Got Nothing Yet," the seminal American garage 45 that made the Stateside Top 5 in 1966. The tempo was lifted from Canned Heat's chugging "On the Road Again," and the title came from an old Arthur Alexander R&B number that had once done sterling duty in Episode Six's live repertoire. From there, it was simply a matter of Gillan and Glover piecing together a lyric that could ride atop this startling mélange. It was an indication of how easily things fit together once the band sensed they were onto something that, within three hours, "Black Night" was completed.

Scornfully dismissing the track as nothing more than a creative icebreaker, Deep Purple's initial instinct was to use the song as the B-side to a still-unwritten potential hit single. Tony Edwards and John Coletta, however, were adamant that the hard work was over. "Black Night" would be the group's next single, to be released alongside *Deep Purple in Rock* in early June. It would not, however, be included on the LP, a cunning ploy that maximized the potential for success by ensuring fans of the band would have to buy both records, but fans of the song needed only pick up the single.

In the most superserious rock circles, of course, the very existence of a Deep Purple single was frowned upon. Terms such as "sell-out," reserved only for the most heinous of crimes against the underground, were freely bandied about, but Deep Purple were not the only sinners that season. Uriah Heep, too, had a new single out; the opening cut on their landmark *Very 'Eavy . . . Very 'Umble* debut album was "Gypsy," a staccato blues rocker that lurched through a battery of riffs and rhythms before finally unleashing that so distinctive opening line, "When I was only seventeen, I fell in love with . . ." — in Heep's hands, it was a "gypsy queen" but, a few years on, as the band's live stage show grew ever more theatrical, the English *New Musical Express* substituted that last line with "a dry ice machine."

Black Sabbath, who were also experimenting with the intricacies of progressive-rock, even as they purposefully pioneered the mutant strains of primal heavy metal, were on the brink of releasing a 45 of their own as well, as they readied the drilling power chords of "Paranoid" for their own driving spiral into the minds of the record-buying public. And, over the course of a couple of weeks that summer of 1970, the unthinkable happened.

Deep Purple were in the United States, finally playing the shows canceled from March (and giving the concerto its final airing), when both their single and Sabbath's began to move. On August 15, "Black Night" made its entrance into the U.K. Top 50; on August 29, "Paranoid" joined it there, the pair barreling up a listing that creaked beneath such safety-first fodder as the Vegas-bound Elvis Presley and the Beatles-balladeering Shirley Bassey, the perky pop of Pickettywitch and Marmalade, the novelty joys of Hotlegs and Mr. Bloe. As Sabbath's own Ozzy Osbourne remarked at the time, "It's about time groups like [us] had a look in the chart. Up to now, it's been all Tamla and bubblegum that's made the chart. The Deep Purple record is really good."

Deep Purple were less amenable to the inevitable comparisons being made between the two groups. "They're out of the same school, the same time zone, the late '60s," Jon Lord reflected four years later. "But I think they're a group that got trapped by their own image. I think Purple has more humor about it." In fact, Black Sabbath's own Tony Iommi rightly points out that his band were practically rolling in the aisles as they conceived some of their visions, but Lord is correct on one point: Black Sabbath had an image to maintain and, while fellow travelers through the Satanic miasma Bodkin, Coven, and Black Widow all fell by the wayside, Sabbath both protected and prolonged their public persona with a ferocious abandon. Deep Purple, on the other hand, often appeared to be simply making it up as they went along.

For now, of course, their future was still waiting to happen. On September 5, "Black Night" lay at No. 32 and "Paranoid" at No. 47. Deep Purple dipped a couple of places the following week, but, buoyed by the newly returned band's appearance on BBC TV's *Top of the Pops*, it was nothing more than a momentary blip. Leaping first to No. 20, then to No. 9, by early October "Black Night" was No. 5 and preparing to spend two weeks at No. 2, kept from the top slot only by the eternal heartache of Freda Payne's "Band of Gold." "Paranoid" lay immediately behind it and, as though an unspoken Rubicon had finally been crossed, in their wake lay a slew of acts who might never previously have even imagined assaulting the pop charts.

The end of 1970 would see some truly enormous hits drawn from spectacularly unexpected corners. Midlands art-proggers Family, former Fairport folkie Iain Matthews, underground whimsicalists Tyrannosaurus Rex and Spectoresque bluesman Dave Edmunds all toured the Top 10, while jazz-blues fusionist Alexis Korner negated Led Zeppelin's no-singles snobbery by heaving their "Whole Lotta Love" first into the upper echelons of the charts and then, irony of delicious ironies, into television legend, as his cover was adopted as the theme tune to *Top of the Pops* itself.

Deep Purple (and Black Sabbath) certainly were not responsible for this sudden influx. But, by proving that you could have a hit without turning to saccharin overnight, they could be held accountable for lessening the burden of disapproval that had hitherto draped the pop-hit ambitions of an entire generation of rock bands, uncorking a genie that would never sleep again, no matter what excuses the newfound heatseekers may have unveiled. Whether they were "sticking it to the man" or "subverting from within," singles were suddenly sought after again and, still laying in the bed that they had made, the elitist snobbery of the likes of Led Zeppelin now looked very silly indeed.

Heedless of such cultural clashes, Deep Purple barreled on, adding further weight to their already leviathan reputation as *In Rock* set about moving even faster than "Black Night." It would ultimately soar to No. 4 on the U.K. charts, the unimpeachable high point of a residency that saw it remain on the listings for a staggering sixty-eight weeks.

"It opened a lot of doors," Roger Glover said of that manic summer. "I remember thinking *In Rock* was very gratifying to see in the chart, but with 'Black Night,' we were everywhere — the newspapers, the gigs started selling out, crowds started coming. . . ."

Everywhere, word was spreading that Deep Purple were unmissable. As they gigged around the U.K. and Europe through the spring and summer of 1970, in the weeks surrounding the release of both *In Rock* and "Black Night," the band's itinerary revolved almost exclusively around the college circuit: Jesus in Cambridge, John Dalton in

Manchester, University College in Oxford. Status Quo's Rick Parfitt speaks for Deep Purple, and every other band on that circuit, when he remembers, "The places we were playing were the ones where you'd see the geezers with their trenchcoats on, a pint in one hand, an album under the other arm, sitting on the floor nodding their heads. We were very scruffy, and making a noise that went with the look. It was rough, it was raw, and people loved it."

Only occasionally did Deep Purple's grind around such halls of academia break for any higher-profile show, although when it did, the stage was always well-chosen. London's Lyceum Ballroom was one of the capital's highest-profile venues at that time, a vast (by local standards), unseated theater whose dance floor, historically, was frequently so packed that some long-ago renovator had arranged for the venue's roof to slide open, to let in the air. An open-air bash at Bedford Town Football Club paved the way for what would, in later years, become a rock'n'roll passion for performing at soccer grounds. And, two years after their ignominious showing at the eighth National Jazz & Blues Festival, a return booking for the tenth allowed Deep Purple to demonstrate just how far they had grown since they last graced that institution.

Staged at Plumpton Race Track, the 1970 gathering was overshadowed by the truly international events put on at Bath and the Isle of Wight that same summer. The festival spread over an unprecedented four days regardless, with performances from the likes of Jellybread, Family, the Groundhogs, Cat Stevens, Peter Green, Black Sabbath, and the Incredible String Band leading up to the Sunday finale's night of stars. Van Der Graaf Generator and Wishbone Ash, all but unknown to the concert-going public at large, opened the proceedings; Caravan, Juicy Lucy, Yes, and Colosseum highlighted the run-up to the final performance; and, as they left the stage to the flickering flames and billowing smoke of a truly — and literally — incendiary performance, Deep Purple sent the audience shell-shocked back to its cars and tents.

Blackmore had long since mastered the art of what pop-art Who fans used to call "auto-destruction," shattering his guitars on a regular basis and justifying the carnage with a shrugged dismissal — "I play the guitar very well, and I feel I'm entitled to kick it around a little." Tonight, however, it wasn't only his guitar that perished in a shower of shredded wood and tortured electrics, while the strobe lights flashed a funereal tango. "Blackmore set upon his stack with the rage of an executioner," *Melody Maker* reported the following week. "It caught fire and was then hurled across the stage into the crowd. Guitars were flung around the stage in wild abandon. Jon Lord's organ rocked like a boat in a storm." Onlookers had already proclaimed Deep Purple suitable headliners for the festival. The band responded with a performance that was truly headline material.

Smash albums, hit singles, hot headlines — Deep Purple were going stellar. Their song lyrics were reprinted in *Disco 45*, a monthly teen magazine dedicated wholly to the toppermost of the poppermost; and when the *Daily Express* newspaper published a special one-off guide to the premier pacemakers of the new decade, Deep Purple, "one of the most comprehensible of the 'heavy' groups," were included alongside any number of heinous light-entertainment deities. And when the band announced their next tour, eschewing universities for the blast around the traditional theaters that would permit all their newfound fans to experience the show, even veteran promoters were astonished at the hysteria in the ticket queues. The gigs were still a month or more away, and already the little girls were screaming.

Undaunted by their overground popularity, Deep Purple continued courting the underground, their credos taking a major boost when a recording of a German festival performance, at the Aachen Reichstadion on July 11, was immortalized as the first ever Deep Purple bootleg, the appropriately titled *H-Bombs*.

Bootlegging was still a novelty at that time. Barely two years had elapsed since Bob Dylan's *Great White Wonder* first introduced the concept of illegally produced LP records to the rock industry (such things had long existed in the classical and jazz arenas), and only a mere handful of the heaviest hitters had thus far been honored — Dylan was followed by the Beatles, the Rolling Stones, The Who . . . and Deep Purple? Within weeks of *H-Bombs'* appearance on the record racks that catered for such releases, the album was nestling at the top of the best-selling bootleg chart that accompanied a *Melody Maker* investigation into the phenomenon, and Deep Purple were bracing to become one of the most-bootlegged bands in rock history.

Looking back in 1998, Roger Glover professed himself firmly in favor of such recordings, legitimacy be damned. "I could never understand our success," he said. "I could never understand why so many people bought our records, because they were so full of flaws! And then I started listening to bootlegs and to what we really were, and I came to reassess the whole thing. Listening to bootlegs from [the early 1970s], I realized what a dangerous band we were, and how exciting it was not to know what was going to happen next. We walked a very thin line between chaos and order, and that was the magic, that was why people bought our records. I came from a pop band, and when you're a pop band you learn the song and you play it the same way every night. And now there's this band veering off and suddenly the solo's in E when it should be . . . 'Hey, what's happening here?' That's the magic."

Neither did the traditional music-industry complaints against bootlegging hold any water for him: "I had a meeting with some bootleggers many years ago in Germany; we had a big discussion about bootlegs, and they said, 'Listen, bootleggers are not ripping you off, you're not losing money because of bootleggers. The fact that other people are making money from your music is indisputable, but you're not losing money, it's not money out of your pocket. In fact, the people who buy these things have already bought your albums probably two or three times already.'

"It was a potent argument," Glover continued, "and I sympathize with that. Besides, they presented me with something I'd not heard in years, which was a recording of us doing [something] for a BBC session. It was a song that was written on the spur of the moment, just a blues, very fast, and it's great, I love it. But it was never formally written and recorded, that's the only version of it, and I said, 'Wow, it's so wonderful to hear this, I'd forgotten all about it!' So it's through bootlegs, or at least bootleggers, that things like that even exist."

Deep Purple's emergence as a bootleggable force certainly upped their reputation among the folk who cared for such things — primarily journalists and students, of course, but their opinions still counted for something. But, just in case any cynics doubted that Deep Purple remained deeply committed to the serious side of their muse, one year on from the concerto, the group unveiled the second of Jon Lord's classical compositions — that which, twelve months earlier, he had assured his bandmates would be their last delving into such extracurricular depths.

The Gemini Suite was commissioned by the BBC for broadcast in the *South Bank Pops* program on September 17, 1970, and again paired Lord with conductor Malcolm Arnold. As before, the group were very much sidelined during the actual writing of the piece. Lord later admitted he originally didn't even want to involve his bandmates, but the BBC had insisted that they participate. It turned out to be the correct decision. Lord conceived a single piece that, across five movements, was devoted to the musical personalities of each of the group's members, and each titled for its inspiration's star sign.

Whereas Deep Purple's schedule in 1969 had afforded Lord considerable downtime in which to work on the concerto, this time around, matters were considerably different, as the group toured throughout the spring and summer. Much of *The Gemini Suite* was composed on the road, in the back of the bus or late night in hotel rooms, with Gillan again procrastinating before completing his lyrics, scribbling down the last words just as the accompanying Orchestra of the Light Music Society struck up the first bars of the show's overture, George Gershwin's "Rhapsody in Blue."

Again contrasting with the band's last classical sojourn, the publicity and media furor around *The Gemini Suite* was muted — few of the music papers offered it much more than a cursory mention during the run-up to the event, while the national papers scarcely acknowledged its existence. Asked to comment, most journalists of the day simply regarded it as "another" of Deep Purple's little deviations, as though they undertook such extravaganzas every day of the week.

Of course they didn't, but such attitudes contributed much to the less than enthusiastic air with which Gillan and Blackmore, in particular, approached the event. Public perceptions, after all, are a vital component in any band's drive for success and, repeating a fear that had pursued the band following the Royal Albert Hall performance, there again seemed a very real danger that Deep Purple might become known simply as "the band that does stuff with orchestras."

Despite such, and so many, pitfalls, *The Gemini Suite* emerged an absolute triumph. Whereas its predecessor was very much an attempt to marry a rock band with a classical orchestra, this time the emphasis lay in fusing the best qualities of both into a seamless whole that wasn't afraid to acknowledge Deep Purple's own work in the same musical breath as the classical influences that hung over the proceedings.

Sharp ears can pick up more than a handful of archetypal Purple passages within the piece, including several ghosts recalled from the symphonic "Child in Time." Blackmore's guitar-led movement that opened the suite readily echoed some of the spectacular moments he'd already incorporated into the band's regular live set, while Paice's movement emerged a thunderously percussive duel between the two musical disciplines, going a long way toward proving that, in terms of sheer dynamism, rock and the classics have a lot more in common than the Concerto's audiences might ever have imagined.

Indeed, though it would undoubtedly have necessitated the refurbishment of Deep Purple's entire future career, one can only regret that it was the concerto that received all the attention, while *The Gemini Suite* was allowed to slip into absolute anonymity. Although Lord would stage repeat performances in Munich in January 1972 and October 1973, both with conductor Eberhard Schoener, it would be twenty-eight years before a recording of the live performance made it onto the official release schedules, and, while a studio rendering of the suite was issued within a year of the original South Bank show, Glover and Paice alone joined Lord to reprise their roles. Blackmore was replaced by Albert Lee, Gillan by Tony Ashton and another *Jesus Christ Superstar* superstar, Yvonne Elliman. (Intriguingly, Lord also offered a role to Keith Emerson, but the maestro's commitments to Lake and Palmer forced him to turn it down.)

Yet Lord admitted that maybe things had turned out for the best. Although *In Rock* was still selling strongly, Deep Purple's thoughts were already turning toward their next album, and he told *Beat Instrumental* magazine, "We've now reached a point where we are perfectly happy and content to develop naturally. We were trying to develop unnaturally before — we would grasp at all sorts of different ideas at once. We were searching for a group identity. *In Rock* is the only [album] we've made [which has] a strong direction, [and] on the next one we'll use what we have learned, and progress from there."

The intention was to avoid the piecemeal construction of the last album, by laying the new one down in as few separate sessions as possible. As early as September 1970, the band was back in the studio, recording the first of the songs destined for the new record, the country-flavored (and lightheartedly Dylanish) "Anyone's Daughter." It was a major departure from the expected Deep Purple sound, and one that was ironically recorded, Glover revealed, "the day after we'd had a big discussion about being excited and heavy. We were sitting around the studio waiting for inspiration when Ritchie just started tinkling around with that chord thing and we joined in."

Such moments, however, were little more than brief respites in the band's live agenda. Days after the session, Deep Purple set out on their long-awaited British tour — and found themselves face-to-face with the audience that sent "Black Night" riding so high up the charts.

The tour kicked off in Romford, East London, on September 25, moving on through Liverpool, Cardiff, Southampton, Leeds, and Sheffield, before hitting Scotland on October 12. And it was there that the phenomenon that *Melody Maker*, with some aid from the Scottish constabulary, coined the term that remained with Deep Purple for much of the next two years: Purplemania. "We're becoming a regular teenybop attraction," Jon Lord agreed. "I notice we are getting a younger element coming to see us now. It seems that today a progressive band can get into the chart without detriment to 'live' appeal as seemed to happen to Free. If you like your music liberally laced with showmanship, you will be a Deep Purple fan — I think. And if you like it not so heavy, but with showmanship, then you will like Elton John. And I notice audiences are quite prepared to wear different (metaphorical) hats for different bands."

The opening show, in Edinburgh, was staged at the local Tiffany's ballroom, a northern outpost of a chain of venues regarded among the cream of British concert halls. From the stage, the event seemed to pass off triumphantly. Outside, however, it was chaos, with as many fans locked out as were able to gain entrance. The following night in Glasgow, as word spread of the previous evening's seething sellout, it seemed that every music lover in the city was besieging the scheduled venue, the six-hundred capacity Electric Garden, blocking the traffic on busy Sauchiehall Street, jamming doorways, and making it impossible for anybody to even get near to the club.

Overwhelmed by the response, the promoter somehow managed to switch the show to Glasgow's own branch of Tiffany's, more than double the size of the Electric Garden — and still there were an estimated 3,000 people who weren't able to get in. Five were arrested, more were evicted from the roof of the venue where they were trying to break into the building, and more still simply ran riot on the streets. "It was unbelievable," Gillan recalled, astonished that any so-called rock band could provoke such a hysterical response simply by playing a concert. But it was the Glasgow police, press-ganged at the last minute into providing the group with an escort simply to get them into the club, who truly nailed the passion of the evening. In a statement issued to *Record Mirror* magazine, a spokesperson confessed, "We've seen nothing like this since the heyday of the Beatles."

Neither was the excitement limited to Scotland. Across the U.K., police and dogs became a common sight at venues the band was performing at, while the national press looked on with horrified fascination. "Deep Purple are a group new to me," admitted the *Daily Mirror*'s pop correspondent. "Their stock-in-trade includes orgiastic antics of a kind that made me fear for their well-being. And when, at the close, they knocked their electronic equipment over, I wondered if they had lost their wits."

The continent, too, fell to the band. Deep Purple's visit to France later in October culminated with a show at the legendary Paris Olympia, which sold out within hours. It was in West Germany in November and December, however, that the madness that now attended the band truly reached its peak.

Nineteen-seventy was a year of considerable tumult, as that still-divided nation witnessed the culmination of the (primarily) student revolt that had shaken most of Western Europe over the past two or three years. The flashpoints for the fighting were manifold. Vietnam protests, civil rights strikes, antipoverty demonstrations, peace marchers — all played their roles within the ferment that saw the streets of Rome, Paris, London, and Berlin brought to raucous standstill by rebellious youth. And rock'n'roll played its own part in fanning the flames.

The rhetoric of the American '60s bands — the Doors, the Airplane, the Fugs, and so forth — had given way to an even more inflammatory mood, as the next generation of psychedelic warlords — the likes of

Hawkwind, the Pink Fairies, and Deep Purple's own Harvest labelmates, the Edgar Broughton Band — rose from the most reactionary poles of the British counterculture to espouse an entirely new world order.

Establishing themselves at the forefront of the battle, physically as well as culturally, their battle cries encompassed everything from the legalization of drugs to the redistribution of wealth, and, in drawing up the battle lines along which this new revolution was fought, rock'n'roll itself was co-opted as the insurgents' most powerful weapon — one which would be available to everyone, free of charge.

The problem with this, of course, was that, while bands like the Fairies and the Broughtons might have been happy to spend their summers tramping from free festival to free festival, living off the largesse of the revolution, other bands were less idealistic — were, in fact, adamant that a fair day's pay should accompany a fair day's work. It was simply Deep Purple's bad luck that they should arrive in Germany, with that moral in mind, just weeks after the Broughton Band had passed through to disseminate precisely the opposite message.

For many visiting groups, fractious audiences were already a fact of life — kids who bought their tickets begrudgingly and wanted to make damn sure they got their money's worth in return. But Deep Purple's tour seemed somehow heavier. Every night brought the band face-to-face with one of the local counterculture's less appealing faces — or one of the establishment's less understanding responses. In Heidelberg, the band found itself competing with a demonstration by the local branch of the Black Panthers; in Hamburg, the police turned up at the venue with a water cannon; in Hanover, an overexuberant crowd was dispersed with tear gas.

Deep Purple had remained largely untouched by such disturbances, but they knew they were seated on a powder keg, and that it was only a matter of time before it exploded.

The flashpoint arrived in Ludenscheid, on December 8. Shortly before the band was to play, Ritchie Blackmore was taken ill. An attempt was made to cancel and reschedule the concert, but the crowd ruthlessly howled down the announcement. They had paid for a concert, and they were going to get one. One frontline dispatch even remarked how, from the back of the hall, but quickly spreading throughout the building, the telltale imprimatur of the Broughton Band's influence began to rise, the chant of "Out, demons, out" that was intended to exorcise "the man," in all his money-grabbing, freedom-crushing, lifeblood-draining guises, from every walk of life.

Deep Purple had no choice but to play. Hastily improvising a set that could withstand the absence of Blackmore's guitar, the four musicians delivered an hourlong show, then left the stage. An encore was demanded, but the band had already returned to their hotel, satisfied that they had discharged their duties for the evening. There was to be no more music that night.

Out front, however, the crowd remained restless — especially after one of their number took to the stage to inform the seething masses that the band were heading back in an hour to perform another, longer set. When that deadline elapsed, so did the throng's patience. Having already torn the theater apart, smashing seats and breaking doors and windows, the rampaging horde then leaped onto the stage to take their fury out on Deep Purple's equipment. Roadies, hanging nervously around backstage throughout the drama, fled to a bathroom and escaped through the window. But the sirens howled all night, and, when Deep Purple turned up at their next show in Stuttgart, the venue's customary posse of security guards had been replaced by a detachment of German soldiers.

Another facet of contemporary youth culture awaited the band in Switzerland — a phalanx of Hell's Angels who, in the traditional style of that movement, pronounced themselves Deep Purple's friends, protectors, and security guards for the duration of their stay. In scenes reminiscent of the nightmarish brutality that attended the Rolling Stones at events as far afield as Hyde Park, London, and Altamont, California, the Angels then set about their self-appointed task with absolute gusto, lining the front of the stage, backs to the band, and whacking any concertgoer foolish enough to stray within an outstretched arm's reach.

Finally, Gillan had seen enough. He was already convinced that the rioting that beset so many of the band's shows was the result of "Communist propaganda," designed to bring Western Europe's youth into decisive political warfare with the authorities. Now it was time to put a stop to it. Raising his mike stand, he began laying into the Angels and was, doubtless, stunned to see the whole lot of them beat a hasty retreat long before the show was over. Clearly, they weren't as tough as they liked to make out — or so it seemed. The moment the band stepped out of the theater at the end of the evening, however, they learned the fragility of such hopes. The Angels were there waiting for them. The band and crew leaped onto the tour bus and hit the road, with the Angels in furious pursuit, literally chasing them out of town.

Chapter 7

A Strange Kind of Fireball

Despite the massive success that had so rapidly enfolded the group, Deep Purple was never a happy unit. Ritchie Blackmore and Ian Gillan were constantly at loggerheads over the group's leadership, the guitarist insisting that it was his drive into hard-rock territory that had established the band, the singer equally adamant that, as the frontman, voice, and chief lyricist, his opinion and decisions should count for just as much.

Neither were such turf battles the only agonies that strained at the group's boundaries. Jon Lord seemed to be in constant pain from a back injury he sustained during the early days of the Artwoods, carrying his own equipment in and out of so many subterranean clubs and bars, while Roger Glover was martyr to a stomach ailment which, in the years before stress was recognized as the cause of so many bodily ills, simply baffled the medical establishment. Needless to say, the friction sparked by his warring bandmates and the constant calls for support from the rest of the group, probably caused a goodly proportion of that stress.

Few groups function at their best under such circumstances. Add, however, an exhausting live itinerary that continued yawning ever further ahead, rendering it near impossible for bandmates to get a break from one another; add to that the increasingly urgent need to finish recording the follow-up to *In Rock*; and it is no surprise that, already, the tensions that would ultimately sunder this lineup of the group were making themselves felt.

The new album was an especial bugbear. Despite the promising start to the sessions back in September 1970, the band's schedule didn't allow them to return to the studio; they'd scarcely even got any writing done. The only significant addition to their live repertoire in recent months was an improvisational leviathan built around the Rolling Stones' "Paint It Black," which itself was little more than the framework for a marathon drum solo. It was certainly exciting in concert, but it neither said nor did anything for Deep Purple's hopes of advancing their own art. Increasingly, it seemed that the band had reached a creative impasse, finding it easier to allow existing numbers to grow in length than concoct new material.

A live recording made for Swedish radio broadcast at the Konserthuset in Stockholm, on November 12, 1970, captures the dilemma. The band's classical excursions notwithstanding, this remains one of the earliest Mark II concert recordings to have been officially released, in 1988, as the *Scandinavian Nights* album; it was, in fact, one of the earliest of their concerts to even be recorded (only a February 1970 BBC broadcast and that dynamic Aachen festival show from July predate it).

Scandinavian Nights highlights a live set that comprised just seven numbers, including a mere three from *In Rock* (admittedly volcanic assaults on "Child in Time" and "Into the Fire," and an impossibly over-wrought "Speed King"), three that were little more than endless jams ("Mandrake Root," "Paint It Black," and a full thirty minutes of "Wring That Neck"), and, finally, the encore hit "Black Night." It is an exhausting listen and, in purely musical terms, an exhilarating one — the Bagshot Bullet, as the rest of Deep Purple nicknamed Blackmore's most frenetic playing, ricocheted wildly that night. But it is also the sound of a group that was swiftly vanishing up its own backside.

As conscious of this as the meanest of their critics, Deep Purple finally brought all procrastination to a halt by canceling their last few shows, in Britain in December 1970, and decamping, with roadies and families in tow, to the Hermitage, which Jon Lord recalls as a "derelict, damp, and slightly haunted" farmhouse in Welcombe, Cornwall. There, the band intended writing and rehearsing a new album that would allow them to completely realign their repertoire. And, although Glover later recalled spending as much time in the local pub as in the rehearsal room, they came close to pulling it off. "Strange Kind of Woman" (its opening guitar riff a vague echo of Mark I's "The Painter"), "Freedom," and "Slow Train" were all written at the farmhouse; "The Mule" — a Paice-powered replacement for "Paint It Black" — was formulated there; and "I'm Alone" was sketched from the remains of an earlier instrumental, "Grabsplatter."

Further material was put together back in London when the band reunited with engineer Martin Birch at whichever studios they could book into — they visited De Lane Lea, Olympia, and Abbey Road during January and February 1971 — and hindsight, both among fans and the band, insists that so scattershot an approach did not work this time to the band's benefit. For now, however, it sounded great; so much so that the band almost impatiently agreed to Harvest's request for a prerelease single, something that would whet the audience's appetite for the main attraction. They selected "Strange Kind of Woman," a song that would consequently be absented from British pressings of the new album, but which was the sound of Deep Purple at their best, regardless.

Blackmore recalled this latest record's genesis: "We got that whole call-and-response guitar thing from Edgar Winter's 'Tobacco Road.' He and Rick Derringer used to trade off on that, and we were into that band [Winter's White Trash] at the time. I turned Ian Gillan onto Edgar Winter. 'Listen to this scream,' I said. And Ian's like, 'Who's that?' and I said, 'Edgar Winter — Johnny Winter's brother.' And all of a sudden Ian started screaming [giggles]. That's where the scream at the end of the song comes from."

In strictly dynamic terms, the recorded version of "Strange Kind of Woman" was a far cry from the spellbinding duet for voice and guitar it would rapidly become. But, on a U.K. chart that, only vaguely incidentally, skewed toward sales in London alone as a nationwide postal strike cut the compilers off from the provincial retailers they normally worked with, "Strange Kind of Woman" was all but unstoppable.

Having entered at No. 29 in early March, within two weeks it lay at No. 8, a vivid blur of sound in a British Top 10 that otherwise rejoiced in such joys as country singer Lynn Anderson's "Rose Garden," solo shots by ex-Beatles Harrison and McCartney, veteran crooner Perry Como, and, lying immediately behind Deep Purple in that week's listing, two artists whose own places in the Deep Purple story are all but inviolate: Neil Diamond, one of the earliest lineup's most favored composers, now stepping out on his own career as a performer, and Ashton, Gardner and Dyke, the support act on Deep Purple's latest British tour.

Like Deep Purple, all three members of the trio had sizable pedigrees within the British club and sessions scene. Keyboard player Tony Ashton, of course, was one of Blackmore and Paice's colleagues in the *Green Bullfrog* sessions the previous year and was counted among Jon Lord's closest friends; prior to that, he and drummer Roy Dyke were members of the Remo Four, a Liverpool-based band whose credentials reached back to the days of skiffle when, as the Remo Quartet, they plowed the same circuit as the early Beatles. Bassist Kim Gardner, meanwhile, was a former member of freakbeat legends the Creation — whose "Making Time" was so memorably assaulted by the *Green Bullfrog* crew. Each of these earlier bands had their moments of sublime magic, but none cracked the U.K. market and, by 1968, all had shattered.

(Ashton, Gardner and Dyke's decision to name their new band after its members was an unusual step. Even in a musical age when individual virtuosos were truly coming to the fore, none had hitherto taken such a step. Even the legendary ménage of Baker, Bruce, and Clapton opted for the monolithic Cream, when the BBC would have fit just as memorably.)

Within months of Ashton, Gardner and Dyke's emergence, however, Keith Emerson quit the Nice and formed ELP, a group that not only shared the same nomenclatural ideals, but utilized a similar instrumental punch as well — organ and rhythm section only. But whereas ELP intended taking music to heights as lofty as the members' individual reputations (Greg Lake was ex-King Crimson, Carl Palmer hailed from Atomic Rooster), Ashton, Gardner and Dyke remained precociously rootsy, a decision that swiftly paid off when, in December 1969, they were invited to tour the U.S. as opening act on Delaney & Bonnie's star-studded "And Friends" tour.

The trio's debut album, that same year, oddly failed to move, even in the aftermath of the Delaney & Bonnie tour. But their reputation was established anyway, when Ashton found himself among the swarm of musicians appearing on George Harrison's latest solo album, the triple *All Things Must Pass* (that's him playing keyboards on "Isn't It a Pity"). For whatever reason, he wasn't credited on the album, but Harrison repaid him generously, teaming up with Eric Clapton to join Ashton, Gardner and Dyke as they set to work on their sophomore album. Under the not especially mysterious pseudonyms of George O'Hara Smith and Sir Cedric Clayton, Harrison and Clapton appear on the track "I'm Your Spiritual Breadman."

According to Ashton, Harrison "just did general production and helped out with some of the lyrics on the middle eight." Nevertheless, for some time, "I'm Your Spiritual Breadman" was scheduled to become Ashton, Gardner and Dyke's next single. At the last minute, however, Capitol announced they preferred another Ashton composition, the gritty, horn-laden R&B shouter "Resurrection Shuffle" and were rewarded with a worldwide hit.

The trio were already on the road with Deep Purple when "Resurrection Shuffle" began to move, and were forced to depart the tour long before its end. Ashton recalled, "We were going onstage and the whole place would start calling for 'Resurrection Shuffle.' It was amazing — all of a sudden, every show was filled with what you'd have to call teenyboppers, and all they wanted to hear was 'Resurrection Shuffle.' It was gratifying, but it pissed us off a bit — and I can only imagine how Purple felt!" In fact, they probably weren't even listening — their own crowd was now screaming for both "Black Night" and "Strange Kind of Woman."

Ashton, Gardner and Dyke promptly moved off to headline their own tour, replaced on the Deep Purple tour by fellow *Green Bullfrog* veterans Albert Lee and Chas Hodges' Heads Hands & Feet. (One excellent and utterly representative show from this period is captured on the *Let It Roll Live* album. Roger Glover, whose friendship with Ashton would see the pair work together on many subsequent occasions, remembers another, at Ronnie Scott's, which to this day sums up the group's appeal to him. "Between songs, Tony would talk," Glover recalled. "He came out with a long speech about the duty of performers. He rambled on at length that people who go onstage should be aware of their responsibilities as role models and that bad language is something that should be avoided at all costs, because who knew what effect that might have on younger ears, and that when anyone had a microphone they should refrain from such language, and on and on, etc. Then he said, 'Oh, I've talked enough, fuck it' — and the band kicked in.")

Deep Purple's U.K. tour was scheduled to close on March 8 in Aberdeen — in fact, this incarnation of the band came close to folding that night as well, as Glover collapsed onstage. His stomach pains had been worsening throughout the tour. Some nights he was so ill that Chas Hodges would stand in for him to perform the evening's encore, an increasingly riotous rendition of "Lucille." Sympathy from certain of his bandmates, however, was not always forthcoming; it was Blackmore who, pondering whether the bassist's ailments were fatal, suggested that Glover drop dead onstage and allow them to cremate his corpse as part of the show.

In fact, Glover was astonished to discover the cure lay in nothing more than a course of hypnotherapy, targeted at releasing the stress in his abdomen. Blackmore, however, was not so fortunate. Just days later, he went down with appendicitis.

With *Fireball* now approaching completion (the final sessions would take place in May, shortly before the band's first visit to Australia), the group returned to the road to — as Gillan put it — "give *In Rock* a last fling." Despite its patchiness, confidence in the forthcoming *Fireball* was initially high. "We've kept the same basic theme of the rock album, but we've extended it a wee bit," Gillan continued. He admitted that many of the new songs "would have been out of place on *In Rock*, but they seem to be a natural progression."

The full extent of that progression was only partially visible in the band's live show. Having previously been attacked for not varying their set, Deep Purple now found audiences extraordinarily resistant to fresh material. Several "Here's a new song" introductions went down like lead zeppelins in the U.K. and Europe, and the United States would get the first opportunity to fully inspect the new album, as Warner scheduled its release for July, a full eight weeks before its European debut, to coincide with Deep Purple's next American tour.

American reviews of the album were generally good. As is often the case, it was some time before hindsight swooped down to condemn *Fireball* as something less than brilliant, a consensus frequently backed up by the band members themselves. Within a year, Ian Paice was telling

Music Scene magazine, "I don't think it was a particularly good album for us. It was a time when we were each getting financially stable and resting back on our laurels."

Roger Glover agreed. Looking back from the late 1990s, he reflected, "One tends to think of [the albums] in terms of hits, [and because *Fireball*] wasn't as successful as *In Rock*, it tends to dim by comparison. It was a good album, but I find it a little stodgy. Considering the freshness and fire of *In Rock*, *Fireball* is very self-conscious. *In Rock* was the one before success, and there was nothing to lose on that, whereas *Fireball* was done knowing that *In Rock* had been not just a success, but a huge success; that obviously people were going to be listening to *Fireball*; and I think there was a self-consciousness there, thinking that we had to prove ourselves, prove that we were better than just one album."

Elsewhere, he singled out "No No No" as one of the album's worst offenders. Although, in 1971, he'd been quick to acknowledge the song's innate funkiness, he later reflected, "I thought it dragged a bit, it went on too long and it could have been written better." It was also suspiciously close in musical intent to the last album's "Into the Fire."

Lord and Gillan, however, seemed content with what they had accomplished. With hindsight, Lord admitted, "It could have done with another steamer. But I still think it's a better album than *In Rock*." In terms of variety, inventiveness, and intensity, he was correct. The title track, one of the last numbers to be recorded, was astonishing, a super-sonic rocker whose so-distinctive opening moments — a roar that could indeed be a passing fireball — was as distinctive an intro as the clatter of "Speed King." How disappointing it was, years later, to discover that, far from pointing a microphone at the mysteries of the heavens, Martin Birch had simply recorded the studio air-conditioning clicking on.

"Demon's Eye," built around an extraordinarily slippery riff, followed the funkier inclinations of "No No No" — which, for all of Glover's misgivings, is fabulously atmospheric, with the bassist himself nailing down the kind of earth-beat rhythm that the next, so-funkily flavored Mark III and IV incarnations of the band would, ironically, rarely find themselves within reach of. Plus, the lyric enabled Gillan to indulge in some delightfully playful ad-libbing in concert, as American audiences were now discovering.

With becoming (if, perhaps, obscure) irony, Deep Purple's latest Stateside sojourn found them joining the already in-progress tour by the Faces, the riotous good-time rock'n'roll combo fronted by the selfsame Rod Stewart who'd been passed over as Deep Purple's vocalist back in the group's formative weeks.

It was an intriguing match — the only thing the two bands had in common was a propensity for partying, but Deep Purple swiftly discovered they had much to learn in that department. One infamous evening, at the culmination of a typically frantic show, Stewart invited the entire audience back to the hotel for an all-night rock'n'roll rave-up. What he didn't let on was, it was Deep Purple's hotel that was the unsuspecting venue for the event. On another occasion, in Minneapolis, Warner Brothers unadvisedly threw a joint party for both groups — and wound up footing the bill for $25,000 in damages, after Blackmore and Stewart joined forces to ignite a wild food fight.

If it was riotous offstage and backstage, however, onstage Deep Purple pulled out all the stops. "America is so vast that, I think people there buy records mainly by bands they've seen," Ritchie Blackmore reasoned. To have any kind of impact, then, a band had to make certain that people remembered what they'd witnessed. The guitarist admitted that he was baffled by the massive success of Grand Funk Railroad. "I've never met one person who liked [them]," he marveled. But he also acknowledged, "I should imagine they've seen Grand Funk all over America. So they buy their records."

Deep Purple had just forty-five minutes to make a similar impression on some of America's largest auditoriums, sandwiched between the Faces and the deceptive balminess of the opening Matthews Southern Comfort — three-quarters of an hour that left little room for the unending improvisation of old, forcing Deep Purple to look instead toward an internal discipline that would hit as many people as hard as possible.

It worked. *Fireball* entered America's *Billboard* chart on August 21. Within days, it had surpassed the No. 143 peak attained by *Deep Purple in Rock*; within weeks, it was knocking on the door of the Top 30, the best performance by any Deep Purple album since their debut, four long years before. The fact that the Faces' own latest, *Long Player*, peaked only three places higher, at No. 29, only amplified Deep Purple's triumph.

The band returned home at the end of July, to find themselves faced with a full six weeks off before Harvest released *Fireball* in the U.K.. For Lord, Paice, and Glover, however, the break was little more than a busman's holiday, as they set to work recording the studio version of *The Gemini Suite*. But they returned refreshed in mid-September to kick off the British tour — so refreshed that, as they motored down to the first date in Portsmouth, they found themselves writing a new song after one of the journalists traveling with them asked Gillan how he went about writing lyrics. So Gillan showed them; then, in honor of the surroundings, he titled it "Highway Star."

Once at the venue, the band gave the new arrival a few rehearsals during the sound check, then dropped it into the live set that same evening. Before the month was out, "Highway Star" would even have found its way onto television, as a luridly lit band previewed it (alongside an abundantly ad-libbed "No No No") on German television's *Beat Club*.

Onstage, meanwhile, "Highway Star" was swiftly joined by another new song, "Lazy" (at last allowing "Mandrake Root" to be retired), as the band responded to possibly the most pertinent of all the criticisms targeted at *Fireball* — that the new material had journeyed straight from notebook to studio, without first detouring via the concert setting. Deep Purple would not make (or, recalling prerelease audience responses, be forced to make) that same mistake again.

As the band toured, the album sales rocketed. Effortlessly improving upon its American showing, *Fireball* raced to No. 1 in Britain, squeezing in a week at the top between The Who's megalithic *Who's Next* and Rod Stewart's solo *Every Picture Tells a Story*. Ultimately, however, sales would prove disappointing when compared to *In Rock*. In Germany in the new year, the band's record company intended staging a ceremony at which Deep Purple would be presented with gold discs, but were forced into a last-minute rethink when it transpired that *Fireball* had sold no more than half the number required for such an award.

But with the event already organized, the invitations in the mail, and the caterers hard at work, a cancellation was unthinkable. So the label took the only option left to them. They cut each of the prepared gold discs in half, and presented the band with those instead.

The single of "Fireball," too, sold only a fraction of "Black Night," although here, at least, all concerned could take solace in the knowledge that its final placing of No. 15 was still a respectable showing for a group whose most natural constituency was within the LP charts that remained so impervious to the ebbs and flows of the singles market.

Late 1971, after all, witnessed the dawning of an entire new fashion in British pop, as the glam-rock movement, spearheaded over the previous year by T. Rex and Slade, picked up the kind of speed that ensured, within six months, that the likes of Deep Purple, Black Sabbath, Curved Air, Free, Family, and Argent — all the so-called progressive, metal and hard-rock bands that scored monster hit singles during the first gleaming of the new decade — would likely not strike a similar chord in the future.

It was not, necessarily, a failing the bands themselves regretted. True, journalist Andrew Weiner did mourn, with tongue only partially in cheek, that "if Black Sabbath had followed up 'Paranoid,' they could well have established themselves as the biggest singles band since the Stones"; true, too, that Atomic Rooster's Vincent Crane once acknowledged, "There's a certain joy to seeing your audience filled with teenyboppers, and telling them 'this next song's called "Death Walks Behind You".'"

The notion, however, of Deep Purple competing with the spangled likes of Marc Bolan, David Bowie, Slade, and Gary Glitter — or (again in Weiner's words) "of Black Sabbath [appearing] on *Top of the Pops* month after month, churning out their awful warnings" — suddenly seemed as preposterous as the makeup, platforms, and sparkles that were now de rigueur for every aspiring pop band.

Yet the gulf between the glam-rock crew and their apparently more down-to-earth (and certainly less flamboyant) counterparts was considerably smaller than many people, the bands' fans included, were willing to admit. Many of the participating musicians had known one another back in the 1960s; some had even worked together in different studios and bands; and many remained friends for years after.

The Sweet's Brian Connolly — Ian Gillan's replacement in Wainwright's Gentlemen back in the mid-1960s — recalled, "We used to run into Purple a lot on the road, and we'd always spend time together." And occasionally such fraternization led to some raised eyebrows. The Sweet, in 1971, were widely regarded as little more than puppets for songwriters Nicky Chinn and Mike Chapman — puppets who weren't even permitted to play on their own hit singles. Connolly remembered one late-night meeting at a motorway café, the two bands bent over plates of whatever greasy sustenance they could bring themselves to order, when three or four bikers walked in, recognized both sets of musicians in a heartbeat, then demanded to know how Deep Purple could degrade themselves by hanging out with a "fucking crappy pop group."

The two bands did their best to ignore them, but finally one of the taunters went too far. Connolly continued, "One of them said how much he loved 'Strange Kind of Woman' and asked Jon [Lord] when Purple's next single was coming out. Jon didn't even look up. He just said, 'Oh, I don't think we're going to release any more singles. We'd hate you to think we were a fucking crappy pop group.'"

Deep Purple's U.K. tour wrapped up in Southampton, just a few miles from where it began, on October 11; ten days later, the band were in New York City to kick off their latest American tour at the Felt Forum. Ahead of them stretched a monthlong outing that, for the first time, would see them headlining arenas and stadiums. But the following night's show, in Williamsburg, Virginia, was to be the last they would play all year. Feeling ill even before he went onstage, by the end of the show Gillan was deathly sick.

He remained with the band as they traveled to the next show, in Chicago; once there, however, he was rushed to hospital where he was diagnosed with hepatitis. The rest of the tour would have to be canceled, but, having at least made it to the Windy City, the rest of the group opted to go out in style. With Glover stepping up to the microphone, Deep Purple performed that night as a quartet. Then they flew home, the tour in shreds and their immediate future in a shambles.

With Gillan cooling his heels in recuperation, Deep Purple were out of action for two months. Unable to gig, and unwilling to even write much without Gillan's input, then, the members scattered.

Most groups would have embraced such a break as a welcome, if wholly unexpected, respite from the business of the band. For Ritchie Blackmore, however, it offered up another opportunity altogether. Still chafing over Gillan's perceived challenge to his self-appointed role as band leader, the guitarist had begun entertaining solo ambitions, undecided only as to whether or not they might take place within the overall framework of Deep Purple. Back in London, with Ian Paice alongside him, Blackmore booked into De Lane Lea studios for the first of what would become known as the Babyface sessions — a name Blackmore biographer Roy Davies suggests might well have been inspired by Paice's choirboy looks.

To complete what the guitarist intended as a very basic power trio, Blackmore invited along Phil Lynott, bassist with the then little-known (but definitely fast-rising) Thin Lizzy. It would be several months before the Irish hard rockers scored their first hit single, with a stunning rearrangement of the traditional "Whisky in the Jar," but, with two highly acclaimed albums already behind them, Thin Lizzy were certainly attracting attention, and Blackmore was as enthused as anybody. Catching the band in concert during the summer, he had earmarked Lynott for some future project, long before he decided on the project itself.

Of course, Blackmore's interest did not at all please Thin Lizzy's manager, Chris Donnell, all the more so since he was painfully aware just how difficult it was to keep Lynott's feet firmly on the ground. The bassist had already mused aloud about conducting a solo career alongside his duties with Thin Lizzy, and O'Donnell later summed up this latest pipedream as "a few rehearsals that had Phil thinking he [really] could live out his Rod Stewart/Faces fantasy."

"I wanted to form a band with Phil Lynott," Blackmore acknowledged. "It would consist of Phil, Ian Paice, and myself. We would be a trio. We [would] have made a few albums. That was in 1972–73. I said to Ian, 'Well, that was it. I'm leaving.' And he said he would stay with me and asked me if it was a wise decision. [But] I was just fed up with everybody."

As it transpired, Babyface was doomed to obscurity. Although Lynott later recalled recording as many as five songs with Blackmore and Paice, Blackmore remembered no more than a couple (including a version of Johnny Winter's "Dying to Live"), then damned them with faint praise: "They were good, but it may have been a bit near Hendrix. I was playing that way and Phil was singing that way." In fact, Roy Davies is adamant that "the only known reels of master tape found archived thus far . . . contain just three disappointingly rudimentary and incomplete backing tracks."

Glover and Paice, too, were busy during the band's layoff, heading down to Atlanta, Georgia, to produce the first album by the American band Elf — and igniting, though they could never have known it, one of the longest-standing relationships in the Deep Purple family tree, as they were introduced to that band's vocalist, Ronnie Dio.

Ronald James Padavona had been styling himself Dio since a childhood infatuation with the Mafia introduced him to the legend of Florida gangster Johnny Dio ("Second-generation Italians growing up in America . . . don't have that many heroes," the boy later explained). A performer since childhood, an accomplished trumpeter and possessor of a one-and-one-half-octave vocal range, Dio formed his first band, the Vegas Kings, in the late 1950s to pursue the doo-wop boom of the age. As Ronnie and the Ramblers, they released their first single, "Lover," in 1958 when (according to his official birthdate) Dio was just 11.

Over the next decade or so, the basic Vegas Kings unit of Dio and guitarist Nick Pantas underwent a chain of further name and lineup changes, before settling on the Electric Elves in self-deprecating recognition of the entire group's diminutive stature. They cut a few more 45s as well, and ultimately found themselves a major draw on the East Coast college circuit, where their finely honed eye for covers saw them unveiling great swaths of *Tommy* and Jethro Tull's *Aqualung* within weeks of the original albums' release — and certainly before the songs' originators had taken them to the stage.

This period of gentle achievement was rudely shattered in 1970. Returning from a show, the band was involved in an horrific car accident. Nick Pantas was killed, and pianist Doug Thaler was hospitalized for a year. It was mid-1971 before the group, now operating under the truncated name of Elf, reignited around original members Dio, Thaler, guitarist Dave Feinstein, and drummer Gary Driscoll, plus new member Mickey Lee Soule, but their momentum had slowed considerably. So, when they were invited down to New York City to audition for Columbia Records chief Clive Davis late that October, it was a big deal — and it was about to get even bigger.

"At the same time as we were coming down for this audition," Dio recalled, "as luck would have it for us — and bad luck would have it for them — Deep Purple had just had to cancel their American tour after Ian

[Gillan] came down with hepatitis. So our manager, who was also Purple's agent on that tour, was talking to Roger and Ian [Paice], and said to them, 'I have this band that are coming to audition for Clive Davis. Perhaps you'd be interested in coming up to see them.' So Roger and Ian came to the audition as well.

"Now, Clive Davis was obviously an important man, and we were very impressed by him. But when we found out that Roger and Ian were going to come as well — two of our heroes — any nervousness that we didn't have suddenly appeared!"

The audition required Elf to run through four or five songs, after which, Dio continued, "Clive Davis said, 'Great, I'm gonna sign you.' And then Roger came up to us and said, 'Yeah, I absolutely love this band, and I want to produce you. . . .' Because that's where Roger's at, Roger really loves bands like Little Feat, and we fit into that at the time, so he was really taken by us. So we went on to record our first album in Atlanta with Roger and Ian Paice." The result of those sessions, *Elf*, was released in America the following summer, as the band prepared for their first-ever nationwide tour, opening for Deep Purple themselves. In the meantime, Deep Purple would reconvene to record the album — and the song — that would ensure their immortality.

Chapter 8

Smoking Heads Out of Control

Having spent two weeks in hospital, Gillan was back home in Fulham, London. The doctor's recommendation that he devote the next three months to recuperating seemed more unreasonable every day. Prior to his falling ill, Deep Purple intended to spend December in the Swiss resort town of Montreaux, recording their next album at the Casino, a cavernous arena on the ground floor of an ornate, prepossessing complex of casinos, restaurants, theaters, and bars. These surroundings would hopefully permit them to recapture all the excitement of a live performance without actually making a live record. The Rolling Stones' mobile recording studio had already been booked, the hotel reservations were made, and the band members were heartily enthused by the project.

They'd already played the Casino once before, in May, and had fallen in love both with the venue itself and with its owner, Claude Nobs. It was he who established the Montreaux Casino, among the foremost spots on both the rock and jazz circuits of the day — Led Zeppelin, Pink Floyd, and Black Sabbath had all visited the venue over the last year or so, although Deep Purple were the first to record there. The Casino was closed for concerts through much of December and, so long as the band didn't mind working around the refurbishing that took place every winter, it was theirs for the taking. There was just one more concert on the schedule, a matinee by Frank Zappa and the Mothers of Invention on December 4; after that, the place was the band's.

With Gillan apparently out for the count, those plans had been placed on hold. Now, however, the singer was demanding that the schedule be brought back to life and, on December 3, band and crew flew out to Montreaux, checked into the Hotel Eden au Lac, then set off to check out the Casino.

For Zappa and his band, the Montreaux show was just one more night in the last leg of a European tour that, following an exhaustive U.S. outing, had kept them on the road for three months. *200 Motels*, Zappa's first feature film, had just been released to critical quizzicality, but public support — it effortlessly breached *Variety*'s Top 50. The combination of the tightest musicians the Mothers had ever employed, and the near slapstick ribaldry of auxiliary frontmen Flo and Eddie, had hauled Zappa's oft-impenetrable muse onto a new plateau of wisdom, wit, and weirdness.

Certainly Gillan was entranced by the show, although he would later "vaguely" recall "a guy of Mediterranean appearance walking in" and pointing something toward the ceiling. Still, he thought nothing of it until he heard a sudden crack, saw a brilliant flash — and the building began to burn. This concertgoer, for no reason other than a sense of fun and occasion, had arrived at the concert armed with a flare gun, which he fired into the tinder-dry roof of the old hall.

The flames took hold immediately. From the stage, Zappa attempted to marshal shocked and horrified fans out of the building, before departing himself with the words "Arthur Brown in person!" At every exit, meanwhile, the venue's staff worked to push and pull people through the doors, even as panicked fans began smashing through the massive plate-glass windows to make their escape. Amazingly, nobody was killed, but the Mothers lost $50,000 worth of equipment, and the Casino was left a ruin. Deep Purple's plans went up in smoke with it.

Somehow placing his own problems to one side, Claude Nobs salvaged the situation, arranging for the band to relocate instead to the Pavilion, another Montreaux theater that closed down for the winter season. Just one night there, however, proved the unsuitability of the venue. Located in the heart of one of the city's residential neighborhoods, the Pavilion might have worked for occasional concerts and productions, but it was in no way appropriate for a bunch of heavily amplified, nocturnal rock'n'rollers. Within hours of the band plugging in for the first time, the switchboard at the local police station was screaming in protest as the entire neighborhood, it seemed, phoned in to complain about the noise. And the band had only just got started.

Glover recalled, "The only thing we recorded there was a riff of Ritchie's, which we called 'Title No. 1.' The police were actually outside banging on the doors; the roadies were holding the doors shut until we finished recording it. One can almost hear the banging as the song fades out." The group was evicted on the spot.

What the good people of Montreaux did not know was just how privileged they were that night. The pounding racket that had roused them from their slumbers was, in fact, the maiden performance of a song that, within months, would enshrine their town as firmly into rock'n'roll legend as Route 66 or Strawberry Fields. It would take its place among the all-time classic rock anthems, to nestle alongside the likes of "Stairway to Heaven," "Free Bird," and "Hotel California" in that rarified pantheon of songs that even rock'n'roll's most devoted foes have to acknowledge have *something* in their favor.

At the time, however, Deep Purple shared the disdainful opinions of the sleepless Swiss. "We finished the track, but we really didn't think much of it," Glover recalled. "When we went back to it a week later, it was, 'Oh, what are we going to write over this?' So we wrote something, put it on the album, and that was it."

"It," of course, was "Smoke on the Water."

It was Glover who came up with the title, awakening from a dream with the words on his lips. His initial impression was that it would make a great tag for a drug song; it was several days before he and Gillan decided instead to utilize it as a description of their own experiences of the Casino conflagration. One of the most pervasive images of the disaster, after all, was the sight of smoke from the fire, caught by the downdraft from the surrounding mountains, billowing out across the waters of Lake Geneva.

The riff was simplicity itself — so much so that, in later years,

Blackmore found himself having to defend it against the musical snobs who insisted that, because it *was* so simple, just four notes, it couldn't be any good. His response threw that argument straight back in his interrogators' faces. He suggested they go home and listen to the opening moments of Beethoven's Fifth Symphony.

Close to thirty years after "Smoke on the Water" was released, *Goldmine* pointed out that the song represented the first occasion upon which Frank Zappa and the Mothers of Invention got their name into the American Top 40. It was not, however, the only song on this latest Deep Purple album to mention Zappa. As news of the Mothers' subsequent adventures made its way back to Montreaux, Gillan would drop a friendly ad lib into another song, "Lazy."

Stunned by the fire, and the loss of so much equipment, Zappa wanted to return to the U.S. immediately after the Montreaux disaster and shelve what was left of the Mothers' European tour. The remainder of his band, however, disagreed, and on December 10, three canceled concerts later, the Mothers returned to action at London's Rainbow Theatre.

Zappa's presentiments were not misguided. As the London show reached its conclusion, one of the audience members, the jealous boyfriend of a besotted fan, leaped onstage and shoved Zappa twelve feet into the orchestra pit. The fall knocked him unconscious, causing injuries that included a broken leg and ankle, a crushed larynx, a fractured skull, and spinal damage. Zappa was confined to a wheelchair for nine months, although Gillan was not to know that when, ironically rewiring a traditional showbiz greeting, he simply shouted out, "Break a leg, Frank!"

Following their eviction from the Pavilion, Deep Purple scoured Montreaux in search of a new base, checking out everything from a nuclear fallout shelter to the vast subterranean vaults constructed to store art treasures during World War II. Finally they settled on another hotel, the vast, Victorian-style Grand, sited on the very outskirts of Montreaux, with scarcely a neighbor in sight.

The band set up their gear in one of the corridors, converted from its normal austerity by banks of red lights and insulating mattresses, and so closed off from the rest of the hotel that they were forced to cross through bedrooms and leap across balconies simply to leave the room.

Making their way to the mobile unit, parked outside in the main court-yard, was such a major undertaking that, after just a handful of journeys, the band eschewed the luxury of playbacks altogether. They would record until a take sounded right, then worry about how it really turned out later.

The sessions were fast; within two weeks of finally getting to work, the album was done. "What you get is what we did," explained Glover. "There were no outtakes, no alternate versions. When I came to remaster *Machine Head* for the anniversary edition, that was the challenge. All there was were those eight songs and a little bit of banter. Right at the end of "Lazy" you hear somebody — I think it's me — go 'Wooh!' And that speaks volumes, because there's so little else."

But there was no need for anything else. From "Pictures of Home," its riff built upon a fragment of melody that Blackmore picked up on his shortwave radio one night, floating out of a Bulgarian or Turkish broad-cast, to the hyperanthem "Space Truckin'," its lyric a seamless porcupine of interstellar punning, *Machine Head* was a monster from the moment it hit stores in May 1972. And that was before "Smoke on the Water" coiled out of the grooves to captivate every ear that encountered it — just as it has continued doing ever since. "I heard some live version of 'Smoke on the Water' and [Ritchie Blackmore] just kicked up this rocking guitar solo," Smashing Pumpkins guitarist James Iha remarked at the height of his own band's mid-1990s popularity. "It was really cool."

In 1998, Glover even joked, "The new name of the band, by the way, is Deep Purple Oh Yes 'Smoke on the Water' I Went to College With That." And he marveled, "The funny thing is, when *Machine Head* came out, the song we thought was going to be big was 'Never Before.' We put a lot of work into that, a nice middle eight, polished performances, properly mixed." They were correct to be so proud. With a funky intro that sets up the groove, and a positively Beatlesesque midriff, "Never Before" raised Deep Purple's own performance bar as high as anything they had released so far and, two months before the album was issued, "Never Before" was earmarked not only as the band's latest single, but also as their first release on the newly formed Purple label.

Though Deep Purple were scarcely stepping into uncharted waters with this latest venture, still the creation of a new record label, ostensibly administered according to a single band's own decisions and preferences, was a remarkable achievement in the early 1970s. Both the Beatles' Apple label and the Rolling Stones' eponymous imprint had, after a brief flurry of excitement and high promise, settled down to become nothing more than outlets for the parent bands alone — such Apple signings as James Taylor, Mary Hopkin, and Hot Chocolate had all moved on to other pastures, while the only outside recruit to Rolling Stones Records, Kracker, had vanished without trace.

Elsewhere, the Moody Blues' Threshold Records signed Glenn Hughes' highly fancied Trapeze and came close to picking up the then-unknown Genesis, but ultimately followed the Stones' wisdom, while Marc Bolan's Hot Wax label never even suggested adding other artists to the roster. Later, too, the likes of Emerson Lake & Palmer (Manticore) and Led Zeppelin (Swansong) found it considerably easier to sell their own wares than to market other people's.

Purple Records would ultimately wind up walking a path similar to its predecessors'. But its first two years of operation would, nevertheless, see a remarkable array of talents — all fellow clients of HEC management — share its distinctive logo with Deep Purple themselves.

The studio recording of Jon Lord's *Gemini Suite* launched the label in October 1971, alongside releases by Rupert Hine (produced by Roger Glover), Buddy Bohn, and Curtiss Muldoon, the new band led by Dave Curtiss, the man who came so close to fronting the original Deep Purple. Further old pals followed. Johnny Gustafson, who replaced Roger Glover in Episode Six and then formed Quatermass with drummer Mick Underwood, had recently birthed a new band, Bullet, with a couple of members of Atomic Rooster. These hard rockers, who swiftly changed their name to Hard Stuff, debuted on Purple Records in November 1971 with their first single, "Hobo."

Yvonne Elliman, one of Gillan's compatriots in *Jesus Christ Superstar*, and Tony Ashton both came on board, while other signings included Silverhead, the Martin Birch–produced metallic glam band that launched vocalist Michael Des Barres to a degree of fame, Bill Wyman protégés Tucky Buzzard, and even actor Jon Pertwee — television's Doctor Who. But Deep Purple remained the label's only guaranteed chartmakers, and it was "Never Before" that marked Purple Records' debut on the U.K. listings when it limped, in April 1972, to No. 35.

Of course, such unpromising beginnings were instantly swept away with the release of *Machine Head*. The album entered the British charts two weeks after "Never Before," and was No. 1 just seven days later. It remained at the top for two weeks, then returned for a further week in mid-May. It was a similar story in the United States — although *Machine Head* never topped the charts, it rose swiftly to No. 7 and spent more than two years on the poll, turning double platinum in the process.

Deep Purple were on top of the world. Even before the album was released, their latest American tour, two weeks during January, had confirmed the headline superstatus that their so cruelly curtailed visit in October ought to have conferred. Isolated dates around the U.K. and Scandinavia then preceded a second short U.S. visit in March, before they returned for a longer circuit in May. In fact, Deep Purple undertook a full half-dozen American tours during 1972, as their stock soared even higher. Looking back from the end of the year, Jon Lord told the *New Musical Express*, "Chicago used to be a cold town for us, but the last gig we did was a beauty. Ian Gillan ended up dancing in the crowd. It was just a friendly, happy thing, but it could never have happened two years ago."

But the U.S. was only the tip of the iceberg that masqueraded as the band's work schedule. There was a three-date Japanese visit in August and a full British tour in October. They then found time to record a new studio album, mix and master a pre-Christmas live souvenir of the Japanese shows, and somehow survive the kinds of crises that might well have floored a lesser band.

Machine Head was still awaiting release when Blackmore let slip, in an interview, that it wasn't simply Deep Purple's best album, it might also prove to be their last. For any number of reasons, but with the workload paramount among them, the band, he said, would be lucky to survive the year. This prophecy was promptly given further currency when, for the second time in six months, hepatitis forced the group to cancel a string of American dates. This time Blackmore was stricken, and again the group attempted to soldier on shorthanded. Their scheduled show in Flint, Michigan, on March 31, 1972, went ahead without any lead guitar whatsoever; then, with a few days' break before their next show in Quebec, the group set about finding a temporary replacement.

Their first choice was Al Kooper — a keyboard player, of course (it is his distinctive organ sound that drives Bob Dylan's "Like a Rolling Stone"), but a useful guitarist, too. However, a day of rehearsals proved that the union was never likely to get off the ground, a point reinforced when Kooper succumbed to food poisoning that same evening and was forced to bow out of the proceedings.

They turned next to Randy California, mercurial guitarist with the American band Spirit, and decamped to the old Fillmore East theater in New York City for two days of rehearsals. There, California proved he was anything but a stand-in, realigning a showstopping "Child in Time" around his slide-guitar-playing and persuading the band to introduce "When a Blind Man Cries," a song otherwise renowned only as the non-album B-side to "Never Before," into the live set.

A strong, bluesy number, it allowed California to sparkle as only he could. Talking shortly before his death in 1997, California admitted, "If Purple had had more songs like that, things we could have really gone to town on, it might have worked out. But I would have got so bored just playing 'Smoke on the Water' every night, and I think they'd have got tired of not playing it. We did one show together and it was okay. But they missed what Ritchie could do, and I missed being able to do what I could." Just as they had during Gillan's incapacitation, Deep Purple canceled the remainder of the tour and returned home to await Blackmore's recovery.

They were back on the road at the end of May, touring through June and July, an itinerary highlighted by the reopening of another of London's most venerable venues, the old Finsbury Park Astoria, on June 30, 1972. Though new owners had renamed the place the Rainbow, still Deep Purple believed that an old friend deserved special treatment, and they celebrated the opening by journeying where no band had traveled before, creating a new entry in the *Guiness Book of Records* as the loudest rock'n'roll band in the world. Some 117 decibels, three unconscious fans, and who knows how many bleeding eardrums later, they got their entry.

It was a record Deep Purple would retain for the next four years, until The Who topped their output by cranking up to 120 decibels at Charlton Athletic Football Club's Valley Stadium in May 1976 — but, with all due respect to The Who, Deep Purple were still louder. The Who, after all, were playing an outdoor venue, with nothing to keep the sound from sailing free. The two-thousand-capacity Rainbow was completely enclosed. There was no escape for a single note.

Roger Glover reflected on the honor with reservation: "It wasn't something we wanted or designed or even felt proud of, to be honest, it was just one of those quirks of fate. We were loud that night, but we'd just come from America and we had all this new equipment. We'd just been playing to 15,000 people, 20,000 people a night, in places like the Spectrum Philadelphia, with this huge wall of amplifiers. Then we came back to London and we still had this wall. And they were ours. And we wanted to show them to people."

Amid all this activity, Deep Purple managed to wrangle a few days off in mid-June, embarking on what Blackmore described as "our summer holidays," but what was, in reality, an opportunity to recharge batteries before the band returned to the studio to begin work on their next album.

The recording sessions promised to be a fractious affair. Relations between Gillan and Blackmore were at an all-time low, with the key dispute, incredibly, Blackmore's insistence that Gillan's vocal style was holding him back — and vice versa. The fact that, nightly, they combined to pull off musical feats that no other pairing on earth could have emulated, from the chilling dynamics of "Child in Time" to the duel that bisected "Strange Kind of Woman," seemed to escape both men's attention, and the notion that either could find a sparring partner of equal dexterity seemed absurd.

Yet Gillan was already flexing independent muscles he had only previously contemplated. He drew from a pool of musicians both within and without the immediate Deep Purple family, and summer 1972 saw him turn his full attention back to a project he had named (but scarcely elaborated upon) the previous year, *Cherkazoo*. It was, he now explained, "an animal/space/musical travelogue fantasy" that he loosely envisioned converting into a movie. Answering a query on his own Caramba Web site almost thirty years later, Gillan recalled "a meeting in the '70s with all the senior people at Disney. I did a presentation at their studios in Hollywood and they were very enthusiastic. However, it coincided with a sea change of company policy and they were in production with *Robin Hood*, having decided to go back to classic stories as the basis for their films, due to bad figures on some recent contemporary stuff."

The movie project wound up a nonstarter. But *Cherkazoo* also became the umbrella title for a string of sessions undertaken during 1972 and beyond, with Roger Glover, Jon Lord, and producer Martin Birch joined as the singer's most loyal collaborators by keyboard player Mike Moran, drummers Pete York and Mike Giles, and guitarist Ray Fenwick, the brilliant young player in the most recent incarnation of the Spencer Davis Group — whom Glover was currently producing.

Fenwick recalled, "At the time, it was kind of strange. But it was one of those [projects] that you could see somewhere along the line, there was some connection." Indeed there was. Both Fenwick and Moran would later return to Gillan's side as members of his first Ian Gillan Band, and hindsight proves that much of that group's early momentum was, in turn, provided by the *Cherkazoo* sessions. Fenwick continued, "One of the songs that we did for *Cherkazoo* was 'You Make Me Feel So Good,' which we [rerecorded] on the first Gillan Band album."

Another song from the sessions, "Monster in Paradise," was gifted to Hard Stuff for inclusion on their *Bulletproof* album — the group's bassist, Johnny Gustafson, cowrote the number with Gillan and Glover. Ultimately, in sessions that stretched disconnectedly throughout the next two or three years, sufficient material was laid down to compile a full CD, 1992's *Cherkazoo and Other Stories*.

Nothing was released at the time, however, and when the time came to reconvene with his bandmates, Gillan put the project on hold. The intention was to record the next Deep Purple album in Italy. Glover explained, "After the rigors of the hotel corridor in Montreaux, we decided to have the easy life, so we went to this villa outside Rome, with a swimming pool and a chef and a huge basement full of wine . . . and, of course, no work got done at all." In fact, the most productive single day of the sessions seems to have been the very first, after the band took delivery of the mobile studio but had yet to see their instruments arrive. "There was this empty room with mikes, and this dodgy old piano, so we did a couple of comedy tracks [Lord's ribald 'Smelly Botty' and Gillan's cringeworthy cabaret turn through Conway Twitty's 'It's Only Make Believe'], just for fun, and they are quite priceless."

Glover, Gillan, Paice, and Lord alone feature on these recordings;

Blackmore tellingly absented himself from this initial playfulness, and then proceeded to avoid the rest of the band at every other opportunity that presented itself. Even during the actual recording, he preferred to sit with Martin Birch in the mobile rather than play alongside Deep Purple and, when the Rome sessions concluded with just two completed songs in the can, "Woman from Tokyo" and the oddly, distinctly Sweet-like "Painted Horse," the guitarist was thankful not only to see the back of the villa, but also the back of the studio process itself.

His discontent, Blackmore admitted to the *New Musical Express*, revolved around his firm belief that Deep Purple had taken their music as far as they could — or, perhaps more accurately, as far as their audience would allow them. He explained, "The whole scene now is waiting for something to happen, but I don't know quite what, because in the last four years, [rock has] progressed a hell of a lot, and it can't really go much further. Well, it could go a hell of a lot farther musically, but I don't think that's what people want."

Gillan agreed that the band had suffered an absolute breakdown in envisioning their future direction. Blackmore argued that Deep Purple's fans would not let the group shift in the directions it needed to; in Gillan's mind, it was the band members themselves who had slipped into cruise control. *In Rock* had been a success and, the moment the band's next move — the more adventurous *Fireball* — fell short of their standards, they had simply returned, for *Machine Head*, to what they knew would sell. Now they had the opportunity to try moving on again — and it wasn't happening.

With the benefits of hindsight, it is easy to see where the band went wrong. Past albums had come together around the musicians' love of jamming, taking an idea and then running with it until it reached what all agreed was its ultimate destination. Indeed, Blackmore once insisted, "Personally, I play better if we're having a jam session because the stuff we play onstage is always basically the same, and I know beforehand that it's going to sound more or less the same every night. So I like a jam now and again, to keep in shape."

On a battlefield that had now shattered even the pretense of camaraderie, there was no space for such luxuries. Songs were recorded much as they were written, and Blackmore distributed his guitar lines without his bandmates even hearing them. It was no way to make a record — it was no way to run a band. But any possibility that they might simply put the brakes on their workload and take the time to rediscover the group's original spark was dismissed with one glance at their itinerary for the next twelve months. They were booked solid.

On August 9, 1972, Deep Purple flew to Japan for the first time, a week-long visit that culminated with three concerts, in Osaka on August 15–16 and in Tokyo the following evening. All three dates were sold-out long in advance — without ever having set foot in the country, Deep Purple were huge in Japan, crowned amid a hard-rocking triumvirate completed by Free and (though it would surely have made Ritchie Blackmore smile wryly) Grand Funk.

A string of singles had pursued *In Rock*, *Fireball*, and *Machine Head* up the Japanese charts: "Black Night," "Strange Kind of Woman," "Fireball," "Never Before," and "Highway Star" were all hits, with another, "Lazy," set to coincide with the visit. Media coverage, meanwhile, approached saturation point, with *Music Life* — a magazine whose Anglo bias was already so powerful that homegrown talent found it hard to even get mentioned within its pages — leading the way with vivid color spreads.

Warner Brothers' Japanese wing intended to record Deep Purple's forthcoming concerts, for release, in Japan alone, as a live album, but still the band members were stunned by the sheer weight of the support that awaited them at the airport on arrival. Flowers, gifts, and banners piled up both inside and outside their hotel rooms and, when they performed live, it was as though the entire auditorium — 12,000-plus at the Tokyo Budokan — was singing along with them. They probably were.

Even off-duty, Deep Purple were superstars. If the largesse directed toward them during that first trip to Los Angeles, back in 1968, had over-whelmed the group, Japan shattered even the most jaded palate. For Warner Brothers and tour promoters Universal alike, nothing was too good for the band members, whether it was a visit to a geisha bathhouse (the details of which, one American magazine reported, "could fill half a dozen dirty books") or a night out at the Tokyo disco Byblos, where the cream of the local music scene turned out to pay tribute to the masters.

Despite the success of the outing, Deep Purple were not entirely enthusiastic about the prospect of recording, let alone releasing, the concerts. Although live albums were no longer the sonic minefield of tinny bands and screaming teens that once characterized the genre — had, in fact, gained a considerable measure of respect and success via such milestones as Hendrix's *Band of Gypsies*, Cream's *Wheels of Fire*, The Who's *Live at Leeds*, and the Rolling Stones' *Get Yer Ya-Ya's Out* — still there was great uncertainty as to what a live album was meant to represent. A never-to-be repeated peak in a band's performing abilities? A punctuation point in a career that required such a thing? Or a way of waving goodbye to one record label, en route to a better deal elsewhere?

Hindsight suggests that a Deep Purple live album, recorded at this precise juncture in time, would fulfill at least the first two of those criteria. But hindsight always boasts perfect vision. At the time, the situation was less clear-cut — so much so that, with the concerts over and the tapes back in London, neither Gillan nor Blackmore even bothered dropping by the studios to hear them.

The portents were dubious from the outset. The band was not even unpacked when Martin Birch called with the news that the proffered recording unit was utterly unsuitable for the job at hand. At least, that's what he thought. In fact, *Made in Japan* (*Live in Japan*, as it was called in Japan itself) would emerge as one of the all-time greatest live albums, a masterpiece from both performance and sonic perspectives, and, even amid the veritable ocean of Deep Purple live albums that have since flooded the market, still the only in-concert document of the band that one truly needs to experience.

Looking back from over thirty years distant, Jon Lord enthused, "I've always felt that the great thing about Purple, and one of the reasons I'm so proud of the band, is that it by far outstrips its recorded work as a live animal. Purple has always been a live band, and I don't think we've ever been particularly great in the studio. So, *Made in Japan* was fortuitously able to capture that incredible energy, and it still sells truckloads because of that. It's one of the best-selling live rock albums ever, and I think that it's one of the best-sounding, too. We made it for only $3,000 — it took just four nights of live recording onto an 8-track, with Martin Birch at the helm. The weird thing was that we were all so unconcerned about the whole thing that nobody was actually aware of being recorded. We were never thinking, 'God, we've really got to get this right because this is going down on tape,' so there was no diminution of the interplay, spontaneity, and feeling that we usually got onstage."

Swayed by the dynamic quality of both the recording and the performances, the band promptly agreed to the Japanese release, then okayed its appearance elsewhere, too. A little disingenuously, Glover told the British weekly *Sounds*, "There are so many bootlegs of us going around [that], if we put out our own live set, it should kill their market." But he also acknowledged, "Another reason . . . is that the stage act we've been using . . . will be dropped next year." *Made in Japan* would preserve it for all time.

So, that was it — a nice gesture for the fans, and a kick in the teeth for the bootleggers? Think again. All but single-handedly, *Made in Japan* was the spark that ignited what rapidly became one of the most fail-safe marketing devices of the 1970s.

Only the Allman Brothers' breakthrough *At Fillmore East* had previously packed the nerve to spread a full (or thereabouts) concert over four sides of vinyl; in the wake of the similarly sprawling *Made in Japan*, however, virtually any artist capable of sustaining a concert over the required seventy minutes would venture onto the racks with the ubiquitous double live album, and anybody seeking a measure of just how successful the format was needs only recall Peter Frampton's *Frampton Comes Alive!* Six million people purchased that album in America alone — which is almost six million more than picked up any of his earlier records.

Made in Japan would not prove so vastly popular as that. But still, with its retail price held down to little more than the cost of a regular single album (£3.10 in the U.K., compared to an average £2.99), it readily outsold any similarly styled album of the age, and deservedly so.

Immaculately recorded, drawing the very best performances from three nights of unbridled hysteria, and still home to the definitive versions of so many Deep Purple classics, *Made in Japan* perhaps received the ultimate accolade when Warners drew the live "Smoke on the Water" out as a single, emerging with Deep Purple's first U.S. hit since "Black Night" rose to No. 66 in 1970 and their biggest since "Hush" two years before that. "Smoke on the Water" billowed all the way to No. 4

and, two years later, when Purple compiled their own first "best of" collection, 1975's *24 Carat Purple*, that steaming version of "Smoke" was joined by two more cuts from the live album, "Strange Kind of Woman" and "Child in Time." The radio-friendlier studio versions didn't even get a look in.

Of course, there was no time for Deep Purple to sit back and congratulate themselves on *Made in Japan*, even if they had wanted to — even if they'd actually *listened* to it (according to Martin Birch, only Glover, Lord, and Paice even turned up for the final playback). From Tokyo, the band flew straight into the their next American tour, a week or so of shows in the company of Fleetwood Mac.

It was a family affair of sorts — Birch was set to produce Fleetwood Mac's next album, *Mystery to Me*. But there was another connection as well, although it scarcely made for happy chatter on the road. Like Deep Purple, Fleetwood Mac seemed constantly to be tearing itself viciously apart. Only, whereas Deep Purple was content to grin and bear the ructions and eruptions, Fleetwood Mac's constitution was revised with near-clockwork regularity.

On this occasion, the group's problems revolved around guitarist Danny Kirwan, who had managed to alienate every one of his bandmates. Only Mick Fleetwood, in whose hands lay the power of hiring and firing, was willing to persevere with the prodigal, but finally even he had had enough. It was, after all, a difficult enough job having to open for Deep Purple with all cylinders firing. It was nigh-on impossible to face down a yowlingly partisan audience while your lead guitarist skulked sulking at the back of the hall, after one row too many. After the show, Fleetwood recalled, "I had dinner with Jon Lord and, in the restaurant, he gave me a pep talk. I went back to the hotel . . . and Danny was fired." So often the arbiter within Purple's own internal disputes, Lord knew more than a little about crisis management. Yet, as the seemingly endless 1972 wore on, even his powers of diplomacy were about to be tested to their limits.

From the States, Deep Purple returned to Europe. From there, it was back to the studio, this time in Frankfurt, Germany, to try and pick up the sessions that had collapsed so ignominiously three months earlier.

But the spark was gone. "The albums seemed to go in cycles: easy, difficult; easy, difficult," recalled Glover. "This one was difficult. There was not a lot of love in the band at this time — stupidity, little boys really. One person does something bad, and the other person says, 'Well, fuck him, I'm going to do something bad just to show him.' And meanwhile the band's suffering. Very rarely were all five of us in the same room at the same time. It was Ritchie and the musicians in, and we'd do a track almost without any consultation with Ian. Then, when Ritchie was gone, Ian would come in, listen to what we'd done, and that's when he and I would start working out what we were going to do over it. So it was done fairly piecemeal; it wasn't a collaborative effort."

Neither was Gillan the only recipient of Blackmore's apparent collapse of interest. Glover continued, "There were some moments in the studio I'll never forget, trying to get Ritchie to play something. I had an idea for a song, but to get that going, they have to play something, and I was trying to guide him to what I wanted him to play and he just wouldn't play it. Paicey was playing away, Jon was playing away, I was playing away, and Ritchie was just standing there. Then he took off his guitar and walked out of the room. Ten minutes later, he comes back in and starts up this enormous riff which we all joined in, and we go, 'Ah, that's great, Rich, let's do that.' And he goes, 'Nah, I'm keeping that.' And it eventually turned up on the first Rainbow album."

The eighth Deep Purple album, meanwhile, was going nowhere, simply meandering along with little of the fire and, from the sound of it, even less of the commitment that had hitherto been the group's hallmark. "Woman from Tokyo," the first song completed for the album, in Rome during the summer, would remain the best thing in sight; but the second best, "Painted Horse," would not even see the light of day until 1977, when it was selected as a posthumous Deep Purple B-side (ironically, just as Gillan himself was considering rerecording it for inclusion on his *Scarabus* album).

Elsewhere, the pickings were decidedly humdrum. Although Gillan later expressed his own affection for the groupie epic "Rat Bat Blue," and the world in general flocked to dissect "Smooth Dancer" — the singer's barely disguised assault on Ritchie Blackmore — too much of the album faded into a kind of rock-by-numbers trough that bore little of the brittle fury and understated humor of classic Deep Purple. Either that, or it simply served up a faint photocopy of it.

Following the "Painted Horse" outtake into the kind of earnestly over-rocking territory marked out by the Sweet, "Smooth Dancer" was little more than an echo of "Speed King"; the dried-out blues of "Place in Line" were simply blank-faced filler; and "Mary Long," an assault on Mary Whitehouse and Lord Longford, the self-styled guardians of Britain's early-1970s (and beyond!) morality, suffered from a lyric that battered its subject with no more subtlety or insight than you'd hear in the local pub every night. Which isn't to say one expected better from Deep Purple — simply that one expected something different from them.

The band members were well aware of the album's failings, even before it hit the streets. Prior to the release, Jon Lord counseled fans to expect something new from the band, when he reflected, "If you don't do what [people] expect, [they] cry 'cheat,' and if you do what they expect, they shout 'formula.' [But] there's obviously a nice middle passage between those two, and that's what we've tried to get." Warming to his theme, he singled out the album's final track, "Our Lady," as something that might throw up some shocks. "It's very slow," he said, "and concentrates more on the tune and the lyrics, and there are no solos. It's just a song, which is not normally the way Deep Purple seems to work."

Unfortunately, very little about the album was illustrative of the way Deep Purple *normally* worked, a failing the album's eventual title, *Who Do We Think We Are*, echoed with uncanny precision. The phrase, Ian Paice told *Disc*, was originally lifted from the band's postbag — "The angry [letters] generally start off 'Who do Deep Purple think they are?'" Now, however, it was a question the band members themselves were asking, and they were not finding any answers.

Nowhere did *Who Do We Think We Are* even threaten to stand out amid the august company to which its pedigree raised it, with its hopes for a happy landing further dented by its proximity to *Made in Japan*. Issued in October 1972 in Japan, and December in the U.K., the live leviathan was still being digested when *Who Do We Think We Are* was released in February 1973. In fact, while a full six weeks yawned between the new album's U.K. chart entry and the live set's, just three separated their respective departures. Even in America, where *Made in Japan* was purposefully held back until after *Who Do We Think We Are* had made its impact, it was the double album that marched resolutely into the Top 10 and the studio set that faltered at No. 15.

Yet it was not the music's failings alone that condemned *Who Do We Think We Are* to such a fate. Deep Purple were falling apart — for real, this time — and they didn't seem to care who noticed. Gillan, in fact, had already given notice of his intention to quit, making up his mind in Frankfurt and passing the news on to management as the band worked through its sixth and final U.S. tour of the year, again in the company of Fleetwood Mac. From his hotel room in Alexandria, Virginia, on December 9, Gillan outlined in a letter his dissatisfaction with the band, his sense that the entire Deep Purple operation had become stagnant and safe.

Glover remembers reading Gillan's letter and, although he was not quite ready to admit it, agreeing with many of the singer's sentiments. "He hit the nail right on the head," Glover said. "He cited his reasons for leaving as a lack of progression, musically. So his reasons for leaving were not personal, at least according to his letter, he just felt the band had stagnated into a formula. And we were working so ridiculously hard. We did tour after tour after tour after tour. Nineteen-seventy-two was incredibly busy — we did six separate visits to America that year, and we did a couple of albums in that same period, *Made in Japan* and *Who Do We Think We Are*. And we started 1973 right back in the thick of it, touring.

"Looking back on it," the bassist said, "it was a stunning achievement." But their schedule never allowed the band a single moment in which to sit down and iron out any problems the individual members might have been aware of. Even the news of Gillan's departure barely raised any eyebrows. Glover continued, "Ian gave [in] his notice, the management said, 'Ian's leaving,' and that was the end of it. No one bothered to ask, 'Hey, Ian, mate, why'd you want to leave? Stick around, stick it out,' that kind of talk. That didn't happen. It was, 'Oh, Ian's leaving, okay well,' end of discussion."

Jon Lord, too, acknowledged that a lack of communication lay at the heart of the breakdown. As early as 1973, in the aftermath of *Who Do We Think We Are*, he confessed to *Music Scene*, "We've been so busy since we made [*In Rock*] that we haven't really had time to sit down and consider if there was another way to go." And, a decade later, he told *Sounds*, "We were worked out of our brains, used as a license to print money by some people. We were initially willing victims, obviously, but we should have put our collective foots down to stop the bandwagon." Instead they allowed their careers to career out of control, and the only request that management (or anybody else) made of Gillan was that he remain on board until the end of June and the conclusion of the band's scheduled performances. This included lengthy tours of Europe and the U.K., close to three months on the road in the U.S., and another journey to Japan where, less than one year after the Mark II lineup's greatest performances, the same team would play its last shows.

It was an arduous outing. On the road, the band was at breaking point. Blackmore and Gillan were not even on speaking terms anymore, breaking their silences only to discuss the evening's set list. Gillan had abandoned traveling with the band, citing a newfound fear of flying as a reason for making his own way from show to show aboard a smart Fleetwood Cadillac piloted by his personal roadie, Ossie Hoppe, rather than jetting around with his bandmates. All knew that the band was cracking up, and there was nothing they could do about it.

For Ronnie Dio and Elf, watching the disintegration from the wings, the state of Deep Purple was an absolute eye-opener — and an object lesson into the true rigors of life in a successful band. "The first American tour we did with Purple was the last one with Gillan in the band," Dio recalled. "I think you go into things with some perceptions that have already been cemented in your brain, 'This is the way it's supposed to be' — at least, when you're as inexperienced as we were. And the thing that astounded us most was, Ian would stay in a different hotel to the rest of the band; he'd turn up at the gigs in a car, two or three minutes before the gig started, go onstage and do his bit, then as soon as it was over, he'd go back to his hotel again.

"We couldn't understand that. 'This isn't how bands should be!' Especially as we'd been living together in a car for the last thousand years. We just couldn't understand what the hell was going on. And then of course we did. The problems between Ian and Ritchie, that Ian had a commitment to finish the tour and he wanted to, but he didn't want to associate with Ritchie. For me, that was the most unusual thing that ever happened on the Purple tours, seeing a side of things that I just didn't know existed. I thought bands got on really well and stayed together forever. Boy, have I learned that lesson well over the years!"

In the U.S., meanwhile, the band's status as one of the biggest groups in the world — and their apparent willingness to live up to such a lofty billing — brought its own battery of difficulties, self-imposed and otherwise. Flying into the United States from Canada, they were forced to cancel a show in Boise, Idaho, after customs officials at Seattle's SeaTac airport refused to clear the band until every last piece of equipment had been physically searched, an exercise that would take the rest of the day.

Another show was lost in Las Vegas, only this time it was the band who were to blame, staging such a magnificent preshow party at their hotel that Blackmore simply didn't want to end it for the sake of just another concert. The audience responded with a riot of such magnitude that it was five years before the Convention Center organizers were willing to stage another rock'n'roll show.

A third gig, in Ithaca, ended in disarray after the venue was switched from an indoor auditorium to an outdoor football stadium, only for the city to be promptly swamped by a torrential downpour. Opening band ZZ Top played just three minutes before wading off the drenched stage, by which time, power cables were underwater and the amps and monitors were several inches deep. Of course, Deep Purple could not play under such conditions, but 70,000 concertgoers didn't see it that way. The venue was trashed and the bands' equipment looted.

The pressures piled up emotionally as much as physically, however, a disquietingly queer echo of the situation four years earlier, when Gillan (and Glover) first joined Deep Purple. Then, too, there was a sense of impatience swirling around the band as it hastened to complete its responsibilities to the work of a previous lineup and start getting to grips with its future. The big difference was that nobody yet knew exactly what that future entailed.

Back in Britain over Christmas, Blackmore reignited his solo ambitions once more, this time courting Paul Rodgers, vocalist with Free, to front the sessions. Blackmore had long admired Rodgers — back in 1972, he told the *New Musical Express*, "Free . . . are the best band in England. Paul . . . is such a good singer and a brilliant mover. He moves with the music, none of this jumping up in the air and doing the splits and all that. He just moves with the music."

Despite such praise, Rodgers turned Blackmore's offer down, but still Glover recalls, "There was a feeling in the air that Ritchie was going to leave and he was going to take Ian Paice with him. He was pretty open in his intent." So open that, finally, John Coletta and Tony Edwards called Glover and Lord alone together and tried to thrash out some kind of battle plan. Glover recalled, "They told us, 'This is ridiculous. The band's on top of the world and you're falling apart. You've got to keep it going, so see if you can get Paicey to stay with you. If Ian's going to leave and Ritchie's going to leave, fuck them, we'll get two new guys in and carry on. Are you up for it? So we said, 'Yeah.'"

Lord, too, was fully expecting Blackmore to depart: "Ritchie always had a fixed mindset, always with very strong opinions. So he became a prima donna. And when we told him that he was, in fact, part of a group, he used to say, 'So what?' So to avoid friction, we used to say 'Okay' a lot. In the end, he became the person that people thought was the most important part of Deep Purple, that he somehow personified what was Deep Purple. It was a mistake to give him that. But I think he was quite bored with rock when Ian left. . . ."

Lord, however, was not going to allow Blackmore to slip away quite so easily. "Ian Paice and myself tried to perk him up," and that, Glover said, was where things still stood some six months later, as the band moved toward the end of yet another American jaunt. But, in Jacksonville, Florida, on June 15, 1973, Glover recalled, "I just sensed something was amiss. So I cornered the management and refused to leave his room until he told me what was going on, which he did. He said, 'Well, Ritchie's decided to stay in the band . . .' and I said, 'Oh that's great. . . .' Then he said, 'But, only if *you* leave.' 'Okay, what do the others think?' 'Well, the others would like Ritchie to be in the band.'"

Glover was stunned, but not necessarily surprised. Swiftly gathering his wits about him, he simply responded, "Okay, I'm leaving then. This is my notice, thank you. I'll finish the tour, I'll be a gentleman even if you're not." Which is what he did — finished the tour and then, at the end of June, he too quit the band. That final night in Osaka, as Deep Purple left the stage, Blackmore, Lord, and Paice exited together; Gillan and Glover remained behind to bid the largely uncomprehending audience farewell. There was no encore.

Chapter 9

Burned and Mistreated

The decision to compound the loss of Gillan with the dismissal of Glover is one which, even after thirty years, still puzzles observers. On the one hand, the fact that the two had arrived as a package deal and should, therefore, depart as one, does have a strange kind of symmetry, returning the group to its founding trio and allowing them to rebuild Deep Purple according to the purest of their initial intentions.

At the same time, however, they were shedding more than simply a singer and a bass player. Although Deep Purple's writing credits were, by long-held agreement, split between the five musicians, regardless of who actually did the core writing, still Gillan and Glover's individual contributions to the band's repertoire amounted to far more than a mere one-fifth each.

Such an observation does not, of course, detract in the slightest from all that Lord, Paice, and Blackmore brought — and would continue to bring — to the brew. As far back as the band's debut, and for two more albums to come, the trio combined for some of the most spectacular performances in the group's repertoire. There is a world of difference, however, between such instrumental tours de force as "Mandrake Root," "Wring That Neck," and "Child in Time," and the concise, melodic strains of "Black Night," "Smoke on the Water," and

"Woman from Tokyo" — a world upon which Deep Purple would, henceforth, retain only the slenderest of grasps.

Watching from the sidelines, Ray Fenwick mused on the particular magic the departing pair injected into Deep Purple: "What people forget is that Roger and Ian came out of what was essentially a pop band, Episode Six. I used to see them at the Marquee a lot, when they used to support The Who. It was a very strange band, one of those bands that would have been at home in a lounge. They could turn their hands to anything." It was that adaptability that the pair brought to Deep Purple. Without them, it would become a very different band.

Blackmore's dream of getting something together with Paul Rodgers did not die with the abandonment of his solo ambitions. As he, Lord, and Paice sat down to plan the next generation of Deep Purple, the Free vocalist's name moved to the top of their list.

Since their own breakthrough in late 1968, Free had suffered an extraordinarily star-crossed existence. At their peak, during 1969–70, the band formed by four teenaged North London blues fanatics ranked among the most successful groups of the age, let alone the genre. But guitarist Paul Kossoff's battles with both drug and health problems undermined the unity that once bound the band together and, by late 1972, Free had already broken up once and were now preparing to do so again.

Founding bassist Andy Fraser had already walked, while Kossoff grew so unreliable that he, too, was perforcedly replaced. Kossoff played on just five of the eight songs on the band's latest album and, when Free set out for their next American tour in the new year, Osibisa's Wendell Jones had officially taken his place. Even before they left England, though, the band members knew it was the end of the road. Free played their final concert on February 17, 1973, at the Hollywood Sportatorium in Florida, returned home, and announced their breakup. And this time there was no going back.

Despite having been rebuffed in the past, Blackmore contacted Paul Rodgers about Deep Purple's vacant microphone. In the meantime, another piece of the Deep Purple jigsaw appeared to have slotted into place when the U.K. music press declared, in May, that Phil Lynott was being lined to replace Glover. Deep Purple's management were swift to scotch that story; they then denied that the group was also pursuing Trapeze bassist/vocalist Glenn Hughes. That rumor, however, would not lie down quite so easily, even though it sounded grossly improbable.

Born in Cannock, Staffs, on August 21, 1952, the twenty-one-year-old Hughes was certainly one of the country's most respected bassists (he'd already turned down an invitation to join the nascent Electric Light Orchestra). But his style and interests seemed light years removed from Deep Purple's. Trapeze's most recent album, *You Are the Music, We Are the Band*, was little short of a journey into the very heart of American funk, its rhythmic soul — fired by Hughes' deep-seated love of funk and R&B — shaped not only by the endless months the band had spent touring the United States, but also by their decision to relocate to Los Angeles.

Other considerations, too, weighed against the likelihood of Hughes joining Deep Purple. After years of Hughes combining his bass duties with vocals, Trapeze had just recruited a new bassist, Peter Mackie, freeing Hughes to concentrate fully on his singing and indulge in a little rhythm-guitar-playing as well. Asked for his thoughts on his future with the band he'd coformed in 1968, Hughes said simply, "We're really looking forward to getting the new lineup underway." Planning was well-advanced for the band's fourth album, and their American profile was soaring. If Deep Purple — or anybody else, for that matter — were looking for a new bassist, clearly they would have to look elsewhere.

But at the end of May 1973, with the denials still ringing loud in the music press, Blackmore, Lord, and Paice flew Hughes — at that time resting in Texas between shows with Trapeze — to New York, where Deep Purple were wrapping up two nights at the Felt Forum. Meeting at the Plaza Hotel, they formally invited him to join the band.

Hughes accepted, but not quite in the role the trio was expecting. He *would* become the band's new bassist, but only if he could become lead vocalist as well, replicating his original role in Trapeze and reducing Deep Purple to an absolutely unfamiliar quartet.

It was an interesting suggestion, but one that his prospective employers could not go along with. Of all Deep Purple's chosen roles, that of virtuosi was one they simply could not foresee relinquishing. Musicians were recruited to the band on the strengths of their abilities on one chosen instrument. There was no possibility of them dividing that strength in any other way. However, Hughes remained their first — their only — choice to fill Glover's boots, and so a compromise was reached, electing Hughes into what hindsight swiftly revealed to be the inconclusive role of "second" singer, with the promise that his duties would increase as time went by.

Meanwhile, Paul Rodgers was still being actively courted as the band's new lead vocalist and, this time, when the news was leaked to the music press, there were few convincing denials. Only Rodgers himself seemed less than certain — as Free fell apart, he and drummer Simon Kirke had agreed that they, at least, should continue working together. Deep Purple's offer would involve negating that promise, and Rodgers was not at all comfortable about it.

Swaying his opinion, too, was another possibility opened up in recent months, as guitarist Mick Ralphs quit Mott the Hoople and began making his own overtures toward Rodgers. Soon they were writing and demoing together but, more importantly, they had all but grown up alongside one another. As an Island Records labelmate for much of Ralphs' time with Mott, Rodgers instinctively knew he had far more in common with Ralphs' casual bluesiness than he ever would with Deep Purple's bellowing pomp, and while he agreed to think about Blackmore's offer, his mind was already made up. He delivered his decision a few days later, then joined Ralphs and Simon Kirke in Bad Company.

With Rodgers' refusal, Deep Purple's future seemed seriously in doubt — so much so that full "Purple to part" rumors were already circulating both at home and in the U.S. Hastening to calm the uncertainty, the band formally announced Hughes' recruitment on July 10, 1973 — only for Paice to then muddy the speculative waters when he remarked, that same day, that announcements regarding *two* further members would follow shortly.

Two? Behind the scenes, the core of Deep Purple was in absolute disarray. Jon Lord, never comfortable with what he saw as the abrupt dismissal of Glover, and increasingly wary of Blackmore's apparently dictatorial attitude toward the band's leadership, was himself considering his future with Deep Purple. He later admitted that, when he first learned of the departures, his response was, "Well, that's the end of the band." The idea of simply replacing the errant members never even occurred to him: "We'd already replaced [the singer and the bassist] once; we couldn't do it again." Even after his bandmates assured him they could, he remained unconvinced.

Lord's position was strengthened by the knowledge that a new career awaited him in the realm of further classical works. He was already in discussion with German conductor Eberhard Schoener regarding a new work based around a favorite piece by Johann Sebastian Bach, while the clamor for successors to both the concerto and *The Gemini Suite* had never been stilled.

At the same time, however, the arrival of Hughes, and the promise of fresh directions and dimensions calmed his uncertainties somewhat, while management also offered some convincing fiscal arguments for him to hang in there. Finally, Lord agreed not to make any irrevocable decisions until a new vocalist was decided on. Assuming that the band ever found anybody they liked.

Subtle advertisements in the U.K. music press precipitated a flood of cassettes from budding hopefuls, none of whom knew the identity of the group they were trying out for until they walked into the audition room. Other tapes were received from aspirants responding to the continued stories in the music press, a barrage that ranged from the expected battalion of Gillan soundalikes to a fifteen-year-old from Bournemouth who figured that, if you're going to join a band, you should at least start with one that had made it.

Patiently, John Coletta would weed out the most blatant time-wasters before playing the survivors to the band, but still it was an arduous process — so much so that, at one point, Hughes' dream of fronting a four-piece Deep Purple actually returned for serious discussion.

Amid so much swine, however, there lay one pearl — a tape from a Middlesbrough-based singer whose gainful employ at the local 36 Boutique disguised an ambition that was pushed sky-high by a chance comment uttered four years earlier, when his band, the Government, had supported Deep Purple in Bradford. David Coverdale seriously doubted whether Jon Lord would even remember him, but he mentioned the meeting in his cover note regardless. As it turned out, Lord remembered the Government very well indeed. What he could not recall was what the singer looked like — and Coverdale apparently had no intention of reminding him. When the next post brought the requested photograph, it revealed a twelve-year-old clad in his Boy Scouts uniform.

Neither was Coverdale's resumé especially impressive. Born on September 22, 1951, in the northern seaside town of Saltburn, he had spent his entire career flitting between sundry local part-timers: Magdalene, Denver Mule, the Skyliners, the Government — all were little more than covers bands for whom the peak of ambition was a respectable support slot (such as the Deep Purple show) or occasional outings as the backing band for passing singers. Neither could the singer point to any real studio experience. The Government did cut a four-song demo, of which they pressed up twenty-five vinyl copies, but Coverdale's lack of training was revealed by the tape he sent to Deep Purple — an absolute mess built around two songs he had apparently recorded after a few pints too many, and two more cuts with his latest band, the unfortunately named Fabuloso Brothers.

"The song was nothing to remember for very long, but the voice was exactly what we wanted. I remember that there was a horn section and that you could hear people talk," Lord laughed. But, as he, Paice, and Blackmore listened to the cassette, each felt there was sufficient promise in the *feel* of the vocal, if not its actual delivery, to justify inviting Coverdale to London for an audition at the band's chosen retreat, Scorpio Sound, near the Euston railroad station.

All the way down from Middlesbrough, that morning in August 1973, Coverdale was terrified — a mood that was only amplified when he walked into the studio and heard the band jamming. Even words of reassurance from Lord and Blackmore could not kill his nerves; nor could attempts to lead him through a variety of old rock'n'roll numbers. But when things settled down for a relatively straightforward version of Paul McCartney's "Yesterday," Coverdale finally overcame his fears. By the time the band dropped him off at his hotel later that evening, he was already feeling quietly confident — and they were all but convinced they'd found their man.

Only a perceived lack of rock'n'roll style gave them pause for thought. Looking back on Coverdale's audition, everybody present could reel off an apparently damning directory of misgivings, ranging from cross-eyes and spots to a horrendous dress sense and a pronounced weight problem. Clearly, if Coverdale was to become Deep Purple's new frontman, he would require a serious overhaul.

Yet the daunting prospect of that task was overwhelmed by the delightful prospect of having him in the group. Vocally he was everything they had hoped for, and personality-wise he fit right in. With a new wardrobe, a fresh haircut, a sensible diet, and the loss of a few pounds, there was absolutely nothing standing in Coverdale's way. A week after his audition, at the end of August, the singer was asked to join Deep Purple. At almost exactly the same time, Lord announced that he, too, was staying. The infusion of such new blood delivered precisely the fillip he'd been searching for.

Rehearsals for the band's future commenced immediately. By early September, Deep Purple were ensconced within the palatial surroundings of Clearwell Castle in Gloucestershire, rehearsing in the basement of the baronial pile. Having once again drawn Coverdale out of his nervous shell, they were already writing their first songs. Coverdale himself had arrived with a handful of lyrics already in place, "Sail Away" and "Soldier of Fortune" among them. Now, when Blackmore requested accompaniment for a new piece he'd formulated, based around a riff he'd distilled from Glenn Miller's "Fascinating Rhythm," Coverdale leaped into action, handing over not one, not two, but *seven* separate sets of words. One in particular caught everybody's eye. It was called "Burn," and would become the title track of Deep Purple's next album.

Further material followed rapidly. Coverdale's "Sail Away" was vigorously reworked to become a moderately funky workout that more than presages Led Zeppelin's later "Trampled Underfoot." It also raised further wry eyebrows when one compared Coverdale's assuredly bluesy vocals with those of the singer who got away, Paul Rodgers.

"Lay Down Stay Down," a cunning construct that echoed elements of the recently emergent Queen, was another high, while a new live showcase was built around Blackmore's ultra-epic "Mistreated," another bluesy number that quickly erupts into a truly incandescent guitar workout that effortlessly erases the memory of any past Deep Purple party piece. And so on. By the time the band was ready to depart Clearwell, the entire album was all but in place — just one more song arrived once the band was actually in the studio, when Jon Lord decided he wanted to try something on a synthesizer and conjured the instrumental "A 200." (The title, incidentally, referred to an ointment used to soothe nasty infestations of the nether regions.)

After the hellacious atmosphere within which Lord, Paice, and Blackmore had lived for so long, the mood surrounding the new lineup was so buoyant that, when management suggested throwing Clearwell open to the media on September 23, there wasn't even a tremor of misgiving. And so, as the rehearsal period neared its end, Deep Purple Mark III was unveiled to the European and British press, trainloads of reporters and photographers converging upon Clearwell to cast their eyes over the newcomers.

It was Coverdale who received the most attention in the ensuing stories — the Cinderella saga of how he was plucked from absolute obscurity to front one of the biggest rock bands in the world wasn't merely a fairytale, after all. It was all but unheard of — had any band in Deep Purple's position ever foregone the traditional superrecruit route in favor of blooding a total newcomer? Even Gillan was a partially known quantity, at least among the people who take note of such things. Blackmore, however, made it clear that it was the unknown quality he most craved. "I wanted a new band," he said. "I didn't want to [just] get a new singer in and carry on where we'd left off."

That said, plans for the new Deep Purple album rested very much on it retaining the hard-rock sound the band was best associated with — a dismissal not only of the more progressive strains that Gillan had wanted to bring into the band, and which *In Rock* and *Machine Head* had packed in spades, but also of the fundamental body swerve that Hughes envisioned introducing. Indeed, work on *Burn* would even return the group to Montreaux, the scene of their greatest metal triumph, parking the Rolling Stones Mobile outside a recently constructed conference center, wherein the band could simply let rip.

Reflecting on the ensuing sessions later in the year, Lord insisted, "The basic difference [between this album and its predecessors] is the use of the vocals. There is a different vocal approach. It's much freer and looser, a progression that's noticeable to us, though I don't know if it is to the audience. Also, no casino burned down during the recording."

Glenn Hughes had already undertaken his own induction into life within Deep Purple, when he accompanied Lord to Munich for a one-off performance of *The Gemini Suite* at the Circus Krone on October 4; two months later, with *Burn* complete, the entire band flew to Denmark for their full live debut, at Copenhagen's KB Hallen on December 9, 1973 (a show the previous evening, in Aarhus, was canceled after the group's gear failed to turn up).

It was a nerve-racking affair. Coverdale admitted he was terrified, and even Hughes, with all his experience of massive crowds from Trapeze's manifold American tours, seemed taken aback by the sheer magnitude of the event. But they pulled it off. With Hughes and Coverdale forming a full frontal vocal assault, both harmonizing with one another and trading verses ("Smoke on the Water" would develop into a gripping showcase for both men's voices); with Blackmore and Lord pulling out every stop they could lay their hands on; and with Paice laying down a positive barrage of rhythm, all the nervousness in the world could not drag the party down. The night was an unadulterated triumph.

But the event took its toll the following day, when the band dropped by a local studio to cut a new song, "Coronarias Redig," intended as the B-side of their next, oddly chosen single, "Might Just Take Your Life." The backing track was complete when the band suddenly realized that their singer, physically and mentally exhausted by the events of the past twenty-four hours, had slept through almost the entire session. They awoke him, only to discover that his throat had closed up. Hastily, the recording was rearranged as an instrumental, with Blackmore taking a lengthy guitar solo over the melody line, and Coverdale's exertions were restricted to a few ooh's and aah's in tandem with Hughes.

As 1973 drifted into 1974, Deep Purple played a handful more European shows, the prelude to their next American tour. It was a propitious time to visit. According to the trade publication *Billboard*, Deep Purple ended 1973 as the year's best-selling albums act, as *Machine Head* and *Made in Japan* soared beyond platinum status, *Who Do We Think We Are* went gold, and even *Purple Passages*, a compilation drawn from the band's long-deleted first three albums, cracked the Top 60 and spent five months on the charts. In a year that history remembers only for Pink Floyd's *Dark Side of the Moon* commencing its endless chart residency, for Elton John scoring two successive No. 1's, and for Led Zeppelin going reggae on *Houses of the Holy*, Deep Purple trumped them all. And every prediction insisted they could only get bigger.

Once again, however, the band reckoned without the curse of ill health that seemed to haunt their every visit to the United States. This time, it was Jon Lord who succumbed, ignoring a pain in his side for two weeks before all but collapsing following the group's January 26 show at the Dusseldorf Philipshalle. He flew home, where he was diagnosed with acute appendicitis, an ailment that normally requires nothing more than a minor operation, followed by recuperation of a week or so. Unfortunately, the wound turned septic and he ended up flat on his back for five weeks.

"It's getting like a bloody circus," Blackmore bemoaned. "Every time we [come] over to America, somebody would come down with something and we'd have to go home. It was usually me. I couldn't take the American environment. Living in hotels and eating no vegetables was no good for me. Touring used to bring me down mentally, as well, which would lower my resistance, and I'd catch anything that was going around — hepatitis or something like that. And if I didn't get it, somebody else would. . . ."

The American tour was bumped back a full month, finally kicking off in Detroit on March 3, 1974. It was Coverdale's first visit to the United States and, twenty years later, he swore, "I will never forget it. Two nights at Cobo, breathtaking. I landed in New York, and then Blackmore and me flew over together to Detroit. That was in the days when there wasn't enough fuel to get you all the way!" (The OPEC oil embargo was in full swing at that time.)

But while the band's first visit in over six months sold out in near record time, that ill-starred false start quickly assumed darkly portentous overtones. At the earliest shows, audiences started out skeptical and occasionally wound up hostile. The group hadn't simply changed its lineup, it had changed the very character that had once so distinguished it, on vinyl and, more pronouncedly, in concert.

It wasn't something you could precisely place your finger on — more the sense of unease derived from sitting in a sea of several thousand people, for whom the only thing that matters is obeying the repeated demands from the stage: "Have a good time — woooo!"; "Get up on your feet — wooooo!" Once, Deep Purple had moved the crowd with the power of music alone. Now, it seemed, that wasn't enough, and Hughes and Coverdale seemed to spend as much time exhorting the crowd to enjoy themselves ("Wooooo!") as giving them a reason to actually do so.

And it worked. By the end of the decade, and increasingly thereafter, the hard-rock scene positively seethed with apparently successful frontmen who did nothing but remind their audience what a great time they were having, and they sold an awful lot of records doing so. Forget stagecraft, forget dynamics, forget even a modicum of musical personality. So long as it could convince a stadium full of kids that they were having the time of their lives, a plank of wood could become a superstar.

At the outset of the American tour, it was more than likely nerves, as opposed to a lack of nuance, that drew such utterances out of Hughes and Coverdale. Faced with a crowd of 10,000 kids, all baying for a blood rush to the head, if you can convince them that they're having fun, even if it's just the bunch of knuckleheads with the loudest lungs, then it's easier to convince yourself as well. And what better way to find out than to ask them?

But the fans who weren't knuckleheads, though, those who knew something more than "Smoke on the Water" and a clutch of glossy photographs in *Circus* or *Creem*, saw that as the easy way out. Deep Purple's reputation was built on generating flash and excitement by being themselves, on their music's embodiment of all that should be held most precious about rock's power to move or soothe the soul. Had all that truly been distilled into nothing more than a routine series of shouts and gestures?

From the stage, such discontent might have been muted, but it was certainly palpable, and it needed to be fixed. Quickly. "Up against the wall of prejudice," *Circus'* Jon Tiven reported, "the new members [have] been pressured by the demand of longtime fans into mimicking the Purple of old — the sounds and pacing of Gillan and Glover." Drop the posturing, cut down on the *wooo*ing and, though it certainly contradicted the band's attempts to make a fresh start, cut out the attempts to take old songs someplace new.

Hughes, in particular, came under the microscope. His vocal range already lent itself to vague comparison; now, the transmutation was almost perfect, as Blackmore marveled later in the tour: "He['s] taken over Gillan's face. He['s] taken that slot."

The ghosts of Deep Purple past were not to have it all their own way, however. Material drawn from the newly (February 1974) released *Burn* dominated the live set, dispatching some of the most sainted songs in the group's entire canon out to grass. Audiences tried resisting that change as well, but on this point, the band's determination was immutable. *Burn* would go on to become Deep Purple's biggest American hit since *Machine Head*.

Elsewhere, too, there was much room for optimism. In the pages of the mainstream music media, the excitement surrounding the induction of two new members was such that, at times, it was difficult to believe there had ever been any other lineup. Roger Glover, following Deep Purple's progress from afar, recalled, "I was most vexed when we became *Billboard*'s biggest-selling artist, and there was a photo of David Coverdale and Glenn Hughes. They hadn't even done a gig yet, and there they were. Because that was my achievement, and Gillan's achievement. They had nothing to do with that."

The bassist was swift, however, to proffer credit where credit was due: "I listened to *Burn* with as open an ear as I could, and I liked some of it. I liked 'Sail Away' and I liked 'Might Just Take Your Life.' I thought those two were very good. After all, I'm a fan of these people, I'm a fan of the way Ritchie played and Jon played and Paicey played, they're my idols. Ritchie's still my idol — what he did with the band back then, it's magnificent."

Compared to past Deep Purple tours, the 1974 American outing was organized with almost military precision. Nothing was left in the lap of the gods, no expense was spared. The band's equipment was upgraded, limousine and hotel bookings were checked and double-checked, media saturation was guaranteed in every town they visited, and the group's comforts were guaranteed with the hiring of what was described as "the largest, most luxurious, and most expensive private jetliner in the world," a hypercustomized Boeing 707 appropriately christened *Starship I*. With the band's name added to the aircraft's already distinctive livery, *Starship I* would become almost as grand an attraction as the band themselves, attracting hordes of sightseers wherever it touched down.

Jon Lord spoke for each of his bandmates as he luxuriated in the aircraft's commodities. "It's a 707 put together by a firm in L.A. that

Sinatra, Dylan, and the Band just used and Elton John uses," he said. "It has a lounge, a bedroom, a shower, a fireplace, and a study. It's supposed to look as little like a plane as possible."

Stretching out over a full month, the spring tour promised many highlights — Madison Square Garden on March 13 and Nassau Coliseum four nights later were early highs, with the latter burning itself into the memory after Carmine Appice and Tim Bogart, former members of long-ago Deep Purple idols Vanilla Fudge, accompanied the band onstage for the encores. In terms of sheer immensity, however, the ultimate peak was reached on April 6, when Deep Purple joined the bill for the largest outdoor festival of the decade so far, a twelve-hour extravaganza called the California Jam.

Staged at the vast Ontario Speedway, the California Jam was the brainchild of the ABC television network, whose weekly *In Concert* broadcast was already one of the most highly regarded rock programs in American TV history. The California Jam would become a part of that series, broadcast in hourlong blocks over the next two months, and the lineup for the event left nobody in any doubt that the expenses involved in setting up the show would easily be recouped.

Modern audiences might remain stoically unmoved at the prospect of spending an evening in the company of funk bands Earth Wind & Fire and Rare Earth, or country-poppers Seals & Croft. But Jim Dandy's hyper-active Black Oak Arkansas had long ago confirmed themselves as among the most exciting live bands in America, the Eagles were reconfirming the ascendancy of what would soon become known as the West Coast sound, and nobody needed convincing of the attributes of the evening's headliners: Deep Purple were joined by Black Sabbath, as they rode the visceral peaks of their *Sabbath Bloody Sabbath* masterpiece, and Emerson Lake & Palmer, at the height of their *Brain Salad Surgery*-inspired extravagance. Add a crowd of over 200,000, paying between $10 and $15 apiece for tickets, and the California Jam didn't simply live up to all the advance hype, it surpassed most expectations before the first band even took the stage.

But the California Jam takes on further-reaching significance with hindsight. Although none could have known it at the time, for each of the three acts topping the bill, the festival represented an *annus mirabilis* to which none would ever return.

Black Sabbath would complete just three more albums, the frankly disappointing *Sabotage* and *Technical Ecstasy*, and the extraordinarily inaptly titled *Never Say Die*, before they did finally cry uncle and shed figurehead vocalist Ozzy Osbourne. Emerson Lake & Palmer would not release another record until 1977, when the overbearing *Works* plopped pompously onto a mainstream that had lost patience with the horse-headed precocity that was the trio's raison d'être. And Deep Purple were about to pitch into a season of such absolute turbulence that, within two years, the group would have utterly imploded.

The California Jam, however, lay far from such dour scenarios. The largest audience any of the participating bands had ever performed before was also the most ecstatic, buoyed not only by the tremendous sense of occasion built up around the event, but also by the sheer efficiency of the day. Dispensing altogether with time-consuming breakdowns or between-act holdups, the organizers had three separate stages chugged around the venue on specially laid railway lines — one being set up, one being dismantled, and one being performed upon. The concert raced past so smoothly that, as the end of the festival came in sight, it was actually running an hour or so *ahead* of schedule.

And that was where the problems began. Negotiating their appearance at the event, for which they were being paid a staggering £135,000, Deep Purple were offered the choice of either closing the show or taking the stage as night began to fall. They opted for the earlier billing, which would allow them to escape the Speedway unencumbered by departing crowds of festivalgoers, yet still employ their full arsenal of pyrotechnic effects.

Now, however, dusk was far from falling when Deep Purple were ordered onstage. So they refused to go — or, at least, Blackmore refused. The remainder of the band simply drifted away or busied themselves making complicated adjustments to their instruments, painstakingly ignoring the increasingly belligerent cajoling of both the festival organizers and their own record company reps.

The minutes ticked by. Outside, the audience had passed beyond restlessness and was now turning decidedly ugly. They had been promised and, thus far received, a day of seamless entertainment — and now this. But Deep Purple would not budge. Finally, after forty-five minutes of fruitless head-butting, the promoters played their final card. If Deep Purple did not take the stage immediately, they would be dropped from the bill.

It was a critical moment. Blackmore remained resolute that the band had been contracted to take the stage at a certain time, and would adhere to that contract, come hell or high water; the promoters were equally adamant that Deep Purple's part in the show was now canceled and the band would pay the consequences. Suddenly, Deep Purple roadie Ossie Hoppe leaped onto the stage, grabbed the microphone, and, with all eyes turned toward him, shouted, "Do you want to see Deep Purple?" The roar that arose from the assembled masses left nobody in doubt as to who had won the backstage impasse. Ten minutes later, as the California skies finally began to darken, Deep Purple stepped out beneath the huge wooden rainbow that spanned the stage, to the loudest reception of the show so far.

The performance that followed was a revelation, certainly one of the finest Mark iii-era outings to have been preserved on either video or audio. From the now-traditional set-opener "Burn" on, Deep Purple are buoyant and playful — "We'd like to play a number from what's-its-name," announced a suddenly stage-front Jon Lord, "and my man Ritchie's gonna play it for you . . . in a minute." Blackmore then launched into a graceful, gentle improvisation, before lurching without warning into a meat-grinding "Smoke on the Water." Later in the show, as "You Fool No One" extended through its marathon midriff, the guitarist came close . . . so close . . . to dropping the anthemic chimes of "School's Out" into the mix; and there were moments during "Space Truckin'" when he looked positively angelic, lost in a world completely of his own as he gently fuzzed "Greensleeves."

The battle between guitarist and organizers, however, was by no means over. As "Space Truckin'" began to think about winding down, a cameraman chose to ignore Blackmore's requests that he stop weaving between the guitarist and the audience — a condition the group had laid down before the performance started.

Blackmore initially seemed determined to ignore the slight, as he launched into the prelude to his grand finale demolition derby, bodily scraping his guitar against the lip of the stage, then dangling it into the pit below. When the lead popped out and the guitar plunged to the ground, Blackmore simply scurried to the back of the stage to collect another instrument, took a few steps toward the cameraman with his face still set in an impassive mask, and then all hell broke loose. Turning on the encroaching camera, he delivered a succession of weighty blows — to its hood, its body, its eye. In the official film of the event, there is one priceless image shot through the offending lens, Blackmore's face a mass of fury, as the guitar neck closes in for the kill.

The attack was over in seconds, the shattered guitar flying into the crowd, while Blackmore collected a third instrument and began grinding it with his boot heel. Then, as if the performance still demanded a spec-tacularly explosive close, Blackmore's roadie, Ron Quinton, put a light to the trays of petrol that had surreptitiously been placed around the speakers. Two massive explosions rent the air, knocking Blackmore off his feet and momentarily igniting his hair. On film, the guitarist seems not to notice, to be simply dancing forward through the flames — it's only in slow motion that you start wondering where Michael Jackson got the idea for that infamous Pepsi commercial. Unperturbed, Blackmore then begins hurling souvenirs off the stage. Pieces of guitar, amps, a monitor, anything he can lift comes hurtling away, while police, fire marshals, and promoters scurry around furiously, threatening every form of retribution they can imagine.

Blackmore only narrowly escaped arrest as John Coletta rushed him off the stage and into a waiting helicopter just moments ahead of the police, flew him to the band's hotel, and then deposited him in a limo, to race out of Ontario County before the law could catch up with him. Elsewhere, however, the legal repercussions of the performance seemed daunting, as a small army of complainants rose up to threaten lawsuits. A stagehand caught off-guard by the explosions led the coterie of onlookers who claimed to have been deafened by the bangs. The cameraman was suing; the promoters, of course, were suing — at one point, even Emerson Lake & Palmer looked like joining the litigious parade, claiming Deep Purple's set had so disrupted the festival that their own performance had suffered.

In fact, Blackmore's antics only pushed ELP to even greater heights than usual. Taking the stage at 1 AM, the trio grasped an audience numbed by the bitterly cold desert night and thrilled them with what drummer Carl Palmer now describes as their greatest performance. Certainly nobody could upstage Keith Emerson's own final party piece, as he strapped himself to a grand piano, levitated several feet off the ground, and then, still playing, proceeded to execute a string of somersaults.

In fact, the entire commotion eventually settled down, until Deep Purple were saddled with nothing more than a $5,000 bill for the broken camera. But for John Coletta, the California Jam was a watershed that he had no intention of revisiting. He would never accompany Deep Purple on the road again.

The California Jam represents a high point not only in the career of the Mark III Deep Purple, but also in that of Deep Purple itself. Never again would they appear before such a vast audience, first onstage, then via the ABC TV broadcasts, and onto a regular stream of home-video, laser-disc, and DVD releases. Unquestionably, too, the sheer theater of the event translated into record sales — *Burn* continued to blaze up the charts, and the band's back catalog spiked sharply as well. As usual, however, the group had little time in which to rest upon its laurels.

At the end of April, Deep Purple launched their longest U.K. tour yet, a month-plus outing that included three separate London shows (at the Hammersmith Odeon, Lewisham Odeon, and the Kilburn Gaumont). The group earned widespread acclaim for doggedly sticking to the traditional circuit of theaters and ballrooms, rather than moving their show into the vast aircraft hangers now favored by so many other bands in their position.

As usual, however (will these people never learn?), the workload had its downside, as tensions that might have been suppressed under more relaxed conditions, began to flare — this time between the two newest members of the band. No longer the shy, fat underachiever who had once needed half an hour of cajoling before he'd even open his mouth, David Coverdale had transformed into the Rock God personified. On and off the road, he lived the lifestyle that his position apparently demanded — "a mass," as one backstage autograph hunter put it, "of ego and testosterone."

No strangers to the carnal (and otherwise) benefits of life in a top rock band, the rest of the band blithely tolerated Coverdale's uninhibited delight in the world that had opened up before him. But they could not deny, either, that Coverdale's embrace of his status was undermining one of the band's own intentions — that Glenn Hughes should occasionally be allowed to move out of the frontman's shadows and take his own turn at the microphone. The bassist had swallowed his discontent during the *Burn* sessions and the ensuing tours, believing that the situation would resolve itself as time passed. In fact, the only concrete resolution that transpired was Coverdale's insistence that, having been recruited as the band's lead singer, that was what he was. The conflict would simmer, increasingly violently, for the remainder of the pair's career together.

Chapter 10

A Rainbow After the Storm

A wealth of more contemporary commentators insist that the most sensible approach to all of the problems that, once again, were building up within Deep Purple would have been for the band to take a break. Gone, after all, were the days when performers were expected to deliver x number of singles and albums a year — by 1974, even a two-year gap between new releases was readily acceptable to an audience conditioned to believe that much of that time was devoted to crafting ever more grandiose projects.

The powers that guided Deep Purple, however, simply would not — or could not — allow the group any such luxury. *Burn* was still high on both the American and U.K. charts, and already the group was preparing to return to Clearwell, to commence rehearsing their next album, which was scheduled for release before the end of the year.

Interviewed backstage at London's Hammersmith Odeon in May 1974, Ritchie Blackmore loudly bemoaned the demands being placed on the band to continue coming up with new material. "I write most of the stuff," he said, then confessed that, in his opinion, "some of it stinks. We only get away with it because we're so good musically." He wanted at least a year between albums, and talked of a time when he could simply play when he wanted to, make records when he wanted to.

He spoke, too, of his longing for a return to a simpler rock'n'roll life, one where he could simply go out there and have some fun, and not feel that his every action had repercussions for a veritable battalion of accomplices and accountants. And it was a longing that was only strengthened every night on tour, as he drifted to the side of the stage to watch Elf, once again booked in as support, run through their paces.

Ronnie Dio recalled, "He loved the attitude we had, because we were just these devil-may-care guys. We had a new drummer on the second Purple tour — we arrived in Amsterdam. He went out and bought some clogs, then fell off and broke his ankle, and this was before the tour even started. But we forgave him because that's who he was.

"He was the kind of guy who . . . at one point he poked himself in the eye with a drumstick while he was playing. We had a gig to do the next day and our thing was, unless your legs and arms have been chopped off, you've got to do the gig. So he went to the doctor and he was given some kind of medication to put in his eye . . . and he put it in the wrong eye! So he couldn't see out of either one. And that's just what Elf were. We were hick-friendly. We persevered through it all, and everybody liked that. They liked our work ethic, the fact we always were happy, the fact we had a good time. Rock'n'roll to us was always supposed to be about being a great band, but if you're not having fun while you're doing it, then what the hell are you out there for?"

That was the question Blackmore was increasingly asking himself — and it was answered when he stumbled into the aftermath of a particularly riotous party at a Coventry hotel the evening before the final show of the May 1974 U.K. tour. The event — a massive affair that took over the hotel ballroom and brought record company executives in from all over the world — was staged to present Deep Purple with all the gold and platinum discs they had accrued since the last such bash. Elf, of course, were among the revelers, but as the rest of the party wound down, theirs was only beginning.

The hotel bar had long since been closed, but Dio was tiny enough to slip through the gate and take up bartending for the rest of the night. By 5 in the morning, Elf and the two bands' road crews were so drunk that it was the most natural thing in the world to find themselves sitting naked in a hotel corridor, watching drummer Gary Driscoll cradle a fire extinguisher.

Only when a fellow guest, a little old lady down the hallway, peeped out of her room to find out what all the noise was about did the party break up, at which point Driscoll slipped into the bathroom of his hotel room and accidentally dropped the fire extinguisher into the toilet bowl. The porcelain shattered, unleashing a flood that soon cascaded into the rooms below, and, just two hours later, the entire Elf crew was being awakened by the local police, summoned not simply to evict the band from the hotel, but from the city of Coventry. And Elf's insistence that they had a concert to play that evening could not sway the lawmen's judgment.

Chastened, Elf retreated to the city airport, where they spent the rest of the day wondering how management would react to news of their behavior, already splashed across local TV and radio, and soon to be all over the national papers as well. And, when they finally arrived at the venue, it was as bad as they'd imagined. "We were sure we were going to get the elbow, sent back to America, dropped from the label," Dio shuddered, "and, sure enough, in came one of the managers and he said, 'That's it, you're out of here.'

"Then, suddenly, he went silent. We turned around, and there was Ritchie in the doorway. 'That was the greatest thing I have ever heard of in my life. Keep doing that, you cannot buy that kind of publicity.' And the manager was, 'Yeah! It was great, keep it up, everything's really cool!' So we never got fired because Ritchie really liked it. He loved us because we did crazy things. . . ." Crazy things that he so rarely got to do himself, because he was too busy buckling down to the demands of simply being in his own band.

For Coverdale and Hughes, such strains were still wildly novel. While Blackmore grabbed what time off he could, they spent the few days' vacation they did have, in late May and early June, working alongside Lord as he brought his latest classical/rock fusion to fruition, staging the now-completed Bach collaboration at the Eurovision presentation of Prix Jeunesse on June 1, 1974, in Munich.

Two pieces were to be premiered: the presumptuously intended "Continuo on B.A.C.H." and "Windows," a lengthy piece built around a Far Eastern renga (a form of chain poetry) and highlighted, for longtime Lord watchers, by large swaths of the vocal segment of his earlier *Gemini Suite*.

It was enacted by both a seven-piece rock band and the orchestra of the Munich Chamber Opera, and the inclusion of Coverdale and Hughes in the band was an intriguing decision that said as much, perhaps, for Lord's talents as a peacemaker as for their suitability to the project. By showing that both men were equally valued, Lord might have hoped to defuse their internecine rivalry. He did so, however, at the expense of the project itself. Though more or less ideal for this latest incarnation of Deep Purple, neither musician was what one would call subtle, with Coverdale's histrionic bellowing, in particular, distracting from the moods the two pieces were so patently attempting to maintain. Indeed, of the photos from the concert that bedeck the ensuing LP jacket, one speaks louder than many words. It depicts Coverdale in full vocal flight, while the horn player beside him raises his eyes, apparently heavenward.

There were other problems, too. Ray Fenwick, guitarist at the event, recalled, "I remember [Eberhard Schoener] saying the orchestra were having great trouble playing with a rhythm section. They were always a bit behind. Eberhard was saying, 'You must listen to the bass drum,' and all these guys were thinking, 'It's not quite the sort of bass drum that we're used to.' But it worked out really well in the end."

The manner in which the performance came together on the night was especially spectacular for the featured players. Jon Lord had *Windows* in mind when he confessed, "I did a couple of pieces after the concerto where I had no chance to hear anything until the first rehearsal . . . and I think all you can do, or what I do, and still do, is if I hear a sound in my head and I can't feel how to make it work — this combination or that combination — I will go back to the masters. . . . I'll read a . . . Tchaikovsky score or Beethoven to find out how they did it. I find that absolutely essential. You have to go back to the [original]. That's how they did it. That's the process. . . . One generation takes from the previous one, builds on it, and passes it on to the next."

"We did some rehearsals beforehand," Fenwick continued. "Jon sent out all the parts, everything was scored, and there were the little ideas that he wanted for it — 'This is where you play a solo,' that sort of thing. Then we got together and worked things out, and it's amazing that, when we got to Munich, it did all fit together. We knew all our bits without the orchestra . . . all the parts were bar-numbered, so you knew that on bar

40, the orchestra was going to come in — and, sure enough, on bar 40 the orchestra appeared.

"So it was all worked out, but it was still an amazing thing when you've rehearsed it without the orchestra, to have them come in on the night, because that was the first time we heard the full thing. And not only was it the orchestra, it was the opera as well. It all came together very well, and what amazed me about the album is there were very few mistakes on it. Nothing was touched up afterward, it was all exactly as it was played on the night."

Ironically, that very proficiency sparked one of the few sour points in the entire affair. There was to be just one performance of the two pieces, and, though the event was recorded, Lord intended that the ensuing album should be issued in Germany alone. As soon as they heard the finished tapes, however, EMI, Purple Records' distributor, disagreed, sensing far wider potential and ultimately arranging a worldwide release. "It was out of my hands," Lord complained to the *New Musical Express*. "I'm not at all positive that it makes a particularly necessary album. I've had less to do with it than any other thing I've done."

Making the most of his free time, Lord also found the opportunity to link with Tony Ashton to record an album of their own, the keyboard extravaganza *First of the Big Bands*. But, finally, Deep Purple reconvened at Clearwell in July 1974, with plans for the new album marching resolutely toward the group's most ambitious offering yet. Having helped pioneer the now-standard notion of double live albums, Deep Purple were considering making their next studio set a similar length. Word was out that both Led Zeppelin (*Physical Graffiti*) and Genesis (*The Lamb Lies Down on Broadway*) were planning similarly vast projects for the new year; Yes (*Tales from Topographic Oceans*) had already unleashed one. It seemed important that Deep Purple take this same step into the realms of creativity-beyond-the-call-of-duty.

There were other forces at work, however, beyond a simple need to keep up with the neighbors. At a time when, again, many of Deep Purple's peers were blithely pumping out solo albums in between their band projects (the Moody Blues and, again, Yes led the charge), Jon Lord alone had found a successful conduit for his private ambitions. But Blackmore continued to harbor notions of a solo album, while Hughes was still chafing over the perceived loss of his promised role as occasional vocalist. A Deep Purple double album, with each band member allotted equal time to shake off all his private demons, before uniting for a massive blowout on the final side of vinyl, seemed to hold the answer to their concerns.

It was not an entirely original idea — Pink Floyd had enacted much the same policy on their *Ummagumma* album four years earlier, and rumor insisted that Emerson, Lake & Palmer were taking a similar course on their next opus. Quite why Deep Purple never followed through on their own grandiose plans, however, remains a mystery. Commercially, artistically, and personally, such a project might have solved many of the problems that now afflicted the group — and it would certainly have spared the world from the album that did eventually emerge, the almost hauntingly lackluster *Stormbringer*.

For anybody seeking preliminary evidence of the band's plight, the title alone spoke volumes. Both folkie John Martyn and science-fiction author Michael Moorcock had already gained considerable mileage from exactly the same name, with Moorcock later musing, "I saw an interview a while back with [David Coverdale]. . . . There's an interview in *NME* that goes, 'Why did you take Mike Moorcock's title for your album?' And he says, 'Well, I didn't. It's just a general name, it's a mythological name.' And the interviewer says, 'No it isn't.' And it's going back and forth, and he says, 'Well, I think it is.'" In fact it isn't, but Moorcock shrugged, "You get used to that after a while. I'm not hugely sensitive about that."

Further appealing to the taste for caustic drama that, throughout the mid-1970s, established the music press as the most powerful independent entity in the U.K. music industry, the difficulties that assailed the *Stormbringer* sessions were headline news throughout August 1974. From Clearwell, the band decamped to Munich and then Los Angeles to record the album, at Musicland and the Record Plant West respectively. No matter the surroundings, however, the mood remained the same — confrontational, even rebellious.

Ironically, considering the vast fortunes Deep Purple were now generating, but understandably, considering the riches at stake, many of the problems assailing the new album came down to money. Throughout the band's first five years, songwriting credits — the single largest and most reliable source of long-term income for a musician — were an equitable five-way split. This arrangement confirmed not only the democracy of a band in which every member played a part in the creation of a new number, but also avoided the kind of simmering and supercostly disputes that would become all too common among successful musicians in later years.

For *Burn*, however, Blackmore had suggested that, henceforth, the credits be applied only to those musicians who actively penned the song — which, in that instance, wound up applying to just three of the eight tracks, "Sail Away" and "Mistreated" (Blackmore/Coverdale) and "A 200" (Blackmore/Lord/Paice). Although Glenn Hughes was forced to forego any credits whatsoever, as his Trapeze-era publishing deal was resolved, the remainder of that album comprised full band compositions in every sense of the word. "You Fool No One" developed from a drum pattern devised by Paice, "Might Just Take Your Life" from an organ chord sequence Lord was tinkering with.

"You start with the basic simple ideas," Paice explained, "then you get five minds together to work with it." This time around, however, such democratic decision-making was thrown to the wind as individual players placed their greatest faith in the songs that they brought to the table, to the exclusion of all else.

Further unseemliness erupted when Blackmore suggested the band try its hand at a pair of covers, the Yardbirds' "Still I'm Sad," and "Black Sheep of the Family," written and recorded by old ally Mick Underwood's early-'70s band (and Harvest Records labelmates) Quatermass. His intentions were shot down immediately, both historically (Deep Purple had not recorded a cover version since the Mark I days) and financially (those pesky songwriting royalties again). "Paicey and Lord . . . were adamant about not doing anybody else's songs," Blackmore told *Record Collector* magazine. "They rejected it because they hadn't written it. I couldn't believe they turned it down because they wouldn't get a writing credit, but that was basically the bottom line."

Incensed, Blackmore vowed to at least record the Quatermass track, if only as a solo single (in fact, he would record both). In the meantime, however, he was seething over the music Deep Purple *were* making of their own volition. "I'm for pretty music or hard rock," Blackmore mused in a period interview. But Deep Purple were getting almost funky — and that, he believed, "can tend to get a bit tedious."

Even more frustrating, his attempts to harden, or at least enliven, the proceedings, with riffs and notions that would once have been seized upon by his bandmates, were being shunted aside, together with the glorious spontaneity that was once guaranteed to erupt from even the most dark-hearted session. Songs that cried out for improvement and improvisation were instead played by the book. In later years, Jon Lord complained that even solos, forever the most inspirational part of the band's entire oeuvre, were now being mapped out beforehand, to forge an album that, viewed dispassionately, may have been technically and musically perfect, but was almost devoid of soul.

The failings continued mounting up. Back during the *Burn* sessions, Blackmore had suggested that Coverdale turn his lyrics away from "traditional" rock'n'roll concerns — groupies, hotels, and rock'n'roll itself — and more toward the kind of imagery that drew people to literature and art. Nobody paid good money to listen to plumbers discuss plumbing, or bank clerks talk about banking. Beyond whatever vicarious thrills might be derived from another churning life-on-the-road song, why should rock'n'rollers be any different?

The guitarist's own interests lay in a Tolkienesque netherworld of dungeons, dragons, and the like, and Coverdale, for a time, followed his suggestions. But the singer never lost his own fascination for girls who never say no and roads that go on forever, and those were the themes now reappearing in the songs. Blackmore later admitted that one number, "High Ball Shooter," so appalled him that he didn't even care to find out what it was called until the album was completed. "But I do recall it's in the key of A," he said.

Two more songs, "Holy Man" and "Hold On," didn't even credit Blackmore as a cowriter, an unheard-of happenstance. And he responded, in the studio, with an almost palpable lack of interest, his guitar barely even chiming through the quirky funk of "Love Don't Mean a Thing," scarcely rousing itself to solo through the macho braggadocio of "Lady Double Dealer." Later, Blackmore would excuse his lack of interest in the album as a consequence of upheavals in his personal life — his six-year marriage was breaking down and, with the best will in the world, his attention was often elsewhere.

But, had Deep Purple been making a great album, the thrill alone would have drawn him out of his shell. The fact they were making a bad one simply drove him further inside, and the more he was rebuffed, the further he retreated — the further he retreated, it seemed, the more he was rebuffed. Gathering up the song ideas that had not made it onto the Deep Purple album, the guitarist asked Coverdale if he'd be interested in adding vocals to a Ritchie Blackmore solo album. Coverdale agreed, but when he played the proffered demos, he withdrew his offer immediately. In a radio interview in 1977, Coverdale explained that he'd been looking for Blackmore's music to move forward. Instead, it had gone backward, and the world already had one *Machine Head*. Blackmore's alienation from the band he'd coformed was complete.

By the time the *Stormbringer* tapes were ready for mixing, Blackmore scarcely seemed to be in the room . . . even when he was. His bandmates retaliated by dropping his playing so deep into the mix that the guitarist actually found himself on the defensive when the subject came up in interviews: "There wasn't as much guitar because, in a way, I was going through more personal problems." But his dissatisfaction with the way everything had turned out was evident nonetheless. "I don't like black funk music, it bores me," he said. He acknowledged Coverdale's description of *Stormbringer* as "a transition," but deliberately left witnesses wondering precisely what it was a transition toward, when he concluded, "Back to rock'n'roll next album." Even he could not have known at the time that there would be no next album. Not for Blackmore, anyway.

Deep Purple set out on their next American tour in November 1974, joined on the bill by the Electric Light Orchestra and the now-inevitable Elf, riding Purple Records' release of their Roger Glover–produced second album, *Carolina Country Ball*. And it was toward them, as opposed to his bandmates, that Blackmore found himself gravitating in search of company. Dio recalled, "We'd been on the road with Purple for a long time and I finally got to meet Ritchie after about a year . . . it's true! We never spoke. He was a very private person and I understood that, I saw everyone around him trying to grab on to him and take a piece of him, and it was wrong, I didn't want any part of that. I thought, 'Okay, you're Ritchie Blackmore and I'm not, so if you want to speak to me, you will.'

"Then, one night, we were playing in Waterbury [Connecticut] and Ritchie came into the dressing room. I was hurriedly changing my clothes so I could go out and see Purple, because we never missed a show. Everyone else had gone, and I suddenly became aware of this figure, and it was Ritchie. He walked in and said, 'You're a great singer' — then he turned around and walked out! And that was my only contact with Ritchie up to that point."

But it broke the ice. "After that we started to hang out a bit," Dio continued. "Then we started to go to clubs and jam. Then he came to me one day and said, 'I want to do a single' — he said it was 'Black Sheep of the Family,' and I was, 'Yes!' I loved Quatermass, I loved that song. And if that didn't stand me in good stead, nothing would! So we had 'Black Sheep of the Family,' and then we needed a B-side. We were in Minneapolis, and Ritchie called me one night and said, 'I've got this little idea, can you do anything with it?' I said, 'Yes, what do you need, when do you need it?' And he said, 'Tomorrow.' So I went back to the one room that all the band and the road crew were staying in — they were all partying and playing around — and I was up in the corner trying to write what became '16th Century Greensleeves.' And the first time Ritchie heard what I'd done was the next day at the studio, when we recorded it."

With Dio and Elf accompanied by Procol Harum's Matthew Fisher and ELO cellist Hugh McDowell, Blackmore booked a single evening session at a Tampa Bay studio on December 12 and nailed the two songs, more or less on the first attempt. Neither was it a stroke of one-off alchemy. By the time the tour ended, in Virginia the week before Christmas 1974, Blackmore and Dio had sketched out a virtual album's worth of songs, some utilizing ideas Blackmore had been carrying around for years, others apparently materializing out of nowhere. At last, the solo album he'd been scheming for so long was taking shape — and with it, a future that would finally allow him to place Deep Purple behind him. Dio — Ronnie *James* Dio, as he would now be known — explained, "He was so disappointed in the music that the band he was in was playing, that he decided he was going to leave. . . ."

Deep Purple's schedule for the new year called for just one concert, at the fourth annual Sunbury Festival, regionally touted as Australia's own Woodstock, in Melbourne on January 25. It wound up a tumultuous affair.

Although Deep Purple had long since agreed to perform, final confirmation of their appearance was so long in arriving that the festival organizers contacted local heroes AC/DC, inviting them to stand in, just in case.

Purple did eventually confirm, but AC/DC offered to appear anyway, taking the stage after the headliners were finished, as a surprise for the homeward-bound crowd. It was an arrangement that Deep Purple apparently knew nothing about and that they furiously resisted when they did find out. They were the headliners; they were the final band of the evening. As the group walked off at the end of their performance, their road crew swarmed on to dismantle the stage as quickly as they could. AC/DC's crew leaped on to try and stop them, and 20,000 concertgoers watched in amazement as a brawl between roadies spread to involve AC/DC themselves and sections of the crowd as well. Even more astonishing, from a local point of view, it was the Englishmen who carried the day. AC/DC left the venue without performing.

Back in Europe a few days later, Blackmore set his sights on his solo project. He did not, as rumor has long insisted, accompany Elf into the studio to work on their next album (again recorded with Roger Glover at the controls). But the moment those sessions were over, he was waiting to whisk the group back to Musicland Studios in Munich, to record.

It was to be a hasty process. Deep Purple's next European tour kicked off in Belgrade, Yugoslavia, on March 16. But Blackmore was accustomed to working quickly, relishing the challenge of laying down some incredibly complex music in as brief a time as possible. In little more than three weeks, the record that at this time was still considered Blackmore's solo debut was completed. Just days later, the guitarist called Deep Purple's management and announced that his time with the band was likewise at an end. He would serve out his notice on the European tour.

Dio recalled, "As time went on, Ritchie got more dissatisfied with Purple. He just got so disenchanted with the R&B flavor that the band was in. So he came to me one night and said, 'I want to put a band together, and I want you to be in it — what do you think?' So I said, 'You take my band and I'll do it.' Elf had been through so much together — deaths in the band and all that terrible, horrible stuff that had happened to us — there was no way I was going to abandon those guys. We'd known each other since we were babies. If he'd said no, I'd have stayed with Elf, because I believed in them. But he said okay, and that was it."

Deep Purple's European tour was short, just a dozen dates across Yugoslavia, Scandinavia, Germany, Austria, and, finally, France, with Blackmore playing his final show with the group he had formed at the Paris Parlays des Sports on April 7, 1975. It was only as the band prepared to go onstage, however, that they were told he was departing. Anxious not to rock what was already a fragile boat, neither management nor Blackmore had breathed a word about his decision, although it was not difficult to grasp that something was in the air.

Pointedly, Blackmore had absented himself from every promotional appearance he could, and when he did speak, his words invariably carried another disgruntled thrust at either the band or their last album. Offstage, he spent as little time as possible with his bandmates; onstage, he threw himself into the set with the passion of a man who knew he might never see another sunrise — or, at least, never have to play another "Smoke on the Water."

At the same time, however, there was clearly more on his mind than just getting another concert out of the way. "You Fool No One," the *Burn* highlight that had become one of Blackmore's most favored virtuoso vehicles, was suddenly alive with absolutely unfamiliar passages and solos. But his bandmates (and audiences, for that matter) didn't realize exactly what he was playing until months later, when they heard his *Ritchie Blackmore's Rainbow* album and recognized elements from both "Man on the Silver Mountain" and "Still I'm Sad" in those wild improvisations.

Uncertain how Deep Purple would weather this latest storm, management booked the Rolling Stones Mobile to record the final three shows on the tour, in Graz, Saarbrücken, and Paris. If worse came to the worst, and Blackmore's departure brought down the final curtain, the band could at least bow out with another live album (the tapes were eventually released as *Made in Europe*). The possibility that they might carry on without him, however, was never far from anyone's mind. Even before Blackmore dropped his bombshell, it was intended for Deep Purple to spend much of 1975 away from the spotlight, and that plan could still be adhered to. The remaining members would just have to broaden their schedule to include some auditions.

Deliberately, no announcement was made to the music press. When the French press rushed into print with the news that Blackmore had quit, EMI were swift to issue a statement pointedly denying the story. But the rumors persisted and, three weeks after the final show, *Sounds* headlined its April 26 issue with the question "Blackmore to quit Purple?"

The article continued, "Rumors concerning this have been rife for some weeks now [and] *Sounds* believes that, following the completion of his solo album, *Rainbow*, in Munich, Blackmore may amicably part from Purple. The remaining Purple members will stay together."

An unnamed spokesman from the band's office was quoted attempting to quell the finality of the story. "The band *is* splitting," he confirmed, "but only for three months, to enable Ritchie to promote his album." The report added that Lord and Hughes, too, were planning to step out of the group for a moment, Lord to record a new classical piece and Hughes to cut a solo album that David Bowie, apparently, was lined up to produce. But the spokesman's last words did little to reassure an anxious fan base: "If one of the solo ventures really took off, especially by one of the older members of the band who has been with them for five or six years, then it could be that someone could leave for good."

Inaugurating a new subsidiary of Purple Records, the Oyster label, *Ritchie Blackmore's Rainbow* was released at the end of May to a generally positive reception. True, a few partisan reviewers professed themselves disappointed at the album's lack of fiery pyrotechnics, but a balanced set traveled, nevertheless, from that so-divisive cover of "Black Sheep of the Family" to the gorgeous "Catch the Rainbow." The latter builds from a base wholly suggested by Jimi Hendrix's "Angel" to say more for Blackmore's love of his old idol than even his most enthusiastic interviews ever did.

Furthermore, by breaching the Top 30 in America, and only just missing the Top 10 at home, *Ritchie Blackmore's Rainbow* would go on to become the guitarist's biggest hit record since *Machine Head*. But it was still rising up the charts when Blackmore insisted that the world be told the truth.

On June 21, 1975, it was finally admitted that every fan's greatest fear had come to pass. "After weeks of rumor, accompanied by wild speculation in some parts of the press," *Sounds* soberly informed its readership, "it was disclosed this week that . . . Ritchie Blackmore is to leave Deep Purple, his replacement being ex–James Gang member Tommy Bolin."

Chapter 11

Come Taste the Band's

News of Ritchie Blackmore's departure made headlines across the rock world. But if you really dug deeply into Deep Purple's back pages, he'd actually been quitting for almost three years, ever since the night in San Antonio, Texas, when keyboardist Jon Lord found himself walking down a hotel corridor with the guitarist, turned around to say something, and, as Lord recalled, "Suddenly he wasn't there. I turned around and he was leaning against a wall with tears running down his cheeks. I asked him if he felt alright, and he said, 'I don't know, I feel weird.' I asked him what he was crying for, and . . . he didn't even know he was crying. I started panicking. I said, 'Call the roadies! Get the manager! Hold the show!'"

In the end, the show went on, of course it did. But the crack in Blackmore's composure revealed more than even the guitarist himself realized at that time, a general discontent that nothing could cure, and that Deep Purple's continued existence seemed only to exacerbate.

Deep Purple was eating him alive and, the worst thing was, he knew it. As Dio reflected, "Ritchie, at heart, he's a really wonderful person, he's a great guy, I always loved him. But I realized what he had to go through when it happened to me — you always have to be on guard, because there's always someone

177

out there who will do something to you. You know, 'The world is full of Kings and Queens who blind your eyes and steal your dreams.' So he had to become less a person who could enjoy himself and more a person who had to become so private. And that's one of the reasons he liked us so much, because we did have a good time, and he was able to do that with us, because we didn't care. We enabled him to become less private than he thought he had to be."

In the end, Blackmore outlived all the prophecies. And so, it appeared, would Deep Purple.

Born in Iowa, deep in the American Midwestern heartland, twenty-four-year-old Tommy Bolin was neither Deep Purple's first-choice guitarist, nor — were one to look out over the full range of available players — the most obvious. He was, however, experienced in the one area that might well have daunted any other applicant, that of stepping into shoes already regarded as legendary. Having made little more than an underground cult of himself with the band Zephyr, in 1974 Bolin became one of the guitarists who replaced the mighty Joe Walsh in the James Gang, a responsibility that, on the American circuit, was at least as forbidding as the Deep Purple job.

Yet it was not that which first attracted Deep Purple. Rather, it was his presence on jazz-rock virtuoso Billy Cobham's *Spectrum* album in 1973 — it was there that David Coverdale first heard his playing, and wasted no time in communicating his discovery to his bandmates.

The decision to contact Bolin could not have arrived at a better time. Since Blackmore's departure, the surviving members of Deep Purple were growing ever more despondent, despairing that they would ever find a suitable replacement. The departures of Gillan and Glover had left Paice and Lord with an unrelenting hatred for both the audition process and the truckloads of demo tapes they felt duty-bound to play through as they searched for a new singer, a new bass player. The idea of repeating the process in search of a guitarist was a nightmare.

For the members who emerged from that torturous audition process, however, Blackmore's departure offered them the chance of a lifetime. Both had joined Deep Purple with only the vaguest notions of what was expected from them on the creative front, but already they had wrested control of the band away from the classically underlined, guitar-heavy epics of fond memory, and into almost revolutionary pastures of soulful derring-do. When Blackmore called them a funk band, it didn't matter that he was scarcely being complimentary. Hughes was secretly satisfied. The opportunity to bring in a new guitarist, one whose heart was not so deeply rooted in the hard rock Blackmore loved, was one he could not — would not — pass up.

The mid-1970s were the era of the guitar hero, but it was also an era in which such creatures seemed in short supply. Every time another vacancy came up, it seemed the same old list of eligible young ax-slingers just went around and around. Jeff Beck, Mick Ronson, Clem Clempson, Rory Gallagher, Harvey Mandel, Wayne Perkins . . . The litany was as short as it was star-studded, and as Deep Purple weighed their options, they found themselves returning, again and again, to the same handful of names.

For anybody following the saga through the media grapevine, there was a distinct taste of déjà vu to the proceedings. Just four months earlier, shortly before Christmas 1974, guitarist Mick Taylor had sensationally upped and quit the Rolling Stones, sending that band, too, scurrying in search of a replacement. They, too, apparently ran a rule over the entire field of guitarists; they, too, contemplated recruiting Gallagher, Ronson, and Clempson, and went so far as to actually call Jeff Beck to jam with them, before finally settling on the Faces' Ronnie Wood — a decision that has sustained the group for close to thirty years.

For Deep Purple, Beck was little more than a pipe dream, and nobody ever really believed he could be persuaded to give up a career of solo dilettantism to wheel out "Smoke on the Water" every night for the foreseeable future. He might well have been the finest guitarist of his generation, but he had a reputation for willful self-sufficiency that made even Blackmore look yielding and downtrodden — one reason, ironically, why Blackmore once proclaimed Beck his favorite guitarist: "He takes a chance every night. Sometimes he's absolutely useless, and you wonder why he's got a name, and other times he pulls things off that sound like nothing you've ever heard before." Deep Purple simply couldn't accommodate that kind of unpredictability. Beck's name was discarded without the group even making contact with him.

So, it seems, was Rory Gallagher's. Years later, the blues maestro recalled, "I read about it somewhere, nobody ever called me . . . but apparently they were thinking about asking me to join. But I had my own career to look out for, it would never have happened." In fact, Gallagher had just signed a new solo record deal that same spring and was about to begin work on his *Against the Grain* album. Flattering though Deep Purple's interest might have been, it had no chance of leading anywhere.

Mick Ronson felt the same way. Guitarist with David Bowie throughout the early '70s glam-rock peak, "Ronno" had more or less drifted since that partnership shattered. A projected solo career had failed to take off, while his much-ballyhooed recruitment into Mott the Hoople lasted just a couple of months before collapsing into a morass of acrimony and recriminations. But he, too, was about to embark on a new phase of his career, piloting Mott's vocalist, Ian Hunter, through his first solo album, before joining up with Bob Dylan's Rolling Thunder Revue for a near-yearlong tour of America. Like Gallagher, Ronson was flattered, but ultimately uninterested: "Somebody told me Purple had mentioned my name, but I never heard anything from them, and I had too much going on anyway."

Other bands, watching as Deep Purple's plight intensified, hastened to hang out their own "hands-off" notices. Four or five years later, Alex Harvey, whose Sensational Alex Harvey Band, in 1975, were at the peak of their powers, told a fan, "Everybody wanted to steal [guitarist Zal Cleminson] away from me. The Rolling Stones, Deep Purple, they were all sniffing around. I just told them to fuck off."

Next in line was Dave "Clem" Clempson, guitarist with the then slowly shattering Humble Pie. Taking over the Pirate Sound rehearsal rooms in Hollywood, a converted movie soundstage operated by one of Deep Purple's former sound engineers, the band spent several days rehearsing with him before it became apparent that not only was Clempson no Ritchie Blackmore, he had no intention of trying to become one. Rob Cooksey, who had now all but taken over the day-to-day running of the band from Coletta and Edwards, told *Circus*, "He was working out really well, but he just didn't have the magic. So we decided to call it a day, and Clem went home."

In desperation, the band then opened the doors to all comers, convinced that somewhere in Los Angeles, there must exist one guitarist

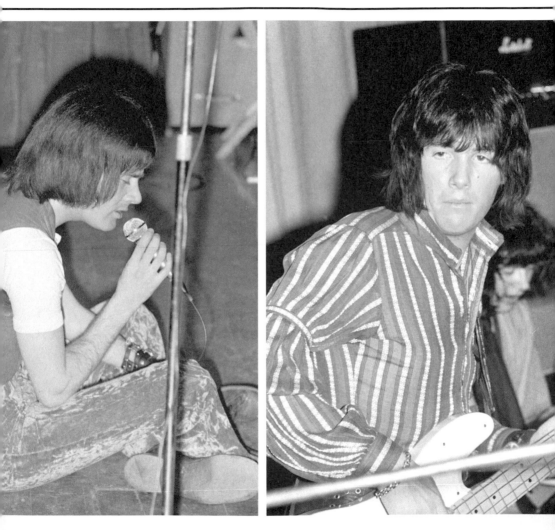

Rod Evans *(left)* and Nick Simper *(right)* onstage at the Gladsaxe TeenClub, Denmark, on February 1, 1969. (Photos by Jorgen Angel)

Ian Gillan *(left)* and Ritchie Blackmore *(right)* at Copenhagen's Club Six, September 7, 1969 (Photos by Jorgen Angel)

Ian Paice *(left)* and Jon Lord *(right)* at Copenhagen's Club Six,
September 7, 1969 (Photos by Jorgen Angel)

The view from the top of the charts — Purple in 1970: *l-r* Ritchie Blackmore, Ian Paice, Jon Lord, Roger Glover, Ian Gillan (Photo by Chris Walter)

Ian Paice *(top)* and Jon Lord *(bottom)* at Copenhagen's KB Hallen on November 14, 1970 (Photos by Jorgen Angel)

Ritchie Blackmore *(left)* and Ian Gillan *(right)* at Copenhagen's KB Hallen on November 14, 1970 (Photos by Jorgen Angel)

Jon Lord and Ian Glover back at Copenhagen's KB Hallen on March 1, 1972

(Photo by Jorgen Angel)

Mark III unveiled – the new boys meet the press for the first time.
L-r David Coverdale *(seated)*, Ritchie Blackmore, Ian Paice, Jon Lord, Glenn Hughes
(Photo by Chris Walter)

(Top left) David Coverdale

(Top right) Ritchie Blackmore

(Bottom) Glenn Hughes
(All photos by Chris Walter)

Mark III in Copenhagen, December 1973 – *l-r* Jon Lord, Glenn Hughes, Ian Paice, David Coverdale, Ritchie Blackmore (Photo by Chris Walter)

Coverdale cuts a shape in Copenhagen, December 9, 1973 (Photo by Jorgen Angel)

(Top left) On his way out –
Ritchie in Copenhagen,
March 20, 1975
(Photo by Jorgen Angel)

(Top right) Tommy Bolin
(Photo by Chris Walter)

(Bottom) Glenn Hughes
(Photo by Chris Walter)

Jon Lord onstage

David Coverdale hits
a high note (Photos
by Chris Walter)

Roger Glover onstage at the Butterfly Ball (Photo by Chris Walter)

Rainbow *(with the rainbow)* in Denmark during the 1976 world tour
(Photo by Jorgen Angel)

Coverdale onstage with Whitesnake, January 1983 (Photo by Jorgen Angel)

Another year, another vocalist: Joe Lynn Turner arrives in 1989
(Photo courtesy Michael Ochs Archives.com)

Don Airey, onstage with the band on June 21, 2002, at Verizon Amphitheatre, Charlotte, North Carolina. (Photo by Daniel Coston)

Steve Morse, with Deep Purple on June 21, 2002, at Verizon Amphitheatre,
Charlotte, North Carolina. (Photo by Daniel Coston)

who they could all agree upon. Weeks passed, however, with barely even a glimmer of hope, and the band's mood was sinking daily — Jon Lord later admitted that he was, once again, on the verge of quitting altogether. But then Tommy Bolin entered the frame and everything fell into place.

It was roadie Nick Bell who made the initial approach, Bolin revealed. In a November 1975 interview with 7HO radio in Melbourne, Australia, he recalled, "David [Coverdale] like, uh, heard me on Cobham albums and stuff, you know, and James Gang albums, and they were looking all over the East Coast: New York and Boston and yadda-yadda, you know; and I live like two minutes from him, in Malibu, in California. It was ridiculous, so. . . ."

Somewhat more coherently, Rob Cooksey continued, "[Tommy's] name was the first that was brought up, but we didn't even know how to get in touch with him. [Finally] we got Tommy's number off some guy in the Rainbow in L.A., and it turned out he was living three miles down the road from us in Malibu."

Bolin wasn't initially certain about the offer: "[Nick Bell] called up and they just said, 'Do you wanna . . . you know, jam a bit,' and I said yeah. You know, I wasn't that enthused about being in an English band. Because English bands tend to be a bit sterile a lot. Every time they play, it's the same jokes, you know it really is, [and] it gets to a point of being really bland, and I just didn't wanna — you know the way I play, I didn't wanna be a part of that."

The moment he arrived at Pirate Sound, however, Bolin admitted that what he heard blew him away. He had never actually listened to Deep Purple in the past: "I'd heard 'Smoke on the Water,' and I'd heard 'Highway Star.'" Now he discovered that, although Deep Purple may have been an English band, "they're a very Americanized English band. I mean, they grew up with the same roots as I grew up with, which really amazed me, playing R&B stuff, Sam and Dave, Motown, you know, yadda-yadda."

If what the guitarist saw of Deep Purple that first evening was a revelation to him, Lord remembered the band being equally taken aback by Bolin — and that was before they even heard him play. "He walked in, thin as a rake, his hair colored green, yellow, and blue with feathers in it," Lord said. "Slinking along beside him was this stunning Hawaiian girl in a crochet dress with nothing on underneath."

Bolin, on the other hand, remembered only that "when Purple first called me for an audition, I hadn't slept in a couple of days, not a wink, because I'd been up writing stuff." He told *Creem*, "The rehearsal was for 4 o'clock and I was lying there thinking, 'I gotta figure a way to tell them, y'know, tomorrow or something.' And [then] I thought, 'Well, fuck it, I'll just go down.' So I walked in and I was like a zombie. But, in the first tune, right away it was smiles all around."

And once he plugged in, blasting through four Marshall 100-watt stacks, Deep Purple were sold. Even as he played, Bolin could hear Coverdale excitedly asking the others, "What did I tell you? What did I tell you?" The guitarist was invited to join on the spot. "He came down and it was instant magic," Cooksey confirmed. "From the first couple of bars we could tell immediately he was the guy. He liked us, we liked him, and we just took it from there."

Bolin continued, "The whole band . . . they asked, 'Would you like to, you know' . . . So then I started thinking, 'Well, okay . . .' I started presenting tunes to them, some of my songs, and things went really well. I mean, they accepted the majority of things that I thought would be . . . I didn't know, like, what vein to really go into. Those two tunes were actually the only ones I really knew of, you know?"

Watching from afar, Ritchie Blackmore was astonished to hear that Bolin was his replacement, but thrilled as well. "I originally heard him on Billy Cobham's *Spectrum* album, and thought, 'Who is this guy?'" Blackmore recalled. "Then I saw him on television and he looked incredible — like Elvis Presley. I knew he was gonna be big.

"When I heard that Purple hired him, I thought it was great. He was always so humble. I remember he would always invite me out to his house in Hollywood to see his guitar. One day I went to his place. I walked in and tried to find him, but no one was around. There were no furnishings — nothing. I stayed there for ten minutes before he finally appeared. He showed me his guitar, and the strings must have had a quarter-inch of grime on them, as though he hadn't changed them in four years. I asked him when was the last time he'd changed strings, and he said very seriously, 'Gee, I don't know. Do you think I should change them?'"

Bolin and his new bandmates spent the best part of the next three weeks simply jamming, feeling one another out and making sure the chemistry worked before they informed the press of his arrival — tapes of those sessions were preserved and later released as the album *Days May Come*. They are rough and, more often than not, as self-indulgent as one would expect from such an occasion. But they are littered, nevertheless, with moments of such sublime beauty that it's obvious the delay in announcing Bolin's recruitment was a needless precaution. Long before that period was up, Bolin and Coverdale had put almost half an album's worth of songs together, and now all that needed to be sorted out were the business arrangements.

"At the moment Tommy's pursuing two entirely different careers," Cooksey confirmed to *Circus*. "But one complements the other. His coming into Deep Purple has certainly given him an eighteen-month to two-year start on his solo career. He's ambitious and together and he's got youth on his side."

In fact, Bolin was racing to wrap up his projected solo record so that he could devote every spare moment to Deep Purple. At the same time he was frantically trying to juggle contracts and commitments so that his new bandmates could join him on his record, before he joined them on theirs! As it turned out, only Glenn Hughes was free to stop by, contributing backing vocals to one track, while Jon Lord was also spotted hanging out at the studio. For the most part, Bolin relied on older friends: Jan Hammer, Bobby Berge, Stanley Sheldon, and Genesis drummer Phil Collins. Over the next month or so, *Teaser* was completed.

Bolin rejoined Deep Purple in July, slipping into the band's schedule with remarkable ease, instinctively linking with Glenn Hughes on the funkier end of things and bringing a new vision to what had become, as Blackmore's interest in Purple declined, an increasingly stale side of the band. Of the ten tracks recorded at Munich's Musicland Studios through August and September 1975, Bolin had a hand in writing seven, including two of the album's finest, the Bolin/Coverdale–penned "Dealer" ("It's about junk," Bolin helpfully acknowledged) and "Gettin' Tighter," a stunning collaboration with Hughes.

"I wrote that at one of the rehearsals," Bolin revealed. "I just thought . . . 'Oh, man, you know they would probably enjoy' . . . you know, because I was starting to feel them out, and they were starting to feel me out, and it was like . . . a give-and-take situation, even musically. And . . . I just kind of presented [them] with all the tunes, mostly; I just presented . . . the music, a riff, or whatever. And I would construct the tune around it, and David would take it from there and do the lyrics, or Glenn would do the lyrics, or you know, whatever."

Another number, "Lady Luck," had been knocking around Bolin's live set for the past four years, requiring only that final fine-tuning Coverdale could offer. "It's good to play . . . in a new environment with new people, because it brings a certain life out of a tune," Bolin explained. "Writing with David is great. And also with Glenn. I'll probably be writing a lot more with Glenn on the next one."

"Owed to G," meanwhile, evolved from a jam between Bolin and Lord, which in turn developed into the album's showpiece ballad, "This Time Around." The piece had a Gershwinesque air and it was readily acknowledged that the G of the title was, in fact, George Gershwin. The album's standout track, however, was the sinewy six minutes of "You Keep on Moving" and, while Bolin was not actually credited with the songwriting, he wrapped some delightful leads around it.

Described by Ian Paice, in a Radio Luxembourg interview, as the album's runaway classic, "You Keep on Moving" would, as everyone involved was aware, completely alienate the majority of "Child in Time"–loving old-time Purple fans. But it was also uniquely capable of introducing the band to a whole new crowd, listeners who maybe hadn't hit puberty midway through "Smoke on the Water" and who didn't share Ritchie Blackmore's distaste for funky music. If any song on what became the *Come Taste the Band* album indicated the true depth of promise encapsulated within the so-called Mark IV lineup, that was it.

It was not only in the studio, however, that Bolin seemed set to usher Deep Purple to new heights of musical creativity and development. Visually, too, he promised to bring an element of flash into a band whose fans had grown way too accustomed to having an introvert Man in Black on stage left. This was one of the leading topics of conversation when Bolin was interviewed by Melbourne's 7HO radio barely ten days into his first tour with the band.

"The only time I saw [Blackmore]," Bolin said, "was the California

Jam thing, where . . . it was a TV thing. There was like a huge flamethrower or something like that, and somebody loaded it too much, and it about burned Ritchie's britches off! And you could tell it on TV, you know, it was like, uh . . ." Words apparently failed Bolin there, but if he thought that was the standard he had to follow, then it's no wonder he seemed so hyperactive onstage. It was one mighty surprise for the fans, though.

Bolin made his live debut as a member of Deep Purple on November 2 in Honolulu, then spent the next week relaxing by the hotel pool. Talking over a year later to his hometown Sioux City radio station KMNS, he laughed, "[Honolulu] was the first Purple concert. But it was kind of — I got my smallpox shot. It was like, aw, the smallpox shot and the TDT also. My week in Hawaii was watching everybody swim."

From Hawaii, the band traveled to New Zealand for two shows, on November 13 and 17, before touching down in Australia for six nights: three in Sydney, two in Melbourne, and one in Auckland. It was the first night of the Melbourne engagements that spawned the earliest known live tape of this incarnation of the band, a fiery sprint through all but two tracks from the new album ("Comin' Home" and "Dealer" were omitted), together with Bolin's own "Wild Dogs" and, finally, a clutch of old faithfuls: "Burn," "Smoke on the Water," "Lazy," "Stormbringer," and "Highway Star."

From Australia, the band hit Indonesia for two shows in Jakarta in early December, then moved on to that most faithful of Purple strongholds, Japan, for four shows that made a mockery of Western critics' claims that the band's appeal had diminished in the years since the epochal *Machine Head*. Gigs in Nagoya, Osaka, and Fukuoka led up to a riotous homecoming at Tokyo's Budokan, and just as they had four years previous, when the *Made in Japan* double album set new standards for in-concert recordings, the band's record company made sure the event was preserved for posterity.

They shouldn't have bothered. Despite the inclusion of both the *Stormbringer* favorite "Soldier of Fortune" and the (for obvious reasons) crowd-pleasing "Woman from Tokyo" in the set, the show that eventually emerged as the *Last Concert in Japan* live album was not one of Deep Purple's greatest. Few people around the band would have denied that as a guitarist, Tommy Bolin was a genius; unfortunately, that genius came at a price — one that was collected every evening by the drug dealers who seemed to be in permanent attendance around him. As the tour progressed, Bolin's chemical unpredictability would play havoc with the band's performance, but the Tokyo gig surely marked a nadir of sorts.

Before the show, a bad fix damaged Bolin's left arm, weakening it to such an extent that he probably shouldn't have even attempted to play, let alone record a showpiece album in front of his band's most fanatical supporters. Filtering down from Bolin's obvious incapacitation, the entire performance is ragged, stilted, and dull, and the band felt nothing but relief when, just one show (in Hong Kong) later, they were freed for their Christmas vacations.

The tour resumed on January 14, 1976, in Fort Bragg, North Carolina. It was to be a fraught reunion. Bolin's suddenly revealed capacity for screwing up had haunted his bandmates throughout their break, yet if ever the group needed to present a united front to the world, it was now. Commercially, *Come Taste the Band* was dying on its feet. Although it fared well in Europe (No. 14 in Britain, Top 10 in Sweden), days before the tour kicked off, Deep Purple's twelfth album struggled to its American chart peak of No. 43, the band's lowest ranking since 1970's *In Rock* had scaled the now-unimaginably ignominious depths of No. 143.

Back then, though, they had expected little better. In a land which knew them for nothing more challenging than a Top 5 cover of "Hush," Deep Purple's sudden embracing of the hard-rocking blues of "Speed King," "Flight of the Rat," and "Into the Fire" caught people unawares. It did not take America long to catch up with them, though, with tireless touring ensuring that there could not have been a rock fan in the land who hadn't seen them play. And the band knew exactly what those fans wanted from them. "The average age of our audience is about nineteen," Ritchie Blackmore once said, "and you must accept that they really don't understand music that much. They're trying to understand it, but . . . if they were really hip, they wouldn't like us. They wouldn't like Led Zeppelin, they wouldn't like anybody. They'd be into Yehudi Menuhin."

So Deep Purple played to that audience's expectations, at the same time trying to extend and expand them, conjuring vast sonic epics out of the basic soup of riff-laden blues, then taking even their own expectations to new limits. The partial disintegration that shook Deep Purple in

1973 barely registered on this following. Maybe David Coverdale didn't have the vocal range of Ian Gillan, and certainly Glenn Hughes didn't have the melodic touch of Roger Glover. But *Burn* still had its share of Purple classics and, though *Stormbringer* had scarcely lived up to even the most generous expectations, the fans were willing to hang on and hope.

Come Taste the Band shattered those hopes. Although it didn't land a really scathing review or serve up any substandard songs, and it wasn't a *bad* album, it just didn't sound like Deep Purple anymore. And with only two members of the classic lineup still around, Jon Lord and Ian Paice, who could be surprised at that?

The January 1976 American tour, then, was the band's chance to redeem themselves in their audience's eyes, to prove the true pedigree of their new songs and line them up alongside the old — new songs like "Drifter," riding on a riff that was second cousin to "Mistreated"; like the Zeppelinesque "Love Child," with its classic Purple chorus built around an old James Gang riff Bolin had hung on to; like "This Time Around," the ghostly, stately ballad with a touch of Queen around its phrasing.

They failed. Jon Lord explained, "I can say, hand-on-heart, we were never really a drug band. My dad bought me my first pint and I was still very much a lad from Leicester, you know. I experimented with drugs, of course I did. I smoked grass, but it left me sitting in a corner, introspective and giggling to myself. To be honest, I don't really like being out of control."

Requesting anonymity not out of fear or malice, but because he claims to still really love the musicians involved, one former Deep Purple retainer agreed. He told *Goldmine*, "The problem wasn't so much that Tommy was into drugs, it was that the rest of the group weren't, which meant he was off in his own world a lot of the time, and the others didn't understand where he was coming from."

In other words, the drugs didn't affect the quality of Bolin's performance, so much as its nature and intent. "Tommy was like Hendrix in a lot of ways," the former employee continued, "in that he could be completely out of his head, and he'd still leave your jaw on the floor. The difference was, Hendrix only had two other musicians with him, and they knew their job was to follow him and make sure what he was playing always had a firm base beneath it. Deep Purple didn't work like that. You couldn't just go wandering off at a moment's notice, because

Jon would be playing his part, or Ian or Glenn or David, and Tommy just didn't get that."

Yet Bolin was not alone in his chemical peregrinations, as Glenn Hughes later admitted to *Metal CD* magazine. As far back as his first American tour with Deep Purple, he acknowledged, "I started using coke, and it started getting heavy. I was a millionaire at twenty-one, coked out of my mind, with my own limo, Rolls Royces everywhere. I could have shot somebody and got away with it. I never did a bad show, but I was a little bit erratic to be around." It was just that Bolin was even more erratic.

If some nights (Tokyo included) resulted in musical chaos, however, others caught the band attaining heights that even the so-called classic Mark II machine of Gillan, Blackmore and Co. would have been hard-pressed to reach. One of these came in Miami on February 9, a night that was surreptitiously, but so fortuitously, recorded for eventual release as the *In Deep Grief* bootleg. From the opening salvo of "Burn" and "Lady Luck," through a thunderously claustrophobic "Smoke on the Water," and on to Bolin's "Owed to G" solo showcase, the band was firing on every cylinder they could find.

Three weeks later, in Long Beach, Deep Purple were in fine form once again, this time for the benefit of the *King Biscuit Flour Hour* radio broadcast. An earlier show on the tour, in Springfield on January 26, was recorded but never aired. Competent though the performance was, and remarkable for the one-night-only inclusion of the playfully "Speed King"-ish "Comin' Home" in the set, it lacked excitement and punch, and was marred by poor sound throughout. The tapes were shelved, and the *Biscuit* people were invited to try again later. And this time their efforts paid off.

Originally available only as the *On the Wings of a Russian Foxbat* bootleg, but subsequently granted an official release in KBFH's own archive series (European releases wryly retain the old bootleg title), the Long Beach set list does not substantially deviate from any other. The set had already been heard at some twenty-eight past shows and would be heard again at four more, as the band's American tour wound up. But the group was smoking that night, the individual pieces slotting together so firmly that, even today, seasoned Purple people pull out the tapes as an indication of precisely how much this incarnation of the band was capable of. Stepping out of the shadows of Deep Purple's history, out from under the imponderable weight of all they had accomplished in the past, that night in Long Beach returned Deep Purple to the very top of the game — which makes the events of the next three weeks appear all the more inexplicable, all the more tragic.

The American tour closed on March 4 in Denver, Colorado; seven days later, Deep Purple were back on the road in Britain. Like *Come Taste the Band*, *Teaser* was newly released in the U.K. — full-page advertisements for the band's album, in fact, were appearing in the U.K. music press alongside reviews of Bolin's record, and the *New Musical Express* spoke for many listeners when reviewer Tony Stewart observed of the guitarist's record, "Bolin is as much a rock'n'roller in solo as he indicated that he was in a group situation on *Come Taste the Band*."

A kind review ("there is a lot of good in the set") could not help, then, but raise expectations for the tour to come, a long-since sold-out outing that opened in Jon Lord's hometown of Leicester, headed south for two nights in London, moved north across the border to Glasgow, then came to a close in Liverpool on March 15. From there, they'd move on to Germany, with the rest of Europe scheduled for the summer. Unfortunately, they would never make it that far.

The musicians were bored. Worse than that, they were miserable. And while they all thought they were keeping their feelings to themselves, all they were really doing was dragging one another down.

In an interview with *Melody Maker*'s Chris Welch, Coverdale mused, "It's really unnecessary to overindulge to the point we do . . . the solo spots where everybody does their own things. I think we should just go on and play. The messing about can be done in the studio."

Glenn Hughes, looking back from two decades' distance, agreed, admitting that, almost from the beginning, he found Deep Purple to be "rather boring onstage. It wasn't really challenging for me. I didn't enjoy the square-sounding . . . stuff they did, à la 'Space Truckin'.' I felt like a B act in a B movie. It was nice singing with David Coverdale, and the *Burn* record worked very well, but this big live thing of five guys doing solos was the most boring shit. We got away with it, but I didn't like it."

Ian Paice, too, was finding the situation intolerable, albeit for different reasons. He told *Modern Drummer*, "What should have happened was, when Ritchie said he wanted to quit, we should have said, 'Let's just stop and look at this.' He, Jon, and I should have sat down and said, 'Look, if it's because of Glenn Hughes and David Coverdale and what they're doing, then let's change the band again, or let's just take two years off. We'll all do what we want, come back in two years' time, and look at it again.' That's what we should have done, because if we had, it would have continued through . . . and we'd have had a lot of fun all along. We would have done a tour every two years, made a record, and still had a nice social circle.

"But when Ritchie left," Paice continued, "we were a bit silly. We were determined to carry on and we brought Tommy Bolin in. As good a player as he was in the studio, he was hopeless onstage. When he got on a big stage, he just seemed to freeze up. Instead of playing a solo, he'd end up shouting at the audience and arguing with them" — usually about Ritchie Blackmore.

Bolin told *Circus*, "If someone yells, 'Where's Blackmore?' at one of our concerts, I'll just do what I did when people yelled, 'Where's Joe Walsh?' at me while I was with the James Gang. I'll have cards printed up with his address and throw them out to the audience."

The band could deal with that side of Bolin's personality. They didn't like it, but they understood it. Besides, time would soon sort it out, and once the audience got accustomed to seeing him there, the Blackmore brigade would soon shut up. What they couldn't handle was his drug intake — "his personal problems," as Paice so delicately put it. "That's when it became too much."

Jon Lord concurred. The band just wasn't any fun anymore, and if he was really honest about it, it hadn't been any fun since Gillan and Glover departed. "Of course," he said, "I know we carried on for a few years after with David and Glenn and then Tommy, but . . . I don't know, it was never quite the same. It became comfortable and its roots got bent. A sort of soul element came into it, which finally took over and destroyed it when Glenn decided he was God — the 'G' on his T-shirt didn't stand for Glenn! And poor old Tommy . . . was out of his depth with this kind of music. He didn't understand what Purple audiences wanted and needed, and we ended up with an album that was absolutely nothing to do with Deep Purple."

But it was David Coverdale who finally gave vent to the emotions everyone else was busily bottling up. At Leicester's Granby Hall on March 11, "[Tommy] got a bit uptight . . . he was doing a solo piece and it could only take one guy or chick to shout 'Blackmore' to blow it." It was, the singer continued, "something you have to live with and get over." But Bolin was simply not doing that and, when he dropped another egg onstage at Wembley two nights later, tempers burned closer than ever to breaking point. Another two nights later, at the last of the British dates, at the Liverpool Empire, they finally snapped for good.

The show itself was dreadful. Uninspired and uninspiring, the band wasn't even going through its paces anymore. Bolin had pretty much given up playing guitar, and a fractious crowd, howling for Blackmore, only added to the suffering. And then Bolin froze completely, right as he was about to launch into his showpiece solo. It was the final straw. Walking offstage in tears, Coverdale turned to Paice and Lord, and completely broke down: "I just can't take this anymore." They could only agree with him.

Hughes and Bolin were never officially informed of Deep Purple's demise. As far as they were concerned, the tour was over. The German gigs had been canceled due to band members' exhaustion, but the group intended honoring them later, when they reconvened after a few months off. Then it would be time to begin work on another record, and the pair were still looking forward to writing more together. It was another four months, July 19, 1976, before the pair learned they were, in fact, out of a job. Deep Purple had broken up for the last time.

Although rumor immediately began circulating that Blackmore and Gillan were about to return to the fold to relaunch the band into classic mode, the members scattered to the winds.

Jon Lord and Ian Paice did briefly consider some kind of reignition, falling into conversation with David Coverdale and mooting a new partnership that would sail beneath the abbreviated name of Purple. But the singer had tired of band life, was already planning a solo career, and the duo shifted their attention elsewhere. As Lord wrapped up fall 1976's *Sarabande*, a combination of a (surprisingly Purple-free) four-piece rock band and the Hungarian Symphony Orchestra he'd been toying with since the previous year, the pair teamed with Tony Ashton as the singularly named Paice, Ashton & Lord.

Ads in *Melody Maker* and *Sounds* added former Colosseum II guitarist Bernie Marsden and bassist Paul Martinez to the lineup, and the team cut the *Malice in Wonderland* album — a promising brew, but one, sadly, that wound up as little more than a frustrating blend of musicianly funk and pubby licks that could (and usually did) swing from exhilarating highs to maudlin lows in the course of one song. Perhaps unsurprisingly, it passed by all but unnoticed, while Paice, Ashton & Lord struggled to stay afloat. A projected tour fell apart with only one concert played and a London show broadcast on BBC radio's *In Concert* program. Recordings intended for a second album, in spring 1977, were also abandoned and, by early summer, the group was no more.

"I still think that Tony is one of the finest performers Britain has ever had," Lord lamented. "But he had this nervous breakdown, which is why we had to stop. He was just a nervous wreck. He couldn't face the public again. We were going to record a second album but then he didn't even work in the studio anymore. Ian Paice and myself paid the bills, and it was a lot of money."

Neither were their fellows from the final incarnation of Deep Purple enjoying any greater rewards. Glenn Hughes returned to Trapeze, the band he'd left when Purple first came calling, but little resulted from the combination. David Coverdale plunged into his promised solo career, but the prophetically titled blues-rock jamboree *David Coverdale's Whitesnake* was perhaps most remarkable in that it eschewed almost all evidence of Coverdale's better-known past persona.

It was true that "Sunny Days," recalling Deep Purple's final American tour, at least proved that he remembered who that persona was. But more than one reviewer sat through the album and professed himself thankful that the old band split when it did. According to Coverdale, "Lady" and "Time on My Side" were both written for what would have been the follow-up to *Come Taste the Band*. Highlights of *Whitesnake* though they unquestionably were, they would certainly have given Purple people a lot to swallow.

Only Tommy Bolin landed on his feet, returning to America to pick up the momentum of his solo career, apparently utterly unbowed by his recent experiences. Discussing Deep Purple on his hometown radio station on November 26, 1976, he shrugged, "They were together what, like eight, nine years, so . . . they're all doing like solo albums. Jon and Ian have a group; David is attempting to do a solo album; and Glenn said he did a double album which I've yet to see, but I wish him all the luck in the world."

The Tommy Bolin Band hit the U.S. concert circuit within weeks of his return from England, touring with Steve Marriott and Robin Trower. From there, it was into the studio to record *Private Eyes*, the follow-up to *Teaser*. He played some sessions with Moxy; he reunited with Billy Cobham on the proposed successor to the groundbreaking *Spectrum*; and once the Purple split was confirmed, he linked up with Glenn Hughes to discuss forming a new band together. Amidst rehearsals for Bolin's own next tours (back-to-back outings with Jeff Beck and Fleetwood Mac), the pair jammed and there seemed a real possibility that something would come of their efforts.

With all these projects boiling around him, Bolin flew to Miami in late November, ready for the first night of the Jeff Beck tour, and on December 3, 1976, he returned to the Jai Alai Fronton Hall, scene of a less-than-stunning Purple gig earlier in the year, for a performance which this time left everybody speechless. It was the last show he would ever play.

Following the concert, and a photo call with Beck himself, Bolin and his girlfriend returned to their Miami Beach hotel, the Newport. Bolin had spent the evening doing drugs, but when he passed out in the early hours of the morning, nobody wanted to call a doctor. Everybody in his entourage had seen this happen before; doubtless they would see it again, and besides that, the thought of the adverse publicity which would assuredly follow was enough to keep them away from the telephone. Instead, they simply bundled Bolin into bed, watched while his breathing normalized and his color started returning, then left him alone to sleep it off.

The following morning dawned, and Bolin looked dreadful. Finally, around 8 AM, his girlfriend called for an ambulance — but it was too late. Bolin died from what the coroner's report called "multiple drug intoxication" shortly before help arrived.

Close to thirty years on, Bolin's death remains a dreadful coda to the bitter demise of the original Deep Purple. Of course, it is unlikely that he would have played any part in the band's subsequent reunion, but *Come Taste the Band* at least paints a promising picture of what Bolin and Glenn Hughes might have accomplished had their own reunion taken place. Indeed, history has been surprisingly kind to *Come Taste the Band* — certainly kinder than the band's fans were at the time of its release — while the KBFH release proves that, no matter what problems Deep Purple Mark IV were dragging around with them, when everything clicked onstage, they were easily the equal of most past incarnations.

Roger Glover, watching Purple's collapse from the sidelines, admitted as much when he reflected, "When you do something in a band, it's only afterward, when it's a failure, that you can come up with the reasons for that. But at the time you're doing it, you don't know what's going to work and what isn't going to work. The Tommy Bolin version of the band — who knows? It might have been huge. And if it had been, how different would the stories have been then? It's all in the lap of the gods."

Chapter 12

An Invitation to the Ball

The breakup of Deep Purple in July 1976 marked more than the end of an era, more than the demise of a group. It also created a massive vacuum at the forefront of the hard-rock scene — one that Ritchie Blackmore's Rainbow were effortlessly poised to fill. Building on the success of what was still regarded as a virtual solo album, but unhappy about simply slipping into a reconfigured Elf lineup, Blackmore had begun redesigning his group as early as August 1975.

Bassist Craig Gruber was first to depart, to be replaced by Jimmy Bain from the Scottish band Harlot — whose drummer, Ricky Munro, quite coincidentally, was one of the myriad musicians who'd passed through Blackmore's Mandrake Root fantasy eight years earlier. Next out were Mickey Lee Soule and Gary Driscoll; in their place came unknown keyboard player Tony Carey, and veteran drummer Cozy Powell, a graduate not only of the Jeff Beck Group and Bedlam, but also the creator of a string of unexpected U.K. hit singles over the previous couple of years. By early October, and despite all his earlier protestations of loyalty, only Dio survived from Elf. But Blackmore's vision remained intact.

Rainbow made their live debut in Montreal, Canada, on November 10, 1975, performing beneath the arch of a vast computer-operated, illuminated rainbow, 40 feet across, 3,000 lightbulbs strong, and costing close to $100,000. A similar motif had decorated the stage at the California Jam a year before, but that was simply a wooden facsimile, a gaily painted backdrop. Rainbow's rainbow flashed, flickered, lit the stage like no light show on earth — and generated almost as much press interest as the band itself.

Well-received though it was, Rainbow's twenty-show skip through North America at the tail end of 1975 was simply a warm-up for a world tour already being scheduled for the following year. The new band's inaugural album, *Rainbow Rising*, was recorded in February in Munich with the ever-faithful Martin Birch, and it was clear that Blackmore knew exactly where his audience — like his heart — lay.

Rising, he explained in interviews, was "a high-level energy affair, an aggressive thing," everything his last album with Deep Purple had failed to deliver. And the future looked even more promising, as he swore, "Our next LP will be based on a hypothetical meeting between Led Zeppelin and Deep Purple." The incorporation of "Mistreated" into Rainbow's live set, stretching now toward the quarter-hour mark and frequently over-shadowing the very best of Deep Purple's own renditions, only added further evidence to the file.

Although Blackmore was already well aware of all that was happening in the Deep Purple camp, Rainbow were a dozen or so shows into the *Rising* world tour when news of Deep Purple's breakup was made public, and at least one fan present at the next show, in Rochester, New York, remembered Blackmore spending the entire show with a look of supreme satisfaction spread across his face: "The entire audience was going wild all night. If you had to put it into words, it really was a case of 'the King is dead, long live the King.'"

Blackmore's gamble — for such it was, walking out on a highly successful business to set up shop just a couple of doors down the road — had paid off. With *Rising* and the following year's public-demanded live album *On Stage*, and on through the (appallingly titled) *Long Live Rock'n'Roll* album that followed, Rainbow effortlessly consolidated their initial status and promise.

Even more importantly, however, they were also able to weather one of the most concerted attacks on their entire raison d'être that the music scene had ever produced, the punk-rock explosion of 1977–78, and emerge out the other side to celebrate the birth of a new wave of heavy-metal stylists. That one is hard-pressed to name a single other British band that made the same journey unscathed is tribute enough to Rainbow's accomplishment — the fact that not one of Blackmore's erst-while bandmates effected the same transition so gracefully is only gratuitous amplification of the original achievement.

That said, little of the music spilling out of the other former Deep Purplers seemed, at that time, at all interested in pursuing Blackmore over the rainbow.

As far back as 1970, when Rod Evans and Nicky Simper took their own first steps out of the band, the branches of the Deep Purple family tree had almost deliberately reached away from the main trunk. Evans' Captain Beyond, a collaboration with blues drummer Bobby Caldwell and Iron Butterfly refugees Larry Rheinhart and Lee Dorman, mustered a couple of albums of ponderous psychedelia before Evans faded from the music scene for the remainder of the decade.

Simper's Warhorse, on the other hand, were somewhat closer to the Purple ideal, but only in as much as volume and intensity were as impor-tant to one as to the other. Besides, if (as seems probable) most modern listeners are most familiar with Warhorse only as an especially thun-derous branch of the Deep Purple family tree, in reality, the group's roots were equally appropriately traced back to the Rolling Stones. After all, if Mick Jagger had not impregnated singer Marsha Hunt and caused her to take a few months off the road, her backing band (which Simper joined following his departure from Purple) might never have found the time to strike out alone.

Three members of Hunt's group would become Warhorse: Simper, guitarist Ged Peck, and drummer Mac Poole. A fourth musician, a young pianist named Rick Wakeman, was also along for some of the band's earliest rehearsals, but that turned out to be a problem. They needed him at all the rehearsals, not just some of them, so Wakeman was bid farewell (he promptly joined Yes), and replaced by ex-Rumble keyboardist Frank Wilson.

In search of a vocalist, Simper returned to Ashley Holt, the singer who came so close to joining the original Deep Purple, and in April 1970

Warhorse cut their first demo, "Miss Jane." A surprisingly melodic number, full of fancy guitar frills and harmonies, it loped along on a remarkably jolly rhythm track and was certainly enough to interest a string of progressively minded record labels. By midsummer, Warhorse had signed with the swirly-logo'd Vertigo.

Armed with a budget of £1,500 and producer Ian Kimmet, and with just five days to complete their record, Warhorse turned in a seven-track behemoth that remains one of the most startling albums Vertigo would sign all year. The fun faded in on neoclassical Hammond organ, a dark lilt that sounded as though it was recorded from an immense distance — so immense, in fact, that when the rest of the band burst in, a minute into the melody, even the needle jumped in shock.

Then there were the songs. The first line of the first song of the first Warhorse album announces, "You drink my blood." A few minutes later, Holt unleashes precisely the sort of spine-curdling scream that would have given Ian Gillan pause for thought, and for reasons which probably don't deserve to be thought about too much, contemporary reviews promptly compared *Warhorse* to labelmates Black Sabbath and, of course, Deep Purple. Their first post-Simper album, *In Rock*, was still being digested at the time and, playing Warhorse's *Warhorse* and Deep Purple's *In Rock* side by side, one could be excused for wondering just what musical differences truly separated Simper from his old bandmates.

Despite a fine reception (particularly on the European mainland), *Warhorse* did little in Britain. Neither did its general excellence do anything to paper over the very serious cracks appearing in the band's makeup. The problems apparently stemmed from a leadership tussle between Simper and Peck that was finally resolved only when Peck quit in 1971, on the eve of a major European tour.

He was replaced by Peter Parks, and that summer the new boy made his recorded debut with Warhorse, when they premiered two new songs for BBC radio's Stuart Henry. Then, with the European tour having established Germany as the band's No. 1 market, Warhorse returned to the studio in late 1971 to begin work on their sophomore album. They were informed, midway through the sessions, that their budget was being slashed and they needed to finish up quickly.

Red Sea, Warhorse's second album, would appear in early 1972, showing few of the wounds its rushed completion must have inflicted. Parks proved to be at least as virtuosic as his predecessor, while the band's songwriting was, if anything, even tighter than the first time around. Again the Deep Purple comparisons are valid, but again, too, Warhorse's unique identity is stamped across the record. Who else, after all, could have handled the classic "I (Who Have Nothing)" with such soul-shaking aplomb?

Unfortunately, *Red Sea* sold no more strongly than its predecessor, while the band's hopes of enlarging their appeal were stymied even further by their failure to find an American outlet. By early 1973, Vertigo had parted company with the group; Mac Poole had quit (he would subsequently surface amid the unlikely pastures of Gong); and the surviving band members were cast adrift to carry on as best they could.

Recruiting drummer Barney James, Warhorse set about recording the clutch of demos that ultimately surfaced as bonus tracks on the late-1990s *Red Sea* CD reissue. These four tracks demonstrated a far more mature side to the band than had hitherto been revealed, with finely worked harmonies, rich, restrained arrangements, and a general mood that had more in common with the Doobie Brothers than any home-grown influences. It was excellent stuff, and deservedly Warhorse looked as though they were going to land on their feet. In fact, as 1973 wore on, Warner Brothers expressed very sincere interest in the band, going so far as to stage a champagne-heavy handshaking ceremony, only to draw its hands back as the Western worldwide energy crisis began to bite.

It was a devastating blow, and though the possibility of another deal soon surfaced, with one of Tamla Motown's subsidiaries, Ashley Holt had had enough. Now established among the world's leading keyboard wizards, as opposed to a passing near-unknown, Rick Wakeman had recently been in touch, offering him a role in one of his forthcoming extravaganzas, a musical reenactment of Jules Verne's *Journey to the Centre of the Earth*. Holt accepted, and not only that, he also brought Barney James, Warhorse's newly acquired drummer, along with him. It was just unfortunate that the pair should announce their departure on the very day the Motown contract was delivered. After that, Warhorse's demise was probably inevitable.

The band members drifted. Holt and James would remain part of the

Rick Wakeman setup for the next couple of years, contributing to both *Journey to the Centre of the Earth* and the *King Arthur* musical adventure, while Frank Wilson would subsequently work with singer-songwriter Alan Ross, both in Ross' own band and alongside fellow keyboard player Kevin Gale, in the fondly remembered Wilson/Gale.

Simper, however, left the music business altogether. In partnership with Carlo Little, his old ally from the Billie Davis/Flowerpot Men days, he opened a greengrocer's shop in Wembley, North London, and, though the venture lasted little more than a year, to all musical ends he faded from view.

His disappearance seemed all the more absurd given the continued high profile Simper's years with Deep Purple enjoyed in the United States. Although the group's first three albums had long since been deleted, the compilation *Purple Passages* was still selling and, as the latest Deep Purple lineup hit towns on tour, local DJs would frequently dig out "Hush" to help celebrate their arrival, maybe reminiscing about the group's first visit to town.

"We were megastars in America," Simper said of the earliest Deep Purple. "Today, all you hear is people mentioning that one single, 'Hush.' But we had five consecutive releases in the U.S. charts at one time, and we were doing a six-month tour there, playing to big audiences." That he could be forgotten so swiftly seems incredible — and the stuff, perhaps, of grand conspiracy theories. Simper's own simmering legal disagreements with Deep Purple were common knowledge at the time; the possibility that the industry had simply dropped him into the bag marked "Troublemaker," regardless of his musical talents, is one that has been murmured on more than one occasion.

By the time Gillan and Glover quit the band in 1973, Deep Purple's public persona, both individually and collectively, was considerably higher than it had ever been in their predecessor's day, and their renown was sufficient to ensure that future departures would not be allowed to vanish so precipitously.

Having always taken a larger share of Deep Purple's production credits than his customary one-fifth allotment suggested, Glover moved effortlessly onto the other side of the mixing desk following his removal from the group. He moved effortlessly, too, into a position of major renown.

Roger Glover's partnership with the Scottish hard-rock band Nazareth was one of those glorious collaborations that could never have been predicted, but which, afterward, could never have been imagined otherwise. Nazareth had already been knocking around for some four years by the time they first hitched up with Glover in early 1973, turning out a pair of well-received but commercially unremarkable albums of churning blues rock before this latest partnership began work on a new LP, *Razamanaz*.

The alchemy sparked immediately. "Broken Down Angel" burst out of nowhere to slam the U.K. Top 10 in May 1973, "Bad Bad Boy" followed it in July, and in between times, *Razamanaz* unleashed a monstrously loud, ferociously paced statement of intent, an invitation to a party, a showdown, a bacchanalian revelry at which the band was gonna "razamanaz you alright . . . all night." And all was delivered with such unaffected joy that it was impossible to view it through the same jaundiced eyes that one normally turned upon exhortations of that ilk. "Razamanaz" itself may not be a verb that many English speakers were familiar with, but the flurry of almost-audible rock'n'roll oldies that flashes through the fading guitar lines that scythed the song to its conclusion let you know you wouldn't be sending the invitation back.

The *New Musical Express*' Julie Webb later hypothesized that Deep Purple's "lapse from the limelight" during those critical breakthrough months helped Nazareth on their way, "because colleges and, indeed, the majority of record buyers were to some extent starved of a British band catering to the heavy-metal brigade." If that was the case, then it was a fitting reward for Glover and, over the next year, he would produce two further, superlative albums for Nazareth.

That same fall's *Loud'n'Proud* and the following spring's *Rampant* both flung out further hit singles, then slammed the band into rock immortality with an absolutely startling reinvention of Joni Mitchell's "This Flight Tonight." In fact, though fans of Mitchell probably wouldn't have recognized it, Nazareth did more than rock up one of her most distinctive songs. They also created a hybrid as potent as anything the Byrds ever did to Bob Dylan — or even Jon Lord to Bach. While guitars keened and panned eerily behind the relentless motorik of the bass and drums, Dan McCafferty's almost metallically treated vocal sounded as dislocated within its thoughts as the airplane in the darkened skies.

A deserved No. 11 hit in the U.K., "This Flight Tonight" was an incredibly atmospheric performance, surrendering even the strength of the so-visual lyric to the weightless tumult of the band, allowing the vocals to slash forth only once, as the harmonies illustrated the sound of the singer's headphones with a snatch of some pure pop oldie. Nazareth were far more than simply a hard-rocking blues band.

Nazareth did not consume all of Glover's attention. He remained an active presence within the Purple Records setup and, just weeks after the release of *Rampant* in June 1974, he was on the new-release racks as one-half of Marlon, a collaboration with Ray Fenwick that the latter recalls with undisguised affection.

"Roger was a great lover of pop songs," Fenwick said. "Me too. And we said, 'Why don't we write a very structured song, along the lines of doo wop, but perhaps with a bit of a disco flavor?' So we came up with 'Let's Go to the Disco.' It was great fun. It was me and Roger indulging ourselves — Roger is and was a great producer, he always had an ear for what was right, and he never did anything he didn't want to do."

Marlon's one and only single sadly failed to follow Nazareth into the charts, but its makers had no time to despair as they moved immediately on to another of Glover's pet projects, a musical adaptation of illustrator Alan Aldridge and poet William Plomer's *The Butterfly Ball & the Grasshopper's Feast*, a delightful tale that combined semipsychedelic intent and art into one of the most enduring children's books of the age.

Glover was still a member of Deep Purple when he was first offered the *Butterfly Ball* project. Apparently, Pink Floyd had already turned it down, but he didn't mind being second choice, even if he was a little puzzled about how he came to be chosen in the first place: "Being the bass player of a hard-rock band, it . . . was very odd."

An admirer of Aldridge's work since encountering it, he said, in a Sunday newspaper supplement a year earlier (although surely he remembered the artist's distinctive work on the Beatles' *Illustrated Song Lyrics* portfolio), Glover contacted Aldridge and was immediately given a list of albums he needed to listen to, if he was to capture the moods the artist intended.

Devouring the book and discussing its characters with Aldridge, Glover started the songwriting with no set notions of who would voice the characters. Only as songs were completed did he mull over the possibilities — Ronnie Dio was involved virtually from the outset, while Glover also contacted Ian Gillan to ask if he'd be interested in appearing. He wasn't, but wound up playing a part regardless, as Glover booked the *Butterfly Ball* sessions into the recording studios that Gillan — resolutely keeping away from the stage, but unable to wholly sever his involvement with the music industry — now co-owned.

Alongside Martin Birch, Gillan had become a partner in a new studio being built around the old De Lane Lea setup in central London's Holborn district, where so many of Deep Purple's own records were recorded. Gillan recalled, "De Lane Lea . . . had moved their operation to Wembley, [but] had left Holborn with all its gear in place and, apart from still paying the rent of about £25,000 a year, they had basically locked the doors and thrown away the key."

The total cost of the venture, including the procurement of a handful of parking spaces, was around £15,000, and immediately the investment began paying off. Leo Sayer and Gillan's old friends in the Sweet both recorded at the newly rechristened Kingsway Studios, while the opportunity to watch as *The Butterfly Ball* came to fruition brought its own rewards, a reminder "of what I'd walked away from." And right now, he didn't regret that decision for a second.

Through the summer of 1974, Glover surrounded himself with familiar faces. Most were musicians with whom he'd worked in the past, although there were a couple that circumstance naturally dictated he never had — Purple's own new arrivals, David Coverdale and Glenn Hughes. Elf's Mickey Lee Soule came aboard, not only contributing some magnificent keyboards, but also cowriting (with Dio and Glover) two of the songs, "Harlequin Hare" and "Together Again."

Tony Ashton, soul singer Jimmy Helms, Roxy Music's Eddie Jobson, former (and future) Peter Green collaborator Nigel Watson, Eddie Hardin, Quatermass' John Gustafson, and keyboard player Mike Moran were all involved, while Ray Fenwick introduced the rhythm section of Les Binks and Mo Foster — his partners in Fancy, a band that was currently riding high on the American charts with a deeply squelchy and seductively groaned rendition of the Troggs' "Wild Thing."

For many of the musicians involved, the *Ball* marked their first ever exposure to Ronnie Dio, and Fenwick recalled, "I couldn't believe it when I first heard Ronnie sing. I was stunned by him, such an enormous voice. He was a New York guy, brought up on Dion DiMucci — he was a very powerful singer, but he was also a very tuneful one." Taking the role of the frog, Dio's showpiece, "Love Is All," remains many people's fondest memory of the project ("Such a great song," agreed Fenwick), but the guitarist continued, "The entire *Butterfly Ball* was such a great project to be involved in."

A massive hit in the Benelux countries, "Love Is All" earned Dio his first gold disc, and the singer unequivocally agreed with Fenwick's enthusiasm. Only Glover himself seems less certain of *The Butterfly Ball*'s charms: "It's an album that, when I finished it, I didn't like it. I always see the flaws. I put six months' work into it, and we had a party for the finished product. But I'd been working forty-eight hours straight, no sleep, to finish, so I was rather stressed. And all the people were there, all the artists and musicians who sang and played on it, the publishers, the record company. It was all at my house, it was catered, it was a big huge celebration and I was so upset! We played the stuff, and everyone was, 'Oh, that sounds great, Rog,' and I just went to my room and burst into tears."

A projected animated movie version of *The Butterfly Ball* never came to pass — only one piece of footage ever made it out into the public, a short clip that accompanied "Love Is All," and which became a regular sight on Saturday-morning children's TV. However, for all his misgivings over the project, when Glover was approached the following November 1975 to stage a live performance of *The Butterfly Ball*, in aid of charity, he readily agreed.

Recalling as many of the original cast of musicians as he could, and adding one new song to the production, "Little Chalk Blue," Glover pieced together a minor masterpiece. Even the absence of Dio could not hold him back — the singer's three songs were performed instead by Lucifer's Friend (and future Uriah Heep) frontman John Lawton ("Love Is All"), supermodel-turned-superb-singer Twiggy ("Homeward"), and, taking his first public steps in more than two years, Ian Gillan ("Sitting in a Dream").

Dio reflected, "We'd just got Rainbow off the ground when Roger came to me about the concert, and at first I said okay. But then I mentioned it to Ritchie, and he said, 'No, I don't think you should do that. We're a new band, we're just starting, we want to not have any side roads going on.' So . . . I didn't quite understand that, but it's your band, mate . . . So I had to refuse."

Gillan, on the other hand, was more than ready to throw himself into the fray. In the months following the *Butterfly Ball* studio sessions, he had grown increasingly restless, haunted by a sense of absolute unfulfillment. Any number of different ventures had occupied his time since departing Deep Purple; aside from his co-ownership of Kingsway Studios, he also enjoyed stints as a hotelier, travel agent, and motorcycle marketer.

Of course, he toyed with a little recording. Very early on in *The Butterfly Ball*'s gestation, even after Gillan had turned down the chance to appear in it, he and Glover took advantage of some downtime at Kingsway to knock off a handful of recordings together, including another stab at the *Cherkazoo*-era rocker "Driving Me Wild" and a couple of cover versions — Elvis' "Trying to Get to You" and Cliff Bennett's "Ain't That Lovin' You Baby."

Ray Fenwick, guitarist at the session, recalled, "I remember we did a great version of 'Trying to Get to You.' Ian always loved that song, and I think that was his background. If he hadn't been in Deep Purple, I always thought he'd make a great rock'n'roll singer, going down the Tom Jones route. He always used to say that in his record collection he only had rock'n'roll records — Little Richard, Jerry Lee Lewis, and Elvis." Gillan himself once claimed he knew "every word, tune, and arrangement, and what song follows what on all [Presley's] albums up to *Blue Hawaii*."

Since that time, though he was aching to do something else, Gillan was not ready to consider a full return to music, he insisted, until he was called to a series of meetings with managers Tony Edwards and John Coletta and accountant Bill Reid in Paris.

Reid had spent the past year or so agitating for the various members of the Deep Purple family to relocate to Europe, to escape the then-incumbent Labour government's latest ploy to prop up the dramatically ailing British economy, a so-called supertax that would devour a full 90 per cent of its victims' earnings. Of course, this savage device applied only to the country's richest earners, but that was no consolation to those earners. And Gillan was one of them.

It wasn't his own ventures that were the problem — in fact, with the exception of the studios, most of them were teetering on the edge of collapse. It was his Deep Purple-related earnings that were mounting up, and while various legal loopholes had so far protected him from the harshest extremes of the new tax laws, the government was methodically moving in to close them down.

Suddenly, and seemingly without warning, Gillan was advised that his best option was to enter voluntary liquidation. He might also want to consider resuming his musical career. It wouldn't stave off the bankruptcy, but it would allow him to get back on his financial feet with a minimum of fuss. Even as Reid was explaining the situation to the stunned Gillan, other members of the organization were preparing the way — and, perhaps just as importantly, negotiating the fees — for the singer's return to action.

His mind made up, Gillan first called Ray Fenwick. "He just suddenly said, 'I want to perform again,'" recalled Fenwick. He hadn't seen Gillan in close to a year, and he barely recognized him when he did. "When I first saw Ian again, he'd cut all his hair, he had a car coat on . . . he could have been a car salesman. He really didn't look like the Ian Gillan of the rock-star thing. He'd gone into business. And suddenly it was, 'Hey, guys, do you want to form a band?' and 'Let's do the show right here.'"

Fenwick's own group, Fancy, had just completed a well-received U.K. tour with 10cc, and the guitarist recalled, "I can remember still being contracted to the Fancy situation and having discussions with [manager] Mike Hurst — 'Look, I've got this chance. . . .' Mike was great about it. They did some kind of settlement thing, and we just got on with it."

Joining Fenwick were Mike Moran, Elf's Mark Nauseef, and, briefly, Roger Glover — although, as Fenwick recalled, "Roger was never intended to be the bass player, he was really a producer at that time. I think his heart really wasn't in it, and he didn't really want to go on the road again, so we got John Gustafson in." Ian Gillan's Shand Grenade, as the singer initially intended christening the group, was unveiled to management in Paris in September 1975. A month later, the quintet hit

The Butterfly Ball for what — though few in the audience were aware of the fact — was their debut performance.

Some twenty-eight months had elapsed since Gillan last appeared on a public stage and, ahead of his midshow performance, he reduced himself to an absolute bundle of nerves. He was convinced, he explained later, that after he'd been so long away from the spotlight, not a soul in the room would remember him. Instead, "at the announcement of my name, the audience rose and gave me a standing ovation!" Even the show's narrator, Vincent Price, resplendent in a peacock chair up in the organ loft, was forced to pause while the roars echoed around the hall. Gillan was back — and he knew it.

With David Coverdale and Glenn Hughes also making appearances at the show, and Jon Lord a permanent presence in the accompanying band, the *Butterfly Ball* concert brought a massive turnout of Deep Purple fans, none of whom were destined to be disappointed. Tightening some of the album's more florid arrangements, and stepping back from the occasionally self-conscious whimsy of the recorded set, Glover realigned *The Butterfly Ball* in such a way that further performances seemed guaranteed.

But it was not to be. The *Ball* has never been restaged, while a movie of the concert, subsequently given a brief theatrical release (and an even briefer home-video lifespan), somehow manages to upstage the actual music with insertions that virtually everybody associated with the project still find utterly unpalatable. Bassist Mo Foster explained, "The main reason the movie is bad is the director [Tony Klinger] intercut it with people walking around in what looks like rolls of carpet. They're meant to be little animals, but it actually looks like they've fallen into a carpet shop and walked out with the stock." Referring to a then-prominent chain of U.K. carpet stores, Fenwick quipped, "We used to say the movie was directed by Cyril Lord's."

Glover, too, shuddered at the thought of the movie, but insisted that *The Butterfly Ball* is not dead: "It's one of those projects that has a life of its own, although it's got one fatal flaw in my view, and that's the fact it's not much of a story. It's just a day when the animals forgot their differences and had a party. I've actually attempted to write a storyline through it, because I do think there's a future for it. So many people have had an interest over the years in reviving it, either as a stage play or a full animated cartoon. Sundance were looking at it [in the early 1990s]. But I've heard nothing else since, so obviously it's died — but, in the process of that Sundance thing, I've done a synopsis. It could be a *Cats*-style musical, I can see that. . . ."

Chapter 13

A New Wave to Surf

Having recorded their debut album at studios as far afield as Munich, Montreaux, and the faithful old Kingsway, Ian Gillan's Shand Grenade made their world television debut shortly before Christmas, appearing on German TV with Roger Glover standing in for Gustafson on bass. Four months later, with first Mickey Lee Soule (like Nauseef, a refugee from the hijacked Elf), then Colin Towns, replacing Mike Moran on keyboards, the now-renamed Ian Gillan Band made a low-key live debut in Scandinavia, moved on to a strangely underpromoted (and heartbreakingly underattended) tour of France during April 1976, and finally marched into an American tour opening for Nazareth.

Just as it had for Rainbow, the shadow of the newly dismantled Deep Purple loomed expectantly over this group. However, while Ritchie Blackmore made no secret of his desire to seize that crown for his own, Gillan was steaming out of his way to avoid it.

Gillan recalled the band's first show: "The audience went berserk as soon as we walked out onstage; they were hyped up, ready to headbang and everything else. And our opening number went, 'Dink-dink-a-dink, dink-dink-a-dink,' it was a jazzy, funky thing. And the crowd didn't know what was happening. They were going, 'Eh? What the hell's *that*?' But we stuck with it. You've got to do what you believe in. You've got to take risks."

And they continued taking risks for the next two years. Between spring 1976 and early 1978, the Ian Gillan Band released three albums (and recorded sufficient material for several more besides) and enjoyed, according to Gillan's autobiography, as wild a rock'n'roll time as ever Deep Purple had experienced. However, while they made no bones whatsoever about their frontman's past, titling their debut album after "Child in Time" and allowing both "Smoke on the Water" and "Woman from Tokyo" to take pride of place in their live set, the group's approach was far from the rumbling attack of old. Abandoning his initial inclination to finally complete and release the rock'n'rolling *Cherkazoo*-era material, Gillan chose to pursue, instead, a gritty jazz-funk hybrid that he knew — and critics agreed — would effectively defuse expectations.

Ray Fenwick looked back on this period of phenomenal adventuring with undisguised pride: "The first album was very, very good, I thought. The thing with it was, Ian suddenly found himself in a band with a bunch of session guys and, of course, session guys like to play as much as they can when they get a chance. In that situation, we were given a bit of room and rope, so we let the rope out a bit."

Unfortunately, they picked precisely the wrong time to do so. The punk scene that Rainbow, by spending so much of their time in America and Japan, had so neatly sidestepped was, contrarily, all around the Ian Gillan Band. After the American tour, the group spent much of the next two years in the U.K., amid a musical sea change that painstakingly rejected every value — any value — that the likes of Gillan had ever espoused.

The Adverts, by far the finest of all the bands emerging in the wake of the Sex Pistols/Clash/Damned axis, drew a barrage of raised eyebrows when they had the audacity to throw a brief guitar solo into one song, while Newcastle band Penetration went even further. Vocalist Pauline Murray recalled the band dropping the "Smoke on the Water" riff unannounced into their live repertoire and watching as the serried ranks of punks pogoed wildly to its punching rhythm — right up until the band stopped playing and told them what they'd been dancing to. Then the booing rose from the pit, a furious disdain that didn't care a hoot for what the disgraced dinosaurs of an earlier age sounded like. It was what they represented that was under attack — the exaggeration, the profligacy, the sheer arrogance of being "a famous rock'n'roll star."

The Ian Gillan Band, with their apparently heedless delight in musical values, and nuances that flew far over the heads of the "kids on the street," were a prime target for punk's acrimony. And, of course, where fashion led, the media followed — a hailstorm of scorn from a music press that had once tripped over its own shoelaces in its haste to confer ever greater honors upon the purveyors of such convolutions.

Neither was Gillan's own traditional constituency any less bemused by the singer's change in direction. They had never truly accepted, after all, the final incarnation of Deep Purple — it was reputation and the band's penchant for playing lots of oldies in concert that gave the Bolin-era version the majority of its staying power. Had Deep Purple not shattered when they did, the law of diminishing returns might ultimately have snatched away even those consolations. The question that the Ian Gillan Band seemed to be asking was, how much of a betrayal was *Come Taste the Band*, and how much a harbinger of the familiar brand name's future?

Looking back on the Deep Purple story so far, it's the arrival of Coverdale and Hughes that heralded the band's flirtation with R&B and da funk, and the departure of Gillan and Glover — producer of *Child in Time* — that allowed them into the family in the first place. But you'd never guess that from *Child in Time* as it bounded turbulently from the full-on crunch of "Lay Me Down," through the Sly Stone-ish "You Make Me Feel So Good." and on to "Let It Slide," apparently a song about premature ejaculation that contrarily slid on for eleven-plus minutes.

Deeply atmospheric, lighter-wavingly anthemic, "Let It Slide" was more a showcase for the band than for its singer, both confirming the democracy of this new group and going some way toward explaining the "jazz-rock" label that *Child in Time* is still frequently saddled with. In fact, *Child in Time* remains one of the hardest, loudest, and most exciting of all the mothership's myriad offspring, and the fact that it was such a brutally funky album only amplified its achievements.

How easy it would have been, after all, for Gillan to simply fall back on all the past glories his audience hoped he'd be replaying. Instead, the album has more in common with band members Fenwick and Gustafson's recent pasts with Fancy and Roxy Music (the dance-floor stuffing "Love Is the Drug") respectively than any of Gillan's best-known triumphs. Even the album's title was a joke of sorts. "Child in Time" was replayed within, of course, but you'd have a hard time recognizing it, as it flows over a luxurious quiet-storm landscape, to squeeze an almost heartbreaking guitar solo out of Fenwick. Other versions of the song are more powerful, but this remains the most emotional, and that's what the song has always demanded.

Fenwick remembered, "A lot of the Deep Purple fans *were* getting a little unhappy — 'Hey, Ian's getting funky!' — and, of course, by the time of the second album [*Clear Air Turbulence*], that terrible word 'jazz' was coming in. But the worst thing we could have done was be another Deep Purple. We started to really experiment and, by the time we got to the third album [*Scarabus*], although we started doing shorter songs because we were thinking about radio play, we were also getting into some really strange stuff."

Unfortunately, that strangeness was even further removed from both the commercial and the critical radar than ever before. Released in late 1977, *Scarabus* was the Ian Gillan Band's final album — ahead lay nothing more than relentless gigging at home and, with alarmingly less frequency, abroad, until the group played its last concert at the London Marquee on June 14, 1978.

"It really just ended," said Fenwick. "Ian was deciding he needed to get back to a more commercial sound, and we were just locked into what we were doing. I started doing sessions again; Mark [Nauseef] went back to the States. We just fell back into the lives we had before. You can't remember a single day when everyone said, 'The band's broken up' — it just drifted apart. Everyone went and picked up their stuff, and Ian went and formed another band." Only Colin Towns, the keyboard player who moved into the band on the eve of the Nazareth tour, would remain by Gillan's side.

The "commercial sound" for which Gillan was now hankering was one he knew very well — both from his own past and, strangely, from meetings and conversations he was having now. Punk was dead; power pop — the quirky mutant Monkees revival that the U.K. press championed with such rare delight through early 1978 — had not even come to life.

But it wouldn't have mattered much if it had. Deep in the English heartland, in the industrial midlands cities that had never had much time for the arty pronouncements of the capital-centric music papers and certainly weren't crazy about London's attempts to foist fresh "fashions" upon them, a new musical breed was fermenting. It was, to those first observers, a most peculiar underworld, one where the posters of Zeppelin, Sabbath, and Heep still hung on bedroom walls, where it wasn't fashionably de rigueur to hide *Deep Purple in Rock* behind a Sex Pistols LP, where sew-on patches were still a proud flag of allegiance and denim remained the color of choice — and where beginner bands thought there was still some accomplishment to be gained from learning "Highway Star" and "Trampled Underfoot."

It was another year or so before anybody actually named this new breed — and, of course, it was one of the London-based papers that did so. *Sounds* not only christened the ferment as the new wave of British heavy metal, it also, ultimately, spawned a new magazine to cater exclusively to it. *Kerrang!* would grow to become the single most influential publication in metal's entire history.

Although history tends to record the new wave of British heavy metal (customarily abbreviated to the only marginally less cumbersome NWOBHM) as just one among several musical insurgencies washing around the U.K. scene in the aftermath of punk, one underestimates it at one's peril.

True, only two genuinely new acts — Iron Maiden and Def Leppard — would emerge from its ranks as truly international superstars (with two more, Saxon and Venom, closing in behind them), but Metallica were born as little more than severely relocated NWOBHM clones, while Motörhead rose from five years of directionless crunching to become the role model for an even newer wave of amphetamined noise merchants.

Ethel the Frog, the Tygers of Pan Tang, Demon, AIIZ, Witchfynde, Vardis, Tank, Diamond Head, Samson, Girlschool, Angel Witch . . . every week, a new band seemed to form and fly immediately up onstage, to pummel another clubful of willing victims with Panzerfaust riffs and leviathan rhythms. But the ruthless surge of creativity unleashed as the movement gathered pace was responsible not only for a clutch of still-much-loved "new" music, but also for regenerating a battalion of veteran names: UFO, Atomic Rooster, Uriah Heep, and Budgie were all either reborn or rejuvenated by the NWOBHM's search for its own heritage. That only a handful of these acts had ever truly adhered to the tenets of heavy metal was irrelevant. It was perception, not purpose, that fueled the new movement's admiration, and a night out at a late-1970s headbanger's ball was as likely to find the assembled masses shaking their dandruff to the near-folky tones of Wishbone Ash's *Argus* as to the primal battering of Black Sabbath's *Volume Four*.

The groups that emerged from these forgotten hinterlands, however, were anything but relics of rock's hoary past. Rather, they represented a reaction to its spiky present, as Iron Maiden's Steve Harris pointed out when he complained that anyone could cut their hair and look like a punk, but it takes years to grow it long.

Punk's thirsty insistence for musical change, too, was echoed in the new bands' strivings. Even among the movement's staunchest adherents, the awareness was inescapable that too many "classic" groups had made too many albums that simply vanished up their own well-lined rectums. Purple's *Come Taste the Band*, Zeppelin's *Presence*, Sabbath's *Technical Ecstasy* — the musicians themselves were sainted, but they were sainted for what they accomplished in the years before art succumbed to artifice; for "Smoke on the Water," not "Gettin' Tighter," for "Iron Man," not "Rock'n'Roll Doctor." More than any other consideration, the NWOBHM represented the return of the riff. And the louder, heavier, and doomier, the better.

It was a divide that Ray Fenwick readily acknowledged as he mused on the inevitability of the breakup of the Ian Gillan Band: "We weren't those kind of people, we were more thoughtful musicians, very careful about everything we played. And what Ian wanted was a bit more energy."

Gillan, the newly realigned quintet the singer formed around himself and Colin Towns, certainly offered that. In mid-1978, a new band lineup featuring bassist John McCoy, guitarist Steve Byrd, and drummer Pete Barnacle cut an album for the Japanese market alone, then hit the road in Britain, promising a resolute return to both the actual and the perceived hard core at the center of classic Deep Purple.

Neither was Gillan alone in pursuing that goal. David Coverdale, likewise, was reinventing a hitherto hesitant solo career toward this new and astoundingly voracious metal audience, with his two solo albums to date,

1977's *David Coverdale's Whitesnake* and 1978's Roger Glover–produced *Northwinds*, standing as ample evidence of just how swiftly this new constituency had emerged.

In the company of guitarist Bernie Marsden, fresh from the Paice, Ashton & Lord misadventure, alongside his Colosseum II bandmate bassist Neil Murray, plus keyboardist Brian Johnson and drummer David Dowell, from the post-Family band Chapman Whitney Streetwalkers, Coverdale had walked a solid line of melodic, Bad Companyesque blues rock, a competent crew, an enjoyable brew. But where was the flash? Where was the bluster? Where were the power chords?

As it transpired, they were merely biding their time. *Northwinds* was still fresh on the racks when Coverdale relaunched virtually the same lineup of musicians as Whitesnake, a hard-hitting dreadnought of fiercesome riffs and brilliantine rhythms that not only echoed every last preoccupation of the still-burgeoning NWOBHM, it expanded the frontiers a little, as well, by revealing a salacious line in both lyric and imagery that would set the antisexist lobby up for life.

It never took much imagination, after all, to visualize precisely what kind of serpent a *white snake* was — but just in case there was room for doubt, Coverdale gleefully banged the message home in every arena he could. From an on- and offstage persona that blueprinted "Cock Rock" for an entire generation of drooling teenage admirers, to the *Love Hunter* album art that depicted a naked lovely astride a massive coiled snake, there was no attempt at apology, no shade of camouflage, and certainly no room for subtlety. No cliché was too cumbersome, no molehill too mountainous — and the more outcry the band ran up against, the more Coverdale seemed to love it.

And why not? In a career that stretched unbroken into mid-1984 and delivered six consecutive U.K. hit albums, Whitesnake constructed, for their own use and their audiences', a world of unfettered revelry, where the shot glass is always full, the women always willing, and the trouser fly always strained to bursting point.

The newly aligned Whitesnake issued their initial declaration of intent, the *Snakebite* EP, in June 1978, immediately shattering the security of the hip London scene. To the tastemakers of the age, after all, the NWOBHM was little more than a nightmarish anachronism, crewed by inbred mutants who missed the chimes of musical change because they were too busy listening to twenty-minute guitar solos. But the lead track from *Snakebite*, the anthemic "Ain't No Love in the Heart of the City," was already proving that the NWOBHM could sustain a chart hit. When Whitesnake announced that their next London show would be staged at the 2,000-plus-capacity Lyceum, the intention was to prove that neither their success nor their followers were a mere provincial phenomenon. The NWOBHM had gone nationwide.

It was a Lyceum tradition — Sunday-night concerts that packed three bands onto the bill, frequently mixing and matching both style and approach to entertain as many people as possible. (Or, at least, sell more tickets.) Tonight, Whitesnake were taking the stage following perform-ances by new-wave arty types Dead Fingers Talk and, straight out of the spittle-sodden meccas of punk central, the Bernie Tormé Band.

For over a year, guitar wizard Tormé's eponymous band had been driving an energetic swath through such hallowed halls of infamy as the Roxy and the Vortex, and scything through the punk medium's tradi-tional province of three-chords-and-a-prayer with some really rather remarkably guitar-heavy rock. If any of the bands that circumstance had labeled "punk rock" could succeed in front of a David Coverdale audi-ence, and maybe knock these metalheads down a few pegs, it was the Bernie Tormé Band.

Only it wasn't a Coverdale audience that they faced. Or rather, it was, but scarcely one that anybody would recognize. The denim-clad, hippie-haired, button-bedecked regulars were out in force, of course. But so was a whole new crowd — still hairy, still denimed, still laden down with the logos of a dozen extinct bands. But they were younger, louder, harder, and impatient as all buggery. Even before the Lyceum doors opened, as the crowd straggled round the corner onto the Strand, the low chant of "Whitesnake . . . Whitesnake . . ." was audible. By the time the dancefloor was filled, even the DJ was fighting to make himself heard.

What followed, Tormé recalled, was the mismatch from hell — for his band, and for Dead Fingers Talk. In the lair of the Whitesnake, nothing else could exist. From the moment the Bernie Tormé Band took the stage, the barracking was palpable. "We opened, struggled, and died," he said. And, though Dead Fingers Talk fared even worse ("They did a few pro-gay songs and really went down well . . . *not*. They were lucky to get out alive and, as I've never heard of them since, maybe they didn't"), Tormé was unforgiving. He was never going to be shown up by a metal band again.

If Whitesnake were surfing a wave of unprecedented proportions, Ian Gillan had cause for confidence, too — so much so, in fact, that when Ritchie Blackmore dropped by the Marquee on December 27, 1978, to catch the band in concert, Gillan happily welcomed his old adversary onstage to jam through the Deep Purple–era encore of "Lucille." Then, as the crowd filed out at the end of the night, any fans hanging around the club as it closed up would have seen the two old warhorses still deep in conversation. It didn't require many brain cells to surmise what they were talking about, either.

Just months earlier, Jon Lord had slipped into the heart of Whitesnake's neo-bacchanalian revelry, replacing newcomer Pete Solley as the band worked toward the successor to the *Snakebite* breakthrough, fall 1978's *Trouble*. He and Coverdale had remained in touch throughout the past two years — there was even a suggestion, at one point, that Coverdale would voice the unfinished backing tracks on what would have been the second Paice, Ashton & Lord album. That never happened, and over the past few months, Lord had all but left the music business, later confessing, "I had a nervous breakdown. I sat at home and felt sorry for myself. And the longer you do that the harder it is to walk out that door again. I stopped writing, playing, listening. It happens to a lot of people."

Certainly, when the first phone call came in from Coverdale, asking him to join this new band, Lord refused outright, and continued refusing for another month or so. Finally, however, the vocalist's persistent entreaties wore him down. That summer, Lord resumed his partnerships with both Coverdale and Marsden; but, perhaps more significantly, he proved that former members of Deep Purple could reunite without having to reignite all the old rumors and whispers. Now Blackmore was wondering whether Gillan might be interested in staging their own minireconciliation.

Just weeks earlier, as Ian Gillan first deflated and then relaunched his solo dreams, Ritchie Blackmore's Rainbow was undergoing convolutions of its own. It became a standing joke within those circles who spend their time perusing the Musicians Wanted ads that Rainbow would never record two successive albums with the same lineup, and so it proved. By the time of summer 1978's *Long Live Rock*, only Dio and Cozy Powell remained from the outfit that toured so impressively during 1976; by late 1978, even Dio had departed, en route to rejuvenating Black Sabbath. Now Blackmore was on the prowl for a new singer and the Marquee was where he hoped to find one. The guitarist told *Sounds*, "I said to Ian Gillan, 'Let's get together,' [but] he said, 'I can't.' So we got drunk together and I . . . left it at that."

In fact, Blackmore's offer to Gillan, that he disband his own group and join Rainbow, simply mirrored an idea Gillan himself had been mulling over — that Blackmore scrap Rainbow and join Gillan. The present incumbent, Steve Byrd, was not working out, and Gillan was looking for a new guitarist. Blackmore, however, was no more interested in joining one band than Gillan was the other, and the pair parted as friends — who would quickly become rivals. For, no sooner had both bands been brought back to full strength than they embarked, in tandem with Whitesnake, on a campaign of U.K. chart dominance that made Deep Purple's past accomplishments seem a very long way away.

Gillan was the first to get off the starting blocks. Byrd was still aboard when, in early spring 1979, John McCoy introduced him to one of his old friends (and former bandmates), Bernie Tormé. And Tormé, still seething over his treatment at the hands of the Whitesnake crowd, was happy to be introduced.

Tormé had caught the Gillan band live just once, at the London Music Machine the previous year. "I was a big fan of Ian's at the time," he remembered, "but . . . I thought they were really boring, and very rock/conservative, which I didn't like much. I thought [Gillan] didn't work very well, which has always separated me from the Ian/Purple fans at the time, who were the only people around who seemed to like it! I thought it was a bit of a 'dad's band,' if you know what I mean. Very good players, but really just boring."

However, he also remembered thinking, "in a very drunken state at the back of the hall, that I would like to be in that band, because I could give it something it didn't have, a bit of punky violence and rebelliousness, a bit of chaos. Maybe not improve it musically, but make it more interesting. I thought that would make it far more saleable, far more accessible to the people I knew and hung around with. And make it a foil for Ian, which the band was not at that stage."

At least one person, McCoy, apparently agreed with him, wrangling Tormé's band a few support slots with Gillan, opening in such far-flung paradises as Colchester and Aberystwyth University. "John had obviously planned it all," Tormé continued. "He got me to show off at a sound check and armwrestled Ian out to see me. Thank you, man. I knew nothing about it, I just wanted to show what I had started to regard as a bunch of old wankers how it really should be done! Humility was not my strong suit in those days. I had no idea that I was, in fact, being auditioned. It never crossed my mind, I never even thought about it."

As Byrd moved aside to admit Bernie Tormé, drummer Barnacle, too, passed out of the group, and there was talk, for a time, of recruiting Ian Paice to the band — he even auditioned. Finally, however, Gillan turned to a player he'd known for even longer, his old Episode 6 colleague Mick Underwood and, having already entered into a new era of nonstop gigging, the newly constituted Gillan cut their first album, *Mr. Universe*, that summer 1979.

The band were still pounding the clubs when they received the first inkling that, after three years, Gillan was back where he belonged. Tormé recalled, "We were in this shitty bed and breakfast in Carlisle (which is a pretty grim town at the best of times), with an instant coffee/tea machine in place of a breakfast room in the hall, which was the size of a broom cupboard, and also had a broken window with cardboard in it. A call came through on the payphone from our agent, telling us that *Mr. Universe* had gone straight in [the U.K. chart] at no. 11. 'Yes! Victory, justification, suck on that one, shitheads! I'm a rock star, riches beyond our wildest dreams, all those hellish years paying dues, and now we need never ever worry again, especially about money. . . .' As if. It was a very sweet moment, if somewhat illusory."

The band's next album, *Glory Road*, climbed to No. 3, while the single "Trouble" rose to No. 14. "New Orleans" only just missed topping the U.K. charts in March 1981, and the following month, the *Future Shock* album (Tormé's last studio recording, before his replacement by Janick

Gers) similarly pulled up just one place short. And, on the occasions when neither Gillan nor Whitesnake were sniffing the peak of the chart pile, Rainbow were patrolling it instead.

Though he was rebuffed by Gillan, Blackmore continued looking backward as he sought to ease the prospect of rebuilding Rainbow during those first months of 1979. He invited Roger Glover into the band, both as producer and bass player — an offer Glover promptly accepted.

Since *The Butterfly Ball*, Glover had continued in production work, handling new albums by Rory Gallagher, Nazareth vocalist Dan McCafferty, and, of course, David Coverdale, but otherwise breaking cover only once, in 1978, to deliver his first solo album, *Elements* (early press reports titled it *Eyes of Omega*). A concept album built around the properties and powers of the four elements — earth, wind, water, and fire — with the four tracks dedicated to each one, *Elements* was recorded with the Munich Philharmonic, plus an impressive arsenal of keyboards, percussion and wind. (Ronnie James Dio cut vocal tracks for a couple of numbers, but was ultimately dropped in favor of a full instrumental approach.)

It was an ambitious set, yet never so prepossessing as to leave the listener feeling alienated by another ham-fisted attempt to meld rock with the classics. Rather, the Wagnerian scope of the music and the immensity of the orchestra were both wholly ingested into Glover's traditional knack for writing well-arranged, dynamic pop-prog-rock. Thus, the riff that was central to "The First Ring Made of Clay" could, with only minor readjustment, have driven a hard-rocking Purple classic, while some of the shifts in tempo and mood put one in mind of early albums by Steve Hackett and/or Godley-Creme, with the link to the latter further cemented by the thematic similarities between *Elements* and the duo's own *Consequences*.

"The Next a Ring of Fire," too, rattled along like a well-oiled prog jam, with the sax and drum duel amidships conjuring images of mid-'70s King Crimson. To dwell on such reference points, however, was to overlook the sheer originality, excitement, and overall exuberance that were the hallmarks of *Elements* — an album that, though decidedly late in the day by conventional prog-rock standards, nevertheless represented a towering achievement. It also contributed to the surprise that greeted Glover's recruitment to Rainbow.

Such emotions, however, were swiftly suppressed as Rainbow returned to action in summer 1979. With Glover joined in the new-arrivals box by former Marbles singer Graham Bonnet and, echoing Whitesnake's fondness for former members of Colosseum II, keyboard player Don Airey (also formerly of Cozy Powell's early '70s band Hammer), the Glover-produced *Down to Earth* went on to become Rainbow's most successful, and most commercial, album yet, not only sailing up the LP charts worldwide, but breaking the band on the singles listings, too.

Past Rainbow 45s were little more than tasters for the LPs, and August 1979's "Since You've Been Gone" was initially regarded as nothing more than that. Buoyed by the gathering mainstream impetus of the NWOBHM, however, the song that would almost single-handedly invent the so-called "power ballad" of the next decade soared to No. 6 in Britain and brought Blackmore and Glover back to British TV's *Top of the Pops* for the first time in eight years. Six months later, a remixed edit of the album's "All Night Long" became their first Top 5 hit single in almost a decade.

No matter that neither song, exquisitely classy pop though they were, could ever hold their ground in any true competition of all-time heavy-metal anthems. Together, they established Rainbow alongside anybody else you could mention at the top of the resurgent metal boom — and proved what a laugh any attempts to so ruthlessly pigeonhole artists can be.

One might have expected this incarnation of Rainbow to follow through with even greater glories. Instead, true to form, the lineup shattered as Cozy Powell — the last remaining veteran member — quit during what were, from all accounts, a series of absolutely lifeless rehearsals for the next album. He was swiftly followed by Bonnett, passing out with the savage rejoinder, "If Rainbow had worked at it a bit more, they could have been as big as Zeppelin. But Ritchie throws his talent away onstage, and after Cozy left, it took a real dive." Glover responded, "God gave [Bonnett] a great voice — but took away everything else."

Powell was replaced (or, at least, succeeded) by Bobby Rondinelli; Bonnett by Joe Lynn Turner. Born in Hackensack, New Jersey, on August 2, 1951, Turner, early in his musical career, played guitar alongside future Kool & the Gang star JT Taylor in the local band Filet of Soul. From there, he moved to Ezra, a chiefly covers band whose repertoire stretched, ambitiously, through Hendrix, Yes, and (don't they always!) Deep Purple.

Turner had little intention of becoming a professional musician. Armed with a degree in education, Turner spent much of the 1970s teaching English literature. In 1977, however, he joined another local band, Fandango, as guitarist and occasional vocalist. Over the next three years, Fandango released four albums, cut in a reasonably pleasant Steely-Dan-meets-the-Allman-Brothers mold, but broke up shortly after a Chicago festival disaster, when their equipment was stolen from the back of a truck. (Coincidentally, ex-Purpler Nick Simper and fellow Warhorse renegade Pete Parks were simultaneously working with their own Fandango, cutting two albums of considerably harder intent.)

Returning to the northeast, Turner was playing low-key shows on the New York club circuit when he received word that Ritchie Blackmore wanted to meet with him. The guitarist had recently been introduced to Fandango's back catalog and was so impressed that, within hours of their meeting, the two were writing their first songs together.

Turner's first recording with Rainbow was "I Surrender," a magnificently melodic offering from ex-Zombies songwriter Russ Ballard. Rainbow had already recorded the number with Bonnett, but thought nothing of replacing the errant singer's vocals with the newcomer's. And immediately Blackmore's instincts were proven correct — "I Surrender" saw Rainbow open 1981 with a No. 3 British hit, a placing echoed by the attendant new album, *Difficult to Cure*.

Whitesnake, too, were on an all-time high. Secure within the armor of their audience's unrelenting hatred for anything that stepped outside of the metal framework (for NWOBHM audiences were astonishingly partisan in their tastes), they reveled in the tempest of opprobrium that rained down around 1979's *Love Hunter* artwork. Journalist Mick Wall offered the best riposte when he remarked, "Whatever bile it caused the feminists to spew up, you had to admit that that bird had an arse on her."

It was an attitude that couldn't fail to win the undying support of the band's chosen audience, and when drummer Dowell departed in early 1980, Whitesnake slithered even deeper into metallic iconography with the announcement of his successor. So Ritchie Blackmore thought he was cool for reuniting two former members of Deep Purple? With the arrival of Ian Paice, Whitesnake had three.

Paice had spent the intervening period being associated with seemingly every drumming vacancy in rock. He was widely linked with Paul McCartney's Wings, as replacement for the departed Joe English during the summer of 1977, and with The Who, as they prepared to reanimate in the aftermath of Keith Moon's death. He also spent a few months rehearsing (alongside Jon Lord and fellow PAL pal Paul Martinez) with former Stone the Crows singer Maggie Bell, as she worked toward her planned comeback.

Paice's arrival into Whitesnake was certainly well-timed. His first single with the band, "Fool for Your Loving," readily pursued Rainbow's "All Night Long" into the U.K. Top 20 in April 1980; the next album, *Ready an' Willing*, gatecrashed the Top 10. With Gillan's latest 45, "Sleeping on the Job," then squeaking into the Top 60 just weeks later, the shards of Deep Purple had notched up as many British hits in nine months as the parent band had mustered in nine years. Over the next twelve months, that tally would swell even further.

The year-end readers' polls in the U.K. press echoed this dominance. Throughout the early 1980s, Rainbow, Whitesnake, and Gillan effortlessly held their own against the very best that anyone could pitch at them, including every other star in the NWOBHM firmament.

Such success did not, however, necessarily breed contentment. Within all three bands, there grew the nagging belief that no matter how gloriously certain musicians were feted individually, no matter how well they worked together in simple pairs and partnerships, how much more applause might greet them — how much more magnificence might flow — if they were all to join forces once again?

There was only one way to find out.

Chapter 14

As the Colors Fade

By the early 1980s, rumors of a Deep Purple reunion were as old as dirt. The flurry of speculation that surrounded Jon Lord and Ian Paice's loosely mooted Purple project with David Coverdale in 1976 was followed, in 1978, by reports that the Mark II lineup was set to reconvene for five concerts in Spain in May 1979. Nineteen-eighty brought a fresh bout of whispering following a similar offer from a Japanese promoter.

Barely a year seemed to pass without sundry supposedly informed sources putting it around that one so-and-so was talking to another so-and-so. Of course they usually weren't, but still it came as no surprise, in 1980, to hear that some enterprising American had hit on the notion of eschewing all the usual suspects altogether and reforming Deep Purple from an entirely different direction, with original members Rod Evans and Nick Simper. It didn't matter that, by that time, few people even remembered their tenure with the group.

The inspiration behind this audacious adventure came from a pair of musicians, guitarist Tony Flynn and keyboard player Geoff Emery. Both, as the plan began to take shape, were members of the New Steppenwolf, a group formed in 1977 from, if not the ashes, then at least the memory of John Kay's early-1970s hard-rock band. The New Steppenwolf featured just one original member of the Canadian legends, keyboard player Goldy McJohn, and one latter-day player, bassist Nick St. Nicholas, but audiences raised on the roar of "Born to Be Wild" and "The Pusher" seldom worried about that.

St. Nicholas alone would see out the New Steppenwolf's entire three-year career, while around him spun a revolving door of musicians, several drawn from a pack of jobbing players in the employ of the New Steppenwolf's promoter, Steve Green. His company, Advent Talent Associates, had long since cornered the market in what the concert circuit knew as "revival acts" — bands who, having disbanded or retired, could be reanimated around one or two former members and sent back onto the road.

The New Steppenwolf slid graciously, then, into a roster that already included such legends of classic rock and pop as Canned Heat, Jay and the Americans, the MC5, and Herman's Hermits. Emery himself was a former member of Mike Pinera's New Cactus Band, a revival of a revival of the early-'70s Vanilla Fudge spin-off. And all had one thing in common. Like Steppenwolf, the name was frequently the only "original" thing about the act. Anybody going along in the hope of seeing any of the stars that might have once ridden the band — Heat's Bob Hite, the 5's Wayne Kramer, the Americans' Jay — were out of luck.

As Peter Noone, Herman of the Hermits, explained, "I was receiving letters from fans who'd say, 'I went to see Herman's Hermits last night and you weren't there. . . .' It turned out there were people touring, using the name, playing the songs, who I'd never even heard of! I went to some of the shows, and I'd see these fucking clowns onstage: 'Ah, here's one we recorded in 1965,' and my friends would have to hold me back. I just wanted to run up there and have a tantrum — 'You didn't record it . . . the only one of you who was even in the band back then was the drummer, and he never played on any of the records!'"

Despite such artistic misgivings, the revival circuit these bands plied was both profitable and popular, with American audiences seemingly starving for further nostalgic attractions to drink and dance to. So, when the New Steppenwolf began to wind down in late 1979, Emery and Flynn conceived their next move.

Both were fans of Deep Purple; both were well aware of the avid interest that still swirled around the apparently lifeless corpse of the band. In late 1979, with a third former member of the New Steppenwolf, drummer Dick Jurgens, they began looking to place their plans in motion.

Their first step was to track down a former member of the original group, to add legitimacy to the "new" lineup's existence. They settled on Rod Evans, five years out of the music industry and now, newly acquired medical degree in hand, working as director of respiratory therapy at a California hospital. He, in turn, contacted Nick Simper, only for the bassist to turn the offer down flat. "[Evans] contacted me about it," said Simper, "but I didn't want to know. I was not involved with that in any way at all." The new band was not to be dissuaded, however. From a stream of auditions, bassist Tom DeRivera was procured and, by early 1980, the "new" Deep Purple was locked in rehearsal.

Although those who make their money from it have always regarded rock'n'roll as big business, many aspects of the industry were once surprisingly lax. So many revival acts flourished without fear of legal reprisal because very few original bands ever got around to legally trademarking, or otherwise protecting, their name. The original Steppenwolf's John Kay discovered this when he first became aware of the revived band — with nothing in writing to prove he owned the rights to the name, there was nothing he could do to stop anybody else from using it. Ultimately, he came to an arrangement whereby the name was "leased" to its new proprietors — other artists, however, were not even extended that luxury.

With such precedents behind them, it is unlikely whether anybody involved in reanimating Deep Purple even considered for a moment that this name was better protected than any other. Although Evans might have recalled that the group's name was registered in the U.K. in May 1968, it seems nobody ever dreamed that a registered company, Deep Purple Overseas Ltd., was formed back in 1971 to safeguard it from unwarranted exploitation. And, for the moment at least, Deep Purple Overseas Ltd. never imagined that anybody would be brazen enough to try.

They were wrong. In March 1980, Emery registered the name Deep Purple with both the U.S. Patent and Trademark Office and the State of California, affirming under oath that no other person had a prior right to the same name "either in the identical form or in such near resemblance

. . . as to be likely . . . to cause confusion, or cause mistake or to deceive."

The absence of any of his original bandmates did not, apparently, worry Evans. He told Mexico's *Conecte* magazine that "we talked with Jon Lord . . . and Ritchie Blackmore . . . and they showed no interest in Deep Purple." They had, after all, their own current projects to pursue, and Evans reminded *Sounds*, "It's a shame to kind of knock it . . . for the fact that it isn't everybody together. What seems peculiar to Deep Purple is that there were several formations of the band and it never seemed to really affect the fans of the music, as long as it was played up to a certain par. They just wanted to hear the music."

Other forces in the American music industry agreed. The William Morris Agency, one of the most powerful booking agencies in the country, readily added Deep Purple to its client base and began working on a tour itinerary. That, in turn, led the group into a recording contract with a record company affiliated to Warner Brothers, the original Deep Purple's own American label. Over the next few months, up to half a dozen songs, including the authentically titled "Blood Blister" and a punningly titled Gene Krupa tribute, "Brum Doogie," were recorded at L.A.'s Village Recording Studios, for inclusion on the band's proposed debut album, tentatively scheduled for November 1980 release.

Deep Purple made their live debut at the Amarillo Civic Center on May 17, 1980, the first of several low-key shows in and around Texas that led up to their first major engagement, top of the bill at Mexico City's open-air Estadio Inde on June 28.

Headlining over '60s-era Mexican band Dugs Dugs and the latest incarnation of Black Oak Arkansas, Deep Purple came onstage to a riotous reception. Media coverage of the event was enormous, pumping several thousand onlookers into a state of virtual frenzy. Radio was blaring "Smoke on the Water," journalists were recalling *Machine Head* and *Burn*. Nobody thought to even ask precisely which version of Deep Purple they were witnessing — so long as Blackmore was there, Gillan or Coverdale, Glover or Hughes, Lord and Paice . . .

A rainstorm that struck during the final changeover and delayed for hours Deep Purple's arrival onto the tented stage, couldn't dampen the audience's spirits. They simply sat there soaked, convinced that once the band did arrive onstage, all the discomfort would be worthwhile.

How mistaken they were. Even with the blistering roar of the opening "Highway Star" blaring from the PA, and what was clearly a very expensive light and laser show preparing to kick into gear, from the moment the five unfamiliar faces appeared onstage, you could sense the audience's confusion turning to unrest turning to rage. No Blackmore, no Gillan, no Paice . . . If anybody recognized even the one true Deep Purple member who was on that stage, they kept the knowledge to themselves.

The band played on. Reasonable facsimiles of "Mandrake Root," "Hush," and "Hey Joe" spun out of Evans' own years with the original group, but horrendous approximations of "Space Truckin'" and "Smoke on the Water" confirmed the players' absolute lack of legitimate credentials. So, as they left the stage after just forty minutes, did the brevity of the set. There was no encore — but there was a riot. By the time the police cleared the stadium, the stage was littered with bottles and debris, doors were ripped from their hinges and shattered . . . even the huge American football-style goals that stood at either end of the stadium's playing surface were dismantled and turned into so much scrap wood.

Shaken but not disheartened, Deep Purple were in Phoenix the following night, before moving up to the midwest and the East Coast. By now, the "real" Deep Purple were fully aware of what was taking place in their name and were hurrying to halt it. It was, however, a slow process that the bogus band had no intention of acknowledging. As early as mid-May, the trademark infringement was pointed out to the interlopers, but the only difference it appears to have made was the occasional prefixing of the band's name with the word "New" on concert posters. Otherwise they carried on regardless.

The following month, Tony Edwards and John Coletta, representing HEC Enterprises Ltd. and Deep Purple Overseas Ltd., filed an action in the Los Angeles Federal District Court, seeking an injunction against the fraudulent band and requesting damages under the Lanham Act, a statute governing the sanctity of trademarks and trade names. Again, however, the wheels of justice ground slowly.

Nevertheless, word of the true nature of the band had begun to spread. A gig in Detroit ended with another riot, while an appearance at the Soap Factory on New York's Staten Island was looking shaky before the show even got started, after an already rowdy audience set up a rafter-rocking chant of "We want Blackmore."

In a surely misguided attempt to calm the crowd's expectations, an announcement was made over the PA that only one original Deep Purple member, Rod Evans, was scheduled to appear that night — at which point the audience exploded. With bottles and cans flying, the concert was abandoned on the spot. Somehow, the venue's security prevented an outright reenactment of the scenes in Detroit and Mexico City, instead persuading the crowd to form an orderly line to collect refunds of their ticket money.

And still the sham went on. The following night, the band played in Seaside Heights, then made their way up to Somerset, Massachusetts, en route to shows in Quebec and Anchorage, Alaska. By now the set had expanded to include a lengthy improvisation through "Wring That Neck" and, reaching even further ahead of Evans' own era, "Woman from Tokyo" and "Might Just Take Your Life" — songs whose inclusion, Evans acknowledged, were obligatory. The audience, he said, "expect it. You can sure enough play 'Hush,' but you'll play 'Smoke on the Water,' then someone else will ask for 'Burn.' Even if we came out with a whole bunch of new material, which we're working on now, they'd still want to hear certain songs."

As for the audience's demand for other, perhaps better-known, members of Deep Purple, he continued, "There'll always be people in the crowd looking for Ritchie, or asking, 'Where's Jon?'" He recalled his years with Captain Beyond, a group formed with former members of Iron Butterfly and Johnny Winter's band: "People would come up to me all the time and say, 'Why the hell aren't you playing Purple material?' Or they'd go up to the Iron Butterfly people and say, 'Why aren't you playing "In a Gadda Da Vida?"'" Captain Beyond had eventually shattered under the weight of such audiences' disappointment. Deep Purple were not going to make the same mistake. They were going to make another one entirely.

No matter where the group went, audiences remained furious at the deception. The Quebec show, at the Capitol Theatre on August 12, was punctuated throughout by a hail of chairs raining onto the stage, a dire situation Tony Flynn only exacerbated when he grabbed the microphone to admonish the crowd: "Whoever wants to see the real Deep Purple is welcome to stay . . . the rest of you can fuck off." Inevitably, it was the band who fucked off, downing tools midway through crucifying "Space Truckin'," and returning to their dressing room.

The group played what would become its final show at the Long Beach Arena in Los Angeles on August 19. The "real" Deep Purple's injunction was still tied up in legal red tape, so tangled they were unable even to halt a show in the court's own backyard, and so convoluted that the ticket-buying public could never be warned in time.

Neither, it seemed, did the William Morris Agency want them warned. When the Long Beach show's promoter, Avalon Attractions, requested permission to publicize the membership of the band to avoid the kind of scenes that had marred previous concerts, the agency allegedly threatened to sue for breach of contract.

Coletta and Edwards, however, did at least arrange for a notice to appear in the *L.A. Times* the day before the concert, noting not who *was* in the band, but who wasn't: "The following stars will not perform . . . Ritchie Blackmore, David Coverdale, Ian Gillan, Roger Glover, Glen [sic] Hughes, Jon Lord, Ian Paice." They also made the rounds of local rock critics, informing them of the nature of the evening's entertainment and requesting, according to a report in *Sounds*, that any reviews that might appear should be somewhat less than glowing.

Such bad publicity had little effect on ticket sales. The 9,000-seat arena was filled to at least two-thirds capacity, and *Sounds* reported, "The kids I spoke to were either curious enough to see what was going on, confused, or stupid — expecting anything from Blackmore to a complete reincarnation of all the Purple-ites over the years, including the dead ones." Needless to say, they didn't get them and, just a couple of songs into the performance, there was already a line of disgruntled patrons demanding their money back.

Others, however, seemed content to sit the spectacle out, "content to bang their heads whenever possible, and cheer at the memory of classics that most weren't old enough to remember" — and which some, the *L.A. Times* critic among them, were hard-pressed even to recognize: "The band's playing was so sloppy that . . . [they] got halfway through one of my favorites, 'Woman from Tokyo,' before I realized what it was. Tempos constantly went awry, all sense of dynamics were absent, and the long guitar, organ, and drum solos were pathetic. Flashy laser and light effects couldn't hide the fact that the whole thing was a sham."

Finally a date was announced for the court case, and as the day approached, Evans began to consider the future of the group. Interviewed by *Sounds*, he spoke hopefully of continuing the band, either under the Deep Purple name, if the court decided in his favor, or under a new one, if it didn't. In the event, the group shattered beneath the colossal weight of the judge's decision. On October 3, 1980, a verdict was delivered that unconditionally upheld the "real" Deep Purple's rights to the band name, awarding punitive damages of $672,000 against the impersonators. The quintet disbanded immediately.

The entire exercise, Jon Lord growled, "was a very silly thing to do, an example of poor judgment, I would say. [Rod] was an idiot. He was misled by people that wanted to cash in on the name, with no regard to quality. They didn't care that it could hurt the name, the reputation that we spent years in building. We felt very sad about that. Had we not fought them according to American law for six months, they could have recorded as Deep Purple, which would have been the worst lie."

In fact, the material the group recorded, that much-vaunted debut album, was scrapped. The following year, interviewed in *Conecte*, Tony Flynn talked of plans to "release a solo album" which would feature guests appearances from Rod Evans and Geoff Emery — clearly a reference to the Deep Purple material — but nothing ever came of it. Flynn remains in the music industry, however, performing in and around Acapulco, Mexico. Emery, too, remains active, as vice president of the independent California record label Statue Records. Dick Jurgens, however, quit and now runs a motorcycle repair and customizing store in Hawaii, while DeRivera returned to the obscurity from which he came and Rod Evans, to all intents and purposes, has vanished off the face of the earth.

That was then, this was now. Picking up where they'd left off at the Marquee at Christmas 1978, Gillan and Blackmore were talking again in mid-1982, casually inquiring of one another whether they'd be interested in putting something together. Both, of course, knew what that "something" would be, and so feelers began extending toward other Purple alumni — Glover, of course; Paice and Lord inevitably.

Of the five, Blackmore seemed to have the most to gain from

returning to the familiar waters of Purplehood. The peaks that Rainbow had touched with *Down to Earth* and *Difficult to Cure* had proven alarmingly illusory; though the band returned to the U.K. Top 5 with 1982's essentially forgettable *Straight Between the Eyes*, personnel clashes and changes continued to claim both musicians and, increasingly, the music. Keyboard player Don Airey hit the nail at least partially on the head when he quit in early 1982, claiming he'd finally had enough of "bashing our way through old Rainbow and even old Purple material." He moved on to the now-reenergized Ozzy Osbourne's new band — where, as every ironist in the world was quick to point out, he commenced bashing his way through old Sabbath material instead, but his earlier point was no less pertinent for that.

Just as Gillan had complained of Deep Purple precisely a decade earlier, Rainbow was flying on autopilot, cranking to a formula and backing it up with the best of the oldies. Ignore the fact that the group was still selling out some of the largest arenas in the world (for since when has that been a guarantee of quality?), and Rainbow had developed into little more than a crowd-pleasing cabaret turn. Blackmore and Glover knew it.

Their conversations with their former bandmates were secret, of course. Rainbow, Whitesnake, and Gillan all had new albums approaching, fresh commitments to fulfill. But, as early as September 1982, whispers began leaking into the music press regardless, with the muttering gathering further momentum after Gillan split his own band in December, at the conclusion of their latest world tour.

Gillan's explanation was that he simply needed a break, that his voice was on the brink of collapse — with the rest of him set to follow. "We ended up in Portsmouth and . . . for the first time in my life, I couldn't even croak my way through a show," he recalled. "There was nothing coming out at all. The audience was great, phenomenal, but . . . I was just knackered. I'd been doing two hundred shows a year for God knows how long, and suddenly the voice had gone."

It really had. But the news could not help but give fresh force to the rumor mill. A European promoter, leaping ahead of any semblance of reality, even provisionally booked the reborn Deep Purple's first concerts. In fact, for the moment, the issue was dead. While Glover and

Paice had pledged their support to a reunion, Lord was proving less enthusiastic.

Always close to Coverdale, Lord valued loyalty to Whitesnake higher than any sentimental attachments to his past — particularly a past that had ended so bitterly a decade before. Besides, a well-received new solo album, *Before I Forget*, the previous year, had already been succeeded by plans for a new one, a musical adaptation of the best-selling *Country Diary of an Edwardian Lady*. Even if he wanted to reform Deep Purple, he would hardly have the time. And so, as Gillan bluntly put it, "Having caused its own public intrigue . . . the idea fizzled out" — and the hard-rock merry-go-round that the various band members had been riding for so long took another unexpected turn. Early into 1983, Ronnie James Dio quit Black Sabbath. He was replaced by Ian Gillan.

When he was first contacted by the band's management, Gillan recalled, "I kept on saying, 'No, no, I'm not interested.' But finally I was persuaded to meet them. I spent an afternoon in a pub with [them] and just got totally arseholed. I thought, "This is just great, I'm really getting on with these guys and . . . wouldn't it be nice to just be a singer in a band once again, with no leadership responsibilities.' So I thought, 'Yeah, I'll do it.'"

Having struggled so dourly through their last years with Ozzy Osbourne, Black Sabbath were utterly reinvented by Dio's arrival. Though admirers of the group's early work — those first five albums remain a benchmark of heavy-metal purity — complained that the two LPS cut under Dio's tutelage, *Heaven and Hell* and *Mob Rules*, served up only crude cartoon caricatures of the venomous brutality the band had once spit so unerringly, still Black Sabbath readily reconfirmed their status as prime exponents of what religiously inclined disbelievers termed "Devil Rock."

The advent of Gillan, though certain to skew the band in another direction entirely — he'd never been one for Black Masses and sacrifice, even when such practices were progressive rock staples — nevertheless filled the fan club with breathless excitement. So many past marriages of super-groups, after all, were made in heaven, but wound up in hell. This one was surely the first to have been consummated the other way around.

Despite his enthusiasm for his new bandmates, however, Gillan could not shake off a sense of uncertainty about this latest adventure, even after the world was informed of his arrival via a press conference at London's Le Beat Route nightclub on April 6.

Some of his unhappiness was rooted in the decision to continue billing the band as Black Sabbath. "Our [individual] music backgrounds and the fans we appealed to were quite different," Gillan reflected, and the inclusion of "Smoke on the Water" in the new band's live set was only going to amplify that gulf. It was an opinion that Sabbath's Tony Iommi would later come to share — he told Sabbath biographer Steve Rosen, "[We] should have been under a different name — Gillan, Iommi, Butler and Whatever." Hindsight, unfortunately, butters few parsnips. Black Sabbath it would remain.

Even more disconcerting was the knowledge that Black Sabbath had, in fact, already disbanded, and that the impetus behind this new incarnation came not from the band members, but from their manager, Don Arden. So the possibility that this much-heralded supergroup was little more than a supermoneymaking machine was never far from anybody's mind — Gillan's included.

At the same time, news that Sabbath's original drummer, Bill Ward, was returning to the fold alongside fellow founders Tony Iommi and Geezer Butler, was the source of considerable optimism. Ward had departed (to be replaced by Vinnie Appice) in 1980, driving another nail into the coffin of the band's early musical potency. His restoration to the engine room might well prove the catalyst so lacking in the group's last couple of albums.

The quartet familiarized themselves with one another with a series of tentative rehearsals, at which the gulf between the musicians' backgrounds and preferences proved less of a stumbling block than Gillan might have imagined. Only the same vocal problems that had forced Gillan to abandon his own band might upset the rhythm. A specialist had diagnosed nodules on the singer's vocal chords, a common problem, but a debilitating one all the same, and recommended that Gillan undergo a minor operation to have them removed. Unfortunately, just as he was ready to go under the knife, the Sabbath offer arrived. Now there simply wasn't the time.

Sessions for the album, now aptly titled *Born Again*, commenced in May 1983 at the Manor Studios, and the sparkling energy of the rehearsals seemed destined to continue. Tony Iommi recalled, "We put some ideas down [in rehearsal], but we didn't exactly know what [Gillan] was going to sing until we got into the studio." In fact, he fulfilled every one of his bandmates' hopes. True, few acolytes of either party would rate *Born Again* among the best records either Gillan or Black Sabbath ever put their name to. But it proved that the partnership was, at least, eminently workable. Or it did in the studio.

Gillan told *Kerrang!,* "[*Born Again*] was brilliant, absolutely fucking sensational . . . until it was mixed, when it was totally destroyed." Trusting in his bandmates to turn in a suitable mix of a magnificent record and approve appropriate cover art, Gillan was on holiday while the finishing touches were cemented into place. "I came back off holiday," he explained, "[and] found they'd sent me a bundle of twenty *Born Again* albums." He looked at the cover, a truly garish portrait of a horn-headed baby, "and puked. [Then] I put the LP on the turntable and was disgusted by it. It was just garbage. In a rage, I smashed all of the twenty albums to pieces."

As his first tour with Black Sabbath approached, Gillan's early faith in the group was shattered even further. The first blow was delivered by Bill Ward's insistence that, though he was happy to record the album, his ongoing battle with alcohol would not permit him to go out on the road. The group promptly drafted in former Electric Light Orchestra drummer Bev Bevan — like the Sabbath team, a child of the late-1960s Birmingham music scene, but born of another school of musical influences and notions altogether.

The group's chosen repertoire, so heavy on Sabbath oldies that even the new album scarcely got a look in, was equally disappointing. Looking on from his newly launched solo career, Ronnie James Dio quipped, "It [is] beyond my comprehension how [Gillan] will possibly sing any of the songs they'll force him to do, such as 'Iron Man' and 'Paranoid.'" Gillan shared his bemusement. Even worse was the band's insistence that Gillan curtail his long-practiced delight in ad-libbing, for fear of upsetting fans who demanded word-perfect renditions of their favorite songs. But the final straw came with the demand that he conform with the band's traditional image and wear all black, all the time. That might have been Black Sabbath's image, but it certainly wasn't his.

This catalog of misgivings notwithstanding, the tour itself was as well-oiled as it could be. "A masterpiece of organization," Gillan marveled, "bigger than anything I'd ever expected." Even the incorporation of a mountainous Stonehenge backdrop, a crew of roadies clad in druidic cowls, and a dwarf dressed as the album sleeve's demonic baby, left him speechlessly impressed, if only from a logistic point of view — carting such a monstrous set around half the world for six full months was an art form in itself. Not, however, until the release of the movie *Spinal Tap*, in which similar props were immortalized for all time as the apex of true rock'n'roll madness, did Gillan come to appreciate them in any other way. The rest of the time, he simply considered it silly.

Gillan told *Classic Rock Revisited*, "We were rehearsing and we went to a company called LSD [Light and Sound Design] in Birmingham to talk about production. The guys said, 'Does anybody have any ideas for a stage set?' We were all looking around at each other and trying to think of something, and Geezer said, 'Stonehenge.' The bloke said, 'What a great idea. How do you visualize it?' Geezer said, 'Life-size, of course.' So they built an exact replica of Stonehenge, which is huge.

"No one gave it any thought, but we could only get it into two of the halls and, even then, it was only three of these things. The rest of them are in containers in a dock somewhere and they have been [ever since]. I remember it being set up at the first gig at Toronto Maple Leaf Gardens. They could only get three of these things up. I remember that there was a dwarf hanging around. The manager looked around like, 'Why is this guy hanging around here?' On the front cover of *Born Again* they had this baby with long fingernails and horns, so we had this dwarf. We had a tape of a baby screaming and the sound was flanged. The dwarf would fall backward about 20 feet and then the bells would toll and the roadies would come out dressed as druids. They looked great. Apart from the Reeboks, they looked authentic.

"I was laughing my fucking socks off. When the dwarf would fall off of Stonehenge, the screaming would fade and the druids would come on to the sounds of the bells tolling. On opening night, we could still hear the screaming after the dwarf fell. He was supposed to fall onto some mattresses, but on opening night somebody had moved the mattresses! We didn't see the dwarf anymore! I think he bounced right out the door."

For all the difficulties, disputes, and minor disasters that charted

Gillan's stint with Black Sabbath, it was at least a commercial success. The tour did phenomenally well, while *Born Again*, a Top 40 American hit, incredibly became Black Sabbath's highest-charting album in the U.K. since the halcyon days of *Sabbath Bloody Sabbath*, a full decade previous.

Gillan, however, knew that life in this most distinctive of bands was never going to become any easier. On the eve of Black Sabbath's second American tour, in October 1983, he announced his intention to quit the group once the outing was over. And three years later, when Black Sabbath returned from a sabbatical that now saw Tony Iommi alone remain from past lineups, he discovered who his replacement was: Glenn Hughes.

Hughes came into the band at a critical juncture in Black Sabbath's now soap-operatic career less than a year after the original, Ozzy-led lineup had reconvened for Live Aid, and encouraged hopes that the partnership might remain permanent. But only a short while after it became apparent that those hopes had already been dashed. Osbourne returned to his solo career, Bill Ward was still absent, and Geezer Butler had opted out of the band altogether.

So, as it happened, had Tony Iommi. When he first made contact with Hughes, he was, in fact, planning a solo album, *Seventh Star*, one that would showcase his guitar-playing abilities alongside a host of guest vocalists. Aside from Hughes, Iommi had also lined up Ronnie James Dio and Rob Halford. Unfortunately, a wealth of attendant contractual difficulties swooped to dismiss that plan, and Hughes wound up singing the whole disc. The solo album was then derailed when management and record-company pressures insisted that it should instead be bundled up under the familiar brand name. Iommi's personal ambitions were appeased with little more than a subtitle — the LP was released as Black Sabbath Featuring Tony Iommi.

Like Gillan, Iommi had known Hughes since their respective "early days" — indeed, he'd known him even longer. Hughes was a fellow Brummie, rattling around the Birmingham music scene at the same time as Sabbath's first incarnation, Earth, were taking their novice steps, while Trapeze had opened for Sabbath on at least one occasion, at the Birmingham Top Rank in 1971.

Neither was Iommi's offer the first time Hughes had been invited into the Black Sabbath family. He and Ozzy Osbourne had talked of forming their own group in 1977. That fell apart for a number of reasons, not least of all Hughes' reluctance to be drawn back into the same situation he'd undergone with Deep Purple, where his own singing abilities would be sidelined by the presence of an acknowledged "vocalist."

The Iommi venture, too, might have foundered had Hughes understood the machinery grinding behind it. As desperate now as he'd ever been to perform music that actually matched his own musical tastes, Hughes had finally commenced making signal advances on that front via his own post-Purple activities. He certainly had no intention of becoming "the new Black Sabbath singer." In the event, it was not until the album was complete — with Hughes very happy with the decidedly non-metallic results — that Sabbath manager Don Arden dropped his advice into the stew. And, as Gillan reflected of his own experiences with the man, "Don tended to get what he wanted."

In early 1986, Hughes, Iommi, and the rest of the newly rebranded band went into North Hollywood's Alley Studios to begin rehearsing for the inevitable tour. It was an awkward few weeks, as Hughes admitted that, though he had no problem performing songs from the Ronnie Dio era of the band, the earlier Ozzy material was another matter entirely. "For Glenn Hughes to sing 'War Pigs' is an absolute crime," he mused later and, when Iommi asked him to commit to the tour, Hughes realized he couldn't do it — and Iommi realized he shouldn't.

Hughes was perfect for the Tony Iommi solo album. But the moment that morphed into another blast from the past, it was clear that other arrangements needed to be made. Although Hughes would perform at the first few shows of the tour, he was swiftly replaced by one Ray Gillen, and this most anonymous version of Black Sabbath trundled on. Hughes, like Ian Gillan before him, was simply glad to see the back of the whole thing.

Of course, the decision to keep the Black Sabbath name alive through the dark years when the band alone seemed to feel it had any value would eventually pay off. The original quartet reconvened once again at the end of the 20th century to pay their own disrespectful respects to the old adage that there really was a time when one became "too old to rock-'n'roll, but too young to die."

By that time, however, that most hoary of clichés had already been laid to rest by a slew of similarly successful (and somewhat longer-lived) reformations — with perhaps the most successful (and certainly the longest-lived) springing from the first of Iommi's post-Ozzy/Dio reanimations. *Born Again* was an appropriate title, after all, for the album that Sabbath cut with Ian Gillan. But it was Gillan who was truly born again.

Chapter 15

The Not-So-Perfect Strangers

Shortly before Christmas 1983, Ritchie Blackmore's manager, Bruce Payne, contacted Ian Gillan to ask if he was interested in reawakening the dormant reunion.

The last months of Rainbow were a nightmare — although, as is so often the way in this story, when the end came it was foreshadowed not by a deliberate decision, but by a happenstance of fate. What turned out to be the band's final U.K. tour, promoting the dismal *Bent Out of Shape* in September 1983, was curtailed — musically if not actually — after Blackmore injured his back playing soccer, sending one of the muscles into spasm. Every time he put on his guitar, a trapped nerve would scream out in protest, and night after night, while a hastily recruited masseur tried to alleviate the guitarist's suffering, his bandmates were on tenterhooks wondering whether the show would even go on.

It did, and by the time the band reached the U.S. in October, buoyed by Blackmore's nomination for a Grammy (for the instrumental track "Anybody There?"), spirits were considerably higher. But not for long. What should have been the compulsive coupling of Rainbow and the Scorpions had signally failed to catch the eye of the ticket-buying public. So poor was the projected turnout that several shows were actually canceled, and, while another set of dates with Blue Öyster Cult took the band through early December on at least an even keel, to Blackmore's bandmates — Joe Lynn Turner, in particular — it was clear that an end (maybe even *the* end) of the Rainbow was in sight. The coup de grâce would be delivered in March 1984, following the band's final scheduled shows in Japan.

In the meantime, Blackmore had already begun thinking about material for a new Deep Purple album and had rallied the support of the rest of the band. Roger Glover, busy with his latest solo album, the masterful *The Mask*, was of two minds, but he agreed to talk about it. Ian Paice, who left Whitesnake after eighteen months ("He became a little lazy when we recorded *Saints An' Sinners* and David took notice," explained Jon Lord) and was now playing alongside Neil Murray in Gary Moore's band (Moore and Murray were Colosseum II bandmates), was up for the challenge, while Lord had thrown in his lot as well, deciding to quit Whitesnake as soon as their latest activities were over. "I enjoyed Whitesnake," Lord reflected later. "I thought it was a wonderful band. But then petty things began creeping in." Like Blackmore, he would clear his desk of prior commitments by the end of March.

Gillan, astonished that so many of the pieces had already fallen into place, leaped on board the moment he heard; balked when Payne announced that Blackmore was demanding 50 per cent of all the band's earnings; then leaped again when Blackmore relented and agreed on equal shares for everybody — a view he later echoed in interviews: "Everybody is as important as the next person. There's five very strong musicians and that's how I like to leave it."

Only in the realm of songwriting would individual credits continue to stand out, although the singer was, perhaps, being a little disingenuous when he remarked, "Writing-wise, it's always been basically three people, and it's still those same three people." Indeed, it was later revealed that two of those three, Gillan and Glover, attempted to return matters to the all-for-one democracy of the band's earliest recordings, but Blackmore held firm. Just one song in the reformed Deep Purple's new repertoire, "Nobody's Home," would be credited to all five band members, and it was not until Blackmore left the group in 1993 that the issue was finally resolved. "Every [Deep Purple] song begins with Ian

Paice," Gillan now swore. "And just because he doesn't write words or play guitar does not mean he has no contribution to make."

These ructions, of course, were far off in the future, as the five sat down for their first face-to-face band meeting in a hired conference room overlooking the harbor in Greenwich, Connecticut. Lord recalled, "Paicey and I walked in [and] I was nervous as a kitten. And then Ian Gillan came in, whom I'd seen recently before that. Roger came in, whom I'd seen about two months before. And who was last? Yes, the man in black. And I hadn't seen him for ten years — only onstage; I'd been to a Rainbow show, but I didn't go backstage afterward, I don't know why. And I was so pleased to see him. When he walked into that room, suddenly these five people were together for the first time in ten years. Everybody just started smiling. And I think it was Ritchie who said, 'Right then, well let's do it.'"

The first rehearsal was magical. Gillan told BBC DJ Tommy Vance, "Everyone started playing and this band was just made to be, it always was. I just sat there on a stool. Jon was late as usual, reading a book or something. And Ritchie sat on a stool and started playing; Ian came in and picked up the rhythm; Roger came in and put his coffee down, cigarette in mouth. I'll never forget the scene! It was just a jam, [but] I just sat there with cold shivers coming down the back, thinking, 'These are the greatest players I've ever worked with.'"

It wasn't all to be quite as simple as that. Five musicians might have been at the core of the reunion, but sure as sedimentation, in the wings there lurked an army of "associates," all anxious to ensure that their own piece of the pie was fully protected.

For Tony Edwards and John Coletta, the management team that nursed Deep Purple through their first eight years of life, there was the realization that new organizations had arisen to oversee the band's future career, Bruce Payne paramount among them. Blackmore told *Kerrang!*, "[They] are very upset with the state of affairs, and there's legal battles going on every day." For Virgin Records, Ian Gillan's home throughout the Gillan band's years of greatest success, there was the knowledge that he was still contracted to deliver one more album, and the insistence that he fulfill that obligation. And so on.

For now, however, Deep Purple put such complications aside and set their minds to what they wanted to do. On April 27, 1984, local London newspaper the *Evening Standard* broke the news to the tube trains full of city commuters; a few hours later, Tommy Vance, a long-standing Purple supporter, revealed the same secret on a nationwide level, crowning an evening of hints and teases by announcing the group's reformation on his *Friday Rock Show* radio program. The remainder of the details — a new record deal (with Polydor), a series of summer festivals, and a world tour — fell into place days later.

Deep Purple weren't simply the biggest band ever to reform with their so-called classic lineup — as of 1983–84, they were also one of the first. True, the NWOBHM era had healed any number of decade-old divides, while the years on either side of that watershed had at least brought about a few renewals. Most, however, were either one-offs or worse. Only Yes, resuming their own 1972–73-era lineup with the return of Rick Wakeman in 1977, could even claim to have both reconfigured and resparked their most glorious age, while other contenders for retroglory were often left pounding precisely the same seedy club-circuit boards they'd broken up to escape from in the first place.

Rather, any taste for reunions that might have circulated in the early 1980s had instead been supplanted by a new generation of so-called supergroups — the much-storied likes of Foreigner (ex-Spooky Tooth, King Crimson, and the Ian Hunter Band), Asia (Uriah Heep, Yes, ELP, and Buggles . . . er, Buggles?) and Fastway (Motörhead, Humble Pie, UFO). Such broad cross-pollination, of course, was cut across the boundaries of band (or, perhaps, *brand*) loyalty. There also occurred, however, another, less predictable consequence, as Foreigner and Asia delved not into the dramatic annals of the members' past accomplishments, but into the newly charted waters of AOR — adult-oriented rock: soft, smooth sounds for soft, smooth living.

From the outset, Deep Purple were adamant that there was no place in their repertoire for a similar curdling of the spirits. Maybe it would have sold through the roof, just as those bands had. But Deep Purple had more than a reputation to live up to. They had standards, as well.

At the same time, Ritchie Blackmore was only partly jesting when he suggested Deep Purple title their "comeback" LP *At Last, the 1974 Album*. He knew, as well as the critics lining up to knock the band down and the fans patiently congregating to lap it all up, that Deep Purple had left a lot of unfinished business when they splintered in 1973 — that there were a lot of people who really were still awaiting the follow-up to *Who Do We Think We Are*. But Jon Lord was adamant: "We didn't want to sound like 1974. We wanted to sound like 1984."

Ian Paice agreed with him. Interviewed by Tommy Vance, he mused, "All we can do is what we did then and realize that we have to be in the eighties now and not in the seventies. I wouldn't say we actually play any differently, but we have to realize that the needs are different now.

"For instance, I don't believe you can do fifteen- or twenty-minute drum solos. I don't believe you can leave the guitarist on his own for half an hour onstage, you can't do that. Then you could, because then you were breaking down all the boundaries and all the things that people said you couldn't do. We said, 'Yes, we can! We can do what hell we want!' [But] that's been done, the boundaries have now been broken down. I think we all realize that and that's why it will work. I don't think we're trying to sell them 1972 or 1973 again. That would be criminal!"

The group was also adamant that the reunion be built around something more than the monstrous payday that inevitably awaited their return to the frontlines. Lord told *Sounds*, "With monotonous regularity, people have said, 'Why don't you [reform],' but the only reason they ever gave me was, 'You'll make a fortune, man.' True enough if it works, but that was the only reason that was ever given — not by the members of the band, but by outside interests. And . . . no matter how tantalizing that may appear, it would be a disaster if that were the only reason."

As things now stood, the band remained becomingly modest about its ambitions. Although Blackmore acknowledged, "I could be very arrogant and say we wanted to create another milestone in the history of rock," he told *Sounds'* Sylvie Simmons. "We put [Deep Purple] back together to annoy the press, basically. Give them something to bitch about. That really is our No. 1 priority — to upset the critics."

That, after all, was a topic very dear to his heart. The press, he swore, "always tried to humiliate us, but in the meantime I started to realize that they can't harm us anymore. We have proven that we're right. But they haven't given up. They now attack the people around us, who work with us. This is really pathetic . . . but I can laugh about it.

"That's why I never go to press conferences and stuff," Blackmore continued. "You'll never see me as a spokesman for the band either. The English press in my eyes means nothing. I remember a story about Paul McCartney in *Melody Maker*, in which they almost nailed him to the cross. Would you believe, the best songwriter we've had this century and then dare to say that he has too much money and make up some bull about him. They would've done the same shit to Beethoven, I think."

He admitted, however, that the reunion could go one of two ways — either a magnificent success, or a colossal failure: "If the fans or the mass in general turn around and give it a definite thumbs-down, then we might all go, 'Ah, we weren't right to come back together.' You can never sit back and say, 'This will obviously be a success because it's good.' In this day and age, being good and being musical and in tune usually goes against you, and that's what throws the whole thing. [But] it would be a thrill to have it accepted without all the bullshit of 'They're too old to do this.'"

Deep Purple played their first official show at a tiny club in Hamburg, Germany, having spent much of the summer of 1984 recording their "comeback" album. From there, the itinerary spread across the globe. The group's first tour together in eleven years would open in Perth, Australia, on November 27, 1984, travel that continent for much of the next month, then swing into a four month trip through American arenas in the new year.

From there, the ever-loyal Japan and Sweden would get their first glimpses of the group, before June 22, 1985, brought Deep Purple before the largest (and, possibly, the most demanding) audience of all, as they headlined the Knebworth Festival in England. Then it was back into Europe, and one more short swing through the United States that wound up in August. And then they would have nine months off before they returned to the recording studio.

Compared to the kind of itinerary they'd endured in the past, it was almost relaxing.

Perfect Strangers, as the new album wound up being titled, absolutely vindicated the musicians' stance. Ian Paice told *Kerrang!*, "To me, it's a natural progression from [the] earlier records, but with a ten-year growth period in between." He acknowledged, "It was a revelation to capture the spirit of the Mark II Purple once again . . . very refreshing."

Glover, in the same interview, said, "Someone told me the other day that, listening to *Perfect Strangers*, he could hear all the influences of the various projects we'd been involved with in the intervening period — Rainbow, Whitesnake, the Gary Moore Band, whatever. I don't know if I can hear that myself, but I'm quite prepared to believe it's true."

Glover was also willing to admit, "It'll never be the same [as the original Mark II]. We're not trying to recreate what we did in the past, there's no way we could ever compete with that. But if we can just recapture the spirit of the way we felt back then, then that'll be just great. And the spirit can be summed up in two words — *fuck it*." As in, "Fuck it, we're going to do what we want."

The group certainly set their sights high. According to legend, one of Blackmore's first demands was that his bandmates sit down and listen to Yes' *90125* album before they started work on their own. Although Yes' own most recent split had lasted but two years before they reformed in 1983, still the group's Trevor Horn–produced "comeback" album mercilessly derailed each and every prediction of how the archetypal '70s prog band would cope with life (and a wholly rearranged lineup) in the early '80s. In fact, in the face of the musical success of the set, its commercial reception — a worldwide chart-topping album, with a No. 1 single on top — was almost irrelevant.

Most bands could only dream of scaling the same heights. Deep Purple were one of the few who were convinced they could do it — and they were going to do it on their own. Although vague consideration was given to drawing in an outside producer to give the album some contemporary sheen, ultimately they opted to let Glover do the honors. As Blackmore sniffed, "We don't want a glossy sound. We want the album to be an '80s version of *Machine Head*. And . . . I think we've struck the right chord."

Outside of the band, of course, opinions were divided as to whether *Perfect Strangers* truly touched that ideal. *Kerrang!*'s Geoff Barton spoke for the majority when he described it as "a safe, solid effort, neither mind-blowingly magnificent nor trite, tedious, and interminable." But still, he concluded, "It's Purple back at, if not their very best, then certainly goddamn close to it."

It certainly was. From the suggestively Zeppelinesque title track's opening demand of "Do you remember my name?" and on to the evocatively, gorgeously Rainbowesque "Son of Alerik" instrumental that was appended to the album's CD edition, *Perfect Strangers* positioned its makers not as old heroes returning to reclaim their throne but — and this was a far greater accomplishment — as a band that hadn't even noticed it had been away.

Cynics, of course, would have a high old time isolating all the little moments that they recognized from the past — Deep Purple's, and the metal/prog hybrid's alike. There was the hint of the primal chaos of "Highway Star" that kicked "Perfect Strangers" into gear; the staccato shudder that gave "Hungry Daze" an unmistakable flavor of old Uriah Heep; the synthed-out "Fireball" that set "Nobody's Home" in motion — you could (and people did) make lists of such things.

But you could balance these against the rival lists of all that Deep Purple brought in that was new. Textures had changed, of course; techniques had altered; timbre had shifted. The humming organ overture that sounded as "Knocking on Your Back Door" creaked into life was as instantly recognizable as any Lord had enacted before, without him ever having played such a drone before, while the first sounds out of Gillan's mouth sent the listener's ears spinning back to the first time they'd heard them. They were that fresh.

Besides, if *Perfect Strangers* failed to fully impress, the accompanying concerts left few people in any doubt. American audiences seemed initially uncertain whether they were being treated to a rebirth or simply an oldies-stuffed revival, but they were swiftly put right on that score. Though no more than one-third of the live show was dedicated to new material, still the impression was of a band as confident in its present as its past.

Not every concert on that maiden tour was a sellout. On more than one occasion, especially on the early American dates, the band took the stage to find the crowd rattling around a half-empty stadium — and the Kansas Coliseum in Wichita wasn't even that full. But, as *Perfect Strangers* rose toward its Top 20 chart peak, two solidly packed nights at the Long Beach Arena and one more at San Francisco's Cow Palace sent the group's confidence soaring, while close to 15,000 people stuffed the McNichols Sports Arena in Denver, the band's biggest audience yet.

By the time the (comparatively) veteran NWOBHM band Girlschool joined the tour in mid-February (earlier shows were opened by Giuffria), the word was out — Deep Purple were back, and so were the crowds. Deep Purple's spring tour was suddenly one of the hottest tickets on the road and the sense of supremacy echoing through the band now was a far cry from the vague uncertainties that had niggled in the months before the tour started. They hadn't simply reconquered America, it was as though they'd never been away.

A very different state of affairs, however, awaited them at home, when Deep Purple's solitary British date, headlining the Knebworth Festival on June 22, 1985, went head-to-head with U2's similarly daylong bash at nearby Milton Keynes. It was a fascinating clash, no contest for the hard-core committed, of course, but a dilemma for the multitudes who simply descend on festivals for a day of music and would be hard-pressed to determine a favorite band from any of the legion on display.

Of course, Britain had taken to the new album with open arms. While *Perfect Strangers* marched into the Top 5, the title track (itself truly a return to classic form) had reached the Top 50 singles chart and, as Knebworth drew closer, a new 45, "Knocking at Your Back Door," looked set to follow it. U2, however, were still coming down from the chart-topping *The Unforgettable Fire*, and a Top 10 placing for its own drab old title track. Quite frankly, U2 were enormous, and the bills backed up behind the respective headliners were just as impressive as the bill-toppers themselves. Knebworth offered 80,000 ticket holders the chance to see the Scorpions, Meat Loaf, UFO, Blackfoot, Mountain, and Mama's Boys; Milton Keynes responded with the Faith Brothers, Billy Bragg, the Ramones, Spear of Destiny, and REM.

Fears of splitting audiences between the two bands proved ground-less, however. Both festivals sold out, and both disgorged satisfied audiences at the end of the day. And, while U2 got on with establishing themselves as the showbiz personalities from hell, Deep Purple simply continued with business as usual — onstage, where the North American dates alone wound up earning some $7 million, and off, where cavorting demons both old and new were preparing to raise their horned little heads. (A shattering souvenir of the Knebworth concert, the live album *In the Absence of Pink*, was released in 1991.)

Of the voices that rose most vociferously in protest at the revival of Deep Purple, the loudest was not the music press, yawning at the thought of another blood revival, but a body that, back in Deep Purple's original life-time, could scarcely have been further removed from rock if they'd tried.

Elements of America's religious right had long kept at least half a disapproving eye on rock'n'roll music, and there'd always been a few placard-waving missionaries lined up outside Deep Purple's mid-'70s concerts, warning ticket holders to Repent the Rock or Burn in Hell.

Into the early 1980s, however, rock'n'roll shifted from being a mere irritant in the side of this shockingly influential body of opinion to being the target of a relentless campaign. From the Beatles' flirtations with Transcendental Meditation through to the purposefully provoking road-shows ringmastered by Ozzy Osbourne, Judas Priest, Dio, and — gasp — worse, the music was Satan's own plaything and it had to be stopped.

Accepting that the loudest voices raised against rock tended to be those that listened least to its lyrics, Deep Purple had long hovered on the fringe of the crusaders' gun sights. With song titles like "Mandrake Root," "Black Night," "Demon's Eye," and "Might Just Take Your Life," how could they have failed to do so? Gillan's brief but visible sojourn with Black Sabbath added further fuel to the not-so-figurative fire.

But the most baleful glares were directed at Ritchie Blackmore, the self-styled Man in Black whose crimes included (but were, by no means, confined to) a long-rumored fascination with the occult, charms, and psychic phenomena, summed up by a 1978 interview with *Circus*, in which he all but laid out the ideal conditions to conduct a séance: "You can't be very tired. You can't have weak personalities present. . . ."

He spoke from experience, too. As a teen, Blackmore had witnessed the escalating degeneration of Joe Meek, as the producer placed more and more faith in (and drew more and more fear from) his own fascina-tion with the so-called black arts. And, as an adult, Blackmore had his own brush with those fears, when he staged a séance at the Hermitage, during the recording of *Fireball*.

"Imagine yourself," wrote Roger Glover, "lying in bed reading at about 3 in the morning, when an ax-head smashes through your door, disappears, then smashes through again and again, making matchwood of it." Leaping from his bed clad only in his underwear, Glover grabbed a handy chair leg and set off in pursuit of the ax-man. It was Blackmore, but that did not deter Glover from seeking vengeance. Having discovered the guitarist "hiding in a darkened part of the house, [I] stopped mercifully short of clubbing him to death." Blackmore and Ian Paice's girlfriend, Wendy, were conducting a séance in the next room, "and it had apparently taken control of their senses. Or maybe mine."

Small wonder, then, that Blackmore cautioned his audience to take care when holding séances of their own. "Unfortunately," thundered Dan and Steve Peters, Christian ministers whose "Truth About Rock" seminars took credit for the destruction of "over $10 million worth of rock music paraphernalia," "Blackmore doesn't realize that people should not attend séances at all, for God has often warned of the results of such practices."

There was more! As they wrote the book *Why Knock Rock*, a 1984 assault on the evils of rock in all its guises, the Peters brothers found further ammunition in the two-page anti-Blackmore spread that Britain's tabloid the *Sun* ran beneath the headline "He looks evil, even Satanic." *Why Knock Rock* gleefully summarized some of its most salient points: "Blackmore likes to record his music in a supposedly haunted 17th-century castle, and his interest in Black Magic has been the inspiration for much of his music. The moody singer [sic], who dresses in black, says that during his live performances, he astral-projects to float above his audiences."

Neither were the rest of Deep Purple going to get away with associating with such a sinister being. Routinely described in the Peters' pages as "mystical," the band was elsewhere cited among the crop of British groups who "brought the macabre into metal music — Satanic Rock."

At the time the book was written, of course, Deep Purple remained securely locked inside their coffin. Now they had risen again, and a fearful world waited tremulously to discover what fresh depravities they intended wreaking.

In fact, there wouldn't be any. But why let reality impinge on such a nicely boiling horror story?

In the months following the world tour, through the winter of 1985, Gillan and Glover were busy together, working on what they assumed were the rudiments of the band's next album. In much the same manner as they had prepared for past Deep Purple recordings, they sketched out songs, drafting a sense of the record's dynamic.

Amid so much preparatory work, however, the duo reckoned without one thing — Ritchie Blackmore. Gillan recalled, "We did a great deal of preparation . . . only to discover that Ritchie wasn't really interested in listening to us." They returned in May 1986 to the small Vermont town of Stowe, where they'd recorded *Perfect Strangers* in such grand spirits, but the sessions for this next album swiftly degenerated to the point where Gillan swore, "There was no spirit, no cohesion — it reminded me of Rome, all those years ago, and making *Who Do We Think We Are.*"

Glover, again cast as the album's producer, readily agreed. "The *Perfect Strangers* tour was actually a good tour," he recalled, "and that was a good time for us. But making *The House of Blue Light* was a struggle between the musicians, and it kinda shows on the album. There's some great bits in it, but . . . it's spotty. You can hear flashes of brilliance, but it doesn't really hold together as an album."

Even as apparently simple a matter as titling the record proved problematic, as Glover later recalled: "When you start an album with a title, somehow it gives you a framework within which to work. We started *Purpendicular* knowing it was going to be called *Purpendicular*, and that was . . . a great move because it then gave us license — 'purpendicular' is one of those words, it makes you think sideways and that's what we did. When you've done a bunch of songs and you're trying to work out what they're going to be called collectively, it's sometimes very difficult to come up with something that encapsulates what they are.

"*Perfect Strangers,*" Glover continued, "we kind of knew what the album was going to be called, very early on in the album, it was one of the hot contenders. But *The House of Blue Light* — we finished the album and we didn't have a title. I was producing, so I was, 'Okay, what are we going to call it?' And there were lots of suggestions, but no one could agree. In the end, we were getting really desperate — we needed a title, so I came up with *The House of Blue Light*, which of course is a line from 'Speed King.' . . . Everyone kinda went, 'Oooer, yeah, it's okay'; and because everyone went, 'It's okay,' that was the one. It wasn't the best one, it wasn't the most appropriate. It was simply the only one everyone seemed to agree on, and that's not a pleasant thing to do. If you have a title at the beginning, it gives you a landscape for what you're doing."

And a landscape was very much absent from the finished album. There were any number of flashpoints as the sessions ground bad-temperedly on, not least when Gillan presented the song "Mitzi Dupree" to the band. Mitzi was a fellow entertainer Gillan had encountered while flying between Los Angeles and Salt Lake City during his Black Sabbath days, a woman who employed her nether regions to fire ping-pong balls with unerring accuracy.

Gillan and Glover roughly demoed the song, fully expecting it to be given the full Deep Purple treatment before it made its way onto the next record. Instead, Blackmore refused point-blank to have anything to do with it, and so vehemently that, although the writers succeeded in getting it onto the record, the version they used was, in fact, the original demo. It's an indication of the mood of the sessions that, at the end of the day, the track's lazy, bluesy mood and gleefully ribald lyric painted it among the finest on the record.

Elsewhere, almost every place one turned, a definite sense of under-accomplishment permeated the disc, grimacing from the rock-by-numbers bombast of "Call of the Wild" and churning around the mundane sexual athleticism of "Hard Lovin' Woman."

There were moments of brilliance — excise the torturously '80s keyboards that skipped around "Strangeways" and the actual arrangement, all ghostly harmonies and slip-sliding rhythm, really was rather delightful. A neat Blackmore solo skated through "Black and White," lit by a burst of mouth harp, and "Bad Attitude" was contrarily the home of the best attitude on the entire record, as Lord's finest Phantom of the Opera keyboard set the stage for a bruising hard-rock battering ram. "The Spanish Archer" was a genuine highlight, and "The Unwritten Law" had a frenetic air that tempted one to forgive the rest of the album almost all of its sins.

Nevertheless, by the time Glover returned from executing the final mix of the album, Gillan laughed, "his brains were like scrambled eggs. I looked at [him] and said, 'You look fucking drained.' He said he was, so I came back with, 'I tell you what . . . I've got an idea. Let's go and make a record.'" The abandoned sketch for what *should* have been the new Deep Purple album was still fresh in his mind; Nick Balogna, the Russian-Canadian engineer who'd put up with so much in Vermont, was still available. And Deep Purple weren't due to stir again until the next tour kicked off in Hungary in January 1987.

Fall 1986, then, saw the trio ensconced within the palatial surroundings of George Martin's AIR Studios in Montserrat, working their material at a lighthearted pace and kicking so readily into joyous, uplifting overdrive that they'd already completed half an album by the time they had to break for the tour.

Compared to the response that greeted *Perfect Strangers*, *The House of Blue Light* was barely applauded by the critics, a low-key reception matched by its chart performances. On the road, however, the tensions that had rendered the record so unappealing seemed a lifetime away. True, Glover and Gillan killed as much time as they could plotting the completion of their own album, but still, the bassist insisted, "The tour . . . was a healing process for the band, and it was great. The band was in great form, everything was going great."

Through Europe Deep Purple rumbled, across to the U.K. in March and April, then on to the U.S. Of course there were occasional flashpoints, but in an odd way, they served only to increase the expectations of the following night's audience. For some fans, after all, a Ritchie Blackmore tantrum was worth the price of admission. And Wembley Arena on March 4 delivered a real doozy.

A tight, competent show was into its closing straight, with Blackmore launching into his showpiece solo at the end of "Space Truckin'," when it became apparent that all was not going to plan. The sound quality, more than adequate all evening long, suddenly nosedived and, with it, the audience reaction. By the time the show was over and the crowd was on its feet demanding an encore, Blackmore had convinced himself that he wasn't going to play another note that night.

The minutes passed. Backstage, the rest of the band did their best to persuade Blackmore to relent, but he refused. Finally, knowing that if they didn't go back out soon, there'd be no point in returning to the stage at all, Lord, Paice, Gillan, and Glover alone stepped out, to offer the audience a pointedly guitarless version of "Smoke on the Water" — punctuated, the sharp-eyed noticed, by Gillan directing a favorite rude hand gesture toward the wings where Blackmore presumably still lurked.

Such incidents, however, were rare. With the album's rancorous creation and poor performance behind them, Deep Purple were facing the future with as much optimism as they had known in a long time.

They really ought to have known better.

Chapter 16

Inadvertent Deliberation

No less than on any previous occasion, Deep Purple's spring 1987 American tour was more or less solidly sold out. A few early shows, with Joan Jett and the Blackhearts a mismatched opening act, clocked in at less than capacity, but from the moment the reformed (if, sadly, Paul Rodgersless) Bad Company replaced them on the bill in Philadelphia, ticket sales never looked back.

Deep Purple rewarded audiences with some truly fiery performances. With the tapes rolling for a new live album, the Irvine Meadows show on May 23 was described by more than one onlooker as one of the greatest shows Deep Purple — *any* version — had ever played. Just a week later, on May 30, however, the band's world turned upside down.

Glover explained: "We were something like two or three weeks into the tour when we played in Phoenix. Ritchie threw his guitar up, got blinded by a light, and it came down — *boof* — and broke his finger. And that was it, end of tour.

"It was a horrible experience to go through, because a tour is like a family, you get to know everyone, it's like a circus of thirty people, riggers and drivers and truckers and caterers, all kinds of stuff. I left for the hotel that night knowing Ritchie had gone to the hospital to have his finger checked out; I woke up the next morning to find no tour and a ticket home. That was so utterly depressing. I didn't even get to say goodbye to the crew."

Blackmore was out of action throughout the summer, a period which saw the ill-feeling contained within *The House of Blue Light* sessions break into the public domain as rumors of a full-fledged split began to circulate. Blackmore did nothing to quell the chatter, admitting that he had originally considered the Deep Purple reunion a one-off celebration that would be shelved again after just a single album and a tour. It had dragged on longer, he laughed, because he'd grown lazy.

Now, however, the grapevine rustled with reports of his latest activities — a revived Rainbow with a returning Joe Lynn Turner; meetings with Kingdom Come vocalist Lenny Wolf; even a collaboration with Brian Howe, then making a grand success of the unenviable task of replacing Paul Rodgers in the reactivated Bad Company and previously schooled in the white heat of Ted Nugent's band.

Further mileage was drawn from these latest legends as Gillan and Glover made their way to New York to complete work on their own record. *Accidentally on Purpose*, titled for the all but unintentional genesis of the record itself, was finished off with the likes of Andy Newmark, Randy Brecker, and Dr. John adding their own frills to the duo's otherwise complete domination of the instrumentation. It was already on the release schedules when the recuperated Blackmore returned to action and Deep Purple launched another European tour in August 1987. The mythmakers widely prophesied that it was their last.

Within the eye of the purple storm itself, the resumption of business as usual did little for any chance of success that *Accidentally on Purpose* might have had — it would be close to six months before the Gillan/ Glover duo even got the chance to perform any of the new songs live, when they appeared on British television's *Friday Night Live* on March 25, 1988. But, while Gillan insisted that a straightforward collaboration with Glover had always been high on his list of ambitions, it was also true that *Accidentally on Purpose* had very little in common with Deep Purple.

True, several of the songs on the album would not have seemed amiss on a full Deep Purple album (and several more would readily have improved *The House of Blue Light*). But the mood of *Accidentally on Purpose* was lighter, brighter, than any album Gillan, at least, had been involved with since the still-archived *Cherkazoo*. As he lets rip across Little Richard's "Can't Believe You Wanna Leave," the memory of those long-ago sessions must have torn back with a vengeance.

But there was no time for regrets or even reminiscence. The touring continued until early September, with shows in Norway and Italy adding to the stockpile of tapes from which the live album would be culled. Even the realization, somewhere down the line, that the group was on the eve of its twentieth birthday drew no more vivacious a celebration than a quick visit to the so-picturesque Hook End Manor Studios in Oxfordshire in February 1988, to record a twentieth-anniversary rendering of the hit that started it all, "Hush."

Gillan later admitted that the recording made him uneasy; that the only person who he wanted to hear singing "Hush" was Rod Evans. But the release did bring Deep Purple their third U.K. hit since reforming — and gave "Hush" its first outing on the U.K. listings, albeit at a lowly No. 62. (Another nine years elapsed before "Hush" finally became a major British smash, when the band Kula Shaker took a virtual photocopy of Deep Purple's original version to No. 2.)

Any sense of optimism that might still have swirled around Deep Purple, however — any notion that the excitement of the first leg of the tour might be extended into its second stage, through August/September, 1988 — was swiftly disabused. That digit-damaging night in Phoenix the previous spring could be isolated as the moment when things first began to go awry. Roger Glover mused, "From that point on . . . maybe that was one of those pivotal points that Isaac Asimov would pinpoint in *The End of Infinity* where, if you could go back and change little things, it would change the course of history . . . a burst tire somewhere along the line would end up saving the world from World War III. And maybe that broken finger was the cause of the demise of the band. After that, all I can remember is that there was squabbling, there was a lousy live album, there was three more months of miserable touring. The thing was in tatters."

Gillan, too, dismissed the live album: "The band wanted to use a lot of the *Made in Japan* stuff and add newer songs to show how we had changed. Sadly, it was clear that we'd hardly changed at all. We'd just become more slick."

He was harsh. Although its title would blithely hand Deep Purple's critics yet another stick with which to berate the band, *Nobody's Perfect* ("you can say that again") was by no means a disaster. Although innumerable technical gremlins haunted the recordings — everything from unexpected tape noise, to sudden silence as the tape ran out — the band's classic material had gracefully been upgraded to meet the demands of the late 1980s; more recent songs, though outnumbered two-to-one by the oldies, at least held their ground.

Entertaining, too, was the sleeve design. Recent Deep Purple albums had, for whatever reason, followed the earlier lineups' post-*Machine Head* penchant for covers that seemingly said as little as possible — a fair-enough comment in the mid-1970s, when designers like Roger Dean and Hipgnosis were as well-known as the artists (Yes and Pink Floyd/Led Zeppelin respectively) with whom they frequently worked, but a disappointment as well. Half the fun of picking up a new album in those days lay in losing yourself in the graphics. Deep Purple sleeves were, frankly, utilitarian by the standards of the day.

Now, however, there came a design that offered minutes of diversion, a gatefold that opened up to reveal the unchanging vista of a desert highway, over which hopped a gaudy kaleidoscope of things that weren't, indeed, perfect — spoutless kettles and bearded ladies, circular die and miscolored pencils, a 10-shilling banknote that was worth only nine. . . . And, better late than never, it was the work of Hipgnosis, although the days when albums sold on the strength of their artwork were long gone.

Nobody's Perfect faltered at the decidedly imperfect chart peak of No. 38 in Britain and No. 105 in the United States. To make matters worse, plans to record a new studio disc that could be whacked out as quickly as possible after the live record were in chaos. Having now wrapped up their deal with Polydor, Deep Purple signed to BMG, who were impatient to get a new record onto the shelves. It soon became apparent that they were going to have to wait.

With both Ritchie Blackmore and Roger Glover now permanently based in New York, Ian Gillan suggested that Deep Purple record their next album in that city — only for Jon Lord to shoot down the notion on the spot. Next up for consideration was Los Angeles, but this time it was Blackmore who demurred. Decision after decision was made and then dismissed, and when Gillan looked back on the squabbling, he realized the direction in which Deep Purple were now traveling. The final show of the protracted *The House of Blue Light* tour, in Bremen on September 29, 1988, was still fresh in the memory when Gillan received the phone call he'd been half-expecting for weeks. He'd been fired.

Viewed with lashings of hindsight, Gillan's departure was not too great a surprise. As Lord later mused, "Ian and Ritchie have no love for each other. It's a lost cause trying to put those two in the same city, let alone the same band." What was more difficult to comprehend was, having fought so hard to bring Deep Purple back from the dead and establish it as a band far beyond the plateaus of mere competence that most reunions drifted toward, whatever possessed the rest of the group to let him go?

According to Gillan, the final straw broke one night in Stowe, as the impasse over locating a suitable recording studio brought another quiet discussion to an angry head. His autobiography recalls the fury he was feeling, as the realization that "being with a band I'd die for" was driving him crazy, simply because all he ever heard from its members were negatives: "Finally I said [to the band], 'You are fucking useless,' at which point Ritchie walked out without saying a word. Jon said something I didn't quite catch, and left with Bruce [Payne, manager] not far behind. That left Roger . . . my dear friend of all those years . . . who leaned forward across the table, knuckles bunched, and stared me in the face. 'Ian,' he said, 'you have gone too far this time.'"

But even before that fateful night, there were murmurings — the sense, for example, that Gillan had not been giving his all to Deep Purple; the belief that he was having far more fun with a part-time revival of his first band, Garth Rockett & the Moonshiners, than he'd ever had with his latest. There were so many whispers, so many pointing fingers, and, as Gillan would later come to realize, so much truth. He was miserable as sin. It was time to start enjoying himself again.

If Gillan's eviction — for the second time! — from Deep Purple wasn't a great shock, the band's state of utter unpreparedness certainly was. They were, after all, still on schedule to begin recording a new album in the new year, yet they had no more idea of who would replace Gillan this time than they did fifteen years before, the last time he'd departed.

The projected sessions were canceled, and it was another year before Deep Purple returned to the recording studio. One cannot help but wonder whether such a break, arranged in 1988, might have spared the band this latest tumult. In the meantime, the audition process got under way.

A few names came immediately to mind — including, with grim symmetry, David Coverdale, the man who'd filled Gillan's shoes the last time around. He and Jon Lord had remained close, after all, and Whitesnake had not, of late, seemed the most stable of beasts. But the group's latest album, *Slip of the Tongue*, was selling up a storm and, with guitarist Steve Vai heading up a lineup as dramatic as any that Coverdale had fielded, it was clear this reunion owed more to idle minds in the music press than to any overtures on Deep Purple's part.

Former Rainbow frontman Ronnie James Dio, too, entered the running. Dio, the eponymous band he'd formed following his departure from Black Sabbath, had sundered in late 1987, and the diminutive maestro had scarcely been sighted since then. But, again, no overtures came from Deep Purple's end, while Dio himself hadn't seen Ritchie Blackmore in almost three years, since their respective bands played a German festival together, and he hadn't spoken with him since 1983. Another door slammed closed before it was even opened.

The list went on. Doug Pinnick, vocalist with breakout Missouri metallurgists Kings X, was apparently considered, while the distinctly Coverdaleesque Kal Swann was auditioned after his own band, Lion, folded during 1989. Glaswegian-born, Australian-famed Jimmy Barnes, ex of early-'80s metal merchants Cold Chisel, tried out for the band; so did Terry Brock of Strangeways. Another Australian contender was the Little River Band's John Farnham, while Bad Company's Brian Howe was another close runner.

There was, however, a certain inevitability to what, for a few weeks at least, looked like being the group's final choice: Jimi Jamison, frontman with a latter-day incarnation of American FM radio heroes Survivor. Of all the objections raised to those other contenders, after all, the greatest was their lack of prior recognition — perhaps recalling the breaking in of David Coverdale, Blackmore was very much against the idea of hiring an even-partial unknown.

Jamison, on the other hand, had immense recognition in the United States, from half a decade spent voicing such Survivor smashes as "High on You," "Burning Heart," "Is This Love," and "The Search Is Over." Unfortunately, the search was not over by a long shot. Jamison explained, "I was in the band, or they said that I was in the band . . . and I told my record label, this was around the time I was to do my solo album. . . . The Scotti Brothers said, 'No way we're going to let you be in Deep Purple, we're not going to let you do it.' So I had to call Ritchie Blackmore up to tell him that the Scotti Brothers didn't like it at all. I would have loved playing with them. With all the original members. [But] that record label held me back for so much stuff I can't believe it." Jamison moved on to a solo career; Deep Purple returned to the drawing board.

Finally, Ritchie Blackmore made the suggestion that, perhaps, should have been made in the first place — that they call in the third and last of Rainbow's featured vocalists, Joe Lynn Turner. The singer's recruitment to Deep Purple was formally announced in December 1989, and rehearsals for the group's next album would commence early in the new year.

According to Jon Lord, "[Ritchie] said, 'Why not try it with Joe Lynn Turner?' And the others said: not Joe again! I mean, he once was in Rainbow, then wasn't, and then was — he was a kind of a 'rent-a-singer'! But Joe agreed to the audition, something which surprised me, and he came and he sang like an angel, wonderful!"

Ian Paice, too, seemed initially enthusiastic. Interviewed for Japanese radio in July 1991, he raved, "The thing that's different is that Joe has the ability to sing anything well, and because of that it opens up more possibilities than there were before. I mean, Ian was a great rock'n'roll singer, David was a great blues singer, but Joe has the ability to do anything and everything, so where there were certain limitations on what we could do before, at the moment anything we can think of he can do. . . . The excitement that can happen onstage becomes more varied because we can do something totally off the wall. Sometimes Ritchie will start something, a piece of music that has never existed before, and Joe will sing something — he has the ability to ad-lib and be totally spontaneous about it and create a song from nothing. We couldn't do that before, so it just gives us more things to do."

Following the end of Rainbow, five years earlier, Turner had teamed with former Foreigner keyboardist Al Greenwood and Queen producer Roy Thomas Baker, to cut 1985's solo album *Rescue You*. Plans for a follow-up, however, were abandoned when Turner linked with Swedish guitar legend Yngwie Malmsteen to cut the *Odyssey* album and undertake the world tour that climaxed with Malmsteen's *Live in Leningrad: Trial by Fire* concert album.

Despite its success, Turner's liaison with Malmsteen was to be short-lived — the guitarist has never been rated among the most pliable of musical collaborators, particularly when his own unerring musical vision is the focus of the union. Unable to impress any more of his own personality on the proceedings than Malmsteen saw fit, Turner quit. "He thought he was God," Turner later mused. "I didn't agree. Blackmore's God."

The vocalist was contemplating restarting his solo career when a most peculiar rumor reached his ears — that Ritchie Blackmore was considering reforming Rainbow and wanted to recall Turner for the occasion. Nothing came of that, but clearly Turner remained on Blackmore's mind. Turner reflected, "[Deep Purple] called me up and said, 'Do you want to come and have a sing with us?'" Of course he did. "I walked in ... there's Purple in the corner all set up ... and Ritchie just started playing 'Hey Joe' by Hendrix. . . ." Clearly, Turner was not well-versed in Deep Purple's early repertoire! "I immediately picked up the mike without saying hello and started singing. We started getting into this really long jam. We ended that, started slapping fives and everything, and made our introductions."

Clearly Turner had the job, but it was to be very much on his own terms. "Before I joined," he explained, "there were certain restrictions and conditions that I felt had to be met. One was that I'm not just gonna come into the band singing someone else's drivel . . . and b: I wasn't gonna try and emulate Ian Gillan because I've really no want or desire to emulate [him]. People say I've got big shoes to fill, [but] I say, 'I'm making my own footsteps.'"

Was the recruitment of Joe Lynn Turner the best idea Deep Purple ever had? Probably not. Indeed, his tenure with the group is now filed alongside the similarly short-lived Tommy Bolin–era lineup as one of those journeys Deep Purple should never have embarked upon. Blackmore had already noted, in the aftermath of the last Rainbow lineup, that Turner was less than ideal for the kind of music he most frequently needed to make. He told *Kerrang!*, "Joe's a great singer, but he's too smooth to sing rock'n'roll." Now Blackmore was to experience those same frustrations all over again.

Lord, too, had doubts over Turner's suitability. "I myself was against Joe Lynn Turner from the beginning on," he said. "He just wasn't the singer I imagined. It's funny because in fact none of us wanted him, but he was the only one that was left. The guy we actually wanted, if we *had* to work with a replacement for Gillan, was [Jimi Jamison], a very nice, very quiet, and very pleasant guy. He was an enormous Deep Purple fan and he would happily have taken over the job. But at the time he was afraid of his managers. They were Italo-Americans; that says enough."

The group immediately locked itself into the studio, and there were some classic Purple passages in store as *Slaves and Masters* took shape. Blackmore's solos are seldom less than sublime, Lord's organ thrusts into all the right places, and the rhythm section is tight as a duck's ass. The opportunity to hear the unadorned backing tracks for "Fire in the Basement," "The Cut Run Deeps," and the supremely mood-drenched "Truth Hurts" would reveal the band's sense of instrumental dynamic and construction to be as high as ever.

But the combination of Turner's rent-a-power-balladeer vocal and a shockingly overglossed Glover production lines the experience with so many safety nets that even the almost-frenetic "Wicked Ways" — at six-and-one-half minutes, the closest the album comes to an epic — is left toothless and castrated.

Lord told *Keyboards* magazine, "Joe's vision on this band was not our vision. He wanted to make something out of the band which it couldn't be, and we wanted to change him into something which he couldn't be. It was a marriage made in hell, not in heaven, and this hell became extremely hot very quickly.

"Roger did some real Herculean work at the time to keep everything together," Lord continued. "Sometimes he went to Joe, sometimes to us, always to try and bring us together musically. But it just didn't fit. There was this beautiful piece, which Ritchie and I had written, 'Love Conquers All.' We once played it late at night — that is, Ritchie and I played it together. It was very sad, very melancholy, it was introspective, but it was absolutely a Purple song, a bit like 'When a Blind Man Cries' or the quiet parts in 'Child in Time' or 'Wasted Sunsets' — a ballad of the kind we sometimes play, a blues ballad. But then Joe appeared and turned it into some sort of cabaret song."

Of course, Deep Purple wanted to open their new record deal with a major hit album; and, of course, to do so would entail making a few major concessions to the mood of American broadcasting. But when a Deep Purple song comes on the radio, one at least expects to recognize it *as* Deep Purple. In overlooking that fact, *Slaves and Masters* overlooked the one major advantage Deep Purple had always enjoyed over the competition. Without it, they simply sank into anonymity.

Released in November 1990, *Slaves and Masters* became Deep Purple's least successful studio album since the Mark I days, entering the U.K. chart at No. 45 — and then dropping straight out again. It was a similar story elsewhere. Germany pushed the album to No. 23, Finland to No. 33, and while ever-loyal Sweden hauled it to No. 12, even that was a disappointment — *Nobody's Perfect* had made the Top 5, and *The House of Blue Light* had topped the chart.

Slaves and Masters had a little more life in the United States, where, as planned, Turner's smooth adult-rock tones slipped effortlessly into "classic oldies" radio programming. But still the album took almost five months to drift up to its eventual peak of No. 87. Nine months of almost solid worldwide touring could convince neither Deep Purple's audience of this latest lineup's worth, nor, it seemed, the band members themselves.

An eight-concert swing across the American East Coast, with the dubious charms of Winger in support, was seriously undersubscribed, despite Deep Purple having purposefully switched from stadiums to mere theaters for the occasion. Recession was biting deep into the American pocketbook in the early 1990s and tours were falling by the wayside everywhere. But if Deep Purple couldn't sell out a 2,170-seat hall in Hartford, Connecticut, or a 3,368-seater in Pittsburgh, Pennsylvania, that wasn't only financial hardship talking. Rejection had something to do with it as well. And, though Turner had Blackmore's loyalty, Lord, Paice, and Glover were growing increasingly dissatisfied.

Lord told *Keyboards*, "Since we can never be sure that there'll be another Deep Purple album? We ourselves know best, that the band has been working in situations in which we'd ask who'd leave this time, for the umpteenth time. That's the reason why we have made every album, aware of the fact that it could be our last. We'd never want people to say, 'What a lousy album. They should have thrown in the towel ten years ago.' We've reached this point a few times, but that's the way it is; sometimes the fire is there, sometimes it is not. You can't just go into a store and buy something to light it, like, 'Oh sorry, do you happen to have a Deep Purple lighter on offer?'

"But when you look back, you could find that we haven't recorded many albums in all those years for which we should be ashamed. When I think about the highs and lows we've gone through, I myself am amazed how few there are. This thing from '73, *Who Do We Think We Are*, surely wasn't one of our best moments, [and] *Slaves and Masters* is undoubtedly an album which should never never have been labeled as Deep Purple."

The slackening of the group's studio prowess and in-concert appeal were not, however, the only issues on the band members' minds. Moves had also been made toward treating Deep Purple's traditional songwriting methods with some extra assistance — *not*, the core quartet were assured, because there was anything wrong with what they already did, but because a fresh perspective might well nudge them further toward the promised land of an American smash. That, after all, was where *Slaves and Masters* was heading, wasn't it?

Jim Peterik, Jimi Jamison's colleague in Survivor and the genius behind such all-time stellar gems as "Eye of the Tiger" and "Burning Heart," was the chosen catalyst, and it might have worked. Certainly Turner was relishing the opportunity to work with such an accomplished wordsmith, and apparently Blackmore was equally happy with the way things were going. Two songs, "Stroke of Midnight" and "Lonely for You," were complete, while backing tracks for several more were sounding good as well.

Other members of the band, however, were less impressed at being peremptorily squeezed out of the songwriting process — they were alarmed, too, at the alacrity with which they were expected to surrender what was left of the band's identity for the sake of a slice of the American AOR pie. And slowly, an idea began to ferment.

In 1989, the entire band had been united in the urge to dismiss Gillan — "The chemistry wasn't right," Glover told Q magazine. "We all took part in a very painful decision for the good of the band." Now they were united in the desire to recall him, a mood that both management and the band's record company also shared.

Blackmore, of course, remained opposed. In that same interview with Q, he summed up Gillan as "the most belligerent, awful person ever. I find him a very coarse man, bordering on repulsive. He's obnoxious when he's drunk." But even Blackmore had to acknowledge that bands are not always comprised of friends — and great bands very rarely are. The Deep Purple of *Slaves and Masters* was competent. But the Deep Purple of legend was valued at far more than that. If the group was worth persisting with — and Blackmore's continued presence within its ranks surely suggested it was — then it was worth getting back on track. And there was only one way to do that. Finally, Turner recalled, BMG made Blackmore an offer he couldn't refuse: "BMG went, 'How about $2 million to start your own solo project? We'll put that on the side if you let Gillan come back.' So Ritchie went, 'Two mil? Okay, put it on paper, wire it into my account.'"

"None of us wanted to be the one to show Joe the door, but at the same time, everybody knew that it wouldn't work with him," Lord admitted in a 1994 interview with *Keyboards*. "So Ritchie said, 'Okay, we have a singer whom nobody wants, right? Help me out here!' I knew exactly what he was thinking at the moment. He didn't want to be the doorman again, the bad guy. My heart was pounding in my throat, for I thought the next thing he would say was, 'Let's get Gillan back!' But then he just said, 'We'll have to start looking for a new singer, don't you think so?' I thought, 'Oh man, not again!' So I talked about it to Roger and Ian Paice and said, 'Joe is really not the right singer for us, what do you think?' And both of them said, 'Yes, we should see if we can get Gillan back!'"

Gillan had scarcely taken a back seat since his departure from Deep Purple three years before. Although Garth Rockett & the Moonshiners was scarcely convened as anything more than an enjoyable and extraordinarily hassle-free means of making music, still a fat itinerary of shows and the chance to record a couple of albums was more than sufficient to keep Gillan happy.

He was not, of course, to completely shake off the shadows of his old band. Just weeks after departing Deep Purple, Gillan was among the horde of hard-rock celebrities convened to record an album to raise funds for victims of the earthquake that shook Armenia on December 7, 1988. Over 25,000 people were killed and the region was struggling to get back on its feet.

Organized in the spirit of so many recent rock charity escapades, Rock Aid for Armenia brought together Iron Maiden's Bruce Dickinson, Queen's Roger Taylor, Paul Rodgers, Bryan Adams, and Pink Floyd's Dave Gilmour, then fostered reunions for Gillan with Sabbath's Tony Iommi and Deep Purple's Jon Lord to perform a massive rendition of "Smoke on the Water." Ritchie Blackmore, too, contributed to the proceedings, but characteristically recorded his parts once everyone else had left the studio. The experience, Gillan later wrote, was "perhaps the only real moment of contentment and reunion [I had] with my past" — elsewhere, after all, he was still delightedly tugging away from it.

Launching a new writing partnership with Garth Rockett guitarist Steve Morris, Gillan's next move was to restart his solo career, with a new band that, ironically, looked all the way back to Deep Purple's mid-'70s search for new blood.

Fifteen years before, the Sensational Alex Harvey Band's Zal Cleminson was on the post-*Stormbringer* Deep Purple's shortlist to replace Ritchie Blackmore. Now Cleminson (and the late Harvey) were the only members of that band *not* to be recruited, as SAHB stalwarts Chris Glenn, Ted McKenna, and Tommy Eyre all reunited behind Gillan. With the lineup completed by guitarists Morris and Mick O'Donaghue and percussionist David Lloyd, Gillan began working on his *Naked Thunder* album.

It was, Gillan later confessed, a mediocre record. He wrote in his auto-biography, "The Garth Rockett tour had been a most welcome distraction from the Purple business, but it had not found me reserves of energy and neither had I rediscovered my touch. I should have come out on *Naked Thunder* with both fists flying. [Instead] *Naked Thunder* was a 'hum-dee-hum' album and, while there's a lot about it I'm very happy with, I can see that it disappointed some people."

In concert, too, audience response to the new material was weak, all the more so when compared with the handful of Deep Purple oldies Gillan continued performing: "Demon's Eye," "When a Blind Man Cries," "Speed King," "Knocking at Your Back Door," even "Smoke on the Water" were regulars in the set, while he still encored with "Lucille" as well. By late 1990, both *Naked Thunder* and the band that created it had quietly faded from view, and the Gillan-Morris team was contemplating the follow-up with a star-studded complement of co-conspirators.

Some stayed long enough to play on the album, while others simply met up for a drink and a chat — Bernie Tormé, Mel Galley, Y&T's Lenny Haze, Starship's preternaturally tall Brett Bloomfield, and Leslie West, Mountain's very own man mountain. But all brought something to the proceedings, and the ensuing album, *Toolbox*, effortlessly eclipsed its predecessor — in musical terms, at least. As *Metal Hammer*'s Chris Welch opined, "If *Toolbox* isn't a great success, then maybe rock'n'roll is really dead."

Even as the album hit the streets in October 1991, however, and throughout the sprawling twenty-seven-country tour that accompanied it, Gillan knew he was fighting for a lost cause. For all its manifold good points, *Toolbox* failed to sell as resolutely as its predecessor, a happenstance that was crowned when Gillan's label, East West, announced that they were dropping him from the roster — incredibly, he had not been sacked from a record company since the Episode Six days.

Gillan's attempts to seek out a new deal left him empty-handed, not only because the same recession that scarred Deep Purple's last tour had spread panic waves through the rest of the music industry, but also because the one glimmer of hope the industry did find was so far off the mainstream track that it might take years for its benefit to trickle down elsewhere.

While the so-called grunge explosion leeching out of the Pacific Northwest of Seattle and environs made no attempt to hide its genuflecting debt to the metal monsters of an earlier generation, that's all it did repay. Nirvana, Pearl Jam, Soundgarden, and Mudhoney all acknowledged the formative influence of Deep Purple, Black Sabbath, and many more. But the sounds that influence had mutated into were far removed from anything the musicians could draw compensation from. For an entire generation of worthy antecedents, there would be no tugging the crumbs off the new guard's table, no matter how much they deserved them.

Still, there was safety in numbers and Gillan knew it. Once, when asked whether he would ever contemplate a reunion with Deep Purple, he promised a journalist, "I'd rather slit my throat than work with that band again." Now, although it took some six months of negotiations and discussions for Gillan's return to Deep Purple to finally be confirmed, he knew he'd be slitting his throat if he didn't.

Chapter 17

Farewell to Blackmore's Day

It was Roger Glover who set the wheels in motion. He and Gillan had remained friends throughout the singer's exile, and the bassist explained, "We didn't talk about the band for several years, until I called him up one day and said, 'Hey, I know we're not going to talk about the band, but I do want to talk about the band, [because] I want you back in it.'"

Gillan was under no illusions as to how his return was engineered — it was BMG's money, rather than the rest of the band's friendship, that was responsible. The decision, however, had been made and now all that mattered was to make sure it was the right one.

No matter how much Glover, Lord, and Paice wanted to see Gillan return to the fold, they knew that Gillan was not entirely blameless for his dismissal two years earlier. The singer later described it as "the most disgusting feeling I've ever had in my life" when he realized, a couple of days into an ice-breaking songwriting session with Glover, that he was effectively being auditioned to see if his writing and vocal abilities were still up to scratch. And, though he readily passed every test they set him, there was a bitter irony to the album's ultimate title — *The Battle Rages On.*

"*The Battle Rages On* was a job, not a labor of love," Gillan later remarked. "I was presented with an album that was finished. . . . I was singing on tracks that I had no input in. They were not my songs."

Although the writing credits would note Gillan's contributions, he was well aware that just a few months previous, many of the same songs were destined for an entirely different set of lyrics, courtesy of Jim Peterik and/or Joe Lynn Turner. The original sessions were scrapped, of course. But they lived on regardless.

Recording at Bearsville Studios in upstate New York, before shifting to the Greg Rike Studios in Orlando, Florida, Deep Purple abandoned the notion of bringing in an external songwriter, but, for the first time since the Mark I days, they did employ an outside coproducer. Thom Panunzio was an American whose career dated back to the mid-1970s, when an ambitious college kid working in the tape copy room at New York's Record Plant studio was suddenly promoted to assistant engineer on John Lennon's *Walls and Bridges* album. From there, he went on to similar duties with Bruce Springsteen's *Born to Run* and Patti Smith's *Wave*, before stepping up as a producer in his own right with guitar legend Link Wray's 1979 live album.

By the time Deep Purple came knocking, Panunzio's credits included acts as far afield as Iggy Pop, Gene Loves Jezebel, Joan Jett, and the Jeff Healey Band; most recently, he'd been in the studio with Mother's Finest — all of which added up to a track record that had certainly tasted success, but was rarely caught out begging for it.

Jon Lord was not initially convinced that Panunzio was right for the band. "I . . . thought that Thom was a very strange choice," he recalled. "But it later turned out that it had been exactly the right choice for us. Thom is very reserved, very quiet, but he loves rock'n'roll and he brought along his own engineer, Bill Kennedy. A guy in his thirties who clearly wishes he was still in his twenties, with a punk hairdo and a fifty-ciga-rettes-a-day voice. He insists on raising the recording volume, until right below the point on which everything distorts!

"Thom has really made it work," continued Lord. "His musical contribution had its limits, but he hadn't been hired for that anyway. I mean, nobody tells this band what the songs should look like; when we're good, we're good, and when we're bad, we're bad — I mean really bad! But we're good or bad in the Deep Purple way. What Thom did for us was produce the backing tracks in such a way that the band sounded like a band. That was his job."

For all of Gillan's and Glover's reservations about *The Battle Rages On*, and for how poorly the album sits in many fans' estimation, still it readily drew back from the easy-listening precipice over which *Slaves and Masters* had been so dementedly dangled. As Lord noted, "The first reason that Deep Purple always made new starts is that we always said to ourselves, 'Let's prove ourselves to the people once again and make another really good album!' For example, with *The Battle Rages On* . . . we wanted to show that we can deliver better things than *Slaves and Masters*, which was really not a Deep Purple album at all. It carried the name, but the sleeve was deceiving."

Unfortunately, few of the songs rose to the challenge of Panunzio's production, with the best of them sounding so close to classic Led Zeppelin that one song, the admittedly superlative "Talk About Love," sounded uncertain whether it was going to drive straight into the "Misty Mountain Hop" that Gillan's heavily treated vocals were plainly yearning for, or follow its basic riff's lead and become the Stooges' "No Fun." And is that "Spirit of the Sky" playing underneath "Ramshackle Man"? Or Joe Satriani's "Big Bad Moon"? In the light of what would soon be occurring, the synchronicity that surrounds the latter likeness is almost too delightful to bear.

Its reception surely enhanced by the return of Gillan to the band's ranks, *The Battle Rages On* readily eclipsed *Slaves and Masters'* poor chart performance, at least in Europe (it only narrowly missed the U.K. Top 20). Its immediate American performance was less noteworthy — the album dribbled no higher than No. 192 upon release in August 1993. However, a New Year tour alongside the latest incarnation of Black Sabbath would certainly alter that dour scenario, and Deep Purple Mark II, Version III, kicked off a scheduled nine-month world tour in Rome on September 24, 1993, moving on through Europe and the U.K. en route to Japan at the end of the year. The American dates would follow, and then there was the summer festival season to look forward to. But from the opening shows on, it was apparent that it would take a lot of hard work to make it that far. The mood was taut from the outset, and it grew tighter with every passing performance.

There were moments of incandescent beauty onstage, not least of all the brief passage when Blackmore launched into his rendition of Beethoven's Ninth Symphony to the accompaniment of an ethereal vocal overtone so astonishingly pure that most people assumed that the lurking Lord was generating it from within the battery of keyboards arrayed before him. In fact, the voice was live, performed by twenty-four-year-old former model Candice Night, Blackmore's girlfriend of the past five years and, though nobody knew it at the time, his musical future as well. For his musical past was fast unraveling around him.

Gillan and Blackmore were at complete loggerheads — Gillan later described Deep Purple as "a beautiful meal" with himself and Blackmore as the knife and fork on either side of the plate. What he didn't need to add was, the meal itself was all but forgotten.

Two months of almost nightly concerts did nothing to improve relations between the pair. Even seasoned veterans of Deep Purple's internecine squabbles were adamant that matters were as ugly now as ever they were during the dying days of the original Mark ii lineup. Gillan and Blackmore had long since abandoned traveling together, sending the road crew scurrying to find different routes for the pair to take, simply to walk onstage. Now they scarcely seemed to be playing together either.

Night after night, the only delight they took from one another's presence came in those odd moments when a deliberately misplaced cue or some other figurative banana skin allowed them to trip the other up. Gillan recalled several such moments in his autobiography; Blackmore dropping a "Jesus Christ Superstar" riff into "Black Night," then halting the moment that the singer joined in; Gillan abruptly walking offstage while Blackmore played out "Knocking at Your Back Door."

By the time the tour reached England in November 1993, relations between the pair hadn't simply passed breaking point. They were now irreparable. But Blackmore had learned one valuable lesson from those other occasions when matters had reached such a dire impasse: it wasn't enough to simply get rid of Gillan — he always came back in the end. If this torturous partnership was ever going to shatter, Blackmore was the one who'd have to break it up.

On the eve of the first U.K. date, Blackmore announced that he would not be accompanying the band to Japan the following month, and destroyed his visa to make sure of that. But still the battle was merely simmering. Not until the tour reached Birmingham on November 9, in front of a packed NEC stadium, did it finally hit flashpoint.

The show was to be filmed for home video release, a decision the entire band had taken. Blackmore, however, seemed to be having second thoughts — while the rest of the group walked onstage and kicked into "Highway Star," the guitarist remained backstage, hurling a bucket of water at one of the cameramen. He appeared onstage in time to trip off a perfunctory guitar solo, then disappeared again — an act he repeated throughout the remainder of the show. The concert went on, but it did so, Gillan wrote, with a guitarist who simply "knocked the songs about, ending early, taking lumps out, and generally leaving me stranded whenever possible." As the band's set finally limped to a bedraggled end, Ian Paice spoke for all the musicians when he told the crowd, "We owe you a hell of a lot!"

Backstage, with Blackmore having long since vanished, confusion reigned. Nobody truly understood what was going on; nobody could even begin to try. Clearly Blackmore had reached the end of *a* tether, but which one? Was he tired of the band? Tired of the road? Or just tired? In fact, it was a combination of the three, although he would scarcely admit that for some years to come.

Of course, nobody expressed surprise when he acknowledged, "I really didn't get along with Ian [Gillan] toward the end. I wanted to play good music and he wanted to play bad music. He has a different view, at the different end of the spectrum."

But there were frictions beyond the personality problems that were meat for the watching scandalmongers. "Going on the road is aggravating, and playing through guitar amps very loud was getting sort of banal to me," Blackmore admitted to *Progression* magazine in 1998. "It was getting to the point where playing so loud every night was bothering me after the show. I was having ringing in my ears and I took that as a warning."

He was also tired of going through the motions. Echoing the rage he'd felt onstage at Wembley six years before, he admitted, "I'd come offstage where everybody was screaming for an encore and think, 'This was awful.' Purple had become a security thing, traveling the world in a limousine going, 'This is very safe and secure.' [But] music shouldn't be like that."

Nobody mentioned Birmingham when the band met up two days later to travel to the next show in Copenhagen, Denmark; certainly nobody asked Blackmore to explain his behavior. And there was no repeat of it, either. But hanging over everyone was the knowledge that, once a short swing through Scandinavia was complete, the band's next stop was Japan — and Blackmore had made no attempt to replace his visa. Neither would he. On November 17, 1993, at the Helsinki Ishallen in Finland, Ritchie Blackmore played his final show with Deep Purple. His last words to the band, he later recalled, were "Get yourself another guitar player, because I want out of this."

The group was shattered. "I am never going to describe what went on in that dressing room after Helsinki," Gillan reflected, "because it is deeply personal, but there were some uncontained emotions." He acknowledged, however, that, without Bruce Payne, the band might have broken up there and then. Gillan told *Record Collector*, "He told us about certain things that we weren't aware of, which made up our minds to carry on. Jon, Ian, and Roger had been deeply affected by what had been happening, but had soldiered on. Jon and Ian had some terrible, wicked things done to them, like when they were pushed out of the writing process.

"The problem was that Ritchie thought that what the band had was down to him, but it wasn't," Gillan explained. "He was only a fifth of it. It's not just the goal scorer that makes a good [soccer] team, it is the midfield and the defense." A goal scorer still helps, though. Especially when the next concert is just sixteen days away.

With Blackmore's departure, Deep Purple were poised, once again, on the brink of an uncharted abyss. A few weeks earlier, as the European tour scrambled on, Gillan had told his diary, "With Ritchie Blackmore, Deep Purple has no future." Now he was forced to face the fact that, without him, too, there seemed little room to maneuver.

The group had survived — very briefly — without Blackmore once before, of course. But neither Jon Lord nor Ian Paice looked back on *Come Taste the Band* as a triumph, beyond providing proof of their resilience. They all knew that, in the outside world, the notion of Deep

Purple without Ritchie Blackmore — its founding flame, its guiding light, its spiritual heart — was less than worthless.

To simply collapse around Blackmore's departure, however, was not an option any of the band members could contemplate. "Ritchie's a tragical figure for me," Lord revealed. "Mostly because he is enormously talented. He invented a new style of guitar-playing. He was a man of extraordinary individualism. I said 'was.' Because in the last time, his playing was missing fire, it sounded tired, lustless. And this man was unpredictable. We had to take care all the time. Sometimes he didn't want to play an encore, another time he just walked off the stage during the show. . . . It was hell to bring a good feeling to the audience. . . . Ritchie wanted to transform us into some kind of Rainbow. He refused to accept our ideas, only wanted to play his own stuff."

Lord told Finnish radio, "We'd got very much into a trap, which was that we had come to assume that the band would not exist if it did not have Ritchie Blackmore in it. And . . . we were more and more becoming Ritchie's backing band. And Ritchie — if he didn't write it, he wouldn't play it. It was a very difficult position. And he's a wonderful player and a very good writer — a difficult man, as you know. But I don't want to say anything particularly bad about him, it was just that he was going one way and the rest of us were going the other and he actually did us a real favor when he decided to leave."

Glover saw it this way: "Over the years, we had sunk into a certain state of mind regarding Ritchie, that without Ritchie there couldn't be a band. That was something that was ingrained in all of us, rightly or wrongly, and you know, you do the best you can at the time you're doing it, because you don't seem to have any choice. But here we all were, suddenly presented with a choice, and for the band to have folded at that point, I think, would have given Ritchie some sort of moral victory . . . Ritchie leaves and Purple folds. And that made us extremely determined not to let that happen. We were a bomb ready to blow up . . . No, that's a bad analogy. We were a flower ready to bloom. Again. And that's exactly what happened."

It was the band's Japanese promoter, the eponymous head of Udo Artist Inc., who offered at least a temporary fix to the problem, suggesting they ask guitarist Joe Satriani whether he'd be interested in replacing the errant Blackmore. As it turned out, he *was* interested. His own solo career was flying, so it wouldn't be a permanent arrangement. But he knew Deep Purple's repertoire, and he loved it. Was there any rock guitarist in America who didn't? He had only one question. The tape the band sent him was of a recent show in Stuttgart, during which Blackmore simply stopped playing at one crucial moment. Was Satriani expected to do the same thing?

Born in San Francisco on July 15, 1957, but raised on Long Island, on the opposite side of the country, Joe Satriani had, over the past decade or so, developed into one of the most respected American guitarists ever, a consummate player who was as comfortable with acrobatic flash as with technical excellence. Yet he raised that profile without ever snatching at any of the established guitar-hero crowns.

Only once, with the blistered blues of 1989's "Big Bad Moon," had he really threatened the commercial mainstream on either side of the Atlantic. MTV certainly enjoyed a brief love affair with the accompanying video, in which Satriani challenges none other than Bo Diddley to a game of pool. Yet his albums consistently charted on reputation alone — Deep Purple's call, in fact, came just as his latest release, the *Time Machine* tapestry of old and new material, began its ascent up the charts. As Satriani told the band at the end of their first rehearsal, however, "I never thought I'd get the chance to play 'Smoke on the Water' with Deep Purple onstage!" And now that he had, he wasn't going to surrender it, even if it meant temporarily surrendering some of his own sternest rules.

The man is a genius, but Satriani is becomingly modest about his abilities, sounding more like a determined pupil when he talks guitar than a man whose own past students included Steve Vai and Kirk Hammett. "I studied jazz for a while at home, then I took lessons and it taught me things I'm still working on," Satriani said. "The hardest lesson was, only play what you want to play, make a clear distinction between improvising and simply regurgitating what you've heard other people play. And that is hard, because to be a working musician, like myself, you have to quote other people simply to get people to take you seriously.

"In the world of blues, especially, you have to show people that you know blues, which means you have to play what other people have played. So the theory kind of goes against it — to go against the grain, not to be an automaton. Even if they're your own licks, not other people's, they still become automatic, and trying to get away from that is a challenge. Even down to little things like the way you pick or the way you vibrato, every note that you hit should be new."

Every note he hit with Deep Purple would not, of course, be new — how could it be, in a set that slammed through the past twenty-five years of immortal hit records, from the occasional encore of "Hush" through to the last album's "Anya" and "The Battle Rages On"? But he was determined to enjoy the experience — so much so that, with the Japanese dates complete, Satriani agreed to stay on board for a European tour later in the summer of 1994.

Roger Glover looks back on Satriani's sojourn with the band with immense pleasure: "He came in initially at two weeks' notice, just to save the Japanese tour, and we had so much fun doing those six gigs. What a revelation! It was wonderful to play a gig and not have to worry about politics and bad feelings . . . and so we said, 'This is too good to be true, let's do it again!' And the next opportunity was the summer tour, and that was a lot of fun as well.

"The point of that tour was, we just wanted to get out and prove something to people, we just wanted to play. And it proved various things. It proved that someone else playing guitar would be accepted, and a lot of people liked Satriani. It was a very successful tour and it was a very happy tour.

"But, at the end of it," Glover concluded, "it became apparent that it wasn't Satriani's cup of tea. He loved playing in the band, but I think he felt he'd spent his whole life carving his own niche, and he didn't want it swallowed up by being in a band. And he also felt that he was a generation younger than us, and he wanted to hang on to that few years' difference." Prearranged as it was, Satriani's departure left "no hard feelings at all." Rather, the guitarist's time with the band "was fabulous, and it gave us a taste of what we could be."

So, with their heads still filled by the applause from Satriani's final show, at the Sportplatz in Kapfenberg, Austria, on July 5, 1994, Deep Purple now put those heads together to seek a replacement . . . for Satriani, for Blackmore, and for everything that people believed that Deep Purple stood for.

It would take Ritchie Blackmore close to eighteen months to reemerge following the torrid conclusion to his years with Deep Purple, launching a brand-new incarnation of Rainbow in summer 1995, but ensuring that there could be no comparisons with the past by recruiting an entirely fresh lineup. He had, he later admitted, considered both Ronnie James Dio and Joe Lynn Turner as possible partners, "but not for more than a couple of seconds. I felt I'd done as much with them as I could."

Instead he unveiled former La Paz vocalist Doogie White, ex-Warlock keyboard player Paul Morris, and two sidemen from past Joe Lynn Turner solo projects, bassist Greg Smith and drummer John O'Reilly. All, despite such credentials, were total unknowns and the ensuing album, *Stranger in Us All*, apparently reveled in that anonymity.

Only one element of the entire outing truly stood out, the lyrics that Candice Night spun across four of the songs and the vocals she contributed to the rest. No sooner had Rainbow been laid back to rest than the now betrothed Blackmore and Night were launching their own project, sensibly named Blackmore's Night.

Built upon the solid foundations that Blackmore had always brought to his work, the love of medieval-era music and playing that, even in the firmly rocking grip of Deep Purple and Rainbow, had never strayed too far from view, Blackmore's Night was nevertheless unabashedly targeted far from the visceral riffs and solos of old. Predominantly acoustic, and exploring areas that Blackmore had scarcely been able to pursue in the past — Renaissance melodies, classical motifs, Middle Eastern cadences — Blackmore's Night was nevertheless aimed straight into the heart of his former constituency, confident that listeners who had remained with him for so many years already would appreciate this latest shift. Either that, or they would applaud one of the most bloody-mindedly courageous moves any of rock's old-guard guitar heroes had ever made.

And so they did. Though Blackmore's Night would never set the charts alight, or even aflicker in the manner of recent Deep Purple and Rainbow, still the duo's debut album, *Shadow of the Moon*, proved a roaring success. Sales of 70,000-plus awaited its German release, and loyal Japan purchased 100,000 more. Word spread of the intoxicatingly ethereal journey that flicked aside the occasionally Steve Nicks–shaped specters that some of Night's imagery evoked, delving instead into a parallel universe where music was made for the sheer beauty of it, and critical terms like "folk rock" were so specious as to be utterly redundant.

Touring honed both the music and its makers' understanding of what it meant. Almost bashfully, Blackmore recalled one of Blackmore Night's first live shows, at a Berlin church. Certain that at least part of the audience would go home happy only if he served up some reminder of his past, he readied a pair of Rainbow oldies to wheel out for encores. "And as soon as we started playing the old favorites," Blackmore said, "some people put on their coats to leave!"

If *Shadow of the Moon* was the duo's attempt to prove their credentials within this exciting new arena, Blackmore's Night's second album, 1999's *Under a Violet Moon*, was their stab at seeing what they could do with other people's — and it turned out even grander.

The remarkable "Past Time with Good Company," with its intriguing Henry VIII writing credit, was the first of five overtly traditional airs rearranged and reworked by Blackmore and Night; the daffily Arthurian "Avalon," "March the Heroes Home," the self-defining "Spanish Nights," and the percussive Cossack quick-step "Gone with the Wind" all followed in its footsteps, with the latter also packing one of Blackmore's best guitar solos in years — a gift all the more impressive because it was the only solo on the album.

A guest appearance from the Strawbs' John Ford ("Wind in the Willows") and a surprising version of the *Ritchie Blackmore's Rainbow* standout "Self Portrait" were the album's only other concessions to Blackmore's fabled past, an unselfconscious air of breezy sing-alongability its sole nod to commerciality. Otherwise, *Under a Violet Moon* was that most elusive of all modern musical gestures, an album which existed solely on its own terms, and which rose and fell, similarly, on its own merits. The fact that it succeeded so fabulously on both counts was simply a bonus.

In the face of such dexterity, Blackmore's Night's third album, 2001's *Fires at Midnight*, emerged their most conventional and, correspondingly, most disappointing set. With Blackmore's electric instincts far more to the fore, the opening "Written in the Stars" was the kind of middling AOR-type "epic" that neither Heart nor Stevie Nicks (nor, for that matter, the young Chris DeBurgh) would have balked at creating.

Next up, a version of Dylan's "The Times They Are A-Changin'" was equally disconcerting, most notably via the "I Got You Babe" instrumental hook that swung in to dominate the bridgework. As a wry commentary on the mainstream's co-opting of the folk revival of the Zim-whipped early-1960s, it was a cunning juxtaposition. But somehow one doubts whether such an observation even entered into the equation.

For anybody coming at the album from a point of view enhanced solely by the duo's earlier work, it was difficult to comprehend precisely what *Fires at Midnight*'s purpose was. Blackmore spoke loftily of Central and Eastern European folk traditions as the guiding principle behind Blackmore's Night. But he of all people knew there was more to those disciplines than a few funny-sounding Olde Tyme instruments, especially as the dominant effect on this album was a liquid guitar straight out of the Mike Oldfield school of twiddly influence.

The playing, of course, was superlative, the songs were well-constructed, and there were a few nice flourishes lurking in almost every corner you looked. But whereas Blackmore's Night was once a vehicle for courageous exploration and authentically unlikely esotericism, *Fires at Midnight* suggested it had developed into precisely the kind of fraudulent new-age noodle machine it was previously poised to annihilate. Suddenly, Enya was looking really good again.

It would take a live album to redress the balance, and how ironic was that? With Blackmore's Night stepping into the arena where Blackmore's own reputation was forged amid the most fiery coals, and proving they had nothing to fear from anything they found there, *Past Times with Good Company* might never have made *Made in Japan* quail, but who'd want it if it did? Two discs captured the full melodic power of the duo (and friends), fifteen tracks occasionally extending well beyond their studio parameters, but always remaining true to the air of the original compositions.

Indeed, *Past Times with Good Company* lacked nothing in terms of stirring power and evocation, a point furthered by the handful of songs written around existing traditional memories and then hammered home by the fact that just two tracks harked back to any of Blackmore's own past incarnations. "16th Century Greensleeves," the old Rainbow stand-by, was in any case a stern prophet of where Blackmore's interests lay, while "Soldier of Fortune" (from Deep Purple's *Stormbringer*) always packed a precocious introspection far removed from the problems that scarred the remainder of that benighted disc. The chance to hear it in less prejudicial surroundings rejuvenated it, even before you took in the rearrangements that allowed it to fall so seamlessly into place in these new surroundings.

Regardless of how historically "authentic" Blackmore's Night's interpretation of medieval music might be, it is impossible to overestimate just how profound an impact the group has had on any evaluation of Deep Purple's entire oeuvre — sidelines and solo projects included. Again, the duo imparted nothing that Blackmore's own stated interests had not hinted at in the past; neither would their fourth studio album, 2003's *Ghost of a Rose*, offer anything to change that perspective. (Although what an appropriate choice was Jethro Tull's "Rainbow Blues.") What does confound the doubters is the sheer longevity that the project has enjoyed.

As of late 2003, a decade had elapsed since Ritchie Blackmore left Deep Purple, and it is impossible (if not unnecessary) to say whether time has healed or hardened the rifts that drove him to quit in the first place. In interviews, Blackmore's policy has consistently remained "never say never" — discussing a return to hard rock around the time of *Fires at Midnight*, Blackmore admitted that "further down the line, when my batteries are recharged . . . it's a definite possibility."

Neither has he ever followed Ian Gillan into absolutely denouncing the prospect of returning to Deep Purple. Not for Blackmore, a man who chooses his words carefully at the very best of times, the head-beneath-the-guillotine pledge that "I'd rather slit my throat than work with that band again."

From the fan's point of view, however, maybe sleeping dogs should be left to lie. The second incarnation of the band, through the 1980s and early 1990s, probably didn't disgrace itself any more than the so-called classic lineups ever did — for every *Perfect Strangers*, there was a *Slaves and Masters*, but for every *Machine Head* there was also a *Stormbringer*. But the magisterial energies and Alpine heights to which the 1970–74-era lineups so routinely soared were never more than methodically echoed when the group emerged for a second go-round. Had Deep Purple not reconvened in 1984, their legend today would be no less resonant.

And that was the challenge that faced the band as they steeled themselves for the future. Not to prove, as they had once viewed their task, that life could go on without Ritchie Blackmore, but to prove that things could actually get better.

Viewed from the outside, in the neat choreography of chronological history, there is absolutely no break between the Deep Purple of 1993 and that which swarmed back into action twelve months later — just one more personnel change in a group that had been through eleven already. From the inside, however, the band wasn't simply replacing an errant musician. They were reappraising everything they believed they now stood for. Fans referred to the new lineup as Mark IX. As far as the band was concerned, they were going back to number one.

Chapter 18

Playing in Morse

Summarizing Deep Purple's history for the *Heavy Metal Pioneers* video documentary in 1991, Jon Lord mused aloud that 1993 — the group's twenty-fifth anniversary — loomed as a significant milestone that might, though he left the thought unspoken, inspire him to finally step away from Deep Purple. Instead, an anniversary that had otherwise turned out to be a non-event completely rejuvenated his interest in the group. Now, rather than pack his bags for a career elsewhere, he sat down with the others to compile a wish list of dream guitarists.

Much had changed in the two decades since Deep Purple last found themselves searching for a lead guitar player. There was, of course, no shortage of viable candidates — across the hard-rock spectrum, in particular, heroes continued to abound. The qualifications the group demanded, however, required more than an ability to cut a good shape while laying down some grand riffs.

A player needed to understand both the nature of Deep Purple's music and the weight of history behind it. In terms of modern marketing (a box for everything, and everything in its box), the band was now "classic rock" and, no matter how disgruntled such a label left the musicians (and it did), there was a central truth to that brand that they would never want to shake off. Their music had evolved, of course it had. But it had evolved in directions of the band's own choosing, not in those that the hard-rock scene in general had followed. One would never mistake a Deep Purple track for Helmet. But there was another consideration, as well — to make sure that a *new* Deep Purple track could never be mistaken for an old one. They needed a guitarist, *not* a Ritchie Blackmore clone.

With these and several other strictures in mind, Lord, Paice, Glover, and Gillan compared notes, discovering that, amid their own litanies of favorite guitar players, one name was common to them all — Steve Morse. And when Morse was approached to find out if he felt the same way about Deep Purple, he proved just as enthusiastic.

Born in Hamilton, Ohio, on July 28, 1954, Morse took up the guitar after witnessing a concert by classical player Juan Mercadel (who also gave the teenager some lessons). Linking with high school friends Andy West, a proficient bassist, and keyboard player Mark Parrish, Morse formed his first band, Dixie Grit, while still at school. He was then forced to quit when he was expelled from school for refusing to get a haircut.

Departing Ohio, he enrolled at the University of Miami School of Music. It was there that Morse formed a new band, the Dixie Dregs, with violinist Allen Sloan, drummer Rod Morgenstein, and keyboard player Steve Davidowski; the nature of the group was decided after the quartet caught a campus gig by John McLaughlin's Mahavishnu Orchestra, the hypervirtuoso instrumentalists whose output straddled the twin camps of jazz and rock for much of the early 1970s.

Morse persuaded his old friend Adam West to migrate to Miami, and the Dixie Dregs recorded and self-released their first album, *The Great Spectacular*, as a class project in 1975. Not until they graduated college did the band step out into the wider world, gigging around the American South and finally coming to the attention of Capricorn Records after a string of gigs supporting Randall Bramblett's Southern rock/jazz hybrid Sea Level.

Mark Parrish was the next player to move down from Ohio, to replace Davidowski as the Dixie Dregs set to work on their major-label debut, 1977's *Free Fall*; Parrish was then replaced by one T. Lavitz, and in this form the group became one of the sensations of the 1978 Montreux Jazz Festival — a performance immortalized in part on the *Night of the Living Dregs* live album.

Through the remainder of the 1970s, the Dixie Dregs remained true to their initial vision of instrumental music; having since shortened their name to the Dregs, however, they expanded to feature both vocals and a fiddle (three-time American national champion Mark O'Connor) for what would prove the group's final album (for the time being), 1982's *Industry Standard*.

Morse promptly formed his own eponymous band, cutting three albums (*Two Faces*, *The Introduction*, and *Stand Up*), before 1986 saw him drawn into the newly reformed Kansas, alongside original members Rich Williams, Steve Walsh, and Phil Ehart, and ex-Streets bassist Billy Greer. A major event in the United States (Kansas' decade-old reputation for long-winded art rock was never much of an attraction elsewhere), the reunion spawned an immediate Top 20 hit, "All I Wanted," together with a hit album, *Power*. But subsequent releases fell by the wayside and, when Kansas broke up for a second time in 1988, Morse resumed both his solo career (beginning with the album *High Tension Wires*) and an occasional flirtation with his old Dixie Dregs bandmates. The reconvened band toured during 1988, then again in 1992.

Comprised now of Morse, Lavitz, and Morgenstein, joined by Dave LaRue, from Morse's own band, and a former Mahavishnu Orchestra member Jerry Goodman, the Dixie Dregs maintained a sporadic but well-received career for the next two years, slipping in such albums as the in-concert *Bring 'Em Back Alive* and *Full Circle*. At the same time, Morse continued his own solo tangent with the new-age specialist Windham Hill label. In fact, his latest release, *Structural Damage*, was still fresh when he joined Deep Purple in fall 1994. With just three days of rehearsal under his belt, Morse made his live debut in front of 12,000 fans at Mexico City's Palacio de los Deportes, on November 23, 1994, opening a tour designed to promote the band's latest album, the live *Come Hell or High Water* — Ritchie Blackmore's farewell.

"I think [they wanted] to be adventurous," Morse said of his recruitment. "'Hey, let's have somebody completely different.' A lot of it is that they are so open-minded. The reason they got into the band to begin with, and were pulled in from other bands, is because they are all really good and their talent just shines."

Nevertheless, Morse's first dates with the band were very much a tentative engagement, "a little trial period where both myself and the band were unsure if this was going to work." He told *Guitar Player*, "They were rightfully cautious and so was I. One of the first questions I asked my manager was, 'Are they going to make me wear funny clothes?'" Just four dates into the tour, however, he professed himself "totally blown away that this band, who everybody thinks [of] as the beginning of heavy metal, wanted to improvise more than I did with the Dregs."

Deep Purple gigged sporadically through 1995, paying their first visits to South Korea, South Africa, and India during March and April, but devoting most of their time to preparing for the new album, *Purpendicular* — and doing so with an enthusiasm the group hadn't felt in years.

Watching from afar, Blackmore expressed some astonishment at the band's choice. "I really remember liking [Morse's] work with the Dixie Dregs," he told *Progression*. "But I did kind of wonder what he's doing with [Deep Purple]. But that's for them to figure out."

According to Glover, however, they had long since moved past that point, as he readily credited the arrival of Morse as the wellspring of much of the band's newfound optimism: "From [the moment he joined], it's hard not to exaggerate how good it was. We did a couple of gigs in Mexico, just to feel each other out, as it were, then we went into the studio to start writing songs, and ah, it was magical. Songs just appearing out of thin air. He's such a sympathetic and energetic and supportive guy to have in a band."

Glover recalled how he was tuning up one day, "just playing some silly little pattern, checking my tuning," when Morse walked into the room and started busking along with him. "He goes, 'Hey, that's great!' And I was, 'I'm just tuning up!' But he goes, 'Well, do it again,' so I did, and he played something over it which I could never have thought of, that made it sound wonderful, and, 'Wow! That sounds great!' Then the rest of the band came in and we had a song." The delicately poised "Loosen My Strings," its punchy guitars weaving in and out of a positively yearning but deceptively languorous melody, would emerge as one of the highlights of an album stuffed with such peaks.

"We just wanted to find out who we were," Glover continued, "and the only way to do that is be yourself, and we were completely open to any suggestions Steve could come up with, and it was great for him. He had no idea that we wanted to reinvent ourselves as it were, and I told him this when I first met him — we don't want someone to replace Ritchie or play like him or look like him, we just want someone to give 100per cent of themselves and become part of the five, and he just walked right into that."

Gillan was similarly effusive: "We wanted [the album] to . . . bring a smile back on the faces of those who know and love the band. Terms like 'underground,' even 'dangerous,' were applied to us in the early days, and I never forget what I've said on more than one occasion — that I don't think it's right always to serve up the same old material and play safe, relying on past successes."

But Gillan was adamant that the album wasn't wholly rooted in the new inspiration delivered by Morse. The band's own recent experiences also played a part in shaping their latest adventures. "We went through something in the '80s that was very difficult," explained Gillan. "Our fans have always been totally supportive and very, very loyal. But you had the whole industry and media thing that started in England. They called us dinosaurs. [And] no matter how well you are doing, it does make you think a little bit about the aging process.

"I had quite a long conversation with Roger, [and we agreed] it was very important that we made that step from writing about fast cars and loose women in every song. Well, not every song, but we were thinking about it all the time!"

Possibly casting a wry eye toward the likes of David Coverdale, pushing fifty with a libido half his age, Gillan continued, "Somehow, there is something undignified about a mature guy ranting on about his dick! It is teenage and youthful behavior, [and] people expect a little more from us at our stage. Don't try to do what the kids do. Try and act your age. I think that is exciting."

It was also courageous. The number of bands who not only grew old gracefully, but did so naturally as well, can surely be counted on less than one hand. No matter that rock'n'roll had now been around for forty-plus years, and many of its earliest practitioners were still bashing around the live circuit; the fact is, the genre continues to consider itself a youngster's game, in which youth and, by extension, the obsessions of youth, remain the only universally acceptable currency.

Of course, there are those artists whose personal vision has never been hog-tied to such preoccupations. Dylan, Zappa, Bowie: most of the so-called immortals developed characters and characteristics that owed their genesis to the artist's intellect, as opposed to — as Gillan put it — his dick. But immortality and intellect are scarcely the most abundant qualities in any field; hence, for every act that has succeeded in carving its own furrow through the tempests of changing fashion and demand, there are countless others who either dry up after just a few years in the sun, or who litter the world of oldies-but-goldies, never-changing hulks that won't stop gyrating until even they have to admit they simply can't get it up any longer.

Nobody can blame them, of course. You do what you do because what else *can* you do? But could a painter expect to retain the respect of his public if he spent his entire career simply reworking the first little masterpiece he ever displayed? Would an author still be read if he kept on rewriting his first best-seller?

For an artist to survive, he has to adapt, if not for the sake of the demands of the day, then simply for his own dignity — and that is as true in rock'n'roll as in any other field. How tragic that so few of them seem to realize that. For, as Deep Purple were about to discover, the shift really wasn't that painful. As Gillan put it, "I started thinking that . . . our lyrics have always been expressive concerning things that affect you emotionally, intellectually, and spiritually. We decided to work on that."

But it was not lyrically alone that Deep Purple were abandoning the frivolities of the past. Glover noted, too, that "our playing improved" — although, when he elaborated, it was clear that it was the attitude *behind* the playing that changed, not the mechanics of the musicianship. Gillan's vocals, increasingly pale over his last couple of Deep Purple albums, regained all the fire and vivacity that had once seen him dominate the "Best Rock Vocalist" readers' polls, without ever resorting to the tried-and-trusted characteristics that had helped him rise there — but which, squawked by a fifty-year-old man, could not have sounded so true as they once did. Without sacrificing either his range or his courage, Gillan *sang* again.

Other band members came in for similar praise and, perhaps, reappraisal. Glover marveled, "Paicey was always a very solid guy, very fiery when he was younger. There was always that talk about him playing too much. But, when the '80s came, because it was all bass drum, snare drum, first and third beats on the bar and that was it, usually with a triggered sample, that kind of playing leaves no room for personality. So Paicey's personality disappeared under the direction that the band was going in. He had to be very heavy and clunky, and it just disappeared. But all of a sudden, feeling free in the studio again, he just burst into fire again. And that happened to all of us — we all exploded musically because of the newfound freedom we had, and the happiness, and the peace in the studio, it was just overwhelming. It was a great period."

For Gillan, the first opportunity to put the group's new frame of mind into action came, contrarily, with his next solo album — 1995 saw Gillan record *Dreamcatcher*, widely acknowledged as his best record since the halcyon days of Gillan, and his most adventurous since *Clear Air Turbulence*. Given such a confident kick start, it was no surprise that similar accolades should descend upon *Purpendicular*, the album with which Deep Purple set about restating their position.

With the group returning to the Greg Rike Studios in Orlando, the homey base they discovered during the *Slaves and Masters* sessions, the most immediately apparent aspect of *Purpendicular* was the sheer wealth of styles it broached, without ever leaving recognizable Deep Purple territory. Not since *Fireball* (or, albeit less successfully, *Who Do We Think We Are*), had a Deep Purple album delved so deeply into its membership's influences, without a care for the expectations of its audience.

The jerking, lurching "Soon Forgotten" had a mutant mood that was readily comparable to bands as far afield as Sparks on the one hand, King Crimson on the other. But, if its twitchy rhythms and quirky vocal line put older listeners in mind of something that could have crawled belatedly out of the post-punk art crowd, Steve Morse's guitar quivered with a growling industrial intent that was as fresh as tomorrow.

"Sometimes I Feel Like Screaming," a hybrid ballad bruiser that might once have lived up to its title with a yodeling vengeance, plowed along instead without once raising its voice unnecessarily. Its gentler moments were then taken all the way home by "A Touch Away," a gorgeous slice of acoustic guilelessness that might well qualify as the first true ballad in Deep Purple's entire catalog — just as "The Aviator" was promptly elected their first highland fling.

So much variety was not, however, merely change for change's sake, nor a calculated drive to take Deep Purple as far away from its Ritchie Blackmore–dictated days as possible. Rather, it was the sound of a band relaxing into their music with a carelessness they had forgotten it was legitimate to indulge. "I think we were all so determined to make it work," Glover explained, "and the way to make it work is *not* to try and make it successful, but to shrug your shoulders and say, 'Hey, whatever happens happens.' Deep Purple are not a pop band. We're not about to go and do an Aerosmith, as it were, getting surefire hits and having them produced to perfection. . . . [I'm] not knocking Aerosmith, because they make great records, but for me it's more pop than rock, done for the dollar, not the love."

That said, *Purpendicular* was not to be left wanting dollars in its own right. Immediately upon release in March 1996, the album topped *Kerrang!*'s metal chart, an achievement that far outweighed its less than stellar performance on Britain's national chart — a listing that had, in any case, grown increasingly detached from the reality of what was selling in record stores, placed *Purpendicular* no higher than No. 58.

American sales were less than impressive, as *Purpendicular* became the first Deep Purple studio album ever to fail to make the *Billboard* Top 200. But, though the group's 1996 touring schedule reflected their diminishing American profile, the shows were enjoyable regardless, for fans and band alike.

The brief ride through the country's smaller theaters five years earlier was repeated, as Deep Purple played just a dozen shows, opening at Washington, D.C.'s 9:30 Club, a venue better acquainted with up-and-coming alternative acts of the mid-1990s than with the veteran giants of yesteryear. Two nights at New York's Beacon Theatre were sold-out, but again testified to the fact that Deep Purple, at least in their present state, were far, far away from the stadium-packing demigods of old. Even the seemingly obligatory "festival" date, on December 5 in Auburn Hills, Michigan, was scarcely a monsters-of-rock–style bash. Deep Purple headlined over the Hazies, the Hunger, and punk-metal merchants Danzig.

The audiences that the band did attract, however, reacted with a wild enthusiasm that took even the veteran members by surprise. Past lineup changes, after all, had always generated at least a little hostility, from the diehards who still called for Gillan long after Coverdale had taken over his role, to the packed crowds that all but turned their backs on Tommy Bolin because he wasn't Ritchie Blackmore.

Morse, however, slipped into the setup with scarcely a glitch. Glover mused, "It's wonderful looking out from my vantage point on the stage, and just look at people looking at him. In the early days, the first few dates we did, we started in England, and there'd be all these people coming in with these quizzical expressions on their faces, or maybe just downright hatred. There's a lot of Ritchie Blackmore lovers out there. And within seconds, or minutes, they'd be smiling and nudging each other, 'Wow, did you see that?' And the next song they'd have their fists in the air. It was seamless. People just took to him. He's got his detractors, of course, everyone has, but to most people he's as much a ray of sunshine into their version of Deep Purple as he was to ours."

Away from the actual concert setting, the first chance to check out this newfound live dexterity came with the release of *Live at the Olympia '96*, a two-CD live album recorded at the Paris Olympia on March 24, 1996, and ideally positioned to expunge the memory of the admittedly drab *Come Hell or High Water*. Deep Purple had not, after all, altered their songwriting style alone. Their very approach to music was shifting — not necessarily permanently and not always successfully. But a willingness to experiment had certainly crept in, one that even caught the group operating with a small brass section across two *Purpendicular* songs (the pumping "Cascades" and "Purpendicular Waltz") and two oldies ("No One Came" and "Highway Star"). Other, equally startling adventures would follow.

The purpose of *Live at the Olympia '96* was not, however, solely to document one more night in the life of the band — even if industry onlookers did groan aloud at the news that *another* Deep Purple live album was on its way (including archive releases, this was their sixteenth). It was also intended to counter the tide of bootlegs which, having been unleashed with *H-Bomb* all those years ago, had taken on positively monumental proportions in recent years.

In 1992, the first edition of the *Hot Wacks* guide to bootleg LPs and CDs included details of no fewer than eighty-eight Deep Purple releases. In the years since then, that total had increased by half again, with the first Steve Morse–era bootlegs appearing within weeks of his first shows with the group. Maybe Roger Glover personally did not object to such recordings, but even he acknowledged that, with every other home taper out there making money from Deep Purple's live recordings, the band would be stupid not to join the parade. Besides, although his position was clear, it was not the only one that counted.

"The band doesn't have a position on bootlegs," Glover explained. "The band has five different positions. We all have our own views on it, Steve is adamantly against them. He believes that when he's doing a live performance, it is for the moment, and when he's soaring away and he's doing it for the moment, and he sees the little red light of a video camera, he freezes up because he knows it's going to be dissected later, and it takes away from his performance. His performance is one-time only, it's not there to be pored over and dissected, and that's why he resents it."

There was, however, another consideration to be made when inspecting *Live at the Olympia '96* — the knowledge that without a "new" release for fans to pore over, the future of Deep Purple was very much in danger of being utterly overwhelmed by its past.

Deep Purple had never been strangers to repackages and reissues. As far back as 1972, America was treated to the Top 60 hit *Purple Passages*, a double-album sampling of the band's first three LPs, while barely one year had gone by since the band's 1976 breakup without some new compilation or exhumation hitting the racks.

Several proved major hits. The group was still recovering from the critical mauling of *Stormbringer* when the Mark II lineup was reanimated by *24 Carat Purple*, a Top 20 British hit during summer 1975. In 1980, the height of the new wave of British heavy metal era, saw Deep Purple top the U.K. charts for the first time since *Machine Head*, when the Mark II and III lineups were highlighted for the compilation *Deepest Purple*.

Neither was the archive-trawling confined to greatest hits and old live recordings. The first two EPs in the descriptively titled *New Live and Rare* series made the U.K. Top 50 during 1977–78, while there were plans afoot that same season for a full four-LP Deep Purple anthology, combining two albums' worth of familiar material with two more of rarities and unreleased live — the California Jam tapes among them. This enthralling venture was ultimately boiled down to the somewhat less thrilling *Powerhouse* collection, but clearly the willingness to take a fan's-eye view of the Deep Purple archive was there.

That side of things had slowed somewhat in more recent years, although longtime Deep Purple archivist Simon Robinson was organizing some fascinating reissues of related recordings for the RPM label (Robinson would subsequently reawaken the band's Purple label — dormant since the late 1970s — for a further wealth of treasures). And, while the carefully collector-oriented discs that his operation oversaw were swamped by the more mercenary repackagings that flourished, still it proved that, far away from the new-release racks, Deep Purple thrived with a passion that few bands — even the age's most accredited monsters — could rival.

Through all of this activity, however, one aspect of Deep Purple's career remained unrepresented on the racks — or, at least, so misrepresented that they might as well not have existed. And how ironic that it should be the most important of them all. "When CDs first came out," Roger Glover explained, "I saw *Machine Head* in a store, and it was, 'Wow, look at this! We're on CD!' So I bought it, took it home like a schoolboy, 'Hey, I've got a Deep Purple CD.' But when I played it, I was so disappointed with the pitiful sound that I wrote to Warners and said, 'How can you do this? Please can we remaster?' A three-page letter I sent, and did I even get a reply? Of course not."

Close to a decade after that so-offensive CD was released (to be followed by similarly mishandled reissues of the remainder of the core catalog), the tide finally turned. Nineteen-ninety-five marked the twenty-fifth anniversary of *Deep Purple in Rock*, the album that truly started it all, and to celebrate, EMI commissioned Glover to return the master tapes to the studio and oversee a remastered commemorative edition.

"They sent me the tapes of *In Rock*," Gillan recalled, "and it was revelation just to listen to the individual channels, what people were doing back then. Knowing the record as I do now from twenty-five years of putting it in a certain category, you're suddenly hearing it in a new light. The remastering was beautifully done at Abbey Road, and I had a chance to listen to the multitracks, put on a few jams and outtakes and bits of silliness, and I think it made for a nice package. The more I did it, the more I got into it, pulling together photographs, then I started writing liner notes to go with what I was hearing."

The end result was indeed a jewel, so much so that Glover immediately set to work on a similarly upgraded version of *Fireball*. "And that was a gas," he said, "because we actually found a song ['Freedom'] that had not been released before." (Ironically, but none too disappointingly, an outtake that *had* seen the light of day, Blackmore's somewhat overwrought "Guitar Job" showcase — as released on 1989's *Blackmore Rock Profile* compilation — was surrendered to make room for it.)

Over the next four years, similarly treated editions of *Machine Head*, *Made in Japan*, and *Who Do We Think We Are* followed, each bearing a host of bonus cuts and occasional remixes. It was a fabulous series, with *Made in Japan* in particular shining out. The standing of Deep Purple's first (and finest) live album had scarcely diminished in the quarter-century since its release. True, it was inexplicably overlooked when the British magazine *Vox* came to compile its "Greatest Live Albums of All Time" feature in early 1992 — pushed out, one assumes, to make way for more fashionable documents by the Smiths and Depeche Mode. But the fusillade of complaints that bombarded the magazine's offices in the aftermath spoke as loudly — if not louder — than any so-called critics' choice, a point that the American magazine *Goldmine* reinforced six years later, with its review of the remastered edition.

Reiterating the slew of live Deep Purple albums released in the years since *Made in Japan*, not one, declared *Goldmine*, "will ever be much more than a collectors' curio, because in the world of Deep Purple live albums, there really is only one that truly matters, one which has been recycled, remade, and recreated so often that there can barely be a soul left on the planet without some idea of what it sounds like; but one which is now so relentlessly legendary that life without an umpteenth reissue can barely be called 'life' at all. It is, of course, *Made in Japan*, the two-LP concert recording which defined Deep Purple even as it redefined the concept of the live album."

Of all the albums, however, *Machine Head* is the one Glover himself remembers as being the most challenging. "There were no outtakes," he said. "By the time you've finished an album, you've gone through reels and reels of tape, all of which are covered with outtakes, and what you tend to do is take all the masters and put them on one tape, because that's easier to work with than finding your way among twenty-five reels. And so all those twenty-odd reels have disappeared, leaving only the master reel." He expanded the package, then, with the one B-side recorded during the *Machine Head* sessions, "When a Blind Man Cries," and a couple of mixes drawn from the rare quadraphonic edition of the album — then added an entire bonus disc of 1997 remixes of the original album.

It was a risky undertaking. Just a few years earlier, during the remastering of the Queen back catalog, similar tinkering called down a hail of opprobrium from outraged listeners. Glover's treatments, however, brought nothing but praise. "I think people saw the remixes as a bit of fun," he reasoned. "I was not challenging the old mixes, I was saying, 'Hey, this is the same performance done with '90s technology, or '90s sensibility, because we're actually using a lot of '60s technology to do it, because the sounds are those valve sounds.' And I didn't touch the original mixes, they're still there, they're intact, sounding good.

"But the remixes of *Machine Head* are by far the best of the remixes. In fact, they're better than the originals, and that's something I normally wouldn't say, because the originals have their character. But to me they are, they're just more alive, and they really sound more natural. The first mix always sounded a little muddy to me. So although that album doesn't have the banter and the outtakes and the jams and what-have-you, it does have the absolute 100 per cent truth and true quality. Every song is improved.

"The thing is," Glover continued, "I'm doing [these remasters] from a fan point of view, because I am a fan. In a way, I'm the fan's representative in the mysterious world of the studio and the band. They only see what we give them or what they sneak away from shows. It's a mysterious thing, and everyone wants to understand what goes on inside it. So, because I'm a fan of the music and a fan of the players, I want to do the best job possible for the audience. This is for the fans. This is how I want the band to be remembered, and this is how I want the fans to think of us, in the best light possible."

Buoyant with the success of the remasters so far, Glover even considered taking a fresh look at *Burn*, an album he had hitherto steadfastly avoided paying much attention to. "I always said I wasn't going to do the albums I wasn't on," he maintained, "and it's always been very difficult for me to listen to that particular album, because I was not in a great state when it came out. It was very difficult to listen to it without feeling bitter. But I really enjoyed the anniversary period, and when I heard the song 'Burn' on the radio one day, I listened to it now, and it was, 'Well, that's not a bad song, but boy, it could do with a good mix.' That was my reaction, and I thought, 'Well, maybe I can bring something to this project.'"

Pulling the tapes together for the album took a while — several had gone astray, several more were misfiled. But finally Glover and engineer Peter Denenberg took delivery of the masters. "We went into the studio," Glover recalled, "we put the tapes up, we listened to the originals, and . . . we were getting somewhere, but we weren't getting far enough. Maybe the quality of the tapes we had wasn't very good, I don't know. But what we were coming up with wasn't as revolutionary and mind-blowing as I thought it was going to be. And then I realized, 'Actually, my heart's not in this.' Listening to the atmosphere in the studio, listening to the musicians individually playing, knowing I was not part of it, I just felt like an intruder. I didn't like the atmosphere I was hearing in the studio.

"You can't say why, it was just a feeling. And I turned to Peter and said, 'This doesn't feel right, we're not making any real dent in this, we're not bringing anything to the project.' And that's the only reason to do it, to bring something to it. So I said, 'Well, it's decision time.' And my decision was, 'I'm not going to do this.' And that was the end of it."

In the midst of all this activity, Deep Purple continued rolling on. Early 1997 brought the band's first visit to South America, with gigs in Argentina, Brazil, Peru, and Bolivia; from there, the summer festival circuit saw them visit Lebanon, Germany, and Switzerland; year's end then brought another swing through the United States, for a tour of the country's House of Blues niteries.

After the disappointing turnout last time around, it was an invigorating outing. "Crowds are fantastic," Glover enthused in 1998. "We've not played in America for some time, partly because we're actually pretty dead in America. We're stuck in that 'classic rock' syndrome where [radio] won't play anything new. All they want to play is the old stuff, and it's very difficult to get above that, to get a tour where you can go out and play and say, 'Look, we're not what you think we are.'"

Glover continued on that same theme five years later: "In the States, we're slotted by the media and by everyone into the 'classic rock' thing, which doesn't happen in Europe, doesn't happen in India, doesn't happen in South America. Yes, we're a band with a past, but we're not classic rock, we're just a band that has kept going. So in America, it's a fight to get beyond 'Smoke on the Water' and 'Woman from Tokyo' . . . and how do you beat that? You beat it by doing what we're doing — writing new music and trying to get it across. And how do you get it across? By playing live. And how do you get people to come and see you?"

By playing live. "In Europe, especially, it's very healthy," Glover said. "Right across Europe, we're getting young crowds everywhere. There are obviously some older people who want to see us because they saw us twenty-odd years ago. But by and large, it's a younger crowd." American audiences tended to be a little more traditionalist, although even there, the phrase "older fans" tended to reflect what Glover described as "the sort of thirties set who maybe got into the band during the *Perfect Strangers* time. A few of them know the stuff from the past, like 'Highway Star' and 'Hush' and 'Smoke' and so on, but they haven't been bad. There have been a few places where they've been seated and they've remained seated . . . and that's their right as ticket holders. But that's usually a sign that they're an older crowd, because they need to sit."

Deep Purple, on the other hand, had no intention whatsoever of showing their age. Even when Gillan finally cut the lengthy tresses he'd worn for so long, he did it for what he insisted were the most practical of reasons: "It kept falling in my beer."

Chapter 19

Any Fule Kno What?

"Really," Roger Glover mused in 1998, "I think we did ourselves a disservice, the ten years or so previous to Steve coming into the band." So much had changed — not only within the group's own chemistry, but in their very approach to music — that there were moments when the decade following Deep Purple's reunion seemed little more than a bad dream, one in which the dreamer is well aware of the objectives he needs to achieve, but can't ever come close to them.

Now, however, all the energy and enthusiasm that surrounded the act of reforming back in 1984, and which at least gave *Perfect Strangers* the impetus that made it worthwhile, had returned with added passion — so much so that, as the group worked out the concert repertoire that would sustain Deep Purple through the end of the century, just one song survived from the '80s and '90s pre-Morse era: "Perfect Strangers" itself. The remainder of the group's vocabulary was drawn either from the new material Morse himself had a hand in, or the old favorites that had always been band staples — and even they, enthused Glover, felt like new songs again, as the guitarist set about restyling solos, reinventing riffs, recreating even the hoariest standard to reflect the band's fresh momentum. And that, he said, "has kind of revolutionized everything."

The speed and ease with which new songs and ideas were flowing, meanwhile, sent Deep Purple back into the studio in late 1997, to begin work on their sixteenth studio album — and their first return disc for EMI, the label with which their career had begun, and which saw them through their first ten. They would call it *Abandon*, because that was how they described their approach to writing and recording. Gillan explained, "The definition I favor, from my *Oxford* dictionary, is, 'a) yield oneself completely to a passion or impulse, b) lack of inhibition or restraint; reckless freedom of manner.' In simple terms, it's Fuck Off Rock'n'Roll."

The band returned, once again, to the Greg Rike Studios (now relocated to Altamonte Springs, Florida) where the sessions were fast and ·furious. "It was so easy to record *Abandon*," Gillan celebrated. "We met in the studio, jammed, worked out ideas, and got the flow needed for good songs to come out. Just like when we recorded our classic albums, before a *certain person* started controlling everyone and everything. Now the chemistry between us is back." This point may or may not have been deliberately illustrated by the decision to add, to the eleven new songs, a startling reevaluation of the *In Rock* mainstay "Bloodsucker" — retitled "Bludsucker," and wholly rewired as well.

Overall, it was a less well-balanced album than *Purpendicular* — the hard rock was to the fore once again, although fears that Deep Purple might not have developed their interpretation of the genre were dismissed from the outset, as the opening "Any Fule Kno That" (the title's distinctive spelling lifted from Geoffrey Willans' *Molesworth* books of the 1950s) slammed a hip-hop–heavy "No No No" into a riff reminiscent of Aerosmith's "Walk This Way." Later in the cycle, the raging "Seventh Heaven" made a gallant stab at being acclaimed Deep Purple's heaviest song ever, with the emphasis fully on the word "heavy," as the riffs bordered on discordance, and the hint of melody that played round Gillan's lips was buffeted from all sides by the band in full flood.

Swaths of "Watching the Sky," too, owed more to the inchoate crunchings of the so-called nu-metal scene then engrossing great numbers of musical youth than to anything so traditional as Deep Purple's own origins. The astonishing thing was, no matter how alien such rumblings sounded, they pulled it off with an alacrity that defied the band's veteran status. There is, after all, something extraordinarily pitiful about old dogs attempting to pull off new tricks, and, had advance word of *Abandon* admitted that Deep Purple were mixing it with the young bucks of the late 1990s, the record itself would have been inaudible beneath the chuckling scorn. Instead, they simply got on with it, and *Abandon* hit the unsuspecting listener like a jackknifed tank transporter.

Such an aggressive assault did squeeze out both the variety and the subtlety of *Purpendicular*, a failing Roger Glover would eventually acknowledge: "*Abandon* was a tough album to make. It's a very insular album. . . . I dunno, I've got this pet theory that every time you do a great album, the next one's going to be tough."

Even among the most loyal (older) fans, *Abandon* received a cautious welcome at best, although when it did settle down — the almost-gentle "Don't Make Me Happy," the pointed classicism of "Fingers to the Bone" — it was easy to file alongside several of the band's lesser (but no less admirable) triumphs, a point especially proven in concert. Several of the songs, most notably "Seventh Heaven," had already been established as live crowd-pleasers; now, though the set remained weighted toward the older classics, the very nature of the new material allowed it to join its aging peers in a landscape where every night's performance drew something new out of the hat.

In vivid contrast to the almost calcified appraisals that were trotted out during the late-'80s/early-'90s, arrangements that had once seemed set in stone were fluid once again, and with that fluidity there came a freedom to expand and experiment. The chronological realities of new versus old didn't even enter into the equation. As Glover pointed out, "That's not what people see when they come to see us. What they see is a band that's very vital, and that's the main impression. The band is still a band, and it's better than it's been in many, many years."

That point was one that Deep Purple seemed intent on illustrating with the 2001 release of two separate box sets, between them comprising no fewer than twenty-four CDs, capturing a chain of live performances dating back as far as 1984, but dominated by the Steve Morse era. Four discs within *New, Live & Rare — The Bootleg Collection 1984–2000*, and all twelve within *The Soundboard Series* pursued the group's development over the past six years, and the sheer stand-alone dexterity of each performance was only the first of a myriad surprises.

Like the three-CD *Live in Japan* package — which, a decade previous, had finally liberated every recording made during the shows that produced *Made in Japan* — concerts that, in some instances, were recorded just days apart preserved for all ears the sound of a band firing on all cylinders, relishing once again the simple joy of being onstage and making music. Neither was that sound exclusive merely to the shows that the box sets captured. It was what Deep Purple strived for every night.

The strength of purpose that now bound Deep Purple found no better outlet, perhaps, than the chance to restage at least the final portion of the California Jam, nightly for three weeks through August 1998. A bill that opened with the apparently ill-at-ease Dream Theater was swept into hyperdrive, as Emerson Lake & Palmer reformed to challenge the headlining Deep Purple for every crown they had ever worn.

No matter that the show's physical schedule saw ELP cut their regular show by an hour, and Deep Purple by forty-five minutes. The mere prospect of two of the 1970s' most spectacular live bands, together on a single stage, should have been among the year's most irresistibly mouth-watering, all the more so in the light of *Abandon*'s furious declaration that Deep Purple were offering no quarter to anyone.

Instead, the outing bombed. In Englewood, Colorado, a venue that could comfortably hold close to 20,000 people was attended by just one-tenth that number. Tinley Park's Tweeter Center was barely a quarter full. In Holmdel, New Jersey, and Rochester, New York, two-thirds of the tickets went unsold; even the New York stop, at the Jones Beach Theater, saw half the seats unfilled, while the scheduled show at New Jersey's Camden Center was canceled altogether.

Musically, the show was spectacular. ELP's set, highlighted by a return to live action for the old epic "Tarkus" and the premier of a new piece, "Crossing the Rubicon," was as sensational as anything the trio had attempted in the years since their reunion, while Deep Purple were, simply, Deep Purple. As a business proposition, however, at the bottom line of bums on seats, the venture proved a shocking miscalculation — so shocking that, by the end of the year, ELP had broken up, riven by internal differences and external indifference.

Deep Purple were less susceptible to the whims of the American public. This latest round of gigging opened in Istanbul, Turkey, at the beginning of June 1998, and would run until the end of November. There'd be a break for Christmas, and then it was back onto the road until late July 1999, a fourteen-month extravagance in which the fickleness of one country would always be outweighed by the support of many others.

Neither was the end of the tour the end of the road. September 1999 would mark the passing of three decades since an all but unknown, unappreciated group streaked to U.K. prominence with an audacious attempt to blend a rock band with classical orchestra. And, to mark the occasion, the Royal Albert Hall was rebooked, for two nights this time, and an orchestra, the London Symphony, had been engaged. It was time to do it all again. And this time, everybody was bursting with enthusiasm.

Plans for Deep Purple to restage the epochal *Concerto for Group and Orchestra* were first mooted in the late 1980s, as the twentieth anniversary of the event hove into view — only to be dismissed when Lord realized he didn't actually have a copy of the original score: "[After] we did it at the Hollywood Bowl in 1970 . . . I think someone just forgot [to bring it] as they walked offstage. It's easily done! And really, we were never gonna play it again, I thought, so I never bothered to make sure that the music would come back. I thought it would be in the office. So when somebody said, 'It's the twentieth birthday of the concerto and we should do it again,' [I said], 'Yeah! [But] I don't know where it is!'"

Unwilling to let the event escape his grasp again, Lord began working toward recreating the concerto in 1997 — and he got nowhere. As the deadline drew closer and closer, Lord recalled, "My wife heard me screaming as I tore out my hair, saying, 'I can't make it! It's impossible!'"

Salvation materialized completely out of left field. Unknown to Lord, a Dutch music student, Marco de Goeij, had himself been striving to recreate the concerto for his thesis. "He found out that the score had been lost," Lord marveled, "so he bought the video and he just played it and played it. . . . He was actually . . . pausing the video to see where the players' fingers were." Finally, de Goeij's work was done. Lord told Australian radio station 2JJJ, "In February of 1999, I was getting out of a car in a very rainswept Rotterdam, [and] this young man came up to me and said, 'It's about your concerto. I think I've managed to recreate it!'"

In fact, de Goeij had completed only the first movement, although much of the second was also in place. "He had trouble with the third movement," Lord explained, "because it's so fast." With so much work already done, however, Lord fell back into his own recreation with renewed gusto, rescoring what he could not recall, but finding that much of the missing music came back to him as he worked.

Neither was the concerto the only item on the Albert Hall bill. Group and orchestra together would also run through a full set of Deep Purple classics, while each band member was also allotted ten minutes to perform something from their own extracurricular activities that they felt was important to the overall portrait of the group's last thirty years.

"The idea came together on the tour bus," Gillan explained. "It was the perfect way to end what was a fourteen-month world tour. It was such a party time, a real jamboree. And also a celebration of the fact that, with Steve Morse in the band, we are like a family again." Backed by his own band, Morse aired the theme to DJ Tommy Vance's *Friday Rock Show*, recognizing the program still as one of the band's most solid supporters; Glover, for his part, elected to revisit *The Butterfly Ball*, and recalled Ronnie James Dio for the occasion.

Dio was still fronting his own eponymous band. "We were doing some festivals in Germany [during summer 1999]," he recalled, "and Purple were on the bill at a few of them. One night I was at a bar with Ian Gillan, and he was, 'Has Roger asked you yet?' 'Asked me what?' 'Oh, you don't know about this. . . . ' And he told me about the thirtieth anniversary of the concerto and how each member of the band was going to perform things they had done outside of Purple. 'And Roger wants to ask you if you'll sing "Love Is All" and "Sitting in a Dream."' 'Of course I'll do it, I'll do anything for Rog.' And the next night, at another date, Roger comes up and says, 'I wanted to ask you a question. . . .'

"It was so much fun to do," Dio continued. "It brought back a lot of memories, I don't think I've smiled so much in years, and nor has Roger. It was the easiest gig on the face of the earth, just a wonderful part of my life, making the [original *Butterfly Ball*] album, and then doing it again thirty years later. Wonderful, wonderful times — not just the music, but the camaraderie out there. We just had such a great time."

Compared to the strictures and difficulties that had dogged the original performance, the 1999 concerto went like a dream. Contrasting the

LSO's attitude to the "rather haughty and a little standoffish" Royal Philharmonic Orchestra, Lord reflected, "In 1969 . . . maybe we didn't get everything we might have out of the piece." In 1999, on the other hand, "the orchestra more than met us, the band, halfway. Their attitude was fantastic." Instead of a couple of hurried, last-minute rehearsals, band and orchestra worked with one another constantly, ensuring that every last moment of the music was fully in place. "The whole thing had such a feel of being fun," Lord concluded. "[But] I'm most proud that, in the end, those shows proved that good music is universal."

Deep Purple were originally intended to perform only the two nights at the Royal Albert Hall. So vast was the interest elsewhere around the world, however, that the project was reconvened in March 2000, as the band linked with the Transylvanian Symphony Orchestra for a three-month world tour, for shows in Japan, South America, and all across Europe. Every night was next to flawless.

Evaluating Deep Purple's commercial prospects as the band moved toward the release of *Abandon*, Roger Glover joked, "I had a DJ the other day saying to me, 'I don't see any reason why you classic-rock guys can't go out and have a hit record again.' So I thanked him for that . . . after I'd pulled him up off the floor."

The bassist's aversion to the moniker was readily understandable. Over the years, the term "classic rock" has become increasingly devalued, not only by the traditional marketing machines that manage to degrade everything if they're left alone with it long enough, but also by many of the very musicians who should, in artistic terms at least, have most valued its connotations. Deep Purple were not the only band laboring beneath the classic-rock banner who refused steadfastly to adhere to the lowest common denominator, simply dawdling onto club and casino stages every night to ghost-dance their way through a rabble-rousing routine of nothing-but-the-hits. They weren't the only band who still wrote and recorded new material they believed was as strong as that which came before.

They were, however, in an increasingly endangered minority, their share of the market forever being devoured not only by the myriad cabaret routines that had replaced some of the genre's other great names, but also by a new wave of made-to-order "supergroups."

Inspired by the success, earlier in the decade, of such multifaceted conglomerates as the '60s-flavored British Invasion All-Stars and the revolving roster of former Beatle Ringo's All-Star Band, the Voices of Classic Rock was a sprawling aggregation of, indeed, some of the most distinctive voices in the history of '70s and '80s rock — at least, from an American point of view.

Formed in 1998, the Voices originally intended performing just one show, at an event staged to celebrate the twenty-fifth anniversary of the PGA Masters Tour that March — Starship, Toto, Loverboy, and Survivor were represented on the stage that day, the latter in the form of Jimi Jamison, the vocalist who came so close to joining Deep Purple in 1989. However, the success of the venture was such that, within just three years, the gaggle had swollen beyond its founders' wildest dreams, as such class acts as Gary U.S. Bonds, Leslie West, Pat Travers, John Cafferty, and Spencer Davis threw their lot in with the ever-changing cast that worked beneath the Voices' banner.

It was an occasionally contentious attraction. More than once, presumably well-meaning promoters eschewed the Voices of Classic Rock's own identity in favor of the bands that the featured stars had once represented. So, when Brazilian concertgoers discovered themselves suddenly facing an unannounced and utterly unexpected double bill that apparently comprised Deep Purple and Black Sabbath, many, no doubt, were deeply disappointed when they were instead confronted with a couple of guys who had simply once sung for those two bands — Joe Lynn Turner and Glenn Hughes.

Neither musician, of course, was party to the deception — if deception it was. Certainly, any bitter memories of past not-really-Deep-Purple shows that might have been stirred could immediately be locked back in the trunk. Rather, the pair had ignited a partnership which, shared musical heritage notwithstanding, presented a unified front that could not have been bettered had they actually performed in Deep Purple at the same time.

Both musicians had endured checkered careers in recent years. Alongside Cozy Powell, Hughes enjoyed considerable mainstream success with the semi-supergroup Phenomena, alternating that band's popularity with contributions to sundry Hollywood blockbusters: *Dragnet* and *Highlander II* both featured music by Hughes. He performed alongside the British techno-house band KLF on their "America: What Time Is Love" hit in 1992; released his so-long-awaited third solo album, *From Now on,* in 1994; reformed Trapeze for a short but jubilant tour; and became a regular presence on the American session circuit, both with individual artists and, as the decade progressed, on those classic-rock tribute albums where loose aggregations of name musicians divide into smaller units in honor of a host of supergroups.

Few of these releases offered the listener (let alone the loyal acolyte) much to write home about, although Hughes' performance on the 1994 *Smoke on the Water* Deep Purple tribute album, leading through a credible "Stormbringer," at least brought a touch of authenticity to the proceedings. The project was also the first to unite him with Joe Lynn Turner, as he, too, reveled within much the same circuit.

Only just making his way back into the world following the Deep Purple experience, Turner was now helming the uncompromisingly named JLT & His All Star Band, an act dedicated, it seemed, to reminding him of all that he had lost. The band's repertoire comprised in a large part of old Deep Purple and Rainbow covers. But the version of "Lazy" that Turner gifted to *Smoke on the Water,* like Hughes' contribution, was competent enough, and the pair swiftly became familiar faces at further such sessions. Cream, Queen, Jethro Tull, and Pink Floyd fans have all been tempted by similar excursions, while Turner's own treatments of further Purple classics "Black Night," "Speed King," and (again) "Stormbringer" would emerge on a second tribute to his old band, 1996's *Black Night, Deep Purple Tribute According to New York.*

Turner's own career was not in abeyance throughout such activities. Like Hughes, he continued recording, both solo and as a member of another supergroup, Mother's Army — Carmine Appice, Aynsley Dunbar, and Bob Daisley, all fellow twigs on the Purple family tree, passed through that band's ranks as the 1990s progressed — before 2000 brought not only Turner's induction into the Voices of Classic Rock, but also a full-time pairing with Hughes as Turner prepared to tour Japan in support of his newly released album *The Holy Man.*

That tour, in October, was swiftly followed by the decision to try writing together. The result, *The Hughes-Turner Project*, was finally released in early 2002, a collaborative effort Hughes accurately summed up as a genuinely melodic rock album: "I wouldn't call it metal. I wouldn't call it funky rock. It actually will be a bit commercial, and I do not mean that in a bad way. It will feature more vocals than anything else." In fact, the pair made a point of sharing virtually every song equally. Hughes continued, "[Joe] is really supportive of me and I am supportive of him. It's not at all an ego thing. He's trusted me with [writing] most of the music and he's come in with a lot of the lyrics. I think with the music I have written I have captured what is good for Joe [to sing] as well."

Neither player might today rank as much more than a footnote in the annals of the modern Deep Purple. But, like other former members whose careers have continued unabashed around the parent group's activities — the continued adventures of Blackmore's Night; the reemergence of David Coverdale as the voice of Whitesnake and in partnership with Jimmy Page; the return, even, of Nick Simper in Mick Underwood's brilliantly restyled Quatermass II — their activities highlight the sheer vitality that has linked every member of Deep Purple, past and present. Not every recruit has been ideally well-chosen; not every branch off the main highway leads anywhere interesting. But is there any other band on earth whose family home has so few ghastly skeletons locked away in its closet?

For Deep Purple, the swirling activity of sundry former bandmates was best represented by the activities of the reborn Purple Records, and its gallant scouring of the old imprint's archives. This scouring not only unearthed a clutch of forgotten gems for a reissue of the original label's own *Purple People* various artists sampler, but dug deeper for a companion volume, sensibly titled *Pre-Purple People*.

Other lost jewels were unearthed on Deep Purple's own *Listen, Learn, Read on*, a positively leviathan six-CD box set that traced the first eight years of the band's career through the rarities and outtakes that time itself had forgotten; more still would surface on the millennial remasters of the group's first three albums. As before, however, the current quintet were content to leave their past to look after itself, as a four-month break in the wake of the concert tour was followed by the launch of another world tour, in September 2000.

As always, highlights were manifold. Three jam-packed nights in São Paulo, Brazil. An appearance alongside Luciano Pavarotti at his annual festival in 2001 saw the band performing "Smoke on the Water" before Gillan and Pavarotti dueted on "Nessun Dorma" (the same performance was reprised at Purple's next appearance at the Modena event, in May 2003).

They returned to the United States for an extravagant two-month summertime tour, sharing the top of the bill with southern rockers Lynyrd Skynyrd, while Ted Nugent opened the evening's fare with a carnivorous roar that ensured nobody's ears got out alive. And no sooner had the outing wrapped up, in Athens in September 2001, than the band members were hard at work, expanding their personal resumés.

Steve Morse had already confirmed his independence, first when he took advantage of a short break in Deep Purple's 1999 schedule to reconvene the Dixie Dregs for three nights at the Los Angeles Roxy, celebrated with the *California Screaming* live album; then with *Major Impacts*, a solo album that found him stepping as far away from his own style as one could conceive, by recording eleven instrumentals in the professed manner of eleven *different* guitarists, names whose influence had impacted upon his own playing, even if it rarely showed. John McLaughlin, Eric Clapton, Jeff Beck, Jimi Hendrix, Jimmy Page, Leslie West — track by track, Morse pulled tricks from thin air that, even in the guise of celebrity impersonations, were frequently the equal of the masters themselves.

Now he was at work on a more conventional offering, *Split Decision*, even as Roger Glover set his own mind toward what would emerge as his first solo album since *The Mask*, eighteen years earlier. A gripping excursion into blues-drenched pop, *Snapshot* was recorded with Randall Bramblett, a former member of the Dixie Dregs' old allies, Sea Level and, more recently, the reformed Traffic. With his pedigree to the fore, *The Mask* represented a sizeable break from the Deep Purple sound — what would have been the point otherwise?

Glover explained in an interview with the *Classic Rock Revisited* Web site, "I've always been a fan of JJ Cale, another guy who doesn't have a great voice, but what a great writer. Songwriting is really the core of everything — most of my favorite songs are by songwriters who actually don't have great voices: Bob Dylan, John Hiatt, Ry Cooder . . . Randy Newman.

"They're characters, not singers, [and] I started thinking about character, do I have a character? [But] the character that I hear in my head when I sing isn't the character that comes out when I open my mouth. [So] I had loads of songs, [but] I didn't know what to do with them. They were just sitting there until I heard Randall's voice." Collecting together songs "that I wouldn't even play to my bandmates," Glover was thrilled to discover a spark. "Immediately he got off on the songs" — and, "Boom! Before we knew it . . . I [had] to do an album."

Ian Gillan maintained his longstanding love affair with his earliest musical outlets, as he reconvened the Javelins for what, incredibly, marked their fortieth anniversary, but only their first album, the all-covers *Sole Agency and Representations*. And Jon Lord and Ian Paice regrouped to organize their contributions to a memorial concert for their old PAL-and-more partner, Tony Ashton. After a post-PAL career that saw Ashton establishing himself among the country's most respected session men, he was diagnosed with cancer in the late 1990s. In June 2000, a star-studded array of friends and workmates turned out to perform a benefit concert for Ashton; sadly, though he rallied somewhat over the next year, he finally succumbed to the illness on May 28, 2001.

Staged at the Buxton Opera House, the benefit evening opened with a collection of videos of Ashton, before performances by the Norman Beaker Band, Dave Berry, Neil Murray, Miller Anderson, Colin Hodgkinson, Zoot Money, and more. A short set of Beatles covers featuring Zak Starkey, Bernie Marsden, Mickey Moody, and Phil Spalding recalled Ashton's contributions to sundry ex-Beatles' solo careers, before Lord and Paice emerged, alongside Geraint Watkins and Marsden, for a spirited set of PAL oldies. The evening ended with a monstrous jam through "Smoke on the Water" and Ashton's own "Resurrection Shuffle."

Deep Purple's seemingly never-ending tour continued, kicking off in August 2001 with a clutch of European festivals. On the eve of the opening, however, Lord knew he would be unable to make the first shows. He had recently undergone medical treatment for his knee, and Roger Glover recalled, "We were doing a month out in Europe and the first four dates were in Scandinavia, summer festival type things, with lots of bands on the bill, and he said, 'I can't do the first four dates, but

I'll be able to join you for the fifth.' So we thought, 'Shall we not do the first four dates?' And we were, 'No, they're festivals, get in a temporary replacement, it's fine.' And it worked fine."

Their first — and only — choice for a replacement was Don Airey. Best known to Deep Purple fans for his tenure with Rainbow, Airey was born in Sunderland, England, on June 21, 1948. Early stints with Cozy Powell and Colosseum II (where he struck up his partnership with guitarist Gary Moore) had already established Airey among the classiest players of the late 1970s, a reputation he maintained over the next two decades as he served with Whitesnake (the monster-selling 87 album) and Ozzy Osbourne, regrouped with both Gary Moore and Cozy Powell, and undertook stints with Jethro Tull, Colin Blunstone, and ELO II — the Jeff Lynne-less reincarnation of the 1970s superstars.

Airey was on board Joe Satriani's hyperambitious G3 project, a late-1990s touring retinue of guitar gods (Uli Jon Roth and Michael Schenker completed the triptych), and linked with Bernie Marsden and Mick Moody in a lighthearted tribute to Whitesnake called the Snakes. Most recently, Airey was playing alongside Nick Simper and Mick Underwood in Quatermass II.

Airey had not, however, devoted his entire career to weaving in and out of the Deep Purple family tree. He also made regular session appearances for Katrina and the Waves, the Anglo-American pop band that, having first emerged in the early 1980s, was reborn in 1997 as Britain's representatives in the annual Eurovision Song Contest. Airey both arranged and conducted their contribution to the event, "Love Shine a Light" — and gained, perhaps, the ultimate accolade when the song became the country's first winning entry since 1981. Furthermore, the 227 votes that "Love Shine a Light" accrued remain a Eurovision record, as does the winning margin — second-placed Ireland fell a full 70 votes behind.

Airey's recruitment did more, however, than permit Deep Purple to ally themselves with the likes of Cliff Richard, Céline Dion, Abba, and Bucks Fizz, fellow past winners of the Eurovision event. Glover recalled, "We called Don up because Don was known to us, and he's also got a very good reputation as a handyman, one that can turn his hand to anything when it comes to keyboards. He's supremely talented. So I sent him a tape, he had two days to learn it, and we had one rehearsal at a small club in

Skandeborg — and he'd learned the stuff. We got through it fine; the first gig came, he was very nervous, but it was great. He didn't realize what Deep Purple was like; didn't realize that, though we might appear that way, Deep Purple is not a well-oiled machine. Deep Purple is actually five musicians having fun, and so mistakes are often, but they're not mistakes, they're just interpretations. So, apart from a few panicky looks across the stage and mouthed count-ins — '*Now!* Your solo' — he did it."

Coming offstage, Glover made his way straight over to Airey to congratulate him on his performance: "I was . . . 'Don, I'm so proud of you, that was great,' and he was, 'Well, thanks . . . Actually I tried to play the part of Jon Lord for about twenty seconds and I realized I couldn't do it, so I had to be Don Airey.' And that's the best thing he could have said."

Lord returned to the live show on schedule, but inwardly did not necessarily share his enthusiasm for all that was going on around him. Away from their solo activities, Deep Purple's intentions were turning once again toward a new album. But the keyboard player would not be a part of it. In March 2002, on the eve of the group's next British tour, Lord announced his decision to retire from the band.

"It was one of the hardest decisions I've ever had to make," he confessed. "And it only took about twelve years! I wanted to write more and record more and do other things. And [I just] didn't have the space. And touring . . . eats up a lot of time, and it eats a lot of energy. And it eats up a lot of willpower. So you know, it was very, very hard to make . . . . but I feel good about it. And the rest of the guys said, 'Do you want us to carry on?' [And I said,] 'Well, that's fine,' . . . That's [Deep Purple] . . . an atomic toy — it never stops."

It was Roger Glover who broke the news — his official statement that same month simply noted: "I should inform you that Jon has told us he plans to retire from active participation in Deep Purple. We wish him the best. The moment cannot pass without a personal comment. It is sad that Jon has come to this difficult decision, but every one of us respects his right to determine his own life. I have learned so much from him that I could not possibly do him justice by attempting to quantify it."

For his bandmates, Lord's announcement was a blow, although not exactly a shock. "It's very difficult to pinpoint a time when we knew Jon would be leaving," Glover said. "We kinda knew, even during *Abandon*, that Jon's heart was in his orchestral music and his own music. He loved playing with the band, don't get me wrong, but his heart was somewhere else." The concerto tour, viewed by everybody concerned as "Jon's baby," allowed the band some room in which to relax their worries. Indeed, as Glover put it, "The concerto concerts led to the concerto tour, and all of a sudden, two years had gone by. There was definitely a feeling in the band on the concerto tour that this might be Jon's last tour, but again, I don't know how you can pinpoint that. It's just a feeling, gauging someone's mood, and at the end of the tour, we had a talk — 'Jon, we get the feeling you want to leave.' And he said, 'Absolutely not.'

"Okay, fair enough, we have to take his word for it," continued Glover. "So we kept on keeping on, and then came another tour, and a year later he was ill and Don Airey came in for those four shows. But it got to the point where, really, because we're a working band and we have to play live, we basically had to say to Jon, 'This is what we need to be doing. Does it fit into your sort of time scale?' And finally he said, 'Well, I love Deep Purple, I love playing with Deep Purple, I love you guys. But I can't be away this much.' And that was the point where we knew what was happening."

They also knew what needed to happen next. In the same breath as Glover made Lord's departure public, he also announced his replacement — almost inevitably, Don Airey.

As Deep Purple set out on what was Lord's last, and Airey's first, tour, however, such calculations were the farthest thing from any onlooker's mind. The U.K. and Irish dates, the only ones Lord would be appearing at, kicked off in Dublin, Ireland, in February 2002, yet the solemn significance of the occasion was not about to pass unhindered. Raising specters from another age entirely, the British dates ground to a halt midway through, when Gillan finally succumbed to a cold that had been bothering him for several days. The remainder of the tour was canceled — a total of nine shows, including the second of two nights at the Hammersmith Apollo.

It was an abrupt, heartbreakingly anticlimactic conclusion to the keyboard player's thirty-four years with Deep Purple, but it was surely preferable to the pitiful spectacle Gillan had otherwise presented, coughing and spluttering his way through a two-hour set, clearly feeling as miserable as he sounded. Great swaths of the set were rearranged — "Child in Time," restored to the live show after a seven-year absence, was only the most predictable of the casualties. But harsher still was the belief that Jon Lord had bowed out of Deep Purple not with a bang but a wheeze.

Amid promises that the missing shows would be rescheduled for the fall, Deep Purple were back on the road in March, with a swing through Russia and Eastern Europe. It was a suitably distant spot in which to introduce Don Airey to the setup, far from the prying eyes of the fan clubs and appreciation society — but, of course, there was no need to fear on his behalf.

Playing his first show with the band at the New Ice Arena in St. Petersburg on March 17, 2002, Airey not only blended perfectly in, he stamped his own persona over keyboard lines that *no one* in the entire history of Deep Purple had hitherto had the opportunity to play, including a new solo introduction to "Highway Star" that delighted the local audience with the inclusion of Bach and Mozart, a snatch of the Russian folk song "Kalinka," and even the anthem of St. Petersburg itself.

Asian dates followed before the tour reached the United States in May 2002 for another extravagant triple-header bill, as the band lined up alongside the Scorpions and Ronnie James Dio for a summerlong outing. And finally, it was back to the U.K. to pick up where the band left off in February — and surprise a lot of people by restoring Jon Lord to the lineup alongside Airey.

The retiring veteran did not perform the entire show; indeed, he did not even make his entrance until "Perfect Strangers," as the set went into its final straight. But he was back for the encores and, as the eleven-show tour wound on, it was apparent that the band's British following was pouring out to pay tribute to the passing hero.

Lord played his final Deep Purple concert on September 19 at the Regent in Ipswich. Tonight belonged to him — though Airey took the stage, he happily deferred to Lord, who played almost half the set and was the last to leave the stage at the end of a set that bubbled with emotion. It was the first time, Gillan half-joked, that a member of Deep Purple departed the band still on good terms with his former bandmates.

Liberated at last, Lord swiftly set to work on a new project, touring the concerto around Australia with the local band George in January 2003, then preparing his piano concerto *Boom of the Tingling Strings* for its European premiere on May 31, 2003. Performed by the Luxembourg Philharmonic Orchestra with pianist Michael Kieran Harvey, and conducted by Paul Mann, the concert took place at the Conservatoire de la Ville de Luxembourg.

Lord's erstwhile bandmates, meanwhile, completed their own tour with a handful of shows as far apart as Basel, Dubai, and Athens, before regrouping in November 2002 to plan their seventeenth studio album.

Having already set aside Lord's offer to at least help out on the album, the group also made the decision to work, for the first time since *The Battle Rages on*, with an outside producer. Michael Bradford was better known for unraveling the complexities of '90s rock-rappers Kid Rock than for perpetuating anything so dull as classic rock, but such an unusual move was just one of several that were in the pipeline as 2003's oddly titled *Bananas* took shape.

Bradford was a long-standing Deep Purple fan, despite his renown in those other musical arenas. His involvement with the group, however, was little more than a pipe dream until, as he recalled, his European music publisher set the wheels in motion. "We had the same music publisher in Europe," he recalled. "I had written a song that was a big hit in Europe at the time, and the publisher thought that perhaps a producer who was also a songwriter could help DP with getting their ideas organized. That person sort of acted as a matchmaker between the band and me. Then I called Bruce Payne, Deep Purple's manager, on the phone, and we set up a meeting in England. So calls were going between Germany, London, California, and elsewhere."

"He was a fan, he really wanted to do it," Roger Glover confirmed. "We met him after a show in Brighton on February 19, 2002. He flew over to Brighton to see us, and at first sight, my first thought was, 'My God, he's this huge black guy, what's going to happen here? Are we going to turn into Run-DMC-meets-Aerosmith kind of deal or what?' But that's preconceptions, and very quickly you realize the guy is very intelligent, very erudite, and he's got his directions mapped out. We had a meeting after the show; we pumped him with questions and he said all the right things, he said some great stuff, so we realized this was a serious guy, he wasn't out to change us. He wanted to bring us out, and I think he succeeded admirably."

It was Bradford's enthusiasm for all that the band represented in his own mind that encouraged the musicians to take stock of what Deep Purple meant to others and address themselves to capturing an essence that they had, perhaps, been avoiding for too long.

In the recent past, as Glover explained, the band had always made an effort to avoid what they knew would be described as the "classic" Deep Purple sound, for fear of lapsing into cliché, parody, or worse. Now here was Bradford demanding that they embrace those things. Said Glover, "He came into the project telling us, 'I grew up with Deep Purple, I loved Deep Purple, and that's the sound I love — it's a trademark sound. You should not be scared of it, you should not be worried about being a parody of yourselves, because that's who you are.' And he was right."

Two of the songs the band took into the studio dated back to before Lord's departure. As Glover explained, "We had a couple of writing sessions while Jon was still in the band, and they produced a couple of songs. . . . One was 'Picture of Innocence,' which was actually a jam between Paicey and Steve in the studio from several years ago that I'd recorded on a DAT. I was listening to all the old stuff one day, all the old jam sessions, and I came across this piece. I put it in my computer and chopped it up — I loved the rhythm of it, and Steve plays some great riffs, but he can never remember them. He's got a million of them.

"So I managed to crystalize that in my computer, a rough arrangement for the song, then played it to the rest of the band, and we wrote a song out of it. And the other one, it used to be called 'Up the Wall,' and we actually tried it live a couple of times but it didn't seem finished. It was a complicated little riff, so we dropped it, but we returned to it during these writing sessions, and Michael was great. He said, 'I like the idea, but you're missing the punchline.' And the first thing we played — bang — it fell out. And that's 'I Got Your Number.'"

Don Airey, for his part, contributed as much to the sessions as any player in his position could be expected to. Recalled Glover, "Don was a little shy at first, a little tentative, and he didn't really come up with any original starts, if you know what I mean. When we're writing, we rely on a start, a riff or a chord sequence, or in Paicey's case a rhythm, or in Gillan's case, a title or a couple of words or whatever, a *feel*. But Don was very important as a modifying voice. If it was a choice between one thing or another thing, he'd be, 'I really think you should rock out, forget trying to be clever, just rock out.' Or whatever.

"Stuff like that was very important, because writing in a rock band is not just a matter of writing down notes and words and tunes, it really is a feel. You're trying to create a feel, and it's very difficult to confine that to a series of dots on a piece of paper."

Airey was more at ease when it came to actually recording, said Glover. "The sound that Jon used to have, and somehow didn't have anymore, Don just managed to hit it. He's not playing Jon's role, but he is playing the organ.

"He's got such brilliant technique, and I think that's another thing that's very important to this band," continued Glover. "The action between guitar and keys has to be based on virtuosity, but it is balanced by the simplicity of Paicey, Ian Gillan, and myself — *particularly* Gillan and myself. We're just a couple of naïve, simple writers by comparison, and that's one of the keys to the group, that we have a simplicity and at the same time a complexity."

Even so early in the process, *Bananas* seemed certain to maintain that balance, a discovery that allowed Glover to swiftly inform Purple's own DPAS fan club, "Rest assured that whatever may be going through your imaginations as to what will come out of it is also going through ours, and more. . . . The anticipation level is high."

The first three weeks together, in typical Deep Purple fashion, were spent jamming through ideas and the raw material that the band members brought into the studio. "These guys play like monsters," Bradford told visitors to his Web site. "They've been on tour for two years, so they're tight, but having a break before recording meant they were well-rested and ready to play."

Ideas flew. "We cut about fourteen songs," Bradford continued, "some of which were developed on the road and some of which were written during the month." (Twelve of the fourteen would make it onto the finished record.) The very nature of the ideas that ricocheted around the studio prompted some major departures, including an appearance for the band's first-ever female backing vocalist, Beth Hart.

There was also room for some positively overwhelming orchestrations, undertaken, at Bradford's suggestion, by ace string arranger Paul

Buckmaster, a man whose musical credits date back to the likes of David Bowie and Elton John's earliest hits — and who spent his studio down-time reminiscing with Ian Paice about their childhoods shared in Nottingham. "Small world, indeed," marveled Bradford.

Glover, reveling in the freedom afforded by not even having to copro-duce, was effusive in his praise of Bradford: "It was a pure joy to work with a classy producer. I watched him deal with the pressure, the stress, the heartache, the loneliness of the long-distance runner, and he did it with such style and aplomb."

Gillan continued, "You can't compare it with anything we've done in the past — which is the whole point of doing it as we have done." That much, everyone could agree with. According to a report on the Associated Press, however, no sooner was the album's title revealed than hardcore fans — as the report could not resist putting it — went bananas.

According to Steve Morse, the title was Gillan's idea, inspired by his observation that Morse had "gone bananas" during an instrumental duel with Don Airey — and anything that made the band laugh was usually guaranteed to stick around, particularly when it was compounded by a photograph that Roger Glover uncovered, of a skinny bicyclist loaded down by hundreds of bananas (the album's eventual back cover). Even with the yowling of the outraged multitudes resounding in their ears, Deep Purple remained unrepentant, instead amplifying the title's mani-fold possibilities. When asked when the record would be out, Gillan simply smiled, "It's called *Bananas* and it'll be released when it's ripe."

In fact, the album was finished remarkably quickly, as Deep Purple assimilated newcomer Airey with such alacrity that more than once as the finished album spun past, it was easy to forget Jon Lord had ever gone away. The opening "House of Pain" was a classic workout by any criteria, with Morse and Airey dueling in spellbinding style in the midsection. The blistering rattle of the title track had at least a taste of the old *Fireball* feel playing around its edges (complete with another ster-ling Airey contribution), while the delicate "Haunted" melded a beautiful melody to one of the greatest love songs Deep Purple had ever cut. Lovely, too, were "Never a Word," with its adherence to some distinctly classical guitar themes, and "Walk On," a slow-burning blues-rocker that could have escaped from an early Bad Company album — and which was brought to the sessions by Michael Bradford.

"I had actually written 'Walk On' some time ago, but I never had a use for it," Bradford recalled. "I played it on guitar for Ian and Roger, and they really liked it. Ian rewrote the lyrics in a way that made the song flow better, and had removed some of the bitterness of my original lyrics. In rehearsal, I started the song off by playing that little rhythm part that gets the groove going. We did it that way for so long that we cut it that way as well. That left Steve able to do the other stuff while the track was going down."

There were a few weak moments, though. "Razzle Dazzle" somehow combined the lackluster swagger of Gillan's *Naked Thunder* album with the kind of riff the late-1980s Genesis might have come up with. And the almost-funky "Doing It Tonight" simply sounded rushed, lyrically if not musically. Nevertheless, *Bananas* certainly proved the band to be back on track after the disappointments of *Abandon*, with the swiftness of its creation belied only by the emotion that went into its completion. Playing in Houston, Texas, a couple of years before, the band had struck up a friendship with astronaut Kalpana Chawla and her husband JP Harrison — a relationship that led to Chawla taking copies of *Machine Head* (for "Space Truckin'") and *Purpendicular* (for "The Aviator") with her when she joined the crew of the space shuttle *Columbia* in January 2003. In fact, "Space Truckin'" became one of the crew's regular wakeup calls during the sixteen-day mission.

On February 1, 2003, the crew awoke for the final time. Returning to earth, the space shuttle broke up over Texas, as superheated gases from the earth's atmosphere broke through wing panels damaged during the craft's liftoff. All seven crew members were killed. *Bananas* closes with Morse's brief but so beautiful instrumental "Contact Lost," written as the guitarist watched the tragedy unfolding on television that morning.

Glover recalled, "When we played Houston they came along to see us, Kalpana and her husband JP Harrison, a whole bunch of them came. Initially they made more of a contact with Ian Gillan than with me, talking to him quite a bit that night. . . . But it's always a thrill to meet an astronaut!"

Regular letters from Harrison, detailing the crew's preparations and training, would appear on Gillan's Web site, and the band members had been invited to the shuttle launch. Unfortunately, recording commitments forced them to turn the invitation down, but they followed the mission from their Los Angeles base. "The Saturday morning they were due to come down, we were all in our separate apartments having breakfast," Glover remembered. "We were going to meet in the studio later that day and we were going to do a track or whatever. And of course this horrendous thing happened, and each of us in our own little cell just watched in total disbelief . . . . I called Ian up: 'Did you see that? Oh my God.' We were really shook up."

Looking to bury himself in work, Glover made his way to the studio to find Steve Morse and Michael Bradford already there: "Steve's got his headphones on, his guitar on, Michael's at the controls. . . . I walked in, 'Oh, what are you doing, I didn't mean to interrupt,' and Steve said, 'Oh, I just wrote this tune this morning, watching what was happening. I just want to get it down.'"

At the time, the band was considering recording a succession of brief instrumental interludes as links between the songs on the album, and Morse had that thought in the back of his mind as he played. But the finished piece, Glover marveled, was "so utterly beautiful . . . we all hovered around the studio listening to it, going, 'Jesus, this is great.' So then Michael said, 'Why don't you add to it?' So I put bass on, Don was there putting keyboards on, we all added to it and it just came. . . . It's only a minute and something seconds, but it says what we wanted to say.

"The touching part was . . . we were in contact with JP after the tragedy, of course, and we sent him this piece of music, and he passed it around all the other families and they loved it. He met us in Mexico City that summer and presented us with framed remnants of those CDs that Kalpana had taken up with her, which they found at the crash site — two Deep Purple ones and one Rainbow one. You can't recognize the Deep Purple ones, but the Rainbow one was *Down to Earth*."

Bananas was finally released in August 2003, to immediate European acclaim. It entered the Greek charts at No. 2, the German at No. 3; was a Top 10-er in the Czech Republic and Finland, Top 20 in Switzerland, Italy, Sweden, and Norway. In Britain, however, it struggled no higher than No. 85, in the same week that summer support act the Darkness's album went straight in at No. 1.

Away from the statistics, of course, everything was firing on all cylinders — by the time *Bananas* hit the stores, the group had already been on the road for two months of summer festivals. They were now looking forward to the next scheduled outing, a European tour with Uriah Heep, the band whose first steps, as Spice, back in 1969, had echoed through the soundproofing of the Hanwell Community Center at the same time as Deep Purple Mark II's maiden steps.

Like Deep Purple, Heep had traveled a long, hard road since those naïvely hopeful days potholed with breakups, reformations, and multiple lineup changes. Like Deep Purple, they boasted just one surviving founding member, guitarist Mick Box. But still it was a class reunion that precious few other bands could ever hope to stage, and a classic encounter for anyone who'd spent so many years listening to them — much as, Roger Glover pointed out, every one of Deep Purple's tours seems to be these days.

Days before Christmas 2003, as he looked forward to Deep Purple's upcoming American tour, Glover explained, "The idea was mooted by a promoter, or an agent or someone, that in order to do a decent American tour, you've got to have three good acts on the bill. But that's unwieldy, and it means a lack of time for each of you — seventy-five minutes of greatest hits — because you're essentially playing to people who . . . that's all they know of you.

"So the idea came up that somehow we would perform *Machine Head* in its entirety as a kind of gimmick, and not use one of the other bands. In other words, one support band [the reformed Thin Lizzy, absent the late Phil Lynott], then *Machine Head* as a set piece, and then the new material for the rest of the set."

It was an audacious arrangement, all the more so since what many fans regard as the two principal instruments on that so-revered album, the guitar and the keyboard, are played today by musicians who were nowhere in sight when the LP was recorded. But, as Glover continued, it is that variance that allowed Deep Purple to even consider the idea in the first place, the knowledge that they would not be re*creating* what so many people regard as Deep Purple's finest hour, but re*designing* it. Much of the album was already in the group's live set, after all, in which form it had long since been twisted and turned to fit the lineup's requirements. In an age when so many veteran bands think nothing of presenting flawless reiterations of their classic albums, Deep Purple make the same gesture with almost polar intentions. This is *not* your father's *Machine Head*!

It is, however, the Deep Purple that enters its thirty-sixth year of life — and which, in rock'n'roll terms, has already survived several more lifetimes than most bands dream of. No matter that Don Airey's arrival has reduced the group's membership, for the first time in its history, to just one founding member — Ian Paice; that even Gillan and Glover, for all their historical resonance and subsequent longevity, were members of the original band for no more than four of its eight-year existence, while Morse had recorded fewer "new" Deep Purple albums in six years than either Nick Simper and Rod Evans or David Coverdale and Glenn Hughes cut in one-third as long. In that span, and across so many incarnations, Deep Purple have touched more lives than anybody could possibly count — from the multitude of other groups that lay among the roots and branches of the group's family tree, to the millions of fans who have joined their audience after hearing "Hush," "Black Night," "Smoke on the Water," "Burn," "Knocking on Your Back Door," "King of Dreams," "Fingers to the Bone," "Contact Lost."

It is a legacy that, in terms of sheer longevity, has very few peers. The Rolling Stones, The Who, and Golden Earring can point to even longer careers, but in all honesty, when did any of them last release an album that offered much more than another tired meander through the motions? Chuck Berry, Bo Diddley, and Jerry Lee Lewis can argue that they've had a greater influence, but they'd been firing blanks for close to a decade before Deep Purple even formed. And, of the bands that did rise up alongside Deep Purple — Vanilla Fudge and Led Zeppelin, Barclay James Harvest and, sadly, yes, even Uriah Heep — time and tragedy (and, occasionally, timidity) have taken an all but fatal toll on them.

Deep Purple is an institution. But more than that, it is a way of life, and one that Roger Glover never tires of being reminded he's an integral part of. "The thing I hear more than anything else," he laughed, "is fans saying, 'I grew up to your music.' To which I always reply, 'How interesting, so did I.'"

Discographies

PART ONE: DEEP PURPLE

This discography is designed to document the Deep Purple story in chrono-logical fashion, allowing the collector at-a-glance access to releases as they fall within the band's history. For this reason, compilations and re-issues are noted only when they include unreleased and/or rare material.

MARK I
JON LORD (keyboards); IAN PAICE (drums); RITCHIE BLACK-MORE (guitar); NICK SIMPER (bass); ROD EVANS (vocals)

UK SINGLES
June 1968 Hush; One More Rainy Day (Parlophone R5708)
November 1968 Kentucky Woman; Wring That Neck (Parlophone R5745)
February 1969 Emmaretta; Wring That Neck (Parlophone R5763)

US SINGLES
June 1968 Hush; One More Rainy Day (Tetragrammaton 1503)
November 1968 Kentucky Woman; Hard Road (Tetragrammaton 1508)
June 1969 River Deep Mountain High; Listen, Learn, Read On (Tetgrammaton 1514)
April 1969 Emmaretta; The Bird Has Flown (Tetragrammaton 1519)

UK/US LPS

September 1968 *Shades Of Deep Purple*
And the Address; Hush; One More Rainy Day; Prelude: Happiness; I'm So Glad;
Mandrake Root; Help; Love Help Me; Hey Joe (Parlophone PCS 7055) /
(Tetragrammaton 102)
CD bonus tracks: Shadows (outtake); Love Help Me (instrumental);
Help (alternate); Hey Joe (BBC); Hush (US TV) (Spitfire 6-70211-5062-2)

June 1969 *The Book Of Taliesyn*
Listen, Learn, Read On; Wring That Neck; Kentucky Woman; Shield; Exposition;
We Can Work It Out; The Shield; Anthem; River Deep, Mountain High (Harvest
SHVL 751); (Tetragrammaton 107)
CD bonus tracks: Oh No No No (outtake); It's All Over (BBC); Hey Bop A Re Bop
(BBC); Wring That Neck (BBC); Playground (outtake) (Spitfire 6-70211-5063-2)

November 1969 *Deep Purple*
Chasing Shadows; Blind; Lalena; Faultline; The Painter; Why Didn't Rosemary;
The Bird Has Flown; April (Harvest SHVL 759) / (Tetragrammaton 119)
CD bonus tracks: The Bird Has Flown (single); Emmaretta (single); Emmaretta
(BBC); Lalena (BBC); The Painter (BBC) (Spitfire 6-70211-5064-2)

UK/US LIVE LPS

2002 *Live At The Forum* (Inglewood Forum, Los Angeles, 18 October 1968)
Hush; Kentucky Woman; Mandrake Root; Help; Wring That Neck; River Deep,
Mountain High; Hey Joe (Purple PUR 205)

COMPILATIONS INC UNRELEASED/RARE MATERIAL

1999 *Shades 1968–1998*
Shadows (demo); Love Help Me (instrumental); Kentucky Woman (single version);
River Deep, Mountain High (single version); The Bird Has Flown (single version) +
rare and previously released material Mark II-VII (Warner Archives R2 75556)

2002 *Listen, Learn, Read On*
Playground (outtake); The Bird Has Flown (single version) + rare and previously
released material Mark II–IV (EMI 24354 09732)

MARK II
JON LORD (keyboards); IAN PAICE (drums); RITCHIE BLACKMORE (guitar); ROGER GLOVER (bass); IAN GILLAN (vocals)

UK SINGLES
July 1969 Hallelujah (I Am the Preacher); April (Harvest HAR 5006)

June 1970 Black Night; Speed King (Harvest HAR 5020)

February 1971 Strange Kind of Woman; I'm Alone (Harvest HAR 5033)

October 1971 Fireball; Demon's Eye (Harvest HAR 5045)

March 1972 Never Before; When a Blind Man Cries (Purple 102)

February 1973 Woman from Tokyo; Black Night (live) (Purple 112 – unissued)

September 1977 *New Live & Rare*: Black Night (live); Painted Horse; When a Blind Man Cries (Purple 135)

September 1978 *New Live & Rare Vol. 2*: Burn (edit); Coronarias Redig; Mistreated (live) (Purple 137)

July 1980 *New Live & Rare Vol. 3*: Smoke on the Water (live); The Bird Has Flown; Grabsplatter (Harvest SHEP 101)

US SINGLES
July 1969 Hallelujah (I Am the Preacher); April (Tetragrammaton 1537)

July 1970 Black Night; Into the Fire (Warner 7405)

February 1971 Strange Kind of Woman; I'm Alone (Warner 7493))

October 1971 Fireball; I'm Alone (Warner 7528)

June 1972 Lazy; When a Blind Man Cries (Warner 7595)

October 1972 Highway Star (part one); (part two) (Warner 7643)

April 1973 Woman from Tokyo; Super Trouper (Warner 7672)

May 1973 Smoke on the Water (studio) (live) (Warner 7710)

September 1973 Woman from Tokyo; Super Trouper (Warner 7737)

UK/US LPS
June 1970 *Deep Purple In Rock*

Speed King; Blood Sucker; Child in Time; Flight of the Rat; Into the Fire; Living Wreck; Hard Lovin' Man (Harvest SHVL 777) / (Warner 1877)

CD bonus tracks: Black Night; Speed King (piano version); Cry Free (remix); Jam Stew (outtake); Flight of the Rat (remix); Speed King (remix); Black Night (unedited remix); studio chat (EMI 7243 8 34019 2 5)

September 1971 *Fireball*
Fireball; No No No; Demon's Eye; Anyone's Daughter; The Mule; Fools; No One Came (Harvest SHVL 793) / (Warner 2564)
CD bonus tracks: Strange Kind of Woman (remix); I'm Alone (B-side); Freedom (outtake); Slow Train (outtake); Demon's Eye (remix); The Noise Abatement Society Tapes; Fireball (take one); Backwards Piano; No One Came (remix) (EMI 7243 8 53711 2 7)

April 1972 *Machine Head*
Highway Star; Maybe I'm a Leo; Pictures of Home; Never Before; Smoke on the Water; Lazy; Space Truckin' (Purple TPSA 7504); (Warners 2607)
CD bonus tracks: When a Blind Man Cries (B-side); Maybe I'm a Leo (quad); Lazy (quad); Highway Star; Maybe I'm a Leo; Pictures of Home; Never Before; Smoke on the Water; Lazy; Space Truckin'; When a Blind Man Cries (all remix)

February 1973 *Who Do We Think We Are*
Woman from Tokyo; Mary Long; Super Trouper; Smooth Dancer; Rat Bat Blue; Place in Line; Our Lady (Purple TPSA 7508); (Warners 2678)
CD bonus tracks: Woman from Tokyo (remix); Woman from Tokyo (alt bridge); Painted Horse (outtake); Our Lady (remix); Rat Bat Blue (writing session); Rat Bat Blue (remix); First Day Jam (EMI 5216072)

UK/US LIVE LPS
January 1970 *Concerto for Group and Orchestra with the Royal Philharmonic Orchestra*
First Movement; Second Movement; Third Movement (Harvest SHVL 767) / (Warners 1860)
CD bonus tracks: Hush; Wring That Neck; Child in Time; Encore (Third Movement) (EMI 07243 541006 2 8)
dvd Audio bonus tracks: Arnold's Sixth Symphony First Movement; Second Movement; Third Movement (EV 30030-9)

December 1972 *Made In Japan*
Highway Star; Child in Time; Smoke on the Water; The Mule; Strange Kind of Woman; Lazy; Space Truckin' (Purple TPSA 7351) / (Warner 2701)
CD bonus tracks: Black Night; Speed King; Lucille

326

December 1980 In Concert 1970–72 (BBC concert broadcasts, February 1970 / March 1972)

Speed King; Wring That Neck; Child in Time; Mandrake Root; Highway Star; Strange Kind of Woman; Lazy; Never Before; Space Truckin'; Lucille (Harvest SHDW 412)

CD bonus tracks: Maybe I'm a Leo; Smoke on the Water (EMI CDEM 1434)

October 1988 Scandinavian Nights (Stockholm 1970)

Speed King; Into the Fire; Child in Time; Wring That Neck; Paint It Black; Mandrake Root; Black Night (Connoisseur DPVSOP 125) / (Spitfire SPT 15066)

November 1993 Live in Japan

Highway Star; Child in Time; The Mule; Strange Kind of Woman; Lazy; Space Truckin'; Black Night (Osaka August 15, 1972); Highway Star; Smoke on the Water; Child in Time; The Mule; Strange Kind of Woman; Lazy; Space Truckin' (Osaka August 16, 1972); Highway Star; Smoke on the Water; Child in Time; Strange Kind of Woman; Lazy; Space Truckin'; Speed King (Tokyo August 17, 1972) (EMI CDEM 1510)

1993 *Gemini Suite Live*

First Movement; Second Movement; Third Movement (RPM 114)

2001 Space Vols 1 & 2 (Amsterdam July 1970)

Wring That Neck; Black Night; Paint It Black; Mandrake Root (Purple PUR 202)

COMPILATIONS INC RARE/PREVIOUSLY UNRELEASED MATERIAL

June 1975 *24 Carat Purple*

Black Night (live) + previously released (Purple TPSM 2002)

1977 *Powerhouse*

Painted Horse (outtake); Hush; Wring That Neck; Child in Time (RAH 1969); Black Night (from *24 Carat Purple*); Cry Free (outtake) (Purple TPS 3510)

1985 *Anthology*

Grabsplatter (BBC session); Freedom (outtake); Never Before (quad mix); Smoke on the Water (quad mix) + previously released Mark I–IV (EMI; Harvest PUR-1)

1999 *Shades 1968–1998*
Cry Free (outtake); Jam Stew (outtake); Into the Fire (live); No No No (live); Freedom (outtake); Slow Train (outtake); Painted Horse (outtake) + rare and previously released material Mark II–VII (Warner Archives R2 75556)

2002 *Listen, Learn, Read On*
Ricochet (BBC); The Bird Has Flown (BBC); Hush (RAH); Concerto Third Movement reprise (RAH); Wring That Neck (live); Jam Stew (BBC); Speed King (BBC); Cry Free (outtake); Hard Lovin' Man (BBC); Bloodsucker (BBC); Living Wreck (BBC); studio chat – Jam; Mandrake Root (live); Grabsplatter (BBC); Child in Time (BBC); interview; Black Night (BBC); Into the Fire (BBC); Fools (outtake); No No No (TV); Highway Star (TV); Never Before (quad); When a Blind Man Cries (remix); Strange Kind of Woman (live BBC); Black Night (Tokyo 1972 – last unissued track); Mary Long (remix) + rare and previously released material Mark I; III; IV (EMI 24354 09732)

MARK III
JON LORD (keyboards); IAN PAICE (drums); RITCHIE BLACKMORE (guitar); GLENN HUGHES (bass); DAVID COVERDALE (vocals)

UK SINGLES
March 1974 Might Just Take Your Life; Coronarias Redig (Purple 117)

US SINGLES
March 1974 Might Just Take Your Life; Coronarias Redig (Warner 7784)
May 1974 Burn; Coronarias Redig (Warner 7809)
November 1974 Highball Shooter; You Can't Do It Right (Warner 8049)
January 1975 Stormbringer; Love Don't Mean a Thing (Warner 8069)

UK/US LPS
February 1974 *Burn*
Burn; Might Just Take Your Life; Lay Down Stay Down; Sail Away; You Fool No One; What's Goin' On Here; Mistreated; A 200 (Purple TPS 3505)/(Warner 2766)

November 1974 *Stormbringer*
Stormbringer; Love Don't Mean a Thing; Holy Man; Hold On; Lady Double

Dealer; You Can't Do It Right; High Ball Shooter; The Gypsy; Soldier of Fortune (Purple TPS 3508) / (Warner 2832)

UK/US LIVE LPS

November 1976 *Made In Europe; Deep Purple Live* (Europe 1975)
Burn; Mistreated / Rock Me Baby; Lady Double Dealer; You Fool No One; Stormbringer (Purple 7517) / (Warner 2995)

August 1982 *Deep Purple Live In London* (1974)
Burn; Might Just Take Your Life; Lay Down, Stay Down; Mistreated; Smoke on the Water; You Fool No One (Harvest SHSP 4124)

May 1996 *California Jamming* (California Jam, April 1974)
Burn; Might Just Take Your Life; Mistreated; Smoke on the Water; You Fool No One; The Mule; Space Truckin' (Premier PRMUCD 2)

July 1996 *Mark III: The Final Concerts* (Europe 1975)
Burn; Stormbringer; Gypsy; Lady Double Dealer; Mistreated; Smoke on the Water; You Fool No One; Space Truckin'; Medley: Going Down / Highway Star; Mistreated (alternate version); You Fool No One (alternate version) (Connoisseur DPVSOP 230)

COMPILATIONS INC RARE/PREVIOUSLY UNRELEASED MATERIAL

2002 *Listen, Learn, Read On*
Coronarias Redig; You Fool No One (California Jam); Mistreated (live); Space Truckin' (live); Stormbringer (quad); Soldier Of Fortune (quad); Hold On (quad); Highball Shooter (instrumental); Gypsy (live) + rare and previously released material Mark I/II/IV (EMI 24354 09732)

MARK IV
JON LORD (keyboards); IAN PAICE (drums); TOMMY BOLIN (guitar); GLENN HUGHES (bass); DAVID COVERDALE (vocals)

UK SINGLES

February 1976 scheduled but unissued, unknown tracks (Purple PUR 129)
March 1976 You Keep On Moving; Love Child (Purple PUR 130)

US SINGLE
March 1976 Getting' Tighter; Love Child (Warners 8182)

UK/US LP
October 1975 *Come Taste The Band*
Comin' Home; Lady Luck; Getting Together; Dealer; I Need Love; Drifter; Love Child; This Time Around / Owed To G; You Keep On Moving (Purple TPSA 7515); (Warner 2895)

UK/US LIVE LPS
1977 *Last Concert In Japan* aka *This Time Around* (Budokan, Tokyo, Dec 1975)
Burn; Love Child; You Keep On Moving; Wild Dogs; Lady Luck; Smoke on the Water; Soldier of Fortune; Woman from Tokyo; Highway Star (Warner Bros P-10370-W – Japan)

May 1995 *On The Wings Of A Russian Foxbat / King Biscuit Flour Hour*
(Springfield, January 1976 / Long Beach, February 1976)
Burn; Lady Luck; Getting Tighter; Love Child; Smoke on the Water / Georgia on My Mind; Lazy / The Grind (actually Homeward Strut); This Time Around; Tommy Bolin guitar solo; Stormbringer; Highway Star; Smoke on the Water / Georgia on My Mind (alternate version); Going Down; Highway Star (alternate version) (Connoisseur Collection DPVSOP-CD-217) / (KBFH Records / EMI Canada 70710-88002-2-7)

April 2000 *Days May Come: The 1975 California Rehearsals* (live in studio)
Owed To G; If You Love Me Woman; The Orange Juice Song; I Got Nothing For You; Statesboro Blues; Dance To The Rock & Roll; Drifter (rehearsal sequence); Drifter; The Last Of The Long Jams (Purple PUR 303)

April 2000 1420 Beechwood Drive
Drifter (take 2); Sail Away riff; You Keep On Moving; Pirate Blues; Say You Love Me (Purple PUR 201)

2001 *This Time Around* (Budokan, Tokyo, December 1975)
Burn; Lady Luck; Love Child; Getting' Tighter; Smoke on the Water; Wild Dogs; I Need Love; Soldier Of Fortune; Jon Lord solo; Lazy; This Time Around;

Owed To G; Tommy Bolin guitar solo; Drifter; You Keep On Moving; Stormbringer; Highway Star (Purple PUR 321D)

2002 *Listen, Learn, Read On*
Drifter (rehearsal); Dance To The Rock'n'Roll (rehearsal); Wild Dogs (live); Lady Luck (live); Getting' Tighter (live) + rare and previously released material Mark I–III (EMI 24354 09732)

MARK II (first reunion)
JON LORD (keyboards); IAN PAICE (drums); RITCHIE BLACKMORE (guitar); ROGER GLOVER (bass); IAN GILLAN (vocals)

UK SINGLES
January 1985 Perfect Strangers; Son of Alerik (Polydor POSP 719)
June 1985 Knocking at Your Back Door; Perfect Strangers (Polydor POSP 749)
January 1987 Call of the Wild; Strangeways (Polydor POSP 843)
June 1988 Hush; Dead or Alive; Bad Attitude (all Live) (Polydor POCD 4)

US SINGLES
January 1985 Perfect Strangers; Son of Alerik (Mercury 824003)
June 1985 Knocking at Your Back Door; Perfect Strangers (Mercury 880477)

UK/US LPS
November 1984 *Perfect Strangers*
Knocking at Your Back Door; Under the Gun; Nobody's Home; Mean Streak; Perfect Strangers; A Gypsy's Kiss; Wasted Sunsets; Hungry Daze; Not Responsible (cassette only) (Polydor POLH 16) / (Mercury 824003)

January 1987 *The House Of Blue Light*
Bad Attitude; The Unwritten Law; Call of the Wild; Mad Dog; Black and White; Hard Lovin' Woman; The Spanish Archer; Strangeways; Mitzi Dupree; Dead or Alive (Polydor POLH 32) / (Mercury 831318)

UK/US LIVE LPS
June 1988 *Nobody's Perfect* (Europe/US 1987)
Highway Star; Strange Kind of Woman; Perfect Strangers; Hard Lovin' Woman;

Knocking at Your Back Door; Child in Time; Lazy; Black Night; Woman from Tokyo; Smoke on the Water; Hush; Bad Attitude (LP only); Space Trucking (LP only) (Polydor PODV 10); (Mercury 835897)
CD reissue bonus tracks: Dead Or Alive; Bad Attitude; Space Truckin' (Mercury Records 314546128-2)

August 1991 *In The Absence Of Pink* (Knebworth 1985)
Highway Star; Nobody's Home; Strange Kind of Woman; Gypsy's Kiss; Perfect Strangers; Lazy; Knocking at Your Back Door; Difficult to Cure; Space Truckin'; Speed King; Black Night; Smoke on the Water (Connoisseur DPVSOP 163)

2001 *Highway Stars* – Discs One and Two from 12-CD box set *New, Live & Rare – The Bootleg Collection 1984–2000* (Adelaide, November 1984)
Highway Star; Nobody's Home; Strange Kind of Woman; A Gypsy's Kiss; Perfect Strangers; Under The Gun; Knocking at Your Back Door; Lazy; Child in Time; Beethoven; Organ solo; Space Truckin'; Organ solo; Guitar solo; Space Truckin' cont'd; Black Night; Speed King; Smoke on the Water (Thompson Music Management / Thames Talent DPBSCD001 – Australia)

2001 *Third Night* – Discs Three and Four from 12-CD box set *New, Live & Rare – The Bootleg Collection 1984–2000* (Stockholm, Sweden, June 1985)
Introduction; Highway Star; Nobody's Home; Strange Kind of Woman; A Gypsy's Kiss; Perfect Strangers; Under The Gun; Lazy; Drum solo; Child in Time; Knocking at Your Back Door; Beethoven; Organ solo; Space Truckin'; Woman from Tokyo; Black Night; Smoke on the Water (Thompson Music Management / Thames Talent DPBSCD001 – Australia)

2001 *Hungary Days* – Discs Five and Six from 12-CD box set *New, Live & Rare – The Bootleg Collection 1984–2000* (Budapest, Hungary, January 1987)
Intros; Highway Star; Strange Kind of Woman; The Unwritten Law; Blues; Dead or Alive; Perfect Strangers; Hard Lovin' Woman; Bad Attitude; Child in Time; Difficult to Cure; Organ solo; Knocking at Your Back Door; Hungarian Dance; Lazy; Space Truckin'; Black Night; Smoke on the Water; Speed King; Call of the Wild; Woman from Tokyo; World tour outro (Thompson Music Management / Thames Talent DPBSCD001 – Australia)

MARK V
JON LORD (keyboards); IAN PAICE (drums); RITCHIE BLACKMORE (guitar); ROGER GLOVER (bass); JOE LYNN TURNER (vocals)

UK SINGLES
October 1990 King of Dreams; Fire in the Basement (RCA PB 49247)
February 1991 Love Conquers All; Truth Hurts; Slow Down Sister (RCA PD 49226)

US SINGLES
October 1990 King of Dreams; Fire in the Basement (RCA PB 2703)

UK/US LP
November 1990 *Slaves And Masters*
King of Dreams; The Cut Runs Deep; Fire in the Basement; Truth Hurts; Breakfast in Bed; Love Conquers All; Fortuneteller; Too Much Is Not Enough; Wicked Ways (RCA PD 90535) / (RCA 2421)

MARK II (second reunion)
JON LORD (keyboards); IAN PAICE (drums); RITCHIE BLACKMORE (guitar); ROGER GLOVER (bass); IAN GILLAN (vocals)

UK/US LP
July 1993 *The Battle Rages On*
The Battle Rages On; Lick It Up; Anya; Talk About Love; Time to Kill; Ramshackle Man; A Twist in the Tale; Nasty Piece of Work; Solitaire; One Man's Meat (RCA 74321 15240) / (Giant 24517)

UK/US LIVE LP
November 1994 *Come Hell or High Water* (Germany/UK 1993)
Highway Star; Black Night; A Twist in the Tale; Perfect Strangers; Anyone's Daughter; Child in Time; Anya; Speed King; Smoke on the Water (RCA 74321 15240) / (RCA 74321 15240)
CD reissue bonus tracks: Lazy; Space Truckin'; Woman from Tokyo (BMG Victor BVCP-7478 – Japan)

2001 *In Your Trousers* – Discs Seven and Eight from 12-CD box set *New, Live & Rare – The Bootleg Collection 1984–2000* (Stockholm 1993)
Intro; Highway Star; Black Night; Talk about Love; A Twist in the Tale; Perfect Strangers; Difficult to Cure; Organ solo; Knocking at Your Back Door; Anyone's Daughter; Child in Time; Guitar solo; Anya; The Battle Rages On; Lazy; Drum solo; Space Truckin'; Woman from Tokyo; Paint It Black; Hush; Smoke on the Water (Thompson Music Management / Thames Talent DPBSCD001)

MARK VI
JON LORD (keyboards); IAN PAICE (drums); JOE SATRIANI (guitar); ROGER GLOVER (bass); IAN GILLAN (vocals)
No official releases

MARK VII
JON LORD (keyboards); IAN PAICE (drums); STEVE MORSE (guitar); ROGER GLOVER (bass); IAN GILLAN (vocals)

UK/US LPS
February 1996 *Purpendicular*
Vavoom: Ted the Mechanic; Loosen My Strings; Soon Forgotten; Sometimes I Feel Like Screaming; Cascades: I'm Not Your Lover; The Aviator; Rosa's Cantina; A Castle Full of Rascals; A Touch Away; Hey Cisco; Somebody Stole My Guitar; The Purpendicular Waltz (RCA 74321 33802) / (CMC 86201)

May 1998 *Abandon*
Any Fule Kno That; Almost Human; Don't Make Me Happy; Seventh Heaven; Watching the Sky; Fingers to the Bone; Jack Ruby; She Was; Whatshername; '69; Evil Louie; Bludsucker (RCA 495306) / (CMC 86201)

UK/US LIVE LPs
June 1997 *Live At Olympia* (Paris, France, 1996)
Fireball; Maybe I'm a Leo; Ted the Mechanic; Pictures of Home; Black Night; Cascades: I'm Not Your Lover; Sometimes I Feel Like Screaming; Woman from Tokyo; No One Came; The Purpendicular Waltz; Rosa's Cantina; Smoke on the Water; When a Blind Man Cries; Speed King; Perfect Strangers; Hey Cisco; Highway Star (EMI CDEM 1615)

July 1999 *Total Abandon – Live In Australia* (1999)
Ted the Mechanic; Strange Kind of Woman; Bloodsucker; Pictures of Home; Almost Human; Woman from Tokyo; Watching the Sky; Fireball; Sometimes I Feel Like Screaming; Steve Morse solo; Smoke on the Water; Lazy; Perfect Strangers; Speed King; Black Night; Highway Star; Ian Gillan Interview; Pictorial essay of Deep Purple 1999–2001 (Drew Thompson & Thames Talent DPTA 20 4 99)

January 2000 *Live at The Royal Albert Hall with the London Symphony Orchestra*
Pictured Within; Wait a While; Sitting in a Dream; Love Is All; Via Miami; That's Why God Is Singing the Blues; Take It off the Top; Wring That Neck; Pictures of Home; Concerto for Group and Orchestra – First Movement / Second Movement / Third Movement; Ted the Mechanic; Watching the Sky; Sometimes I Feel Like Screaming; Smoke on the Water; Ted & Them; Ted the Mechanic (mpeg video – US release only); Smoke on the Water (mpeg video – UK release only) (Eagle EDGCD 124) / (Spitfire 15068)

2001 *Live at The Rotterdam Ahoy* (Rotterdam, Holland, 2000)
Introduction; Pictured Within; Sitting in a Dream; Love Is All; Fever Dreams; Rainbow in the Dark; Wring That Neck; Fools; When a Blind Man Cries; Vavoom: Ted the Mechanic; The Well Dressed Guitar; Pictures of Home; Sometimes I Feel Like Screaming; Perfect Strangers; Smoke on the Water; Black Night; Highway Star (Thompson Music Management / Thames Talent TMM003)

2001 *Purple Sunshine* – Discs Nine and Ten from 12-CD box set *New, Live & Rare – The Bootleg Collection 1984–2000* (Ft Lauderdale, March 1995)
Fireball; Black Night; The Battle Rages On; Ted the Mechanic; Woman from Tokyo; The Purpendicular Waltz; When a Blind Man Cries; Perfect Strangers; Pictures of Home; Knocking at Your Back Door; Anyone's Daughter; Child in Time; Anya; Lazy; Speed King; Highway Star; Smoke on the Water (Thompson Music Management / Thames Talent DPBSCD001)

2001 *Made In Japan 2000* – Discs Eleven and Twelve from 12-CD box set *New, Live & Rare – The Bootleg Collection 1984–2000* (Osaka 2000)
Woman from Tokyo; Fireball; Into the Fire; Sometimes I Feel Like Screaming; '69; Smoke on the Water; Fools; Black Night; Watching the Sky; Guitar solo; Any

Fule Kno That; Organ solo; Perfect Strangers; When a Blind Man Cries; Speed
King; Lazy; Hush; Highway Star (Thompson Music Management / Thames Talent
DPBSCD001)

2001 *Australian Tour 2001* – Discs One and Two from 12-CD box set *The
Soundboard Series* Woman from Tokyo; Ted the Mechanic; Mary Long; Lazy; No
One Came; Black Night; Sometimes I Feel Like Screaming; '69; Smoke on the
Water; Perfect Strangers; Hey Cisco; When a Blind Man Cries; Fools; Speed
King; Hush; Highway Star (Thompson Music Management / Thames Talent)

2001 *The Masters Of Rock* – Discs Three and Four from 12-CD box set *The
Soundboard Series* (Woollongong, Australia, 2001)
Woman from Tokyo; Ted the Mechanic; Mary Long; Lazy; No One Came; Black
Night; Sometimes I Feel Like Screaming; Fools; Perfect Strangers; Hey Cisco;
When a Blind Man Cries; Smoke on the Water; Speed King; Hush; Highway Star
(Thompson Music Management / Thames Talent)

2001 *The Masters Of Rock* – Discs Five and Six from 12-CD box set *The
Soundboard Series* (Newcastle, Australia, 2001)
Woman from Tokyo; Ted the Mechanic; Mary Long; Lazy; No One Came; Black
Night; Sometimes I Feel Like Screaming; Fools; Perfect Strangers; Hey Cisco;
When a Blind Man Cries; Smoke on the Water; Speed King; Hush; Highway Star
(Thompson Music Management / Thames Talent)

2001 *Live In Hong Kong* (Discs Seven and Eight from 12-CD box set *The
Soundboard Series*
Woman from Tokyo; Ted the Mechanic; Mary Long; Lazy; No One Came; Black
Night; Sometimes I Feel Like Screaming; Fools; Perfect Strangers; Hey Cisco;
When a Blind Man Cries; Smoke on the Water; Speed King; Hush; Highway Star
(Thompson Music Management / Thames Talent)

2001 *untitled* – Discs Nine and Ten from 12-CD box set *The Soundboard Series*
(Tokyo 2001)
Pictured Within; Sitting In A Dream; Love Is All; Fever Dreams; Rainbow in the
Dark; Watching the Sky; Sometimes I Feel Like Screaming; The Well Dressed
Guitar; Fools; Perfect Strangers; Concerto – First Movement / Second

Movement / Third Movement; When a Blind Man Cries; Pictures of Home; Smoke on the Water (Thompson Music Management / Thames Talent)

2001 *untitled* – Discs Eleven and Twelve from 12-CD box set *The Soundboard Series* (Tokyo 2001)
Pictured Within; Sitting in a Dream; Love Is All; Fever Dreams; Rainbow in the Dark; Sometimes I Feel Like Screaming; The Well Dressed Guitar; Wring That Neck; When a Blind Man Cries; Fools; Perfect Strangers; Concerto – First Movement / Second Movement / Third Movement; Pictures of Home; Smoke on the Water (Thompson Music Management / Thames Talent)

MARK VIII
IAN PAICE (drums); STEVE MORSE (guitar); ROGER GLOVER (bass); IAN GILLAN (vocals); DON AIREY (keyboards)

UK/US LPS
August 2003 *Bananas*
House Of Pain; Sun Goes Down; Haunted; Razzle Dazzle; Silver Tongue; Walk On; Picture of Innocence; I Got Your Number; Never a Word; Bananas; Doing It Tonight; Contact Lost (EMI 7243 5 91049 2 8)

PART TWO: SOLO DISCOGRAPHIES

KEY:
DA = Don Airey, DC = David Coverdale, GH = Glenn Hughes, IG = Ian Gillan, IP = Ian Paice, JL = Jon Lord, JLT = Joe Lynn Turner, JS = Joe Satriani, NS = Nick Simper, RB = Ritchie Blackmore, RE = Rod Evans, RG = Roger Glover, SM = Steve Morse, TB = Tommy Bolin

Note: Although Ritchie Blackmore was a full-time member of Joe Meek's regular studio band, the Outlaws, incomplete record keeping renders it impossible to detail every session in which he appeared. Those noted below should be considered merely a representative sampling.

Release information is for UK issues unless otherwise noted. For further discographical and collector information, see *The Great Rock . . . Metal . . .*

Psychedelic . . . Discography series (various editions) by Martin C. Strong (Canongate Books); the *Record Collector Rare Record price Guide* (various editions) (Diamond Publishing); and the *Goldmine Record Album* and *45 RPM Records Price Guide* (Krause Publications).

1962
MIKE BERRY (RB – Joe Meek session appearance)
Don't You Think It's Time; Loneliness (HMV POP 1105)

1963
BURR BAILEY (RB – Joe Meek session appearance)
San Francisco Bay; Like a Bird without Feathers (Decca F11686)

GLENDA COLLINS (RB – Joe Meek session appearance)
If You Gotta Pick a Baby; In the First Place (HMV POP 1233)

MICHAEL COX (RB – Joe Meek session appearance)
In Sweden EP (HMV 7EGS 296)

HEINZ (RB – Joe Meek session appearance)
Dreams Do Come True; Been Invited to a Party (Decca F11652)
Just Like Eddie; Don't You Knock At My Door (Decca F11693)
Heinz EP (Decca DFE 8545)
Country Boy; Long Tall Jack (Decca F11768)

JOE MEEK ORCHESTRA (RB – Joe Meek session appearance)
The Kennedy March; The Theme Of Freedom (Decca F11801)

THE OUTLAWS (RB)
Return Of The Outlaws; Texan Spiritual (HMV POP 1124)
That Set the Wild West Free; Hobo (HMV POP 1195)

GUNILLA THORNE (RB – Joe Meek session appearance)
Merry Go Round; Go On Then (HMV POP 1239)

GENE VINCENT (RB session appearance)
Rebel Heart Vol. 5 (1963 radio sessions; released 1997) (Magnum CDMF 099)

1964
THE ARTWOODS (JL)
Sweet Mary; If I Ever Get My Hands on You (Decca F12015)

ANDY CAVELL (RB – Joe Meek session appearance)
Tell the Truth; Shut Up (Pye 7N 15610)

HEINZ (RB – Joe Meek session appearance)
You Were There; No Matter What They Say (Decca F11831)
Please Little Girl; For Lovin' Me This Way (Decca F11920)
Questions I Can't Answer; Beating of My Heart (Columbia DB 7374)
A Tribute To Eddie LP (Decca LK 4599)

DAVY KAYE (RB – Joe Meek session appearance)
A Fool such as I; It's Nice Isn't It (Decca F11866)

THE KINKS (JL session)
Long Tall Sally; I Took My Baby Home (Pye 7N 15611)
You Really Got Me; It's All Right (Pye 7N 15673)
The Kinks (Pye NPL 18096)

THE OUTLAWS (RB)
Law and Order; Do Da Day (HMV POP 1241)
Keep a-Knockin'; Shake with Me (HMV POP 1277)

THE RALLY ROUNDERS (a.k.a. THE OUTLAWS) (RB)
The Bike Beat 1; The Bike Beat 2 (Lyntone LYN 574)

HOUSTON WELLS (RB – Joe Meek session appearance)
Galway Bay; Living Alone (Parlophone R5141)
Ramona EP (Parlophone GEP 8914)

1965

THE ARTWOODS (JL)

Big City; Oh My Love (Decca F12091)

Goodbye Sisters; She Knows What to Do (Decca F12206)

If I Ever Get My Hands on You; Sweet Mary; Oh My Love; Big City EP (Decca 457076 – France)

RITCHIE BLACKMORE ORCHESTRA (RB)

Getaway; Little Brown Jug (Oriole CB 314)

GLENDA COLLINS (RB – Joe Meek session appearance)

Thou Shalt Not Steal; Been Invited to a Party (HMV POP 1475)

BUDDY BRITTEN & THE REGENTS (NS)

She's About a Mover; Since You've Gone (Piccadilly 7N 35241)

Right Now; Jailer Bring Me Water (Piccadilly 7N 35257)

JESS CONRAD (RB – Joe Meek session appearance)

Hurt Me; It Can Happen to Anyone

HEINZ (RB – Joe Meek session appearance)

Don't Think Twice; Big Fat Spider (Columbia DB 7559)

THE LANCASTERS (RB session appearance)

Satan's Holiday; Earthshaker (Titan FF 1730 – USA)

THE MURMAIDS (RB session appearance)

To Know Him Is to Love Him; [unknown] (Chattahoochie – USA)

THE OUTLAWS (RB)

Don't Cry; Only for You (Smash S 2025 – USA)

SCREAMING LORD SUTCH & THE SAVAGES (RB session appearance)

The Train Kept A-Rollin'; Honey Hush (CBS 201767)

THE SESSIONS (RB session appearance)
Let Me In; Bouncing Bass (Fontana – USA)

THE SHINDIGS (IP)
One Little Letter; What You Gonna Do (Parlophone R 5316)
A Little While Back; Why Say Goodbye (Parlophone R 5377)

1966
THE ARTWOODS (JL)
I Take What I Want; I'm Looking for a Saxophonist (Decca F12384)
I Feel Good; Molly Anderson's Cookery Book (Decca F12465)
Jazz In Jeans EP (Decca DFE 8654)
Art Gallery (Decca LK 4830)

EPISODE SIX (IG, RG)
Put Yourself in My Place; That's All I Want (Pye 7N 17018)
I Hear Trumpets Blow; True Love Is Funny That Way (Pye 7N 17110)
Here There and Everywhere; Mighty Morris Ten (Pye 7N 17147)
I Will Warm Your Heart; Incense [as sheila carter & episode 6] (Pye 7N17194)

HEINZ (RB session appearance)
I'm Not a Bad Guy; Movin' In (Columbia DB 7942)

RONNIE JONES (RB session appearance)
Satisfy My Soul; My Only Souvenir

JOHNNY KIDD & THE NEW PIRATES (NS)
Send for That Girl; The Fool (HMV POP 1559)

THE MI FIVE (RE, IP)
You'll Never Stop Me Loving You; Only Time Will Tell (Parlophone R5486)

THE MAZE (RE, IP)
Hello Stranger; Telephone (Reaction 591009)

SIMON RAVEN CULT (AKA BUDDY BRITTEN & THE REGENTS) (NS)
I Wonder If She Remembers Me; Sea of Love (Piccadilly 7N 35301)

1967
THE ARTWOODS (JL)
What Shall I Do; In the Deep End (Parlophone R 5590)

EPISODE SIX (IG, RG)
Love Hate Revenge; Baby Baby Baby (Pye 7N 17244)
Morning Dew; Sunshine Girl (Pye 7N 17330)
I Won't Hurt You; U.F.O. [as Neo Maya] (Pye 17371)
I Can See Through You; When I Fall in Love (Pye 7N 17376)

THE MAZE (RE, IP)
Aria Del Sud; Non Fatemio Odiare (Polydor NH 59801 – Italy)
The Maze EP (Vogue Int. 18136 – France)
Catteri, Catteri; Easy Street (MGM 1368)

ST VALENTINE'S DAY MASSACRE (a.k.a. THE ARTWOODS) (JL)
Brother Can You Spare a Dime; Al's Party (Fontana TF.883)

SANTA BARBARA MACHINE HEAD (JL)
Blues Anytime 4 (Immediate IM014/015/019)
(JL appears on "Porcupine Juice," "Albert," and "Rubber Monkey")

SOUL BROTHERS (IP session)
Do Your Own Thing; Goodbye Baby Goodbye

1968
BOZ (RB, JL, IP session appearance)
I Shall Be Released; Down in the Flood (Columbia DB 84006)

NEIL CHRISTIAN & THE CRUSADERS (RB session appearance)
My Baby Left Me; Yakety Yak (Vogue DV 14744)

EPISODE SIX (IG, RG)
Little One; Wide Smiles [as Episode] (MGM Records 1409)
Lucky Sunday; Mr. Universe (Chapter One CH 103)

FINDER'S KEEPERS (GH)
Sadie (The Cleaning Lady); Without Her (Fontana TF-938)

TONY WILSON (IP session)
I Feel Fine; Let Me Love You

1969
EPISODE SIX (IG, RG)
Mozart vs. The Rest; Jack d'Or (Chapter One CH 104)
Music From 'Twisted Nerve' & 'Les Bicyclettes De Belsize' LP (Polydor 583728)

TRAPEZE (GH)
Send Me No More Letters; Another Day (Threshold TH 2)

1970
JESUS CHRIST SUPERSTAR (IG)
Jesus Christ Superstar (MCA Records MKPS 2011; 2)

ELTON JOHN (RG session)
Rock'n'Roll Madonna; Great Deal (DJM Records DJS 222)

TRAPEZE (GH)
Black Cloud; – (Threshold 67005 – USA)
Trapeze (Threshold THS 2)
Medusa (Threshold THS 4)

WARHORSE (NS)
St Louis; No Chance (Vertigo 6059 027)
Warhorse (Vertigo 6360 015)

ZEPHYR (TB)
Zephyr LP (Probe CPLP 4510 – USA)

1971

ROD EVANS (RE)
Hard To Be Without You; You Can't Love a Child Like a Woman (Capitol P-2963 – USA)

GREEN BULLFROG (RB, IP session appearance)
My Baby Left Me; Loving You Is Good for Me Baby (Decca 32831)
Green Bullfrog LP (Decca D 75269)

RUPERT HINE & DAVID MACIVER (RG session)
Pick Up A Bone

MIKE HURST (IP session)
Show Me the Way To Georgia; Over Again (Capitol CL 15681)
I Couldn't Wait To Tell You; Lord I Don't Have the Time (Capitol CL 15688)
In My Time (Capitol ST-21819 – USA)

LORD SUTCH & HEAVY FRIENDS (RB, NS session appearance)
The Hands of Jack the Ripper LP (Cotillion SD 9049 – USA)

ZEPHYR (TB)
Going Back To Colorado LP (Warner WS 1897 – USA)

1972

Ashton, Gardner, Dyke & Co (JL session)
What A Bloody Long Day It's Been (Capitol EA-ST 22862)
(JL appears on "Falling Song")

CAPTAIN BEYOND (RE)
Captain Beyond (Capricorn CPN 0105 – USA)

DAVE COUSINS / The STRAWBS (RG session)
Two Weeks Last Summer (A&M SP 9008)

ELF (RG, IP session; producer)
Elf (Epic 31789)

IAN GILLAN (IG, RG, JL)
Cherkazoo And Other Stories (1972–74 material) (RPM RPM-104)

EDDIE HARDIN (IP session)
Home Is Where You Find It (Decca TXS 106)

JON LORD (RG, JL, IP)
Gemini Suite (Purple TPSA 7501)

TRAPEZE (GH)
Coast To Coast; Your Love Is Right (Threshold TH 11)
You're The Music, We're Just The Band (Threshold THS 8)

VELVET UNDERGROUND (IP session)
Squeeze (Polydor 2383-180 – USA)

WARHORSE (NS)
Red Sea (Vertigo 6360 066)

PETE YORK (IP co-producer)
The Pete York Percussion Band (Decca TXS 109)

1973
Captain Beyond (RE)
Sufficiently Breathless (Capricorn K47503)

BILLY COBHAM (TB session)
Spectrum LP (Atlantic K 40506 – USA)

NAZARETH (RG producer)
Broken Down Angel; Witchdoctor Woman (Mooncrest MOON 1)
Bad Bad Boy; Hard Living (Mooncrest MOON 9)
This Flight Tonight; Called Her Name (Mooncrest MOON 14)
Razamanaz (Mooncrest 1)
Loud 'n' Proud (Mooncrest 4)

RANDY PIE AND FAMILY (RB session appearance)
Hurry to the City; [unknown] (Atlantic 10290 – Germany)

TRAPEZE (GH)
Final Swing (compilation) (Threshold THS 11)

1974
Ashton & Lord (JL)
First Of The Big Bands (Purple TPS 3507)
BBC Radio 1 Live In Concert 1974 (Windsong WINCD 033)

ADAM FAITH (RB session appearance)
I Survive LP (Warner Bros BS 2791 – USA)
(RB appears on "I Survived")

ROGER GLOVER (DC, RG, GH)
Love Is All; Old Blind Mole; Magician Moth (Purple PUR 125)
The Butterfly Ball (Purple TPSA 7514)

HARDIN & YORK, WITH CHARLIE MCCRACKEN (RG producer)
Back Row Movie Star; Wish I'd Never Joined a Band (Vertigo 6147 008)
Hardin & York – Ain't No Breeze (Vertigo 6360 622)

EDDIE HARRIS (IP session)
E.H. in the UK – The Eddie Harris London Sessions (Atlantic ATL 1031)
(IP appears on "He's an Island Man" and "I've Tried Everything")

THE JAMES GANG (TB)
Cruising Down the Highway; Miami Two-Step (Atco 7006 – USA)
Miami (Atco K 50068 – USA)

JON LORD & EBERHARD SCHOENER (DC, JL)
Windows (Purple TPSA 7513)

ANDY MACKAY (RG sesson)
In Search For Eddie Riff (Island ILPS 9278)

MARLON (a.k.a. Roger Glover, Ray Fenwick) (RG)
Let's Go to the Disco; Broken Man (Purple Records PUR 120)

NAZARETH (RG producer; JL session)
Shanghai'd in Shanghai; Love, Now You're Gone (Mooncrest MOON 22)
Rampant (Mooncrest CREST 15)

COZY POWELL'S HAMMER (DA)
Na Na Na; Mistral (RAK 180)

SPENCER DAVIS GROUP (RG producer)
Living in a Back Street (Vertigo 1021)

1975
RITCHIE BLACKMORE'S RAINBOW (RB)
Man on the Silver Mountain; Snake Charmer (Oyster 103)
Ritchie Blackmore's Rainbow (Oyster; Polydor 2490 141)

TOMMY BOLIN (TB, GH)
The Grind; Homeward Strut (Atlantic K10730)
Teaser (Atlantic K 50208 – USA)

ROGER GLOVER (DC, RG, GH)
Little Chalk Blue; Sitting in a Dream (Purple PUR 128)

ROSCO GORDON (NS session)
Roscoe Rocks Again (recorded 1975–76) (JSP Records 1052)

BOBBY HARRISON (IP session)
Funkist (Capitol 11415)

DAN MCCAFFERTY (RG session)
Watcha Gonna Do About It; Nightingale (Mountain Top 5)
Dan McCafferty (Vertigo 6370-409)

ALPHONSE MOUZON (TB session)
Mind Transplant LP (Blue Note BN-LA 398 G)

NATURAL MAGIC (a.k.a. Roger Glover, Eddie Hardin)
Strawberry Fields Forever; Isolated Lady (Oyster Records OYR 102)

RAINBOW CANYON (TB session)
Rollin' in the Rockies LP (Capitol Records 11272)
(TB appears on "Rollin' In The Rockies")

1976
BABE RUTH (DA)
Kid's Stuff (Capitol est 11515)

RITCHIE BLACKMORE'S RAINBOW (RB)
Starstruck; Run With The Wolf (Polydor 2066 709 – Germany)
Rainbow Rising (Polydor 2490 137)

TOMMY BOLIN (TB)
Shake the Devil; Hello Again (CBS Records BA222284 – Australia)
Private Eyes (CBS Records 81612 – USA)

COLOSSEUM II (DA)
Strange New Flesh (WB 2016)

DIXIE DREGS (SM)
The Great Spectacular

RORY GALLAGHER (RG producer)
Calling Card (Chrysalis CHR 1124)

IAN GILLAN; GILLAN (IG, RG)
You Make Me Feel So Good; Shame (Oyster 2066 679)
Child in Time (Polydor ACBR261)

EDDIE HARDIN (DC, RG, GH, JL session)
Wizard's Convention (RCA RS 1085))

JON LORD
Sarabande (Purple TPSA 7516)

MOXY (TB session)
Moxy LP (Mercury SRM-1-1087 – USA)
Moxy II LP (Polydor 2480-372 – Canada)

JOHN PERRY (RG session)
Sunset Wading (Decca SKL 5233)

1977
RITCHIE BLACKMORE'S RAINBOW (RB)
Kill the King; Man on the Silver Mountain; Mistreated (Polydor 2066 845)
Rainbow On Stage (Polydor 2657 016)

COLOSSEUM II (DA)
Electric Savage (MCA 2293)
Wardance (MCA 2310)

DAVID COVERDALE & WHITESNAKE (DC, RG)
Hole in the Sky; Blindman (Purple Records PUR 133)
White Snake (Purple Records TPS 3509)

DIXIE DREGS (sm)
Free Fall (Capricorn CPN 0189)

FANDANGO (JLT)
Fandango (RCA – USA)

IAN GILLAN; GILLAN (IG)
Clear Air Turbulence (Island ILPS 9500)
Scarabus (Island ILPS 9511)
Live at The Budokan (East World EWS-81112)

Ian Gillan Band Live at The Rainbow 1977 (released 1998) Angel Air sjpcd017)
The Rockfield Mixes (*Clear Air Turbulence* sessions, released 1997) (Angel Air sjpcd 007)

EDDIE HARDIN (RG, IP session)
You Can't Teach an Old Dog New Tricks (Attic LAT 1023)

GLENN HUGHES
I Found a Woman; L.A. Cut Off (Safari 6.12098 – Germany)

JUDAS PRIEST (RG co-producer)
Diamonds and Rust; Dissident Aggressor (CBS 5222)
Sin After Sin (CBS 32005)

LIZA MINELLI (SM session)
Tropical Nights (Columbia 34887)

PAICE, ASHTON & LORD (JL)
Malice in Wonderland (Oyster 2391 269)
BBC Radio 1 Live in Concert 1977 (Windsong WINCD 025)

STRAPPS (RG producer)
Child of the City; Soft Touch (Harvest HAR 5119)
Secret Damage (Harvest SHSP 4064)

PAT TRAVERS (GH session)
Makin' Magic (Polydor PD-6103)
(GH appears on "Stevie")

YOUNG & MOODY (RG producer)
Young & Moody (Magnet MAG 5015)

1978
Barbi Benton (RG producer)
Ain't That Just the Way

RITCHIE BLACKMORE'S RAINBOW (RB)
LA Connection; Lady of the Lake (Polydor POSP 275)
Long Live Rock'n'Roll LP (Polydor POLD 5002)

BLACK SABBATH (DA session)
Never Say Die; She's Gone (Vertigo SAB 001)
Hard Road; Symptom of the Universe (Vertigo SAB 002)
Never Say Die (WB 3186)

JOE BREEN (RG producer; JL session)
More Than Meets the Eye (Vertigo 6370 430)

DAVID COVERDALE & WHITESNAKE (DC, RG)
Breakdown; Only My Soul (Purple Records PUR 136)
North Winds (Purple Records TPS 3513)

DAVID COVERDALE & WHITESNAKE (DC)
Snakebite EP (Sunburst INEP 751)

DAVID COVERDALE & WHITESNAKE (DC, JL)
Lie Down; Don't Mess with Me (EMI INT 568)
Trouble (EMI INS 3022)

DIXIE DREGS (sm)
What If (Capricorn CPN 0230)

FANDANGO (JLT)
Last Kiss (RCA – USA)

IAN GILLAN / GILLAN (IG)
Gillan (East World Sound EWS 81120 – Japan)

ROGER GLOVER
Elements (Polydor Super 2391 306)

GLENN HUGHES
Play Me Out (Safari long 2)

KIRBY (IP session)
Composition (Hot Wax Records)

JIM RAFFERTY (DA session)
Don't Talk Back (London 722)

STRIFE (DA)
Back to Thunder (Gull 1029)

BARBARA THOMPSON (DA session)
Jubiaba (MCA MCF 2867)

ANDREW LLOYD WEBBER (DA session)
Variations (MCA 429342))

1979
RITCHIE BLACKMORE'S RAINBOW (DA, RB, RG)
All Night Long; Weiss Heim (Polydor 2095 196)
Since You Been Gone; Bad Girls (Polydor POSP 70 – France)
Down to Earth (Polydor 2391 410)

DAVID COVERDALE & WHITESNAKE (DC, JL)
The Time Is Right for Love; Come On (EMI INT 578)
Long Way from Home; Trouble; Ain't No Love . . . (UA BP 324)
Love Hunter (United Artists Records UAG30264)

RICHARD DIGANCE (JL session)
Commercial Road (Chrysalis CHR 1262)

DIXIE DREGS (sm)
Night of the Living Dregs (Capricorn 216)

FANDANGO (JLT)
One Night Stand (RCA – USA)

FOUR ON THE FLOOR (GH)
Four on the Floor (Casablanca NBLP 7180 – USA)

IAN GILLAN; GILLAN (IG)
Vengeance; Smoke on the Water (Acrobat 1C006-63298 – Germany)
Mr. Universe (Acrobat ACRO 3)
The BBC Tapes Vol 1: Dead of Night 1979 (released 1997) (Purple Records
PUR 319)

GARY MOORE (DA)
Back on the Streets; Track Nine (MCA 386)
Parisienne Walkways; Fanatical Fascists (MCA 419)
Spanish Guitar; Spanish Guitar (instrumental) (MCA 534)
Back on the Streets (MCA MCF 2853)

COZY POWELL (DA)
Theme One; Over the Top (Ariola ARO 189)
The Loner; El Sid (Ariola 205)
Over the Top (Ariola 6312)

JIM RAFFERTY (DA session)
Solid Logic (Decca SKLR 5314)

NICK SIMPER'S FANDANGO (NS)
Slipstreaming (Gull Records GULL-1033)

1980
DAVID COVERDALE & WHITESNAKE (DC, JL, IP)
Fool for Your Loving; Mean Business; Don't Mess with Me (Liberty BP 352)
Ready An' Willing; Nighthawk; We Wish You Well (Liberty BP 363)
Ain't No Love in the Heart of the City; Take Me with You (Liberty BP 381)
Ready An' Willing (Liberty 064-82904)
Live . . . In the Heart of the City (Liberty 138-83023; 4)

DIXIE DREGS (SM)
Dregs of the Earth (Arista 9528)
King Biscuit Flower Hour Presents the Dixie Dregs in Concert 1980 (released 1997) (King Biscuit Entertainment KiX88031)

FANDANGO (JLT)
Cadillac (RCA – USA)

IAN GILLAN / GILLAN (IG)
Sleeping on the Job; Higher and Higher (Virgin VS 355)
No Easy Way; Handles on Her Hips; I Might As Well Go Home (Virgin VS 362)
Mutually Assured Destruction; The Maelstrom (Virgin VS 103)
Trouble; Your Sister's on My List (Virgin VS 377)
Reading Live & More EP (Virgin VIP-5901)
Glory Road (Virgin V2171)
For Gillan Fans Only (Virgin VDJU 32)
The BBC Tapes Vol 2: Unchain Your Brain 1980 (released 1997) (Purple Records PUR 320)
Live At Reading '80 (released 1990) (Raw Fruit FRSCD 002)

JACK GREEN (RB session appearance)
Humanesque LP (RCA Records 5004 – USA)
(RB appears on "I Call, No Answer")

BERNIE MARSDEN (da, JL, IP session)
And About Time Too (Sunburst 1C064-64361)

OZZY OSBOURNE (DA)
Crazy Train; You Looking at Me (Jet 197)
Mr Crowley (live); You Said It All (live) (Jet 7-003)
Blizzard of Oz (Jet 36812)

COZY POWELL (DA)
Heidi Goes to Town; Over the Top (Part 2) (Ariola 222)

JIM RAFFERTY (DA session)
The Bogeyman; Salt Lake City (Charisma CB 377)

MICHAEL SCHENKER GROUP (RG producer; DA session)
Michael Schenker Group (Chrysalis 1302)

NICK SIMPER'S FANDANGO (NS)
Future Times (Shark Records INT-148.506 – Germany)

STEVE WALSH (SM session)
Schemer-Dreamer (Kirshner; CBS Records 36320)

YOUNG & MOODY (RG producer)
All the Good Friends; Playing Your Game (Fabulous JC3)

1981
RITCHIE BLACKMORE'S RAINBOW (DA, RB, RG, JLT)
Can't Happen Here; Jealous Lover (Polydor POSP 251)
I Surrender; Vielleicht Das Naechste Mal (Polydor 2095 339)
Magic; Freedom Fighter (Polydor 7 DM 0033 – Japan)
Difficult To Cure (Polydor 2391 506)

GRAHAM BONNET (JL session)
Line Up (Vertigo 6302 151)
(JL appears on "Don't Stand In The Open")

CLIMAX BLUES BAND (GH session)
Lucky for Some (Warner Bros BSK3623 – USA)
(GH appears on "Shake It Lucy")

DAVID COVERDALE & WHITESNAKE (DC, JL, IP)
Don't Break My Heart Again; Child of Babylon (Liberty BP 395)
Would I Lie to You; Girl (Liberty BP 399)
Come An' Get It (Liberty 062-83134)

DREGS (SM)
Unsung Heroes (Arista)
Live in New York 1981 (Four Aces Records)

IAN GILLAN / GILLAN (IG)
New Orleans; Take a Hold of Yourself (Virgin VS406)
One For The Road EP (Virgin VIP-5911 – Japan)
Nightmare; Bite the Bullet (live) (Virgin VS 441)
Restless; On the Rocks (live) (Virgin VS 465)
Higher and Higher; Spanish Guitar (Flexipop 13)
No Laughing in Heaven EP (Virgin VS 425)
Future Shock (Virgin VH2196)
Double Trouble (Virgin VGD 3506)

KEN HENSLEY (IP session)
Free Spirit (Bronze Records 203-456-320 – Germany)
(IP appears on "Brown Eyed Boy")

BERNIE MARSDEN (JL session)
Look At Me Now (Sunburst 1A064-64454)
(JL appears on "Look at Me Now," "So Far Away," "Who's Foolin' Who?," "Byblos
(Prts 1 & 2)," and "Can You Do It?")

BERNIE MARSDEN (DC session)
The Friday Rock Sessions (released 1992) (Raw Fruit Records FRSCD007)

OZZY OSBOURNE (DA)
Crazy Train; Steal Away (Jet 02079)

COZY POWELL (DA)
Sooner or Later; The Blister (Polydor POSP 328)
Tilt (Polydor 16342)

1982
RITCHIE BLACKMORE'S RAINBOW (RB, RG, JLT)
Death Alley Driver; Power (Polydor 7 DM 0059 – Japan)

Stone Cold; Rock Fever (POSP 421)
Straight Between the Eyes (Polydor 2391 542)

DAVID COVERDALE & WHITESNAKE (DC, JL, IP)
Here I Go Again; Bloody Luxury (Liberty 006-83352)
Saints An' Sinners (Liberty 30354B)

DREGS (SM)
Industry Standard (Arista BVCA 2055 – Japan)

IAN GILLAN / GILLAN (IG)
Living for the City; Breaking Chains (Virgin VS 519)
Long Gone; Fiji (Virgin VS 537)
Magic (Virgin V 2238)

EDDIE HARDIN (RG)
Circumstantial Evidence (RCA 30101)

GEORGE HARRISON (JL session)
Gone Troppo (Dark Horse 23734)
(JL appears on "Circles")

GLENN HUGHES AND PAT THRALL
The Look in Your Eye; Muscle and Blood (Epic A-2795)
Hughes-Thrall (Epic 38116)

JON LORD
Bach onto This Edit; Going Home (Harvest HAR 5220)
Before I Forget (Harvest SHSP 4123)

GARY MOORE BAND (IP, DA)
Always Gonna Love You; Cold Hearted (Virgin VS 528)
Live EP (Virgin Records VDJ34)
Corridors Of Power (Virgin VL2257)

NICOLODEON (NS)
Music, Music, Music; [unknown]

COZY POWELL (DA, JL session)
Octopuss (Polydor POLD 5093)

NICK SIMPER'S FANDANGO (NS)
Just Another Day (In The Life of a Fool); Wish I'd Never Woke Up (Paro Records
Paro-S4)

1983
Black Sabbath (IG)
Trashed; Zero the Hero
Born Again (Vertigo 814 271)

RITCHIE BLACKMORE'S RAINBOW (RB, RG, JLT)
Can't Let You Go; All Night Long (live) (Polydor POSP 654)
Street of Dreams; Anybody There (Polydor POSP 631)
Bent out of Shape (Polydor 815305-1)

DAVID COVERDALE & WHITESNAKE (DC, JL, IP)
Guilty of Love; Gambler (Liberty 006-165208-7)

HEAVEN (GH session)
Where Angels Fear To Tread

GARY MOORE BAND (IP session)
Falling in Love with You EP (Virgin VS564-12)

GARY MOORE BAND (DA, IP session)
Hold on to Love; Devil in my Heart (Ten Records TEN13-12)
Rockin' Every Night (Virgin VIL-6093 – Japan)

NIGHT RANGER (GH session)
Midnight Madness (MCA 5456)

OZZY OSBOURNE (DA)
Bark at the Moon; One Up on the B-Side (Epic 3915)
Bark at the Moon (CBS 38987)

THE ROYAL PHILHARMONIC ORCHESTRA & FRIENDS (DA, IP session)
Arrested (RCA Records RCALP8001)

JOE SATRIANI (JS)
Time Machine (recorded 1983) (Relativity Records – USA)

1984
DAVID COVERDALE & WHITESNAKE (DC, JL)
Give Me More Time; Need Your Love So Bad (Liberty 006-2000027)
Standing in the Shadows; All or Nothing (Liberty BP 423)
Love Ain't No Stranger EP (Liberty BP 20 0555 6 – USA)
Slide It In (UK mix) (Liberty 064-2400001)
Slide It In (US mix) [LP] (Geffen GHS-4018 – USA)

DAVID GILMOUR (JL session)
About Face (EMI 1C 064-2400791)

ROGER GLOVER
The Mask; You're So Remote (Polydor 678)
Gettin' Stranger; Dancing Again (21 Records 21.030 – Holland)
The Mask (Polydor POLD 5139)

GARY MOORE BAND (IP session)
Empty Rooms; Nuclear Attack (live) (Ten Records 106654-100 – Germany)
We Want Moore! (Ten Records 302469-370)
Victims of Future (Virgin OVED 206)

STEVE MORSE (BAND) (SM)
Two Faces (Minotauro Records)
The Introduction (Elektra; Asylum Records 960369 – USA)

1985
ALASKA (DA session)
I Need Your Love; Susie Blue (MFN KUT 108)
Heart of the Storm (MFN 23)

EDDIE HARDIN & ZAK STARKEY (JL session)
Wind in the Willows (President Records PTLS-1078)

GARY MOORE (DA, GH session)
Out in the Fields; Military Man (10 TEN 49)
Empty Rooms; Out of My System (10 TEN 58)
Run for Cover (10 207 283-620)

STEVE MORSE (BAND) (SM)
Stand Up (Elektra; Asulym Records 960448 – USA)

PHENOMENA (DA, GH session)
Phenomena

JOE LYNN TURNER (JLT)
Rescue You (Elektra 9 60449-1 – USA)

1986
Black Sabbath (GH)
Seventh Star (Vertigo 826704)

IAN GILLAN / GILLAN (IG)
What I Did on My Vacation (Ten DIXDCD 39)

KANSAS (SM)
Power (MCA Records MCA-5838)
In The Spirit of Things (MCA Records MCA-6254)
Live on The King Biscuit Flower Hour (released 1998) (King Biscuit Flower Hour
KBFHCD024)

GREG KIHN (JS session)

Love and Rock and Roll (EMI America ST-17180 – USA)
King Biscuit Flower Hour (released 1996) (BMG Music 70710-88004-2 – USA)

T. LAVITZ (SM session)

Story Time (Passport 88012)
(SM appears on "Sparkle Plenty" and "I'm Calling You")

ALVIN LEE (JL session)

Detroit Diesel (Atco; 21 Records 90517 – USA)
(JL appears on "Ordinary Man" and "Let's Go")

GARY MOORE (DA session)

Over the Hills and Far Away; Crying in the Shadows (10 TEN 134)

GILBERT O'SULLIVAN (DA session)

The Way Love Used To Be

JOE SATRIANI (JS)

Not Of This Earth (Relativity REL 462972-1 – USA)

SINNER (DA session)

Comin' Out Fighting (Noise N 0049 – Germany)

WILD STRAWBERRIES (DA session)

Wild Strawberries

ZENO (DA session)

A Little More Love; Signs of the Sky (Parlophone R6123)
Love Will Live; Far Away (EMI 5566)
Zeno (Parlophone PCSD 102)

1987
Michael Bolton (JLT session)

The Hunger (CBS Records 40473)
(JLT appears on "Hot Love" and "Gina")

CHER (JLT session)

Cher (Geffen 924164)

(JLT appears on "We All Sleep Alone," "Bang Bang," "Main Man," "Perfection," and "Working Girl")

DAVID COVERDALE & WHITESNAKE (DC, DA)

Here I Go Again Edit; Slide It In (US Mix) (EMI 006 2020877)

Still Of The Night; Here I Go Again (EMI 5606)

Is This Love; Standing in the Shadows 1987 (EMI 201847-7)

1987 a.k.a. *Serpens Albus* (EMI 064-240737-1)

GILLAN-GLOVER (IG, RG)

Dislocated; Chet (Ten Records TEN 193)

HELIX (DA session)

Wild in the Streets; Kiss It Goodbye (Capitol CL 468)

Wild in the Streets (Capitol 46920)

GLENN HUGHES AND PAT THRALL

Music From The Motion Picture Dragnet (MCA Records MCAD-6210)

(Appear on "City Of Crime")

GARY MOORE (DA)

The Loner; Johnny Boy (10 TEN 178)

Live At The Marquee (Raw Power RAW 034)

MARK O'CONNOR (SM session)

Stone from which The Arch Was Made (Warner Bros 225539)

PHENOMENA II (GH session)

Dream Runner (BMG; Arista 208697)

(GH appears on "Surrender," "Hearts On Fire," and "Double 6 55 Double 4")

JOE SATRIANI (JS)

Surfing with the Alien (Relativity REL 462973-1 – USA)

TRIUMPH (SM session)
Surveillance (MCA MCA-42083)
(SM appears on "Headed For Somewhere" and "All The King's Horses")

JOHN WAITE (JLT session)
Rover's Return (EMI 46332)

PETE YORK'S SUPER DRUMMING (IP session)
Super Drumming (Global 303088-420 – Germany)

1988
DAVID COVERDALE & WHITESNAKE (DC)
Give Me All Your Love EP (EMI 12 EM 23)

DIXIE DREGS (SM)
Off the Records (Ensoniq Keyboards)

FASTWAY (DA session)
A Fine Line; Change of Heart (GWR 8)
On Target (GWR CD 22)

IAN GILLAN / GILLAN (IG)
South Africa; John (Virgin VS 1088)

GILLAN-GLOVER (IG, RG)
I Can't Dance to That; Purple People Eater (Virgin 109 706)
Clouds And Rain; I Thought No (Virgin 109 895)
She Took My Breath Away; Cayman Island (Virgin VS 1041)
Accidentally On Purpose (Virgin 208 737)

STUART HAMM (JS session)
Radio Free Albemuth (Relativity Records 88561-8209-2 – USA)
(JS appears on "Radio Free Albemuth," "Flow My Tears . . . ," and "Sexually Active")

LYNYRD SKYNYRD (SM session)
Southern By The Grace Of God – Tribute Tour '87 (MCA 8027)
(SM appears on "Gimme Back My Bullets")

YNGWIE MALMSTEEN (JLT)
Heaven Tonight; Riot in the Dungeons (Polydor 887518-7 – Germany)
Odyssey (Polydor P2 35451 – USA)

ROSSINGTON BAND (SM session)
Love Your Man (MCA Records MCAAD-42166)

JOE SATRIANI (JS)
Dreamin #11 EP (Food For Thought 12YUM114 – USA)

BONNIE TYLER (JLT session)
Notes from America (Columbia 44163)

1989
PAUL CARRACK (JLT session)
Groove Approved (Capitol 217709 – USA)

DAVID COVERDALE & WHITESNAKE (DC)
Fool for Your Loving; Slow Poke Music (EMI EMP 123)
Slip Of The Tongue (EMI 7-93537-1)

GEORGE HARRISON (IP session)
Cheer Down; Poor Little Girl (Warner; Dark Horse W 2696 CD)

DON JOHNSON (JLT session)
Let It Roll (Epic 460857-1 – USA)

YNGWIE MALMSTEEN (JLT)
Trial By Fire – Live In Leningrad (Polydor 839726-2 – USA)

GARY MOORE (DA)
After the War; This Thing Called Love (Virgin GMS 1)

Ready for Love; Wild Frontier (Virgin GMS 2)
After the War (Virgin V2575)

STEVE MORSE (BAND) (SM)
High Tension Wires (MCA Records 255930)

JOE SATRIANI (JS)
Big Bad Moon; Day at the Beach (Food For Thought Records YUM 118 – USA)
Flying In a Blue Dream (Relativity REL 465995-2 – USA)

SLAVERAIDER (DA session)
Young Blood; [unknown] (Jive 198)
What Do You Know About Rock'n'Roll (Jive HIP 68)

TIGERTAILZ (DA session)
Love Bomb Baby; Love Bomb Baby (MFN KUT 132)

TNT (JLT)
Intuition

XYZ (GH session)
XYZ (Enigma Records 064-773525-1 – Germany)

PETE YORK'S SUPER DRUMMING (JL session)
Super Drumming Vol 2 (Global 209888; 209889 – Germany)

1990
SAM BROWN (JL session)
April Moon (A&M Records 397036)
(JL appears on "Contradictions")

VICKI BROWN (JL session)
About Love And Life (Polydor 847266-2)
(JL appears on "We Are One")

DAVID COVERDALE (DC)

Last Note of Freedom; Last Note of Freedom edit (Epic 656315-3)

Days of Thunder soundtrack LP (Epic 467159-2)

(DC appears on "Last Note of Freedom")

DAVID COVERDALE & WHITESNAKE (DC)

The Deeper the Love; Judgement Day (EMI International 128)

Now You're Gone (remix); Wings of the Storm (EMI Records EM 150)

DON DOKKEN (GH session)

Up from the Ashes (Geffen 24301)

(GH appears on "When Love Finds a Fool")

FASTWAY (DA session)

Bad Bad Girls; [unknown] (Legacy LGY 104)

I've Had Enough; All Shook Up (Legacy LGY 105)

Bad Bad Girls (Legacy LLP 130)

IAN GILLAN / GILLAN (IG, RG)

No Good Luck; Love Gun (Teldec YZ 513 – Germany)

Nothing But the Best; Hole in My West (Teldec 9031 72040 – Germany)

Naked Thunder (Teldec 9031-71899 – Germany)

GLENN HUGHES

Music From And Inspired By The Film Highlander II (Bronze Records 9031-73657)

(GH appears on "Haunted")

GLENN HUGHES & GEOFF DOWNES

The Work Tapes (released 1998) (Blueprint Records BP285CD)

JAGGED EDGE (DA session)

You Don't Love Me; All Through the Night (Polydor PO 97)

Out in the Cold; [unknown] (Polydor PO 105)

Fuel for Your Soul (Polydor 847 201 2)

JUDAS PRIEST (DA session)
Painkiller; United (CBS 656273)
Painkiller (CBS 467290)

GARY MOORE (DA)
Oh Pretty Woman; King of Blues (Virgin VS 1233)
Still Got the Blues; Let Me with the Blues (Virgin VS 1267)
Walking By Myself; All Your Love (Virgin VS 1281)
Too Tired; Texas Strut (Virgin VS 1306)
Still Got the Blues (Virgin V2612)

PERFECT CRIME (DA session)
Blonde On Blonde
Love Me Or Leave Me

PRETTY MAIDS (IG session)
In Santa's Claws (EP) (CBS Records 467744-1)
(IG appears on "A Merry Jingle")

PRETTY MAIDS (RG producer; IP session)
Young Blood; Attention (CBS 655597 7)
Savage Heart; Over and Out (CBS 655884 7)
Jump the Gun (CBS 466365)

ROCK AID ARMENIA (RB, IG, JL session appearance)
Smoke on the Water; Paranoid (Life Aid Armenia Records ARMEN 001)
Smoke on the Water Mega-Rock Remix; Paranoid (Life Aid Armenia Records ARMENTR 001)
The Earthquake Album LP (Life Aid Armenia Records; Harp Beat AID LP001)
(RB, IG, JL appear on "Smoke on the Water")

GARTH ROCKETT & THE MOONSHINERS (IG)
Chris Tetley Presents – The Garth Rockett & The Moonshiners Story (Rock Hard Records ROHA 3)

TIGERTAILZ (DA session)
Noise Level Critical; Murderess (MFN KUT 134)
Berserk (MFN 96)

1991
THE BOLLAND PROJECT (IG session)
Darwin The Evolution (Dino Music 90 70 117 – Holland)
(IG appears on "Overture," "Finale – Suite: The Long Goodbye," "The Final Curtain Falls")

MICHAEL BOLTON (JLT session)
Time Love & Tenderness (Columbia 46771 – USA)

FORCEFIELD (DA session)
Forcefield V

LITA FORD (JLT session)
Dangerous Curves (RCA Records 07863-61025-2)

IAN GILLAN / GILLAN (IG)
Toolbox (East West 9031 75641)

JAGGED EDGE (DA session)
Hell Ain't a Long Way; [unknown] (Polydor PO 132)

STEVE MORSE (BAND) (SM)
Southern Steel (MCA MCAD-10112)

UFO (DA session)
One Of Those Nights; Ain't Life Sweet; Long Gone (Essential ESM 178)

1992
ANTHEM (DA session)
Domestic Booty (Nexus, Japan)

BLUES BUREAU INTERNATIONAL (GH session)

LA Blues Authority (Shrapnel RR 9186 2 – USA)

(GH appears on "Messin' With The Kid")

Glenn Hughes Blues – LA Blues Authority Vol. II (Shrapnel RR 9088-2)

TAYLOR DANE (JLT session)

Soul Dancing (Arista 18705-2)

DIXIE DREGS (SM)

Bring 'Em Back Alive (Capricorn 9-42005-2)

EDDIE HARDIN & ZAK STARKEY (DA, JL session)

Wind In The Willows – A Rock Concert (In-Akustik Records INAK 9010)

KAIZOKU (DA session)

Kaizoku

KLF (GH session)

America What Time Is Love; America No More (Coma Records COMA 7024)

ALVIN LEE (JL session)

Zoom (Mega MRCD 3199 – Germany)

(JL appears on "Real Life Blues" and "Wake Up Moma")

LYNCH MOB (GH session)

Lynch Mob (Elektra 61322-2)

BRIAN MAY (DA session)

Too Much Love Will Kill You; I'm Scared (Parlophone R 6320)

Back to the Light; Nothing But Blue (Parlophone R 6329)

Back to the Light (Parlophone PCCD 123)

STEVE MORSE (BAND) (SM)

Coast to Coast (MCA Records 10565)

JOHN NORUM (GH session)
Face the Truth (Epic EPC 469441-2 – Sweden)

COZY POWELL (DA, JL session)
The Drums Are Back (Electrola 0777-799226-2)
(JL appears on "The Rocket" and "Legend of The Glass Mountain")

JOE SATRIANI (JS)
The Extremist (Relativity 88561)

UFO (DA session)
High Stakes and Dangerous Men (Essential ESM 178)

LAURENT VOULZY (RB session appearance)
Caché Derrière (LP) (BMG; Ariola 3847637622 – France)
(RB appears on "Guitare Héraut")

JEFF WATSON (SM session)
Lone Ranger (Shrapnel SH-1055CD – USA)
(SM appears on "Talking Hands")

1993
COLIN BLUNSTONE (DA session)
Sings His Greatest Hits (Castle CLA 351)

MARC BONILLA (GH session)
American Matador (Warner 9 45329 – USA)
(GH appears on "Whiter Shade of Pale")

COVERDALE-PAGE (DC)
Take Me for a Little While; Waiting on You (EMI 7243-8-80840)
Coverdale-Page (EMI CDEMD-1041)

GEOFF DOWNES & THE NEW DANCE ORCHESTRA (GH session)
Vox Humana (All At Once Records 93212)
(GH appears on "Video Killed The Radio Star")

GEORGE LYNCH (GH session)

Sacred Groove (Elektra 9 61422-2 – USA)

(GH appears on "Not Necessarily Evil" and "Cry Of The Brave")

BRIAN MAY with COZY POWELL (DA session)

Resurrection; Love Token (Parlophone R 6351)

MOTHER'S ARMY (JLT)

Mother's Army (Far East Metal 8129)

MIHALIS RAKINTZHS (IG session)

Getaway (EMI Records 7243-4-78766-1-5 – Greece)

(IG appears on "Getaway," "My Heart Remains the Same," and "I Think I Know")

STEVE SALAS (GH session)

Stevie Salas Presents The Electric Pow-Wow (Aquarius Records Q2-572 – Canada)

(GH appears on "I Was Made to Love Her")

1994

GRAHAM BONNET (DA session)

Here Comes The Night (President 1114)

DIXIE DREGS (SM)

Full Circle (Capricorn 42021-2)

MANFRED EHLERT (GH session)

Amen (recorded 1989-90) (Koch Int. 341372)

(GH appears on "Make My Day," "Child in the Mirror," and "The Mile Worker")

KEN HENSLEY (IP session)

From Time To Time (recorded 1979) (Viceroy Vintage VIN6106-2 – USA)

GLENN HUGHES

Pickin' Up the Pieces; The Liar; Burn (Empire ERCDS 1001 – Sweden)

Why Don't You Stay?; Lay My Body Down (Roadrunner 16861-2372-3 – Hermany)

From Now On . . . (Roadrunner RR-09007)

THE JAVELINS (IG)
Sole Agency and Representation (RPM Records RPM 132)

THE KICK
Tough Trip Through Paradise (Overture 30011)

MICHAEL MANRING (SM session)
Thonk (Windham Hall Records; High Street 10322-2)

MÖTLEY CRÜE (GH session)
Mötley Crüe (Elektra 7559-61534-2)
(GH appears on "Misunderstood")

RIDE (JL session)
Carnival Of Light (Creation CRECD147)
(JL appears on "Moonlight Medicine," "At The End of the Universe," and "Journey to the End of the Universe")

TRIBUTE ALBUMS
Smoke on the Water – A Tribute (Attic; Shrapnel SHR-1076-2)
(GH appears on "Stormbringer"; JLT appears on "Lazy")
Cream of the Crop – L.A. Blues Authority Vol V (Shrapnel; Roadrunner RR 8966 2)
(GH appears on "Born Under a Bad Sign"; JLT appears on "Sitting On Top of the World")

1995
CARMINE APPICE'S GUITAR ZEUS (SM session)
Carmine Appice's Guitar Zeus (No Bull Records; Koch 34336-2)
(SM appears on "4 Miles High")

RITCHIE BLACKMORE'S RAINBOW (RB)
Hunting Humans; Stand and Fight; Black Masquerade (RCA; BMG 74321-30336-2)
Ariel (edit); Ariel; The Temple of the King (live) (RCA; BMG 74321-32982-2)
Stranger In Us All (RCA; BMG 74321-30337-2)

BRAZEN ABBOT (GH session)

Live And Learn (Victor VICP-5607 – Japan)

(GH appears on "Live And Learn," "Clean Up Man," and "Miracle")

GLENN HUGHES

Burning Japan Live (Steamhammer SPV-084-18202)

Feel (Zero; SPV Recordings 085-89762)

STEVE MORSE (BAND) (SM)

Structural Damage (BMG / High Street Records 72902 10332 2)

JOE SATRIANI (JS)

Joe Satriani (Relativity REL 481102-2 – USA)

TRIBUTE ALBUMS

Tales From Yesterday – A View from the South Side of the Sky (Yes tribute)
(Magna Carta RR 8914-2)

(SM appears on "Mood For a Day" and "Clap")

JOE LYNN TURNER (JLT)

Nothing's Changed (Music For Nations CDMFN 189 – USA)

1996

BRAZEN ABBOT (JLT session)

Eye Of The Storm (Victor Entertainment VICP-5757 – Japan)

MARCEL DADI (SM session)

Country Guitar Flavors (EMP Musique 982532)

Nashville Rendez-Vous (EMP Musique 983892)

LIESEGANG (GH session)

No Strings Attached (Alfa-Brunette ALCB-3118)

(GH appears on "King of the Western World," "Cryin' for Love," and "The Night Will Soon Be Gone")

YNGWIE MALMSTEEN (JLT)
Inspiration (Music For Nations CDMFNX-200)

BERNIE MARSDEN (DC session)
And About Time Too (RPM Records RPM-152)
Look at Me Now (RPM Records RPM-153)

STEVE MORSE (BAND) (SM)
StressFest (BMG; High Street Records)

MOTHER'S ARMY (JLT)
Planet Earth (recorded 1994) (Bandai Music Entertainment APCY-8390 – Japan)

TRIBUTE ALBUMS
Twang! A Tribute To Hank Marvin & The Shadows (Pangaea Records 72438-33928-2-7)
(RB performs "Apache"; DA also appears)

To Cry You A Song – A Collection Of Tull Tales (Magna Carta MA-9009-2 – USA)
(GH appears on "To Cry You a Song")

Dragon Attack – A Tribute To Queen (Hawk Records HAWKCD-2166)
(GH appears on "Get Down Make Love")

Working Man (Rush tribute) (Magna Carta MA-9010-2)
(SM appears on "La Villa Strangiato" and "Red Barchetta")

Crossfire – A Salute To Stevie Ray (Blues Bureau Int'l 2031)
(SM appears on "Travis Walk")

Black Night, Deep Purple Tribute According To New York (Revolver Music REV XD 202)
(JLT appears on "Black Night," "Stormbringer," and "Speed King")

1997

BLACKMORE'S NIGHT (RB)

No Second Change; Minstrel Hall (Edel Records 0099365WHE)
Shadow of thc Moon (Edel America 3755)

PAT BOONE (RB session appearance)

Pat Boone In A Metal Mood – No More Mr Nice Guy (Hip-O Records HIPD-40025 – US)
(RB appears on "Smoke on the Water")

BRAZEN ABBOT (jlt session)

Under Cover (Shrapnel Records SH 11122 – USA)
Bad Religion (Victor Entertainment VICP-60057 – Japan)

DAVID COVERDALE & WHITESNAKE (DC)

Too Many Tears Pt 1; Can't Stop Now; Too Many Tears Pt 2 (EMI cds-1)
Too Many Tears Pt 1; The Deeper The Love; Is This Love (EMI cds-2)
Restless Heart (EMI TOCP 50090)
Starkers in Tokyo (EMI Toshiba TOCP-50314 – Japan)

MARCEL DADI (SM session)

Marcel Dadi

G3 (JS)

G3 Live in Concert (Epic Records EPC 487539 2)

IAN GILLAN / GILLAN (IG)

DreaMCAtcher (Ark 21 Records 7243 8 21246 2 7)

IAN GILLAN & RAY SLIJNGAARD (IG)

Smoke on the Water (Original Mix); Smoke on the Water (Club Version) (B&B Records UMD 83065)

KATRINA AND THE WAVES (DA session)

Love Shine a Light; (Eternal)
Walk On Water (Eternal 204)

QUATERMASS II (DA, NS)
Long Road (Thunderbird CSA 108)

GLEN TIPTON (DA session)
Baptism Of Fire (Atlantic 82974)

TRIBUTE ALBUMS
Thunderbolt – A Tribute to AC/DC (D-ROCK 99)
(JLT appears)

JOE LYNN TURNER (JLT)
Under Cover (Pony Canyon PCCY-01074 – Japan)

STEVE VAI (SM session)
Merry Axemas – A Guitar Christmas (Epic Records EK67775)
(SM appears on "Joy to the World"; JS appears on "Silent Night Holy Night Jam")

1998
COLIN BLUNSTONE (DA session)
The Light Inside (Blueprint 125)

THE CAGE (DA session)
The Cage (Nexus KICP 542)

CROSSBONES (DA session)
Crossbones

GLENN HUGHES
Addiction (Shrapnel SH 11132 – USA)

JON LORD
Pictured Within (Virgin Classics 7243 4 93704 2 5 – Germany)

MOTHER'S ARMY (JLT)
Fire on the Moon

STUART SMITH (GH, JLT session)
Heaven and Earth (York Minstrel 103)
(GH appears on "See That My Grave Is Kept Clean"; JLT appears on "Heaven and Earth," "Shadow of the Tyburn Tree," and "I Hate You So Much")

THE SNAKES (DA session)
Live In Europe

TRIBUTE ALBUMS
Tommy Bolin 1997 Tribute (Tommy Bolin Archives TBACD 12)
(GH appears)

Humanary Stew: A Tribute To Alice Cooper
(GH appears on "Only Women Bleed")

JOE LYNN TURNER (JLT)
Hurry Up And Wait (MTM 99558)

1999
BLACKMORE'S NIGHT (RB)
Under a Violet Moon (Cold Harbour Recording)

GLENN HUGHES
The Way It Is (SPV Records SPV 085-21032)

PAUL MCCARTNEY & FRIENDS (IP session)
Run Devil Run (Parlophone 7243 5 22351 2 4)

MILLENNIUM (DA session)
Millennium

JOE LYNN TURNER (JLT)
Under Cover 2 (Pony Canyon PCCY-01354 – Japan)

LESLIE WEST (JLT session)
As Phat As It Gets

2000

COMPANY OF SNAKES (DA session)
Here They Go Again (Steamhammer 7211)

DAVID COVERDALE (DC)
Into The Light (EMI Records 5281242)

DIXIE DREGS (SM)
California Screamin'

GLENN HUGHES
Return of the Chrystal Karma (SPV Records SPV08521812)

THE JAVELINS (IG)
Raving With Ian Gillan & The Javelins (Purple Records PUR 311)

OLAF LENK'S FOOD (DA session)
Fun Stuff

MICK MOODY (DA session)
I Eat 'Em For Breakfast

STEVE MORSE (BAND) (SM)
Major Impacts (Magna Carta MA-9042-2)

GARTH ROCKETT & THE MOONSHINERS (IG)
The Garth Rockett & The Moonshiners Lieve (Purple Records PUR 324)

ULI JON ROTH (DA session)
Transcendental Sky Guitar (Steamhammer 72032)

TEN (DA session)
Babylon AD (Frontiers 46)

JOE LYNN TURNER (JLT)
Holy Man (Pony Canyon 1463)

2001

BLACKMORE'S NIGHT (RB)

Fires At Midnight (Steamhammer SPV 085-72432 CD)

JIM CAPALDI (IP session)

Living On The Outside (SPV Records 72512)

GOV'T MULE (RG session)

The Deep End (ATO 21502)

(RG appears on "Maybe I'm a Leo")

NIKOLO KOTZEV (JLT session)

Nostradamus (SPV 7236)

JORDAN RUDESS (SM session)

Feeding The Wheel (Magna Carta 9055)

2002

BLACKMORE'S NIGHT (RB)

All Because Of You; Home Again (Steamhammer SPV 055-72733CDS)

ROGER GLOVER

Snapshot (Eagle Records EAGCD229)

GLENN HUGHES & JOE LYNN TURNER (GH, JLT)

The Hughes-Turner Project (Pony Canyon PCCY 01556)

STEVE MORSE (BAND) (SM)

Split Decision (Magna Carta MA-9058-2)

Major Impacts 2 (Magna Carta MA-9070-2)

2003

BLACKMORE'S NIGHT (RB)

Past Times with Good Company (Steamhammer SPV 092-74492 DCD)

COMPILATIONS

The following compilations feature rare; unreleased material from throughout the individual members' careers:

RITCHIE BLACKMORE

Ritchie Blackmore Vol. 1 (Connoisseur RP vsop LP; MC; CD 143)
Ritchie Blackmore Vol. 2 (Connoisseur RP vsop LP; MC; CD 157)
The Outlaws Ride Again (LP) (See For Miles CD 303)
The Derek Lawrence Sessions Vol. 1
The Derek Lawrence Sessions Vol. 2
The Derek Lawrence Sessions Vol. 3
The Best of Michael Cox (Sequel nex CD 243)
The Complete Houston Wells (Sequel nex CD 242)
Take It! Sessions 63–68 (RPM Records RPM 120)
This Little Girl Gone Rocking (RPM Records RPM-182)

TOMMY BOLIN

Tommy Bolin – The Ultimate . . . (Geffen 924248-1)
From The Archives Vol. 1 (RPM Records RPM 158)
Live at Ebbets Field, 1974 (Tommy Bolin Archives TBACD 1)
Live at Ebbets Field, 1976 (Tommy Bolin Archives TBACD 2)
The Archives' Bottom Shelf Vol. 1 (Tommy Bolin Archives TBACD 3)
Live at Northern Lights Recording Studios (Tommy Bolin Archives TBACD 4)
Live at Art's Bar & Grill 1973 (Tommy Bolin Archives TBACD 6)
From The Archives Vol. 2 (Tommy Bolin Archives TBACD 7)
In His Own Words (Tommy Bolin Archives TBACD 8; 9)
Energy Radio Broadcasts (TBACD 10-11)
1997 Tribute Concert (TBACD 12)
Energy (TBACD 13)
Snapshot (TBACD 14)
Come Taste the Man Vol. 1 (sampler) (TBACD 15)
Naked Vol. 1 (TBACD 16-17)
First Time Live (TBACD 18-19)
Come Taste the Man Vol. 2 (sampler) (TBACD 20)
Live 9; 19; 76 (TBACD 22)
Naked Vol. 2 (TBACD 23)

After Hours: The Glen Holly Jams Vol. 1 (TBACD 24-25)
Live In Miami at Jai Alai: The Final Show (TBACS 3)
Alive on Long Island, May 22 1976 (TBACS 4)
Energy Live at Tulagi . . . (TBACS 5)

IAN GILLAN; ROGER GLOVER
The Complete Episode Six (Sequel nex CD 156)
Episode Six: The Radio One Club Sessions Live 1968–69 (RPM RPM-178)

PART THREE: PURPLE RECORDS

ORIGINAL RELEASES 1972–79
SINGLES
PUR 101 BULLET: Hobo; Sinister Minister (11/71)
PUR 102 DEEP PURPLE: Never Before; When a Blind Man Cries (3/72)
PUR 103 HARD STUFF: Jay Time; The Orchestrator (4/72)
PUR 104 SILVERHEAD: Oh No No No; Ace Supreme (6/72)
PUR 105 RUPERT HINE: Hamburgers; A Varlet Lad (6/72)
PUR 106 CURTISS MALDOON: One Way Ticket; Next Time (6/72)
PUR 107 BUMBLES: Beep Peep; Buzz Off (6/72)
PUR 108 TONY ASHTON: Surrender Me; Sloeback (unissued)
PUR 109 TONY ASHTON: Celebration; Sloeback (10/72)
PUR 110 SILVERHEAD: In Your Eyes; Rolling With me Baby (11/72)
PUR 111 JON PERTWEE: Who Is the Doctor?; Pure Mystery (11/72)
PUR 112 DEEP PURPLE: Woman from Tokyo; Black Night (live) (unissued)
PUR 113 TUCKY BUZZARD: Gold Medallions; Fast Bluesy Woman (3/73)
PUR 114 YVONNE ELLIMAN: I Can't Explain; Hawaii (7/73)
PUR 115 CAROL HUNTER: Look Out Cleveland; 5-4 March (9/73)
PUR 116 HARD STUFF: Inside Your Life; How You Do It (11/73)
PUR 117 DEEP PURPLE: Might Just Take Your Life; Coronarias Redig (3/74)
PUR 118 ELF: LA 59; Ain't It All Amusing (4/74)
PUR 119 GNASHER: Medina Road; Easy Meat (4/74)
PUR 120 MARLON: Let's Go to the Disco; Broken Man (4/74)
PUR 121 ASHTON; LORD: We're Gonna Make It; Band of the Salvation Army

(7/74)

PUR 122 THE COUNT: Gazaroody; The So-So Song (9/74)

PUR 123 MICHAEL DES BARRES: Leon; New Moon Tonight (10/74)

PUR 124 REFLECTIONS: Love and Affection; No More (11/74)

PUR 125 ROGER GLOVER & FRIENDS: Love Is All; Old Brown Mole (11/74)

PUR 126 BRUTUS: Pay Roll; New Deal Princess (11/74)

PUR 127 REFLECTIONS: Moon Power; Little Star (5/75)

PUR 128 ROGER GLOVER & FRIENDS: Little Chalk Blue; Sitting in a Dream (10/75)

PUR 129 DEEP PURPLE: (titles not announced; unissued)

PUR 130 DEEP PURPLE: You Keep On Moving; Love Child (3/76)

PUR 131 JON LORD: Bouree; Aria (8; 76)

PUR 132 DEEP PURPLE: Smoke on the Water; Child in Time; Woman from Tokyo (3/77)

PUR 133 DAVID COVERDALE: Hole in the Sky; Blindman (5/77)

PUR 134 TUCKY BUZZARD: Gold Medallions; Superbox Rock'n'Roller (8/77)

PUR 135 DEEP PURPLE: *New Live and Rare* (9/77)

PUR 136 DAVID COVERDALE: Breakdown; Only My Soul (2/78)

PUR 137 DEEP PURPLE: *New Live and Rare Vol. 2* (9/78)

ALBUMS

TPS 3501 CURTISS MALDOON: *Curtis Maldoon* (10/71)

TPSA 7501 JON LORD & THE LSO: *Gemini Suite* (10/71)

TPSA 7502 RUPERT HINE: *Pick Up a Bone* (10/71)

TPSA 7503 BUDDY BOHN: *A Drop in the Ocean* (10/71)

TPSA 7504 DEEP PURPLE: *Machine Head* (5/72)

TPSA 7505 HARD STUFF: *Bulletproof* (6/72)

TPSP 351 DEEP PURPLE *Made in Japan* (12/72)

TPSS 1 VARIOUS ARTISTS *Purple People* (12/72)

TPSA 7506 SILVERHEAD: *Silverhead* (1/73)

TPSA 7507 HARD STUFF: *Bolox Dementia* (3/73)

TPSA 7508 DEEP PURPLE: *Who Do We Think We Are* (3/73)

TPSA 7509 RUPERT HINE: *Unfinished Pictures* (3/73)

TPSA 7510 TUCKY BUZZARD: *Alright on the Night* (5/73)

TPSA 7511 SILVERHEAD: *16 and Savaged* (10/73)

TPSA 7512 TUCKY BUZZARD: *Buzzard* (11/73)

TPS 3502 MALDDON: *Maldoon* (11/73)

TPS 3503 CAROL HUNTER: *The Next Voice You Hear* (11/73)

TPS 3504 YVONNE ELLIMAN: *Food of Love* (11/73)

TPS 3505 DEEP PURPLE: *Burn* (2/74)

TPS 3506 ELF: *Carolina County Ball* (4/74)

TPSA 7513 JON LORD: *Windows* (9/73)

TPSA 7514 ROGER GLOVER & FRIENDS *The Butterfly Ball* (12/74)

TPS 3508 DEEP PURPLE: *Stormbringer* (12/74)

TPSM 2001 COLDITZ: *Breakthrough* (5/75)

TPSM 2002 DEEP PURPLE: *24 Carat Purple* (6/75)

TPSA 7515 DEEP PURPLE: *Come Taste the Band* (12/75)

TPSA 7516 JON LORD: *Sarabande* (10/76)

TPSA 7517 DEEP PURPLE: *Made in Europe* (10/76)

TPS 3509 DAVID COVERDALE: *Whitesnake* (5/77)

TPS 3510 DEEP PURPLE: *Powerhouse* (12/77)

TPS 3511 DEEP PURPLE: *Made in Japan Part One* (12/77)

TPS 3512 DEEP PURPLE: *Made in Japan Part Two* (12/77)

TPS 3513 DAVID COVERDALE: *Northwinds* (3/78)

TPS 3514 DEEP PURPLE: *The Mark Two Singles* (4/79)

PURPLE RECORDS REACTIVATED 1999
ALBUMS

PUR 201 Deep Purple: *1420 Beachwood Drive*

PUR 202 Deep Purple: *Space*

PUR 203 Deep Purple: *Live in Denmark 1972*

PUR 205 Deep Purple: *Live at the Forum 1968*

PUR 208 Deep Purple: *Live At Ontario Speedway (California Jam)*

PUR 301 Trapeze: *Welcome to the Real World*

PUR 302 Curtiss Maldoon: *Sepheryn – Ray of Light*

PUR 303 Deep Purple: *Days May Come, Days May Go*

PUR 304 Deep Purple: *Gemini Suite live*

PUR 305 Jon Lord: *Sarabande*

PUR 306 Gillan: *The Japanese Album*

PUR 307 Ashton Gardner & Dyke: *Let It Roll*

PUR 309 Ashton, Gardner & Dyke: *Last Rebel Soundtrack*

PUR 310 Jon Lord: *Before I Forget*

PUR 311 Ian Gillan & the Javelins: *Sole Agency & Representation*

PUR 312 Glenn Hughes: *Play Me Out Special Edition*

PUR 313 Bernie Marsden: *And About Time Too*

PUR 314 Bernie Marsden: *Look at Me Now*

PUR 315 Hardin & York: *Live at the Marquee*

PUR 316 Eddie Hardin & Guests: *The Wizards Convention*

PUR 318 Episode Six: *Live at the BBC*

PUR 319D Episode Six: *Cornflakes and Crazy Foam*

PUR 320 Paice, Ashton, Lord: *Malice in Wonderland*

PUR 321D Deep Purple: *This Time around*

PUR 322 Jon Lord: *Windows*

PUR 323 Hardin & York: *The Best of . . .*

PUR 324 Ian Gillan: *Garth Rockett & the Moonshiners*

PUR 325 Various: *Pre Purple People*

PUR 326 Various: *Purple People*

PUR 327 Eddie Hardin: *Wind in the Willows*

PUR 328 Tiger featuring Big Jim Sullivan: *Burning Bright*

PUR 329 Spencer Davis Group: *Live in Europe 73*

PUR 333 Spencer Davis Group: *Gluggo*

PUR 334 Spencer Davis Group: *Living in a Back Street*

PUR 340D David Coverdale: *The Early Years – Whitesnake; Northwinds*

Although both are concerned only with specific periods of the group's history, the most important books for any Deep Purple fan are, without doubt, *Deep Purple: The Illustrated Biography* by Chris Charlesworth (Omnibus Press, 1983), which takes the group's history up to the 1983 reformation; and *Deep Purple: Listen, Learn, Read On* by Simon Robinson, the monumental booklet included with the box set of the same name (EMI, 2002), which mines the band's story to 1976.

Ian Gillan with David Cohen's *Child in Time* (Smith Gryphon, 1994), the only first-hand recounting of the Deep Purple story to have been published so far, offers a revealing portrait of life in the eye of the storm. Mo Foster's *Play Like Elvis! How British Musicians Bought the American Dream* (Sanctuary, 2000) is an enthralling account of the beginnings of British rock, with first-hand contributions from many of the musicians featured in this book. *Rainbow Rising* by Roy Davies (Helter Skelter, 2002) is an entertainingly thorough account of Ritchie Blackmore's Rainbow days. Finally, Chris Welch's *Deep Purple* HM *Photo Book* offers glorious proof that sometimes pictures are worth a thousand words.

Numerous other volumes detail different aspects of Deep Purple's career. Those I referred to most frequently while writing this book include *Rock Family Trees* by Pete Frame (Omnibus Press, various editions); Martin Strong's *The Great Metal Discography* (Canongate Books, 1998), *The Great Rock Discography* (Mojo Books, 2000), and *The Great Psychedelic Discography* (Canongate, 1997); *Guinness Book of British Hit Singles and Albums* (Guiness, various editions); *Top Pop Singles and Albums* by Joel Whitburn (Record Research, various editions); *In Session Tonight* by Ken Garner (BBC Books, 1992); *The Top 20 Book* by Tony Jasper (Blandford Books, various editions).

Magazines and periodicals: *Circus, Creem, Disc, Live! Music Review, Goldmine, Kerrang!, Melody Maker, Metal Hammer, Mojo, New Musical Express, Record Collector, Rolling Stone, Sounds, ZigZag.*

Web sites:

http://members.aol.com/nigelyoung/mark1.htm — the opening page of an all-encompassing Purple diary.

www.deep-purple.net/ — the Deep Purple Appreciation Society site.

www.thehighwaystar.com — the most complete Purple resource in the world!

www.purplerecords.net/ — home and archive of the band's own label.

Index